T0364130

# International Taxation
# and Multinational Activity

**A National Bureau
of Economic Research
Conference Report**

# International Taxation
# and Multinational Activity

Edited by **James R. Hines Jr.**

**The University of Chicago Press**

Chicago and London

JAMES R. HINES JR. is professor of business economics at the University of Michigan Business School and a research associate of the National Bureau of Economic Research.

The University of Chicago Press, Chicago 60637
The University of Chicago Press, Ltd., London
© 2001 by the National Bureau of Economic Research
All rights reserved. Published 2001
Printed in the United States of America
10 09 08 07 06 05 04 03 02 01     1 2 3 4 5
ISBN: 0-226-34173-9 (cloth)

Library of Congress Cataloging-in-Publication Data

International taxation and multinational activity / edited by James R. Hines Jr.
    p. cm.
    Includes bibliographical references and index.
    ISBN 0-226-34173-9 (cloth : alk. paper)
    1. Investments, Foreign—Congresses. 2. Investments, Foreign—Taxation—Congresses. I. Hines, James R.

HG4538 .I635 2001
336.24′3—dc21
                                                                00-048842

# Contents

# Acknowledgments

This volume contains nine papers that were prepared as part of a research project on the impact of taxation on international capital flows, undertaken by the National Bureau of Economic Research. These papers present new quantitative findings concerning the effects of taxation on foreign direct investment, international tax avoidance, and international productivity spillovers. This research was presented and discussed in a series of meetings that culminated in a conference held in Cambridge, Massachusetts, on 14–15 November 1997.

The work in this volume is part of a broader NBER effort, directed by Martin Feldstein, the goal of which is to understand the determinants and effects of international capital flows. Support for the international capital flows project was provided by the Ford Foundation, the Starr Foundation, and the Center for International Political Economy, for which I am most grateful, and without which this work would not have been possible. Furthermore, the success of the conference and the project depended on the dedicated and extremely capable efforts of Kirsten Foss Davis, Helena Fitz-Patrick, Rob Shannon, and the conference staff of the National Bureau of Economic Research.

# Introduction

James R. Hines Jr.

The ability of modern multinational firms to adjust the scale, character, and location of their worldwide operations creates serious challenges for governments that seek to collect tax revenue from the profits generated by these operations. One of the most important issues that policy makers confront in setting tax policies is to evaluate the extent to which taxation influences the activities of multinational firms. Taxation clearly has the potential to affect the volume of foreign direct investment (FDI), since higher tax rates depress after-tax returns, thereby reducing incentives to commit investment funds. Of course, other considerations are seldom equal: Countries differ in their commercial and regulatory policies, the characteristics of their labor markets, the nature of competition in product markets, the cost and local availability of intermediate supplies, proximity to final markets, and a host of other variables that influence the desirability of an investment location. Until somewhat recently, the obvious relevance of these nontax factors served to convince many observers of the likely unimportance of tax policy in determining the location and character of foreign direct investment.

The hypothesis that tax policies have negligible influence on the activities of multinational firms has been subjected to careful quantitative scrutiny over the last decade, with few (if any) of its implications emerging intact. Recent evidence indicates that taxation significantly influences the location of FDI, corporate borrowing, transfer pricing, dividend and royalty payments, and R&D performance. Much of this evidence has appeared in volumes published by the University of Chicago Press for the

James R. Hines Jr. is professor of business economics at the University of Michigan Business School and a research associate of the National Bureau of Economic Research.

National Bureau of Economic Research.[1] While there is a growing consensus that tax policies affect important observable aspects of FDI and related activity, there remains a great need for answers to numerous more subtle questions, such as whether and how the effects of taxation have changed over time, the impact of interactions between home and host country tax policies, the relationship between tax and nontax factors that influence FDI, the implications of sophisticated tax avoidance techniques, and the role of tax policy in affecting international productivity spillovers due to multinational firms.

The nine chapters in this volume address these issues with careful quantitative analysis of empirical evidence concerning foreign direct investment and the behavior of multinational firms. The chapters of the volume analyze issues that fall into three broad categories. The first is the way in which taxation affects FDI. The second is the effect of tax policies in encouraging international tax avoidance. And the third is the relationship between tax incentives and international spillovers of technology.

### The Effect of Taxation on Foreign Direct Investment

While there exists an emerging consensus that tax policies significantly influence the volume of FDI, there is very little agreement over the precise magnitudes of tax effects and the way in which these magnitudes may have evolved over time. This is an issue of first-order importance, since the effects of tax policies on national welfare depend critically on the extent to which tax rate changes have the ability to influence FDI flows.

Chapter 1, by Rosanne Altshuler, Harry Grubert, and Scott Newlon, analyzes firm-level tax information on the location of foreign investment by American manufacturing firms in 1984 and 1992. The study finds that the location of property, plant, and equipment is highly sensitive to tax rates: Controlling for other considerations, 10 percent higher tax rates are associated with 15 percent less investment in 1984 and 30 percent less investment in 1992. These results are important for at least two reasons. The first is that they document a degree of sensitivity of FDI to local tax rates that is at the very high end of the existing quantitative literature. The second is that they indicate that the sensitivity of FDI to taxation has risen over time. This greater sensitivity is consistent with the incentives created by the U.S. statutory tax rate reductions introduced by the Tax Reform Act of 1986, as well as with the globalization of American business and the consequent greater ability to relocate productive operations in response to tax incentives.

---

1. See Razin and Slemrod (1990), Giovannini, Hubbard, and Slemrod (1993), and Feldstein, Hines, and Hubbard (1995). These and other studies are critically reviewed in Hines (1997, 1999).

Foreign direct investment involves parties in at least two countries, so the tax policies of both home and host governments have the ability to influence the pattern of FDI. These tax policies are often coordinated, as when home governments provide "tax sparing," which is the practice of adjusting home-country taxation of foreign investment income to permit investors to receive the full benefits of any host-country tax reductions. For example, Japanese firms investing in countries with whom Japan has tax sparing agreements are entitled to claim foreign tax credits for income taxes they would have paid to foreign governments in the absence of tax holidays and other special abatements. Most high-income, capital-exporting countries grant tax sparing for FDI in developing countries, while the United States does not.

In chapter 2 I compare Japanese and American investment patterns and find that the ratio of Japanese FDI to American FDI in countries with whom Japan has tax sparing agreements is roughly double what it is elsewhere. In addition, Japanese firms are subject to 23 percent lower tax rates than are their American counterparts in countries with whom Japan has tax sparing agreements. Similar patterns appear when tax sparing agreements with the United Kingdom are used as instruments for Japanese tax sparing agreements. This evidence suggests that tax policy in general, and tax sparing in particular, influences the level and location of FDI. Furthermore, the home-country provision of tax sparing appears to influence the willingness of host governments to offer tax concessions.

Host governments impose on foreign investors various obligations, of which taxes represent a subset (albeit a very important one). Other potentially important obligations and restrictions include capital controls and any obligations to make payments to corrupt government officials.

Chapter 3, by Shang-Jin Wei, analyzes the distribution of foreign direct investment by fourteen major capital-exporting countries in forty-five host countries as of 1991. The patterns are instructive: Countries with higher tax rates, stiffer capital controls, and greater propensity for ordinary business transactions to entail corrupt payments are those that receive the least FDI, controlling for other factors. The estimates imply that the effect of corruption on FDI is so strong that the difference between the environment of Singapore (which has very little official corruption) and that of Mexico has an effect on FDI equivalent to a 29 percent tax rate difference. There is no evidence of any important interactions between the effects of corruption levels and those of tax rates, suggesting that investors are no more able to escape high tax burdens in more corrupt countries than they are in less corrupt countries.

U.S. states tax business activity at different rates, and the responsiveness of foreign direct investment to these tax rate differences offers useful evidence in evaluating both the likely impact of cross-country tax rate differences and the effect of state tax rates on purely domestic investment. The chapter by Deborah Swenson analyzes FDI in the United States between 1984 and 1994, distinguishing investments by type (such as new plants, plant expansions, mergers and acquisitions, joint ventures, and increases in investor equity). The results indicate that FDI types differ greatly in their responsiveness to state tax rates. High state tax rates discourage the location of new plants or expansions of existing plants, while encouraging FDI that takes the form of acquisitions of existing firms. These results are generally consistent with the growing literature on the substantial effects of subnational taxation on the location of FDI, while calling attention to the heterogeneous forms that FDI takes and the likelihood that tax effects vary by type of FDI transaction.

**International Tax Avoidance**

Tax policies affect FDI through the cumulative influence of numerous factors. Firms have incentives to locate assets in low-tax locations because returns to local investments are thereby taxed at low rates. Furthermore, the many tax avoidance methods to which multinational firms have access may provide additional encouragement to locate FDI in low-tax locations in order to facilitate the movement of taxable profits out of high-tax locations. The next three chapters offer quantitative evidence of the importance of international tax avoidance and its potential role in encouraging FDI.

The U.S. Tax Reform Act of 1986 introduced many changes; notable among them was a phased reduction in the statutory corporate tax rate from 46 percent in 1986 to 34 percent by 1988. Based on the tax situations of American firms prior to 1986, it appeared that many American companies would have excess foreign tax credits starting in 1988. Firms with excess foreign tax credits have significantly greater incentives to avoid foreign taxes than do firms with deficit foreign tax credits, and can therefore be expected to reduce their foreign tax obligations through careful use of interest payments, royalty payments, and locally available tax credits and deductions, as well as through other methods. At the same time, host governments have greater incentives to reduce their tax rates in order to compete for investors that have become increasingly tax sensitive.

The chapter by Harry Grubert examines the responses of taxpayers and governments to changed circumstances after 1986 by analyzing individual tax return information for American multinational firms in 1984 and 1992. The results suggest that the average tax rates paid by American firms abroad fell sharply in the years after 1986, with the most pronounced effect on foreign subsidiaries located in countries with the lowest tax rates prior to 1986. These results raise two important possibilities. The first is that American companies responded to the U.S. tax change by economizing on foreign tax payments. The second is that foreign governments changed their own tax practices in the wake of tax reforms in the mid-1980s. These possibilities are not exclusive, of course, and both reveal a process of tax setting and tax avoidance that is considerably subtler than common images of international tax practice.

Tax deferral represents another important opportunity for international tax avoidance. American corporations are required to pay taxes to the U.S. government on their foreign source incomes, but are permitted to defer U.S. tax liabilities on income earned by separately incorporated foreign subsidiaries as long as the income is actively reinvested abroad. The ability to defer U.S. tax obligations on foreign source income is an important component of tax avoidance strategies that include selective timing of dividend repatriations and the possibility that firms will defer repatriations over extended periods of time. Patterns of deferral-based tax avoidance as revealed in the individual tax returns of American multinational companies have been extensively investigated in earlier studies published in the NBER series.

The chapter by Julie Collins, John Hand, and Douglas Shackelford analyzes a new and important indicator of the importance of deferral: stock market reactions to international tax deferral that is reported in the tax footnotes of annual reports. U.S. accounting regulations require firms to report either the tax liabilities they expect to incur when repatriating their currently unrepatriated foreign profits, or to declare such profits to be permanently reinvested. If firms elect to declare their foreign profits permanently reinvested, they are obliged to report elsewhere in a footnote the tax obligation they would incur if these profits were to be repatriated at a later date. Collins, Hand, and Shackelford find that, for firms with deficit foreign tax credits, aggregate share values are depressed by the amounts of any tax liabilities that are reported to be due upon repatriation—even though firms indicate their expectation that profits will be permanently reinvested abroad. This pattern suggests that the market anticipates either the ultimate payment of these tax obligations, or the implicit payment of tax obligations in the form of lower returns to funds that are reinvested abroad to avoid home-country tax liabilities. To the degree that stock market valuations are reliable indicators of corporate opportunities, these results suggest that tax deferral is most valuable as a method of fine-tuning the timing of repatriations, rather than as a method of avoiding altogether any home-country tax liabilities on foreign source income.

The ability of multinational firms to adjust the prices charged in cross-border transactions between members of controlled groups is a widely cited method of reducing total tax liabilities. Most countries require that multinational firms use arm's-length transfer prices for international transactions, but the difficulty of establishing such prices in many realistic situations leaves ample scope for tax-motivated pricing of goods and services bought and sold in jurisdictions with different tax rates. The quantitative literature on international transfer pricing reports evidence suggesting that firms adjust their transfer prices to shift profits from high-tax to low-tax countries, but this evidence is very indirect, typically consisting of reported profit rates that vary inversely with tax rates.

The chapter by Kimberly Clausing analyzes the relationship between tax rates and the reported intrafirm trade volumes of American multinational companies. The results are consistent with significant tax-motivated pricing of transactions between the foreign affiliates of American companies, their parent firms, and other foreign affiliates of the same companies. The evidence indicates that, controlling for other factors, foreign affiliates located in countries with 10 percent lower tax rates have 4.4 percent higher trade surpluses with their American parent companies. In addition, foreign affiliates located in low-tax countries sell unusually high fractions of their total output to other affiliates of the same company. These trade patterns are highly suggestive of tax-motivated transfer pricing, and are therefore consistent with the earlier profitability-based evidence. Clausing's study differs from other transfer pricing investigations in two important ways: first, by examining more direct evidence of transfer pricing methods, and second, by identifying an important impact of tax-motivated transfer pricing on reported trade statistics.

## Tax Policy and International Productivity

The R&D activities of multinational firms contribute significantly to the generation of new technology and its transmission across borders. National tax policies affect the costs and returns to R&D performed by multinational firms, and have the potential to influence the location of innovative activity that these firms undertake.

The chapter by James R. Hines Jr. and Adam Jaffe considers the effect of U.S. tax rules on the distribution of inventive activity between the United States and foreign countries. The chapter analyzes the impact of changes introduced by the U.S. Tax Reform Act of 1986 on the international patenting pattern of a panel of American multinational firms affected by the tax changes. Due to the specifics of U.S. tax law, American firms differed in the extent to which the 1986 tax changes affected their after-tax costs of performing R&D in the United States. Furthermore, there is an important difference between the tax treatment of R&D performed in the United States for use domestically, and R&D performed in the United States for use abroad. The chapter indicates that firms for which the after-tax cost of performing R&D in the United States for use abroad rose most rapidly after 1986 exhibit the slowest subsequent growth of foreign patenting. This finding suggests that tax incentives for R&D influence subsequent patenting, and that foreign and domestic innovative activities are complements rather than substitutes.

The adoption of tax policies that encourage foreign direct investment are likely not only to change the size of a country's capital stock but also thereby to change the age composition of the capital stock. Newer capital generally incorporates advances in learning and technique that make it more productive than older capital, and the productivity differences between capital vintages typically appear in reported productivity figures. To the extent that there are large productivity differences between capital vintages, countries that successfully attract new FDI will exhibit rapid growth of measured economic productivity.

The chapter by Jason Cummins analyzes the sources of firm-level productivity growth in a sample of individual American multinational firms between 1981 and 1995. The results indicate that rapid capital accumulation is more important as a source of productivity growth than is the contribution of other productive factors such as labor and intermediate goods, and that, in particular, investment in foreign operations is associated with rapid growth of productivity. These estimates carry important implications not only for the consequences of foreign direct investment, but also for the implied responsiveness of FDI to tax rate differences.

## Conclusion

Tax policies in the modern world have the potential to influence economic performance far beyond the borders of the countries that enact them. The ability and evident willingness of taxpayers to relocate activity, to shift taxable income between taxing jurisdictions, to adopt technologies developed elsewhere, and to respond to incentives created by the interaction of domestic and foreign tax rules, imply that tax policies must be evaluated at least in part on the basis of their impact on the activity of multinational corporations. The nine chapters in this volume are concerned with measuring the impact of international taxation on multinational activity, using new analytical methods and previously unexamined data to do so. The results of this research serve to reinforce findings by other studies of the importance of tax considerations in affecting the volume and nature of international economic activities. More importantly, the studies in this volume take the important next step of pursuing the investigation of variations in the impact of international taxation over time and between countries and taxpayers in different situations.

There is enormous interest in identifying the impact of tax policies in economies exposed to the rest of the world. In the current American environment, almost every U.S. tax provision influences foreign direct investment or incentives to engage in international tax avoidance. The research reported in this volume reflects the importance of international tax policies and the opportunities they provide to answer old questions in new ways. The ability to look across countries and firms with widely differing tax situations makes it possible to learn a great deal about the responsiveness of economic activity to its tax treatment. The lessons provided by such investigations carry valuable implications for a broad range of domestic and international policies, and deepen our understanding of the operation of modern economies.

# References

Feldstein, Martin, James R. Hines Jr., and R. Glenn Hubbard, eds. 1995. *The effects of taxation on multinational corporations.* Chicago: University of Chicago Press.

Giovannini, Alberto, R. Glenn Hubbard, and Joel Slemrod, eds. 1993. *Studies in international taxation.* Chicago: University of Chicago Press.

Hines, James R., Jr. 1997. Tax policies and the activities of multinational corporations. In *Fiscal policy: Lessons from economic research,* ed. Alan J. Auerbach, 401–45. Cambridge, Mass: MIT Press.

Hines, James R., Jr. 1999. Lessons from behavioral responses to international taxation. *National Tax Journal* 52 (2): 305–22.

Razin, Assaf, and Joel Slemrod, eds. 1990. *Taxation in the global economy.* Chicago: University of Chicago Press.

# 1

# Has U.S. Investment Abroad Become More Sensitive to Tax Rates?

Rosanne Altshuler, Harry Grubert,
and T. Scott Newlon

This paper attempts to address two related questions. The first question is how sensitive U.S. firms' investment location decisions are to tax rate differences across countries. Finding the answer to this question clearly is important for determining the revenue and efficiency consequences of many tax policies. The second question is whether the location of investment abroad by U.S. firms has become more sensitive to tax rate differences across countries. A finding that investment location decisions have become more sensitive to tax rates would be consistent with the view that technological advances and the loosening of trade restrictions and capital controls have in recent years increased the ease with which capital can cross national borders. If different locations became closer substitutes for the location of production, it would not be surprising if investment location decisions became increasingly responsive to tax considerations.

We use data from the U.S. Department of the Treasury corporate tax return files for 1984 and 1992 to address these questions. The use of these data yields two benefits not available to recent cross-sectional studies of the effect of host-country tax rates on the distribution of U.S. direct investment abroad (e.g., Grubert and Mutti 1991, 1997; and Hines and Rice 1994). The first benefit is that, with the time element in our data, we can examine whether investment location choices abroad have in fact become

Rosanne Altshuler is associate professor of economics at Rutgers University. Harry Grubert is an economist in the Office of Tax Analysis in the U.S. Department of the Treasury. T. Scott Newlon is managing director of Horst Frisch Incorporated.

The authors thank Gordon Wilson and Paul Dobbins for providing the data files in a convenient form. They are grateful to James Hines Jr., Jack Mintz, William Randolph, Frank Vella, and conference participants for helpful comments. Any opinions expressed are those of the authors and not of the U.S. Department of the Treasury.

more sensitive to tax rates over the period spanned by our two sample years. The second benefit is that we can control for unmeasured country fixed effects.

Our data come from the information forms filed with the tax returns of U.S. parent corporations on each controlled foreign corporation (CFC) abroad.[1] This information form, to be described more fully later, includes details from the balance sheets and income statements of CFCs. We aggregate these data up to country level and combine it with information from a variety of other sources to control for nontax features of different locations. The data include information for almost sixty countries. We limit our analysis to the manufacturing CFCs of U.S. manufacturing parents.

Following the earlier studies by Grubert and Mutti (1991, 1997) and Hines and Rice (1994), we regress a measure of U.S. multinational firms' real capital in each country on tax rate variables and measures of nontax characteristics of each country. The focus is on the effect of differences in host-country tax rates on investment choices across foreign locations, not on the choice between investing at home or abroad. Our work has two main findings. First, we find large estimated tax elasticities for investment abroad. Controlling for country fixed effects produces tax elasticities that are slightly larger and more precisely estimated than those from our single-year cross sections. Second, our results suggest that the location of real capital in manufacturing affiliates has become more sensitive to tax rates in the period from 1984 to 1992. Our basic estimates indicate that the elasticity of real capital to changes in after-tax returns increased from about 1.5 in 1984 to 2.8 in 1992 (for countries with the most open trade regimes). Both the elasticities and the difference between them are statistically significant at standard levels.

We perform a variety of tests to check the robustness of our elasticity estimates. With few exceptions, the magnitude and significance of our 1992 and 1984 elasticities changes little when we screen our sample in various ways or change the measure of host-country taxes. The difference between the 1984 and 1992 elasticities is large in absolute terms and is statistically significant; and its absolute and statistical significance is robust to our sensitivity checks.

The remainder of the paper is organized as follows. Section 1.1 contains a brief review of studies using cross-sectional data to estimate tax effects on location decisions of U.S. multinational corporations. We highlight the elasticity estimates in previous studies and note that they provide suggestive but inconclusive evidence that investment location has become more sensitive to tax rates in recent years. Section 1.2 describes the data and

---

1. A CFC is a foreign corporation that is at least 50 percent owned by a group of U.S. shareholders, each of whom has at least a 10 percent interest in the company. In fact, most of the CFCs in our sample are 100 percent owned by the U.S. parent corporation.

how our tax and capital measures are constructed from the U.S. Department of the Treasury tax files. Empirical results are contained in section 1.3, and the final section presents our conclusions.

## 1.1  A Brief Review of the Recent Literature

While early studies of the responsiveness of U.S. direct investment to after-tax rates of return used aggregate time series data,[2] the most recent work in this area exploits cross-sectional data. In this section, we review the three studies that relate most directly to our approach: Grubert and Mutti (1991), Hines and Rice (1994), and Grubert and Mutti (1997). All three papers contain estimates of the effect of local taxes on the allocation of real capital. While the tax variable in these papers is similar (each uses a measure of average effective tax rates), it appears in different forms in the estimating equations, making the comparison of estimated tax effects difficult.

Both Grubert and Mutti (1991) and Hines and Rice (1994) use the 1982 benchmark data on U.S. direct investment abroad from the Bureau of Economic Analysis (BEA). One important difference between these two papers is the sample studied. Grubert and Mutti analyze the allocation of capital by manufacturing affiliates of U.S. parents across thirty-three host countries; the focus of Hines and Rice is on the activity of U.S. multinationals in tax havens. Their sample includes all majority owned nonbank affiliates of U.S. parents, which results in a larger set of countries (seventy-three), more than half of which (forty-one) are tax havens with little real capital.[3]

Grubert and Mutti (1991) regress the log of the net stock of property, plant, and equipment (PPE) on two different forms of the average effective tax rate: the log of 1 minus the tax rate, and the inverse of the tax rate. The first specification gives a (constant) tax elasticity that measures the sensitivity of the demand for real capital to changes in after-tax returns (for a given pretax return) or, alternatively, to changes in the cost of capital (for given after-tax returns). The second specification allows for larger tax effects at lower tax rates. Using the first specification, Grubert and Mutti estimate tax elasticities that range from 1.5 (for all manufacturing affiliates) to 2 (for majority owned manufacturing affiliates) but that were statistically not highly significant. The inverse formulation, however, produced a highly significant tax coefficient of $-0.11$. At lower tax rates, this

2. This work includes Hartman (1981), Boskin and Gale (1987), and Newlon (1987). The literature on the effects of taxation on foreign direct investment abroad has been carefully reviewed in Hines (1997). This review does not include the recent work in Grubert and Mutti (1997), however.
3. Hines and Rice report that 4.2 percent of all property, plant, and equipment is located in the tax havens in 1982.

tax effect is particularly strong. Grubert and Mutti report that reducing local tax rates from 20 to 10 percent will increase U.S. affiliates' net plant and equipment in a country by 65 percent.

Hines and Rice (1994) regress the log of PPE on host-country average tax rates. The coefficient on their tax term is $-3.3$ and is significantly different from 0.[4] This coefficient suggests that at their mean tax rate of 31 percent, a 1 percent increase in after-tax returns leads to a 2.3 percent increase in the real capital stock of U.S. affiliates. Hines and Rice's inclusion of the tax haven countries, as well as their examining the allocation of capital in all nonbank affiliates, may be responsible for their higher estimated elasticity.

The most recent analysis of the effects of taxes on investment location decision of U.S. multinational firms is Grubert and Mutti (1997). They estimate tax elasticities using country- and firm-level cross-sectional data on the manufacturing affiliates of U.S. manufacturing parents in sixty locations from the 1992 U.S. Department of the Treasury tax file. As in their previous study, they enter the tax variable in log $(1 - t)$ form.

When compared to the results of their previous paper, the estimates from Grubert and Mutti (1997) suggest that the location of capital may have become more sensitive to differences in after-tax returns between 1982 and 1992. Using the aggregated country-level data, they estimate a tax elasticity that is greater than 3 (for open economies) and is statistically highly significant. Using the firm-level data, they calculate a combined elasticity measure that takes into account the probability of choosing to locate capital in a country and the amount of capital invested into account. They report a combined elasticity of capital to after-tax returns for open economies of about 3.

To summarize, the results of previous work with cross-sectional data indicate that taxes have a significant impact on the investment location decisions of U.S. multinational firms. In addition, a rough comparison of the elasticity estimates suggests that these decisions may have become more sensitive to host-country tax rates in recent years; however, the validity of this comparison is questionable, since the estimates were derived from different data sources.

## 1.2    The Data

Our principal source of data is the body of U.S. Department of the Treasury corporate tax files compiled by the Statistics of Income (SOI)

---

4. Hines and Rice (1994) also report results of regressions that include both the tax rate and the square of the tax rate as explanatory variables. However, the squared tax rate is not significantly different from zero.

division of the Internal Revenue Service. This data set is derived from a variety of tax and information forms filed by U.S. parent corporations. Many of the data necessary for our analysis come from the Form 5471, which reports on the activities of each CFC of a U.S. parent. This form, which U.S. parents must file for each of their CFCs, reports subsidiary-level information on assets, taxes paid, earnings and profits, and other information from balance sheets and income statements.

Information from the Form 5471 is compiled only in even years and was available to us from 1980 through 1992. However, the level of detail recorded from this form on the SOI files differs from year to year. For example, both the 1984 and 1992 files provide information on the composition of assets from the balance sheet portion of the Form 5471, whereas the files from other sample years do not. The interval from 1984 to 1992 is particularly appropriate for our study, since it covers a period of large declines in effective tax rates in some locations abroad.[5] We use the information in the remaining even years between 1980 and 1992 to calculate country average effective tax rates. These effective tax rates are used in various forms as independent variables in our regressions.

We restrict our sample to the manufacturing CFCs of all large U.S. manufacturing corporations.[6] We aggregate the subsidiary-level information from the Form 5471 across parents by country.[7] One advantage of using country-level data is that such data eliminate some of the complicated statistical problems associated with subsidiary-level data—for example, the problems that arise from using data that are truncated at zero when errors may be correlated across observations within a country because of omitted variables. A drawback is that we lose information on the characteristics of the parent corporations that may affect their location decisions.

Aggregating across subsidiaries in each country leaves us with data for

---

5. This period also straddles that of the U.S. Tax Reform Act of 1986, which made significant changes in U.S. taxation of both domestic and international business. Our analysis considers the choice of investment across foreign locations, not between domestic and foreign locations. However, we allow the intercept in our estimates to vary by year, which to some extent may capture the effect of changes in U.S. taxes over the time period. Some evidence of the responsiveness of foreign investment to changes in U.S. tax rates is provided in Harris (1993). He finds that firms that were most negatively impacted by the 1986 tax reform responded by increasing their investment abroad.

6. Although beyond the scope of this project, it is possible that the behavior of firms in the manufacturing industry differs from those in other industries. As discussed in section 1.1, the difference between the estimates of the elasticity of property, plant, and equipment to average host-country tax rates found in Grubert and Mutti (1991) and Hines and Rice (1994) may be due to the inclusion of nonbank affiliates in the latter study. Given the focus of this paper on the location of real capital, it seemed appropriate to limit the sample to data from manufacturing affiliates.

7. The 1984 sample includes all U.S. corporations with at least one CFC and total assets greater than $250 million. All U.S. corporations with at least $500 million in assets were included in the 1992 sample.

fifty-eight locations for 1984 and 1992.[8] Our two cross sections are "unlinked" in that there is no requirement that the same parents (or the same CFCs) appear in both years of data. We also experimented with a sample drawn from a panel that contains *only* those CFCs associated with parents that appear in both years.[9] We report results using this linked data set in our sensitivity analysis.[10]

We augment the Form 5471 data with country-specific information from some other sources to help control for countries' nontax characteristics that may affect location decisions. We obtained population, GDP, and inflation data from the *International Monetary Fund International Financial Statistics* (International Monetary Fund 1984, 1992) supplemented in a few cases by information from statistics from the United Nations. As in Grubert and Mutti (1997), we use the trade regime classification developed in the *World Development Report* (World Bank 1987) to control for the degree of openness of each country's economy. This measure is based on observations from 1973 to 1985 of (1) the country's effective rate of protection, (2) its use of direct controls such as quotas, (3) its use of exports, and (4) the extent of any overvaluation of its exchange rate. The variable runs from 0 (most open) to 3 (most restrictive). Unfortunately, there is only one observation of this measure—it has not been updated for the years after 1985.

Before turning to our empirical results, we briefly discuss how we use the Form 5471 information to calculate effective tax rates and to measure real capital. These variables are reported in appendix tables 1A.1 and 1A.2.

### 1.2.1  Measuring Assets

Our measure of real capital in each year is composed of end-of-year depreciable assets (plant and equipment) and inventories from the balance sheet information reported on the Form 5471. Because parents are required to report subsidiary assets according to U.S. accounting principles, these figures are not distorted by host-country incentives such as accelerated depreciation. However, the asset measures reflect historical book values and therefore may be affected by local inflation and exchange rates.[11]

Another potential problem with our real capital measure is that the

8. Locations for which there were fewer than five CFCs were eliminated from the analysis. This left us with sixty locations. Our analysis was further limited to fifty-eight countries because we were unable to locate complete information for Taiwan and the Cayman Islands.

9. The link is based largely on employer identification numbers (EINs), but a special effort using corporate names was made to identify large companies whose EINs may have changed. Companies may disappear because of mergers and may appear because they moved over the threshold for inclusion during our time interval.

10. Our unlinked panel has, however, some advantages over the linked panel. For example, if a parent disappears due to a merger, the unlinked country totals will contain both the parent's 1984 and 1992 assets and income.

11. In some cases the parent may maintain historical values in terms of dollars originally invested (particularly in locations with hyperinflation), but this is not mandated.

assets reported by a CFC may not be located in the country in which the CFC is incorporated. This problem is especially serious in tax haven countries, which are often hosts to holding companies and financial CFCs. Including only manufacturing affiliates in our country data helps mitigate this problem. In addition, we investigate how our results are affected when we remove countries that are likely to be tax havens from the analysis.

### 1.2.2 Measuring Effective Tax Rates

We calculated the average effective tax rate for manufacturing CFCs incorporated in each country by dividing total income taxes paid by total earnings and profits.[12] Both variables appear on the Form 5471. Parent corporations must report their CFCs' earnings and profits using the definition provided by the U.S. Internal Revenue Code. This measure of earnings and profits is meant to reflect net economic income, not host-country (or domestic U.S.) taxable income, which would be affected by investment incentives such as accelerated depreciation.[13]

One potential problem with our country average effective tax rate calculations, particularly in small countries with few CFCs, is that they appear to contain noise. We were particularly concerned about the 1984 effective tax rates. Appendix table 1A.3 reports the results of regressing previous-year average effective tax rates on 1986 and 1990 average effective tax rates. We found that the 1982 effective tax rates are better predictors of 1986 effective tax rates than are the 1984 rates. To diminish the role of the 1984 effective tax rates in our analysis, we averaged them with effective tax rates from the previous two even years. For consistency, we average the 1992 effective tax rates with those from 1990 and 1988. We also experiment with using lagged effective tax rates.

Another potential problem with our effective tax rate measures is that they may be correlated with inflation, because depreciation allowances are based on the historic costs of assets. In addition to including inflation as an explanatory variable, we also checked the relation between differences in inflation and differences in effective tax rates. We found that the change in inflation between 1984 and 1992 explains less than 4 percent of the variation in our effective tax rate variables.

A further issue is that average effective tax rates are, to some extent, endogenous to investment decisions. The effective tax rate in a country

---

12. Only CFCs with positive income were included in the calculation; otherwise, the tax measure would be biased upward. As indicated, only income taxes are included in the average effective tax rate measure. However, foreign affiliates operating in host countries are sometimes also subject to property and assets taxes. These taxes may also influence the investment patterns of U.S. multinationals. Our data do not permit us to identify these taxes.

13. As noted in Grubert and Mutti (1997), earnings and profits on the Form 5471 seem very close to book income (which is also reported).

may be low in a given year because of a recent increase in investment activity in that country that qualifies for investment incentives, such as accelerated depreciation, that accrue early in an investment's life.[14] One approach to avoiding this potential endogeneity problem is to replace average effective tax rates with statutory rates. Although statutory rates have the virtue of being exogenous to investment decisions, they do not reflect all the variation in the tax advantages of investment in different locations because they do not measure tax base differences across countries. Statutory rates also do not capture ad hoc deals between host countries and individual foreign investors. For this reason, statutory rates are better indicators of the advantages of placing financial capital in a location and the gains to income shifting. Nevertheless, we use statutory rates as well as instrumental variable techniques to test the sensitivity of our results to alternative measures of taxes. We collected country statutory tax rates from the Price Waterhouse (1984, 1992) guides.

Given that we are implicitly modeling investment decisions, it might seem appropriate to use host-country marginal effective tax rates rather than average effective tax rates. Marginal effective tax rates were not available for many of the countries included in our sample. Even if Hall-Jorgenson-King-Fullerton marginal effective tax rates as they are usually modelled were calculated for all the countries and both years in our sample, it is not clear that they would be superior at capturing the effects of taxes on investment location decisions. As discussed previously by others, there are serious drawbacks to the use of marginal effective tax rates. For example, taking into account all of the feature of tax systems that are important for investment decisions in the calculation of marginal effective rates is generally not feasible. There may be features of tax codes that are difficult to model (such as the alternative minimum tax in the United States), tax incentives that apply to only some regions of countries, and ad hoc deals between companies and host countries. Finally, the formulas used to compute Hall-Jorgenson-King-Fullerton tax rates are sensitive to the required rate of return assumed.

The tax variable used in the location equations, the local average effective tax rate, tends to overstate the cross-country variation in tax burdens, and thus to understate the true investment elasticity. For one thing, multinational corporations can allocate more debt to high (statutory) tax locations, diluting the impact of the local tax on net equity income. In addition, the tax variable does not include the residual U.S. tax on repatriations

---

14. Grubert and Mutti (1997) found that recently incorporated CFCs had significantly lower effective tax rates than the country average in the 1992 file. To correct for age effects, they adjust the country average effective tax rates by the age distribution of CFCs in each country. Their tax elasticity estimates were unaffected by this adjustment. Grubert (chap. 5 in this volume) indicates that age effects were the same in 1984 as in 1992.

Table 1.1          **Global Decline in Average Effective Tax Rates, 1980–92 (average effective tax rates for manufacturing in fifty-eight countries)**

| Year | Mean | Standard Deviation |
|------|------|--------------------|
| 1980 | .321 | .115 |
| 1982 | .340 | .131 |
| 1984 | .339 | .134 |
| 1986 | .303 | .133 |
| 1988 | .306 | .155 |
| 1990 | .245 | .119 |
| 1992 | .234 | .113 |

*Note:* The table presents the means and standard deviations of average effective tax rates for U.S. manufacturing subsidiaries in fifty-eight countries. Average effective tax rates in each country are calculated by dividing the total income taxes paid by U.S. controlled foreign corporations in the manufacturing sector by their total earnings and profits.

from each location.[15] If anything, residual U.S. taxes would tend to even out differences in tax rates across the countries; if a company's foreign tax credits do not fully offset its U.S. tax liability on repatriated income, additional repatriations from a low-tax country trigger an additional U.S. tax, while repatriations from countries with a tax rate above the U.S. rate yield a bonus because some of the foreign tax credits can shield other income (see Grubert and Mutti 1997 for a discussion of this issue).

### 1.2.3   Variation in Effective Tax Rates across Countries and Time

Our empirical strategy relies on the existence of variation in effective tax rates across countries and across our time period. Fortunately, this was a period of intense tax reform activity around the world. Along with the United States, many countries reduced their corporate tax rates (including Canada, the United Kingdom, France, Belgium, and the Netherlands). These reforms resulted in substantial declines in average effective tax rates for U.S. CFCs between 1984 and 1992.[16]

Table 1.1 provides information on the mean and standard deviation of average effective tax rates (for manufacturing) for the fifty-eight locations in our data set. The table shows that average effective tax rates in our sample steadily declined between 1980 and 1992. In addition, the standard deviation of average effective tax rates was greater than 11 percent in each year. We also calculated the variation in country average effective tax rates

15. See Altshuler and Newlon (1993) or Grubert (1998) for a detailed description of repatriation taxes.

16. Grubert, Randolph, and Rousslang (1996) found that there was a substantial decrease in the average foreign tax rate faced by U.S. multinationals on repatriated income between 1984 and 1992. They conclude that the decrease in average foreign tax rates (from 36 percent in 1984 to 25 percent in 1992) was due primarily to reductions in country average effective tax rates and not to changes in income repatriation patterns.

across years. We found that average effective tax rates in manufacturing fell by more than 10 percentage points between 1984 and 1992. The standard deviation of the change was 17 percentage points, indicating substantial variation in the change in tax rates.[17]

## 1.3 Estimation Results

For our estimates we use a reduced-form model that follows the model used in Grubert and Mutti (1997) and is similar to the models used in Grubert and Mutti (1991) and Hines and Rice (1994). The model assumes that the derived demand for capital by multinational firms in a country is a function of after-tax rates of return and exogenous country characteristics that affect supply and demand (such as GDP and GDP per capita).[18] This reduced-form relation between tax rates and investment in real capital would result from a standard partial equilibrium economic model in which parent firms allocate capital abroad to maximize after-tax returns.

$$(1) \qquad \log K_{it} = \text{const}_t + a' Z_{it} + \beta \log(1 - t_{it})$$
$$+ \gamma \text{TRADE}_i * \log(1 - t_{it}) + \varepsilon_{it},$$

where $i$ indicates countries, subscript $t$ indicates the year of analysis ($t = $ 1984 or 1992), $K$ is real capital, $Z$ is a vector of nontax country characteristics, $t$ is the tax variable, and TRADE is the trade policy variable. Notice that our tax variable is interacted with the trade variable (which also appears by itself in the vector $Z$) to control for the possibility that the benefit of low tax rates may be smaller in more restrictive trade regimes. Thus, the estimated coefficient $\beta$ describes the elasticity of total real capital with respect to after-tax returns (for a given pretax return), for the most open regimes (in which the trade variable is zero). We use log GDP and log population as scale variables to reflect the economic size of each country. Since we use the log form, we are implicitly controlling for differences in GDP per capita across countries.

---

17. As will be explained shortly, we use differences in effective tax rates averaged over three years, lagged effective tax rates, and statutory tax rates in our regression analysis. The decline in effective tax rates averaged over the years 1980, 1982, and 1984, and in effective tax rates averaged over the years 1988, 1990, and 1992, was 11 percentage points with a standard deviation of 12. Average effective tax rates fell by 9.5 percentage points (with a standard deviation of 15) between 1982 and 1990. Finally, statutory tax rates fell almost 14 percentage points between 1984 and 1992 with a standard deviation of 14.

18. We recognize that there may be general equilibrium responses in factor returns that affect the role of taxes in multinational behavior. As Gordon (1986) shows in a small country model with homogeneous capital and perfect mobility of portfolio capital, any increase in the local tax rate on capital is offset by lower local wage costs; but, as discussed in Grubert and Mutti (1997), many features of a more realistic model would diminish or even reverse this general equilibrium response. In any case, if the Gordon (1986) model is valid, we should observe no effect of local taxes on the location of multinational corporations. Indeed, bringing potential U.S. tax credits into the picture would predict that U.S. companies should locate in high-tax countries.

### 1.3.1  Single-Year Cross-Sectional Analysis

Table 1.2 presents our main results.[19] The first column reports regression results for the 1992 cross section. We include regional dummies to control for unmeasured geographic characteristics.[20] Our results indicate that the open regime tax elasticity is 2.7 and is highly significant. The trade regime variable is also highly significant and negative, indicating the adverse effect of trade restrictions on the desirability of a location for investment. As expected, the presence of trade restrictions lessens the responsiveness to lower tax rates: The trade-tax interaction term is negative and significant at the 5 percent level. Although we included inflation as an independent variable in other estimates, we do not report these results in the table because inflation rates had no effect on the tax variables and were never a significant explanatory variable.

The analogous regression for 1984 is presented in the second column of table 1.2. In contrast to the 1992 results, neither the tax term nor the trade-tax interaction term is significant at conventional levels in the 1984 cross section. In addition, the coefficient on the tax term in the 1984 regression is (about) half the size of that in the 1992 regression.

Before turning to the fixed effects estimates, we pool the data and test whether the coefficients on the $\log(1 - t)$ terms are statistically different from each other in 1984 and 1992. We restrict all of the coefficients except the ones on $\log(1 - t)$ terms to be equal; an $F$-test does not reject this specification.

The pooled regression results appear in column (3) of table 1.2. In these regressions, the tax term $(\log(1 - t))$ appears by itself and interacted with a year variable that equals one in 1984. Therefore the 1992 open economy elasticity is the coefficient on the $\log(1 - t)$ term, the interacted term gives the difference between the 1984 and 1992 open economy elasticities, and the sum of the two terms gives the 1984 open economy elasticity. The bottom two rows of the table report the 1984 and 1992 elasticity estimates with standard errors.[21]

Interestingly, in the pooled regression, the 1992 coefficient decreases in size and significance; the opposite is true of the 1984 coefficient, which is now significant at the 10 percent level. In addition, the difference between the rates, although still large, is not statistically significant. Controlling for country fixed effects will increase the precision of these estimates if our tax terms are correlated with omitted nontax country variables. To the

---

19. Since the number and size of CFCs differ across countries in our data set, we report White-corrected standard errors to correct for heteroskedasticity.

20. The excluded countries are a highly heterogeneous group that includes African, Scandinavian, and Middle Eastern countries, among others.

21. The standard error comes from the analogous regression in which YEAR84 = 1 for the 1992 observations.

**Table 1.2**     **The Effect of Taxes on the Location of Real Capital Abroad by U.S. Manufacturing Companies (results for cross-sectional, pooled, and fixed effects regressions)**

| | Dependent Variable | | | |
|---|---|---|---|---|
| | Log of Capital 1992 (1) | Log of Capital 1984 (2) | Log of Capital (3) | Difference in Log of Capital (4) |
| Log(1−Ave ETR for 1988–92) | 2.68** (.720) | | | |
| Log(1−Ave ETR for 1980–84) | | 1.32 (.874) | | 1.24** (.324) |
| Log(1−Ave ETR) | | | 2.21** (.691) | |
| Log(1−Ave ETR)∗YEAR84 | | | −.795 (.768) | |
| Difference in log(1−Ave ETR) | | | | 2.77** (.744) |
| TRADE | −.719** (.200) | −.638* (.320) | −.630** (.183) | |
| TRADE∗log(1−Ave ETR for 1988–92) | −1.14** (.445) | | | |
| TRADE∗log(1−Ave ETR for 1980–84) | | −.752 (.464) | | |
| TRADE∗log(1−Ave ETR) | | | −.707** (.306) | |
| TRADE∗difference in log(1−Ave ETR) | | | | −.496 (.440) |
| Log GDP, 1992 | 1.08** (.104) | | | |
| Log GDP, 1984 | | 1.18** (.172) | | |
| Log GDP | | | 1.08** (.091) | |
| Difference in log GDP | | | | .580** (.163) |
| Log population, 1992 | −.223** (.111) | | | |
| Log population, 1984 | | −.314 (.193) | | |
| Log population | | | −.230** (.105) | |
| Difference in log population | | | | −.317** (.139) |
| Regional dummies | | | | |
|   North America | 2.04** (.269) | 1.82** (.303) | 1.97** (.194) | |
|   Latin America | 1.18** (.253) | 1.16** (.344) | 1.14** (.213) | |

**Table 1.2**          (continued)

| | Dependent Variable | | | |
|---|---|---|---|---|
| | Log of Capital 1992 (1) | Log of Capital 1984 (2) | Log of Capital (3) | Difference in Log of Capital (4) |
| Asia | .289 | .159 | .200 | |
| | (.306) | (.330) | (.219) | |
| EEC | .410 | .644* | .531** | |
| | (.341) | (.383) | (.260) | |
| YEAR84 | | | −.346 | |
| | | | (.334) | |
| Constant | 4.01** | 3.32** | 3.86** | .782** |
| | (.539) | (.731) | (.512) | (.188) |
| Adjusted $R^2$ | .860 | .755 | .826 | .327 |
| $N$ | 58 | 58 | 116 | 58 |
| 1992 Tax Elasticity | 2.68** | | 2.21** | 2.77** |
| | (.720) | | (.691) | (.744) |
| 1984 Tax Elasticity | | 1.32 | 1.42* | 1.53** |
| | | (.847) | (.741) | (.722) |

*Note:* The columns report estimated OLS coefficients. Columns (1) and (2) present estimated coefficients from regressions using cross-sectional data for 1992 and 1984, respectively. Column (3) presents estimated coefficients using pooled data from the 1984 and 1992 cross sections. Column (4) presents estimated coefficients from a regression of first differences of the 1984 and 1992 cross-sectional data. "Ave ETR for 1988–92" is equal to the country average effective tax rate averaged over 1988, 1990, and 1992. "Ave ETR for 1980–84" is equal to the country average effective tax rate averaged over 1980, 1982, and 1984. "Difference in log(1−Ave ETR)" equals "log(1−Ave ETR for 1988–92)" minus log(1−Ave ETR for 1980–84)." The dummy variable "YEAR84" equals 1 for 1984. The trade regime variable, "TRADE," runs from 0 (most open) to 3 (most restrictive). The bottom panel of the table reports the tax elasticity estimates from each regression. White-corrected standard errors are in parentheses.

*Denotes significance at the 10 percent level.
**Denotes significance at the 5 percent level.

extent that these omitted variables do not vary over time, we can control for their fixed effects by estimating the model in first difference form.

### 1.3.2   Controlling for Permanent Nontax Features of Different Locations

As in the pooled regression, we allow the tax coefficients to differ over time. This gives the following model in difference form:

$$(2) \quad \log K_{i,92} - \log K_{i,84} = \text{const} + \alpha'(\mathbf{Z}_{i,92} - \mathbf{Z}_{i,84})$$

$$+ \beta_{92}\log(1 - t_{i,92}) - \beta_{84}\log(1 - t_{i,84})$$

$$+ \gamma\text{TRADE}_i[\log(1 - t_{i,92}) - \log(1 - t_{i,84})] + \upsilon_t.$$

By rearranging this equation as follows we can test directly whether tax elasticities have changed over time while controlling for country fixed effects:

$$(3) \quad \log K_{i,92} - \log K_{i,84} = \text{const} + \alpha'(\mathbf{Z}_{i,92} - \mathbf{Z}_{i,84})$$
$$+ \beta_{92}[\log(1 - t_{i,92}) - \log(1 - t_{i,84})]$$
$$+ \beta_{\text{diff}} \log(1 - t_{i,84}) + \gamma \text{TRADE}_i[\log(1 - t_{i,92})$$
$$- \log(1 - t_{i,84})] + \iota_t,$$

where $\beta_{\text{diff}} = \beta_{92} - \beta_{84}$.

The fourth column of table 1.2 presents estimates of equation (3); summary statistics on the regression variables are presented in appendix table 1A.4. Three main findings emerge. First, the 1992 elasticity increases substantially in magnitude (from 2.21 to 2.77).[22] Second, the 1984 coefficient also becomes larger (from 1.42 to 1.53) and is more precisely estimated.[23] And finally, the difference in elasticities is greater than 1 and is significant at the 5 percent level, indicating that the location of real manufacturing capital by manufacturing firms may indeed have become more sensitive to tax rates.[24] These results indicate that the estimates in column (3) may have been affected by correlation between the tax rate variable and omitted country characteristics.

Notice that by including a constant term in this regression, we have assumed that the constant terms in the yearly regressions are not identical. It is interesting to note that the constant is positive and highly significant (and remains so in all the estimates). Among other things, this term may be controlling for changes in both tax and nontax factors that affected the

22. We can also calculate a weighted elasticity that reflects the effects of the trade restrictions. Adjusting the elasticity by trade regime using the 1992 real capital stocks as weights gives a slightly lower tax elasticity of 2.64.

23. To test the significance of the 1984 rate we ran the same regression as in equation (3) but with $\log(1 - t_{i,92})$ instead of $\log(1 - t_{i,84})$ entered separately. The result is presented in the last row of table 1.2.

24. Although our estimation results strongly indicate that the tax elasticities are not the same in our two sample years, we also estimated the fixed effects model that constrains the tax elasticities to be equal in 1984 and 1992. To do this we simply dropped the 1984 tax term $\log(1 - t_{i,84})$ from the right-hand side of equation (3). The coefficient on the tax term in this regression was 2.1 (which is the average of the 1984 and 1992 estimated elasticities in column [4] of table 1.2) and was statistically different from zero at the 1 percent confidence level. The estimated coefficients and standard errors on the trade-tax interaction term and the population and GDP variables changed insignificantly. Dropping the trade-tax interaction variable from the constrained model (regressing the difference in capital stocks on a constant term, the difference in the tax terms, the difference in population, and the difference in GDP) lowered both the magnitude and the significance of the tax coefficient (from 2.1 and statistically significant at the 1 percent level to 1.3 and statistically significant at the 10 percent level), had little impact on the size or significance of the population coefficient estimate, and increased both the size and significance of the GDP coefficient estimate.

attractiveness of the United States relative to other countries as a location for investment.

Apart from globalization, another possible explanation for the increased tax sensitivity of investment after 1984 is the change in companies' excess foreign tax credit expectations as a result of the Tax Reform Act of 1986, which lowered the U.S. rate from 46 to 34 percent. If there were no changes in behavior by companies or reactions by foreign governments, the number of companies with excess foreign tax credits would have expanded dramatically. If a company moves into an excess credit position, its effective tax burden in a high-tax country goes up because repatriations do not provide a bonus in terms of usable tax credits, while the effective tax burden in low-tax countries declines because there is no residual U.S. tax. Therefore, a large increase in the proportion of parent companies in excess credit positions could be responsible for the increase in the sensitivity of investment decisions to after-tax returns over our time period. However, research using data from the tax returns of U.S. multinationals shows about the same proportion of foreign source income associated with parents in excess credit positions in 1992 as in 1984. Grubert, Randolph, and Rousslang (1996) report that although the fraction of foreign source income associated with parents in excess credit positions increased from 33 percent in 1984 to 66 percent in 1990, it was only 35 percent by 1992.[25] Although there may have been a temporary effect on investment abroad, it is unlikely that the decrease in the U.S. statutory tax rate plays an important role in explaining our results.[26] In fact, recent research reported in Grubert and Mutti (1999) suggests that repatriation taxes play no role in explaining investment location decisions.

### 1.3.3   Alternative Specifications of the Difference Regression

We experimented with a few different specifications of this regression that are not reported in the table. As was the case in the previous formulation, including the difference in inflation rates in this regression had no effect on the tax elasticities. We also tested whether the trade-tax interaction term is different in the two time periods by adding the 1984 trade-tax term. This additional variable had no impact on the tax effects and was

25. The foreign tax credit is calculated separately for different types ("baskets") of foreign source income. These figures refer to the percentage of foreign source income in the general basket associated with excess credit parents. This basket, which accounted for more than 80 percent of foreign source income in 1992, contains income earned through the active conduct of business abroad. For further details, see Grubert, Randolph, and Rousslang (1996).

26. As mentioned in n. 16, Grubert, Randolph, and Rousslang (1996) conclude from their investigation of multinational tax returns that decreases in country average tax rates are largely responsible for the somewhat surprisingly small increase in the portion of foreign source income held by firms in excess credit positions. The United States was one of many countries that enacted corporate tax–lowering reforms in the late 1980s. For example, as reported in n. 17, we found that statutory tax rates fell by more than 14 percentage points between 1984 and 1992.

not significantly different from zero. In addition, we dropped the trade-tax interaction terms from the regression to determine whether our results are sensitive to their inclusion.[27] Without the trade-tax term, the 1984 elasticity loses its significance (at conventional levels) and the magnitude of both elasticities diminishes slightly: 2.18 for 1992 and .87 for 1984. However, the 1992 elasticity and the difference between the elasticities remain highly significant at above the 5 percent level.

As in Hines and Rice (1994), we also entered our average effective tax rate variables in the linear form. When average effective tax rates appear on the right-hand side instead of the log of 1 minus the average effective tax rate, the coefficients on the 1992, 1984, and difference in tax terms are $-4.23$, $-2.63$, and 1.60, respectively. All three terms are statistically different from zero at the 5 percent level or better. At the mean tax rates for 1992 and 1984 given in table 1.1, these coefficients imply that a 1 percent increase in after-tax returns in a country would increase the real capital stock held by U.S. affiliates in that country by 3.2 percent in 1992 and 1.7 percent in 1984. When squared tax terms are added, their coefficients are positive, not negative as would be expected if the logarithm specification is exactly correct, but they are not statistically significant. There seems to be greater tax sensitivity at low tax rates than would be suggested by the log specification, but in any case, there does not seem to be much substantive difference between the double log and semilog specifications. Given this fact, we prefer the log specification because it yields coefficients that can be directly interpreted as elasticities.

### 1.3.4    Sensitivity Analysis

The remaining two tables test the robustness of the results in column (4) to differences in the tax variables (table 1.3) and the sample (table 1.4) used. In particular, we focus on the significance of the two elasticities and the difference between them. The results are generally consistent with those just presented, although the 1984 tax elasticity is not always statistically significant.

In the first column of table 1.3, we replace the three-year average effective tax rates with lagged effective tax rates. This eliminates the noise contained in the 1984 tax rates, but by eliminating the averaging of tax rates over three years it may also increase the noise in the tax rate variable. Using lagged tax rates yields a slightly smaller tax coefficient for 1992. Although the difference between the two tax coefficients is smaller, it is still statistically different from zero at a 5 percent confidence level. One pos-

---

27. We also ran the regression using only the twenty-two countries for which the trade variable equaled zero. While the difference between the two estimated elasticities remains larger than one, the magnitude of the two elasticities decreases slightly. Both the 1992 tax coefficient and the coefficient on the difference between tax rates remain significant at conventional levels. However, the 1984 tax coefficient loses significance at the 10 percent level.

Table 1.3    **Sensitivity of Results of Regressions in Differences to Changes in the Measure of Tax Rates**

|  | Dependent Variable: Log of Capital in 1992 − Log of Capital in 1984 | | |
|---|---|---|---|
|  | OLS | OLS | IV |
| Tax variables are lagged effective tax rates (ETR) | | | |
| $Log(1-ETR_{1990}) - log(1-ETR_{1982})$ | 2.40** | | |
|  | (.825) | | |
| $Log(1-ETR_{1982})$ | .869** | | |
|  | (.424) | | |
| $Trade*[log(1-ETR_{1990}) - log(1-ETR_{1982})]$ | −.874** | | |
|  | (.401) | | |
| Tax variables are statutory tax rates (t) | | | |
| $Log(1-t_{1992}) - log(1-t_{1984})$ | | 1.87** | 2.49 |
|  | | (.734) | (1.58) |
| $Log(1-t_{1984})$ | | 1.07** | 1.27** |
|  | | (.319) | (.591) |
| $Trade*[log(1-t_{1992}) - log(1-t_{1984})]$ | | −.840** | −.539 |
|  | | (.352) | (.576) |
| $Log\ GDP_{1992} - log\ GDP_{1984}$ | .445** | .490** | .560** |
|  | (.165) | (.150) | (.184) |
| $Log\ population_{1992} - log\ population_{1984}$ | −.227* | −.248** | −.316 |
|  | (.129) | (.096) | (.297) |
| Constant | .775** | 1.02** | .847** |
|  | (.196) | (.204) | (.277) |
| Adjusted $R^2$ | .309 | .315 | .265 |
| N | 58 | 58 | 58 |
| 1992 Tax Elasticity | 2.40** | 1.87** | 2.49 |
|  | (.825) | (.734) | (1.58) |
| 1984 Tax Elasticity | 1.53** | .795 | 1.21 |
|  | (.640) | (.585) | (1.54) |

*Note:* Columns (1) and (2) report estimated OLS coefficients. Column (3) reports estimated coefficients from an instrumental variables regression in which statutory tax rates are used as instruments for country average effective tax rates (ETRs). The trade regime variable, "TRADE," runs from 0 (most open) to 3 (most restrictive). The bottom panel reports tax elasticity estimates from each regression. White-corrected standard errors for the coefficient estimates in the first two columns are in parentheses. The standard errors in the third column are not White-corrected.
*Denotes significance at the 10 percent level.
**Denotes significance at the 5 percent level.

sible reason for the decrease in the magnitude of the difference in elasticities is that the 1988 rates no longer receive any weight in the analysis. Table 1.1 shows that the big drop in rates occurred between 1988 and 1990. Averaging in 1988 with 1990 and 1992 may have led to an underestimation of the tax rate change between 1984 and 1992 and an overestimate of the responsiveness of investment to the change.

As previously discussed, a potential problem with the average effective

**Table 1.4    Sensitivity of Results of Regressions in Differences to Changes in Sample Selection**

| | Dependent Variable = Log of Capital in 1992 − Log of Capital in 1984 | | | |
| --- | --- | --- | --- | --- |
| | Include Only Countries with Populations Greater Than 1 Million | Include Only Countries with Changes in AETRs Between .35 and −.10 | Include Only Countries with Changes in Log of Capital Stocks between 2 and −.5 | Include Only CFCs of Parent Companies in Both the 1984 and 1992 Samples |
| Log(1−Ave ETR $_{1988-92}$) − log(1−Ave ETR $_{1980-84}$) | 2.78** | 2.48** | 2.00** | 2.410** |
| | (.746) | (.870) | (.574) | (.676) |
| Log(1−Ave ETR $_{1980-84}$) | 1.19** | 1.20** | .855** | .873** |
| | (.346) | (.355) | (.258) | (.406) |
| Trade*[log(1−Ave ETR $_{1988-92}$) − log(1−Ave ETR $_{1980-84}$)] | −.507 | −.544 | −.130 | −.119 |
| | (.441) | (.531) | (.283) | (.444) |
| Log GDP $_{1992}$ − log GDP $_{1984}$ | .585** | .558** | .605** | .454** |
| | (.165) | (.173) | (.135) | (.152) |
| Log population $_{1992}$ − log population $_{1984}$ | −.310 | −.304** | −.311** | −.276 |
| | (.200) | (.137) | (.144) | (.181) |
| Constant | .759** | .795** | .679** | .651** |
| | (.141) | (.210) | (.160) | (.214) |
| Adjusted $R^2$ | .314 | .293 | .404 | .251 |
| N | 56 | 55 | 53 | 58 |
| 1992 Tax Elasticity | 2.78** | 2.48** | 2.00** | 2.41** |
| | (.746) | (.870) | (.574) | (.676) |
| 1984 Tax Elasticity | 1.59** | 1.28 | 1.06* | 1.54** |
| | (.737) | (.808) | (.607) | (.608) |

*Note:* "Ave ETR $_{1988-92}$" is the country average effective tax rate averaged over 1988, 1990, and 1992. "Ave ETR $_{1980-84}$" is the country average effective tax rate averaged over 1980, 1982, and 1984. The trade regime variable, "TRADE," runs from 0 (most open) to 3 (most restrictive). The last column excludes the CFCs of parents that were not in both the 1984 and 1992 samples. This screen eliminated about one-third of our parent companies. The bottom panel reports tax elasticity estimates from each regression. The columns report estimated OLS coefficients. White-corrected standard errors are in parentheses.

*Denotes significance at the 10 percent level.

**Denotes significance at the 5 percent level.

tax rates is that they are endogenous to investment decisions. The effective tax rate in a country may be low in one year because of a recent increase in investment activity in that country. Using statutory tax rates eliminates this potential endogeneity problem. At the same time, though, statutory rates do not capture the effects of tax base differences across countries. The second column shows that our qualitative results are unaffected by this measure of taxes—both the 1992 tax elasticity and the difference in elasticities are positive and significant. However, the 1984 elasticity is no longer statistically significant. Notice that the magnitude of the tax coefficients decreases, suggesting that investment location decisions are more responsive to differences in average effective tax rates than to differences in statutory rates.

An alternative way of addressing the endogeneity problem is to use an instrumental variables approach. In column (3), we present estimates that use statutory tax rates as instruments for average effective tax rates. Using instrumented tax rates had little effect on our coefficient estimates but increased our standard errors significantly. In fact, column (3) shows that neither elasticity was significantly different from zero at standard levels. These results suggest that the statutory rates do not adequately capture the variation in the component of effective tax rates that explain location choices.

Table 1.4 shows the results of a series of experiments in which we restrict the sample in different ways. To test whether outliers played a significant role in our regressions we restricted the sample to include only countries with populations greater than 1 million (fifty-six countries), eliminated countries for which the difference of three-year average effective tax rates was greater than 0.35 and less than −0.10 (three countries), and deleted countries for which the difference in the log of the capital stocks between 1992 and 1984 was greater than 2 or less than −0.5 (this eliminates the five countries in which capital stocks grew more than 700 percent or contracted by more than 40 percent). Column (1) shows that our main findings are not the result of activities in tax havens. The elasticities and the difference between them change little in magnitude or statistical significance. Removing countries with large changes in average effective tax rates from the sample decreases the magnitude and significance of the tax coefficients, although the 1992 elasticity and the difference between the two elasticities remain significant at the 5 percent level or better (see column [2]). Countries experiencing large changes in the real capital stocks of U.S. manufacturing affiliates have an impact on the magnitude of our tax elasticity estimates and the difference between them. However, all three coefficients are still significant at the 10 percent level or better.

Finally, in the last column we report results from the linked panel, which contains the same parents in both years. This panel contains about two-thirds of the parents in our unlinked data. Both the 1984 and 1992 elasticities and the difference between them are large and statistically highly significant in this panel.

## 1.4    Conclusion

Measuring the extent to which host-country taxes affect the allocation of multinationals' foreign direct investment across foreign jurisdictions has been an active area of research in international taxation. The most recent studies indicate that taxes exert a strong influence on location decisions. Our estimates, using two years of data from the U.S. Department of the Treasury tax files, provide additional evidence that the foreign investment of manufacturing firms is sensitive to differences in host-country tax rates. Unlike in previous estimates, however, in ours we control for any (permanent) differences in nontax features of countries that may be correlated with host-country tax rates.

Our estimates with country fixed effects produce tax elasticities that are large in magnitude and generally precisely estimated. Our basic estimates yield an elasticity of real capital to after-tax rates of return of close to 3 in 1992 and about 1.5 in 1984; both are significant at standard levels. Comparing these elasticities to those estimated from a model in which the two years of data are simply pooled together without controlling for country fixed effects shows the importance of taking these effects into account. Both the 1984 and 1992 elasticities increase in magnitude and in significance.

The increase of more than one in the estimated elasticities from 1984 to 1992 also suggests that the allocation of real capital held in manufacturing affiliates abroad by manufacturing parents may have become more sensitive to differences in host-country taxes in recent years. This would be consistent with increasing international mobility of capital and globalization of production. Controlling for fixed effects is again important, since the difference between the 1984 and 1992 elasticities is statistically significant when country fixed effects are taken into account, but not otherwise.

# Appendix

**Table 1A.1**      Country Average Effective Tax Rates by Year

|  | 1980 | 1982 | 1984 | 1986 | 1988 | 1990 | 1992 |
|---|---|---|---|---|---|---|---|
| Argentina | 0.2121 | 0.1185 | 0.0377 | 0.1134 | 0.2434 | 0.0483 | 0.1539 |
| Australia | 0.3715 | 0.4071 | 0.4070 | 0.3718 | 0.3426 | 0.3451 | 0.3222 |
| Austria | 0.3548 | 0.2868 | 0.3933 | 0.2347 | 0.7289 | 0.2859 | 0.3258 |
| Belgium | 0.4023 | 0.3457 | 0.3724 | 0.3789 | 0.2895 | 0.2235 | 0.2594 |
| Bermuda | 0.0904 | 0.0841 | 0.0333 | 0.0221 | 0.0099 | 0.0482 | 0.0706 |
| Brazil | 0.3077 | 0.3004 | 0.3140 | 0.2892 | 0.3297 | 0.2335 | 0.1289 |
| Canada | 0.3907 | 0.3594 | 0.3720 | 0.3850 | 0.3434 | 0.3159 | 0.3538 |
| Chile | 0.3181 | 0.4124 | 0.3849 | 0.1167 | 0.0900 | 0.0470 | 0.0978 |
| China | 0.2352 | 0.2059 | 0.1640 | 0.0073 | 0.1170 | 0.0529 | 0.0573 |
| Colombia | 0.3100 | 0.3110 | 0.3534 | 0.3526 | 0.2581 | 0.2929 | 0.2912 |
| Costa Rica | 0.2718 | 0.3984 | 0.3184 | 0.3465 | 0.3189 | 0.0969 | 0.1203 |
| Denmark | 0.3503 | 0.2244 | 0.3583 | 0.4288 | 0.4478 | 0.3181 | 0.3104 |
| Dominican Republic | 0.2234 | 0.3345 | 0.3099 | 0.3287 | 0.0936 | 0.1582 | 0.1196 |
| Ecuador | 0.1639 | 0.1895 | 0.2453 | 0.2300 | 0.2851 | 0.1008 | 0.1714 |
| Egypt | 0.3181 | 0.3181 | 0.3239 | 0.2169 | 0.1310 | 0.1948 | 0.1638 |
| El Salvador | 0.2635 | 0.2427 | 0.3138 | 0.2899 | 0.3194 | 0.2342 | 0.2168 |
| Finland | 0.4354 | 0.4701 | 0.4331 | 0.3558 | 0.2214 | 0.3187 | 0.1584 |
| France | 0.3958 | 0.4511 | 0.4367 | 0.3955 | 0.3775 | 0.2977 | 0.2283 |
| Greece | 0.1947 | 0.3541 | 0.3422 | 0.2247 | 0.2488 | 0.2570 | 0.3338 |
| Guatemala | 0.3620 | 0.3183 | 0.2087 | 0.2906 | 0.3845 | 0.2838 | 0.1828 |
| Honduras | 0.3735 | 0.3980 | 0.4396 | 0.3815 | 0.4615 | 0.3538 | 0.4187 |
| Hong Kong | 0.1338 | 0.1422 | 0.2032 | 0.0936 | 0.1390 | 0.1178 | 0.1011 |
| India | 0.5629 | 0.5691 | 0.5764 | 0.4029 | 0.3919 | 0.3118 | 0.4364 |
| Indonesia | 0.3651 | 0.3478 | 0.3695 | 0.3476 | 0.2632 | 0.3105 | 0.3516 |
| Ireland | 0.0800 | 0.0295 | 0.0293 | 0.0342 | 0.0261 | 0.0324 | 0.0579 |
| Israel | 0.1814 | 0.1687 | 0.0960 | 0.3299 | 0.2016 | 0.0820 | 0.1021 |
| Italy | 0.2861 | 0.3368 | 0.3739 | 0.3623 | 0.3396 | 0.3505 | 0.3256 |
| Jamaica | 0.3767 | 0.3497 | 0.3245 | 0.3508 | 0.3387 | 0.2744 | 0.2621 |
| Japan | 0.4571 | 0.5134 | 0.5265 | 0.5050 | 0.5693 | 0.5201 | 0.5027 |
| Kenya | 0.4106 | 0.4662 | 0.4683 | 0.4592 | 0.4899 | 0.4010 | 0.3585 |
| Luxembourg | 0.3363 | 0.4036 | 0.4957 | 0.3380 | 0.4313 | 0.2871 | 0.2160 |
| Malaysia | 0.1314 | 0.1355 | 0.1717 | 0.2674 | 0.0758 | 0.1394 | 0.0814 |
| Mexico | 0.4346 | 0.3805 | 0.3589 | 0.3011 | 0.3291 | 0.3177 | 0.2766 |
| Morocco | 0.5226 | 0.5029 | 0.5421 | 0.4041 | 0.4908 | 0.3460 | 0.4094 |
| Netherlands | 0.2997 | 0.2623 | 0.1962 | 0.2012 | 0.2480 | 0.2107 | 0.1789 |
| New Zealand | 0.4306 | 0.4064 | 0.3926 | 0.4380 | 0.3702 | 0.2094 | 0.2867 |
| Nigeria | 0.4052 | 0.4006 | 0.3131 | 0.4391 | 0.2855 | 0.2676 | 0.1301 |
| Norway | 0.2860 | 0.4188 | 0.3747 | 0.3618 | 0.1703 | 0.1352 | 0.2904 |
| Pakistan | 0.5365 | 0.6144 | 0.4559 | 0.4397 | 0.4761 | 0.4430 | 0.4367 |
| Panama | 0.1527 | 0.1125 | 0.2599 | 0.0763 | 0.0622 | 0.0603 | 0.0918 |
| Peru | 0.4170 | 0.4887 | 0.4876 | 0.4131 | 0.5914 | 0.1483 | 0.1544 |
| Philippines | 0.3405 | 0.3345 | 0.3618 | 0.3499 | 0.3499 | 0.3257 | 0.3347 |
| Portugal | 0.2867 | 0.3263 | 0.2519 | 0.2421 | 0.2664 | 0.2849 | 0.2530 |
| Singapore | 0.1705 | 0.1734 | 0.0842 | 0.0256 | 0.0402 | 0.0537 | 0.0565 |
| South Africa | 0.2767 | 0.3703 | 0.5021 | 0.2886 | 0.4361 | 0.4175 | 0.4183 |
| South Korea | 0.3112 | 0.4347 | 0.2062 | 0.2986 | 0.3489 | 0.4477 | 0.2575 |
| Spain | 0.1947 | 0.2615 | 0.2836 | 0.2757 | 0.2277 | 0.2669 | 0.2533 |

(*continued*)

**Table 1A.1** (continued)

| | 1980 | 1982 | 1984 | 1986 | 1988 | 1990 | 1992 |
|---|---|---|---|---|---|---|---|
| Sri Lanka | 0.3643 | 0.5563 | 0.2963 | 0.5465 | 0.5164 | 0.4409 | 0.4054 |
| Sweden | 0.4404 | 0.5075 | 0.5734 | 0.5550 | 0.5166 | 0.2024 | 0.1669 |
| Switzerland | 0.2206 | 0.2121 | 0.2062 | 0.1838 | 0.1126 | 0.1538 | 0.1387 |
| Thailand | 0.3843 | 0.3254 | 0.3194 | 0.2828 | 0.3134 | 0.1795 | 0.2465 |
| Turkey | 0.5839 | 0.5628 | 0.4194 | 0.4378 | 0.4223 | 0.3164 | 0.2295 |
| United Kingdom | 0.2749 | 0.2713 | 0.3224 | 0.3713 | 0.2664 | 0.2126 | 0.1929 |
| Uruguay | 0.1837 | 0.2318 | 0.3099 | 0.0809 | 0.2762 | 0.1926 | 0.1897 |
| Venezuela | 0.2796 | 0.2826 | 0.3376 | 0.2990 | 0.3630 | 0.2211 | 0.1973 |
| West Germany | 0.4409 | 0.5049 | 0.5034 | 0.4793 | 0.3281 | 0.3242 | 0.2893 |
| Zambia | 0.4495 | 0.3950 | 0.4728 | 0.3799 | 0.0842 | 0.2804 | 0.2793 |
| Zimbabwe | 0.3312 | 0.3943 | 0.5231 | 0.1984 | 0.5262 | 0.4092 | 0.1203 |

*Note:* The table reports country average effective tax rates for U.S. manufacturing subsidiaries. Average effective tax rates in each country are calculated by dividing the total income taxes paid by controlled foreign corporations in the manufacturing sector by their total earnings and profits. Information on total income taxes paid and earnings and profits comes from the Form 5471 portion of the U.S. Department of the Treasury corporate tax files.

**Table 1A.2**    **Real Capital Stock by Year**

| | Capital Stock (in millions) | | | Capital Stock (in millions) | |
|---|---|---|---|---|---|
| | 1984 | 1992 | | 1984 | 1992 |
| Argentina | 1,536.7 | 2,101.7 | Kenya | 54.7 | 37.9 |
| Australia | 4,174.4 | 8,314.9 | Luxembourg | 225.3 | 710.6 |
| Austria | 477.3 | 834.8 | Malaysia | 493.5 | 1,587.0 |
| Belgium | 2,017.6 | 6,288.6 | Mexico | 3,293.0 | 6,821.4 |
| Bermuda | 132.3 | 533.2 | Morocco | 30.2 | 69.2 |
| Brazil | 5,091.2 | 11,288.7 | Netherlands | 3,735.1 | 10,566.1 |
| Canada | 15,276.0 | 36,573.3 | New Zealand | 1,315.9 | 605.1 |
| Chile | 103.1 | 984.6 | Nigeria | 58.3 | 61.5 |
| China | 206.7 | 494.2 | Norway | 131.4 | 785.2 |
| Colombia | 429.2 | 975.5 | Pakistan | 63.7 | 118.1 |
| Costa Rica | 60.5 | 143.5 | Panama | 259.4 | 630.2 |
| Denmark | 254.3 | 725.9 | Peru | 255.7 | 108.2 |
| Dominican Republic | 12.5 | 25.5 | Philippines | 368.5 | 699.1 |
| Ecuador | 91.3 | 101.9 | Portugal | 201.1 | 912.5 |
| Egypt | 25.7 | 96.3 | Singapore | 719.8 | 3,598.9 |
| El Salvador | 11.3 | 61.5 | South Africa | 1,023.7 | 464.2 |
| Finland | 78.3 | 290.5 | South Korea | 258.1 | 1,721.3 |
| France | 5,631.0 | 19,710.1 | Spain | 4,153.8 | 7,207.5 |
| Greece | 90.2 | 270.7 | Sri Lanka | 10.0 | 11.0 |
| Guatemala | 117.9 | 77.3 | Sweden | 385.7 | 2,290.5 |
| Honduras | 56.9 | 86.9 | Switzerland | 935.0 | 2,489.0 |
| Hong Kong | 242.6 | 635.6 | Thailand | 183.9 | 1,385.3 |
| India | 221.5 | 361.6 | Turkey | 125.0 | 584.2 |
| Indonesia | 138.2 | 279.6 | United Kingdom | 12,632.0 | 32,970.4 |
| Ireland | 470.4 | 1,513.2 | Uruguay | 78.5 | 136.4 |
| Israel | 197.8 | 504.3 | Venezuela | 946.2 | 1,138.0 |
| Italy | 2,871.4 | 12,983.0 | West Germany | 15,176.3 | 28,909.4 |
| Jamaica | 15.6 | 47.6 | Zambia | 10.7 | 15.1 |
| Japan | 8,053.9 | 14,918.9 | Zimbabwe | 43.8 | 30.6 |

*Source:* Form 5471 information from the U.S. Department of the Treasury tax files.

**Table 1A.3**          **Tax Rate Regression Showing Noise in 1984 Effective Tax Rate**

| | Dependent Variable | |
|---|---|---|
| | ETR 1986 | ETR 1990 |
| Constant | .010 | .011 |
| ETR | (.034) | (.032) |
| 1980 | .297 | .037 |
| | (.199) | (.194) |
| 1982 | .426 | .288 |
| | (.197) | (.195) |
| 1984 | .157 | −.019 |
| | (.145) | (.144) |
| 1986 | | .140 |
| | | (.133) |
| 1988 | | .289 |
| | | (.095) |
| Adjusted $R^2$ | .604 | .553 |
| $N$ | 58 | 58 |

*Note:* The columns report estimated ordinary least squares (OLS) coefficients. Standard errors are in parentheses. ETR = effective tax rate.

**Table 1A.4**          **Means and Standard Deviations for Variables in the Difference Regressions**

| Variable | Mean | Standard Deviation |
|---|---|---|
| Log capital, 1992 − log capital, 1984 | 0.812 | 0.684 |
| Log(1 − Ave ETR for 1980–84) | −0.421 | 0.178 |
| Log(1 − Ave ETR for 1988–92) | −0.315 | 0.159 |
| Log(1−Ave ETR for 1988–92) − log(1−Ave ETR for 1980–84) | 0.106 | 0.126 |
| Log population, 1992 − log population, 1984 | 0.153 | 0.255 |
| Log GDP, 1992 − log GDP, 1984 | 0.660 | 0.484 |
| TRADE | 1.160 | 1.150 |
| TRADE*[log(1−Ave ETR for 1988–92) − log(1−Ave ETR for 1980–84)] | 0.155 | 0.270 |

*Note:* "Ave ETR" is the country average effective tax rate. "Ave ETR for 1988–92" is equal to the country average effective tax rate averaged over 1988, 1990, and 1992. "Ave ETR for 1980–84" is equal to the country average effective tax rate averaged over 1980, 1982, and 1984. The trade regime variable, "TRADE," runs from 0 (most open) to 3 (most restrictive).

# References

Altshuler, Rosanne, and T. Scott Newlon. 1993. The effects of U.S. tax policy on the income repatriation patterns of U.S. multinational corporations. In *Studies in international taxation,* ed. Alberto Giovannini, R. Glenn Hubbard, and Joel Slemrod, 77–115. Chicago: University of Chicago Press.

Boskin, Michael J., and William G. Gale. 1987. New results on the effects of tax policy on the international location of investment. In *The effects of taxation on capital accumulation,* ed. Martin Feldstein, 201–19. Chicago: University of Chicago Press.

Gordon, Roger. 1986. Taxation of investment and savings in a world economy. *American Economic Review* 76:1086–1102.

Grubert, Harry. 1998. Taxes and the division of foreign operating income among royalties, interest, dividends and retained earnings. *Journal of Public Economics* 68:269–90.

Grubert, Harry, and John Mutti. 1991. Taxes, tariffs and transfer pricing in multinational corporation decision making. *Review of Economics and Statistics* 33: 285–93.

Grubert, Harry, and John Mutti. 1997. Do taxes influence where U.S. corporations invest? U.S. Department of the Treasury, Office of Tax Analysis. Mimeograph.

Grubert, Harry, and John Mutti. 1999. Dividend exemption versus the current system for taxing foreign business income. U.S. Department of the Treasury, Office of Tax Analysis. Mimeograph.

Grubert, Harry, William Randolph, and Donald Rousslang. 1996. The response of countries and multinational companies to the Tax Reform Act of 1986. *National Tax Journal* 49 (3): 341–58.

Harris, David G. 1993. The impact of U.S. tax law revision on multinational corporations' capital location and income-shifting decisions. *Journal of Accounting Research* 31 (Suppl.): 111–40.

Hartman, David G. 1981. Domestic tax policy and foreign investment: Some evidence. NBER Working Paper no. 784. Cambridge, Mass.: National Bureau of Economic Research, June.

Hines, James R., Jr. 1997. Tax policy and the activities of multinational corporations. In *Fiscal policy: Lessons from economic research,* ed. Alan J. Auerbach, 402–45. Cambridge: MIT Press.

Hines, James R., Jr., and Eric M. Rice. 1994. Fiscal paradise: Foreign tax havens and American business. *Quarterly Journal of Economics* 109:149–82.

International Monetary Fund (IMF). 1984. *International Monetary Fund international financial statistics.* Washington, D.C.: IMF.

———. 1992. *International Monetary Fund international financial statistics.* Washington, D.C.: IMF.

Newlon, T. Scott. 1987. Tax policy and the multinational firm's financial policy and investment decisions. Ph.D. diss. Princeton University.

Price Waterhouse. 1984. *Corporate taxes: A worldwide summary.* New York: Price Waterhouse Center for Transnational Taxation.

———. 1992. *Corporate taxes: A worldwide summary.* New York: Price Waterhouse Center for Transnational Taxation.

World Bank. 1987. *World development report.* Washington, D.C.: World Bank.

# Comment    Jack M. Mintz

### A Eulogy for the Use of Average Tax Rates in Investment Equations

In recent years, there has been considerable effort to model the impact of taxation on the location of investment. These efforts have included

Jack M. Mintz is the Arthur Andersen Professor of Taxation at the Rotman School of Management, University of Toronto.

country cross section and time series studies looking at how taxes impact the investment decisions of firms. Two examples of quite different approaches include Cummins, Hassett, and Hubbard (1996) and Hartman (1984) (see also the survey by Hines 1996). The first uses publicly available data but models the capital decision of the firm based on a cost of capital—taxes are incorporated following the Jorgenson-Hall approach. The second example uses reduced-form equations that look at capital decisions on a more aggregated level (by country), with decisions being related to proxies for the return on capital and the average rate of tax (taxes divided by profits of the firm).

The paper by Altshuler, Grubert, and Newlon is an ambitious study that follows the approach of Grubert and Mutti (1997). It has the advantage of using a rich source of data that provide values of capital, taxes, and profits of U.S. manufacturing subsidiaries operating in close to sixty countries, spanning the years 1980 to 1992. The authors regress investment on average tax rates that are measured as corporate income taxes divided by book profits. In my comments I will provide a brief overview of the econometric model and, thereafter, a critique of the use of average tax rates in investment equations.

The Basic Econometric Model

The econometric model presented in the paper is a parsimonious fixed effects model. It involves regressing the aggregated manufacturing capital stock of a country on tax rate variables, a single-year measure of the openness of the economy, GDP, and regional dummies. Most of the variables had their expected effects on the location of capital.

Rather than try to estimate the impact of taxes on each firm, the authors choose to aggregate data to the country level. It should be noted, however, that it is somewhat unclear whether a link exists between GDP and manufacturing capital stock if industrial structure differs across countries. To the extent that GDP is a poor proxy of the output effect on the demand for manufacturing capital, this may give the average tax rate variable a greater role in the results than appropriate. Moreover, the concentration on manufacturing is a bit unfortunate since, in many countries, resource and service sectors are quite important and country tax systems reflect a particular industrial structure.

The variable capturing openness of the economy is not significant. I suspect that this results from the use of one year of data derived from a World Bank study when many countries throughout the 1980s and early 1990s substantially improved their openness, particularly in Latin America. Another approach would have been to use the difference in a real rate of interest comparable to the U.S. real rate (for example, bank loan rates that are obtainable from International Monetary Fund publications). This variable could be viewed as a measure of risk or credit market inefficiencies.

The general result, that capital is affected by the average tax rate with elasticities of more than 2, is rather surprising, given the level of aggregation. Studies that tend to aggregate data in the cost of capital literature often tend to find lower numbers, if at all significant. I believe that the strong tax effects on investment obtained from these studies result from unwelcome dependency of average tax rates on investment.

### Endogeneity of Average Tax Rates

I have been critical of the use of average tax rates for investment equations in the past because the tax rates are endogenous to the investment decision. Higher investment or growth in capital stocks result in lower average tax rates, assuming that the statutory tax rate is greater than the average tax rate and that tax writeoffs for capital are greater than the economic costs of replacing capital. Therefore, in periods of sustained growth rates for firms, industries, or countries, average tax rates tend to fall when investment increases provided the previous two assumptions hold (and vice versa if the converse holds). The authors wisely anticipated this criticism and therefore used a number of proxies to avoid this endogeneity—these proxies included the statutory tax rates and a tax rate averaged for a period.

These attempts to deal with the limitations of average tax rates are important. Nonetheless, as discussed below, the average tax rates measured for a host country still are truly limited in application, and I will now discuss these issues more fully.

### Complexities of Tax Systems and Limitations
### for the Use of Average Tax Rates

Trying to understand the corporate tax system for one country is difficult enough. Capital is affected not only by corporate income taxes but by a host of other taxes on capital—asset or net worth taxes (as is Canada, Germany, and Italy, for example), sales taxes on capital inputs (Canada and the United States), property taxes, and minimum taxes on profits, assets, turnover, or dividends. Although research has concentrated on the corporate income tax in that it is the largest tax, this is not the case in many countries. For example, in Canada, businesses in 1995 paid close to $19 billion in capital and property taxes and $18 billion in corporate income taxes.

Tax provisions require taking into account rates of tax and detailed aspects of the base, including the treatment of inventory costs, depreciation, interest expense (such as thin capitalization ratios), and losses. The treatment of losses for tax purposes is very important—a profitable corporation may not be paying tax at a point in time because of either current fast writeoffs in the tax system or of using up a bank of past losses reflecting past policies and economic circumstances. Thus, the average tax rate, once aggregated across firms, depends not only on current but also on past tax policy.

More complicated is the relationship between tax systems at the international level. A host country's tax rate influences not only U.S. investments but also the U.S. tax regime. Some of the prominent features include the following:

- The average tax rate for a particular country is not independent of other tax systems because U.S. tax considerations will affect the timing and source of remissions. A U.S. corporation pays tax on income remitted to the United States net of foreign tax credits abroad, and the average tax rate plays a role in determining the amount of the foreign tax credit. Although the United States uses a global tax credit and allows companies to aggregate sources of remitted income and foreign tax credits, restrictions are in place that limit the degree to which this is available, as in the case of interest from high-tax countries. These restrictions apply differently across countries and are further complicated by withholding tax regimes and thin capitalization and other rules in the host country. Generally, however, a firm can manipulate its credits by changing its remissions of types of income to the parent from abroad (Altshuler and Newlon [1993]). For example, when remitting dividends with excess credits, the parent can simultaneously remit other charges deductible from income in the host country to eliminate excess tax credits and to avoid paying U.S. tax on income.

- Average tax rates will depend on past and current policies to remit income from subsidiaries to the U.S. parent. Prior to 1986, the foreign average tax rate could be blown up in years of remitting income by avoiding certain deductions (for example, losses, discretionary capital cost allowances, or tax credits) that would result in lower average tax rates during that year. The following year, the deductions would be claimed if no income was to be remitted, thereby lowering the average tax rate. After 1987, eligible earnings and profits and the foreign tax credit became related to accumulated earnings and taxes paid over time, thereby reducing the scope for manipulating tax credits and average tax rates in this manner.

- An average tax rate in the host country does not capture the full impact of a subsidiary's decision on the taxes paid by the multinational. United States laws are complicated by allocation rules that could result in the allocation of certain costs to foreign source income—especially interest expense—thereby affecting the amount of U.S. tax paid on income earned in the United States. These rules, which require companies to allocate interest expense according the share of foreign to worldwide assets, became more stringent after 1986. Under allocation, an investment decision by a subsidiary can affect the average tax rate in the host country as well as the U.S. tax rate on domestic income, as has been discussed (Altshuler and Mintz 1994).

- Average tax rates of a host country will also depend on the tax planning decisions of multinationals that link foreign tax considerations across a number of countries. Multinationals often use planning techniques, especially with respect to interest expense "double dipping," that can result in a reduction of both foreign and U.S. taxes. With multiple deductions for interest and other expenses, both U.S. and foreign taxes can be reduced, resulting in a lower effective tax rate in both host and home countries. Some of these arrangements have been facilitated by such past U.S. actions as the provision of limited liability partnership status. On the other hand, the United States in the past few years has aggressively limited some of these schemes that result in the reduction of U.S. and foreign taxes. Recent changes to the treatment of active and passive income, including the new "check-the-box" rules, will have a different impact on tax planning that is not yet fully known.

The Pitfalls of Using Average Tax Rates for Empirical Work

The previous discussion illustrates only some of the complications in the foreign and U.S. tax regimes that make one skeptical about using average corporate income tax rates in a host country to determine the impact of tax on investment. More specifically, I would suggest that the results in the paper by Altshuler, Grubert, and Newlon may be overstated for the following possible reasons:

1. Investment depends on other features of a host country's tax system besides the corporate income tax. One does not know if the inclusion of other taxes might have resulted in better or less precise estimates (elasticities could be lower in value as a result). For example, there is not a significant difference between U.S. and Canadian manufacturing corporate income tax provisions—the corporate income tax rates and the present value of tax depreciation rates are similar. However, Canadian average tax rates on manufacturing are higher than those found in the United States, once capital taxes, sales tax on capital inputs, and property taxes are included in the comparison.

2. The average corporate income tax rate for a host country does not take into account the impact of the subsidiary's decisions on corporate income taxes paid by the United States on investments abroad or in the United States. As remarked earlier, the interest allocation rules alone and international double-dipping arrangements are examples whereby the subsidiary's investment decision can impact other taxes paid, not just those to the host country. Also, when the parent is in a deficient tax credit position, the parent's taxes on remitted income will be affected by the subsid-

iary's decisions. In principle one should be measuring a total average tax rate that incorporates the effects of both host and other taxes paid by the U.S. multinational. The bias introduced by leaving out the impact of subsidiary decisions on the overall taxes paid by the multinational is not clear.

3. There seems to be no incorporation of the dramatic changes in the U.S. treatment of foreign income since 1986, including interest allocation rules and foreign tax credit limitations. One would have expected these rules to result in a reduction of foreign tax credits as indicated by the data. I would suspect that parents with excess credits in 1986 would have responded differently and tried to reduce their average tax rates abroad. This and other factors such as leveraged buyouts in the United States could have resulted in a divestment of capital investment and remissions to the parent (thereby resulting in an increasingly negative correlation between average tax rates and capital). Moreover, prior to 1986, many companies, when remitting income back to the U.S. parent, often reduced their reliance on capital investment abroad and blew up their average tax rates in those years. The average corporate income tax rate measure for a host country therefore may overstate the negative correlation between capital investment and taxes.

4. The aggregation of taxes and profits in a country masks the role of tax losses in affecting investment decisions. Since losses have a value in reducing taxes at some point through loss carryforwards (assuming that carry-backs have already been reflected in tax payments), the average tax rate may be overstated in a particular year because taxes should be reduced by the reduced taxes of other years. This is particularly important for cycles—during downturns, when investment slows down, average tax rates aggregated across firms tend to rise, and during upturns, average tax rates tend to be lower when losses are being written off. Although the authors use time-averaged or lagged effective tax rates, it would seem that the 1982, 1990, and 1992 effective tax rates are somewhat high and that a bias may be introduced exaggerating the effects of taxes on investment.

5. Many studies of foreign investment suggest that the anticipated changes in exchange rates can have a significant impact on investment. If a host country's exchange rate is expected to devalue, investment decisions could be discouraged while an anticipated revaluation would attract more capital. If a country's exchange rate declines, a parent may choose to reduce capital expenditures and remit more dividends out of the country for several years—average tax rates may rise during a period when income is remitted.

## Conclusion

As I have tried to illustrate, the use of average corporate income tax rates for a host country in an investment equation may result in a biased estimate of the impact of taxes on investment. The foremost problem is that the average tax rate depends on current and past investment decisions that tend to overstate the impact of taxes on investment. Moreover, many institutional features of the tax system are not incorporated in the measure of the average tax rate. These include the impact of losses in affecting the value of taxes paid in the host country or abroad, the effect of timing of remissions to the parent on average tax rates, and other tax-planning schemes.

The alternative for investment studies is to use the effective tax rate on marginal investments, which may be defined as the amount of tax paid on income earned by the last unit of capital held by the firm. Marginal effective tax rates, in principle, can be derived from a theoretical model that incorporates most of the important features of corporate tax systems, including minimum taxes, tax losses, capital taxes, and home-country taxes on remitted earnings. Theoretically, the marginal effective tax rate is a superior measure because it better characterizes the effect of taxes on capital decisions. However, one could criticize this tax rate measure since it is often difficult to obtain data to incorporate important institutional features in estimates of marginal effective tax rates; yet one should not jump to the conclusion that average tax rates are necessarily any better than marginal effective tax rates. If a complete set of data were available, it would seem that the marginal effective tax rate is clearly the appropriate statistic to use in an investment equation.

## References

Altshuler, Rosanne, and Jack M. Mintz. 1995. Interest allocation rules: Effects and policy. *International Tax and Public Finance* 2 (1): 7–35.
Altshuler, Rosanne, and Scott Newlon. 1993. The effects of U.S. tax policy on the income repatriation patterns of U.S. multinational corporations. In *Studies in international taxation,* ed. Alberto Giovannini, R. Glenn Hubbard, and Joel Slemrod, 77–115. University of Chicago Press, Chicago.
Cummins, Jason, Kevin A. Hassett, and R. Glenn Hubbard. 1996. Tax reforms and investment: A cross-country comparison. *Journal of Public Economics* 62 (1/2): 237–73.
Grubert, Harry, and John Mutti. 1997. Do taxes influence where U.S. corporations invest? U.S. Department of the Treasury. Mimeograph.
Hartman, D. G. 1984. Tax policy and foreign direct investment in the U.S. *National Tax Journal* 37 (4): 475–88.
Hines, James R., Jr. 1999. Lessons from behavioral responses to international taxation. *National Tax Journal* 52 (2): 305–22.

# Tax Sparing and Direct Investment in Developing Countries

James R. Hines Jr.

## 2.1 Introduction

Only a small fraction of the world's foreign direct investment (FDI) is located in developing countries. In 1990, countries that were not members of the OECD received roughly 15 percent of the $200 billion of world FDI. Since these developing countries account for 35 percent of world GDP in 1990 (and 80 percent of the world's population), they received a much smaller fraction of total FDI than even their relatively modest economic activity levels appear to warrant. Numerous explanations have been advanced to account for the unwillingness of investors to locate FDI in the developing world, explanations that typically focus on distances to final markets, the difficulty or cost of obtaining important factors of production, inhospitable legal and regulatory environments, and the relatively undeveloped state of public infrastructure such as roads, port facilities, and telecommunications.[1] Although the large number of available explanations can make it difficult to identify the most important determinants of FDI, many explanations share the feature that poor local economic conditions discourage FDI that might otherwise contribute to local economic development.

James R. Hines Jr. is professor of business economics at the University of Michigan Business School and a research associate of the National Bureau of Economic Research.

The author thanks Austin Nichols for outstanding research assistance, Hisahiro Naito and David Weinstein for expert advice concerning Japanese data, Timothy Goodspeed for helpful comments on an earlier draft, and the NBER for financial support.

1. See, e.g., Calvo, Leiderman, and Reinhart (1996), who note that the share of world FDI received by developing countries has risen since 1990. Data reported by the United Nations (1997, 303) indicate that the developing countries received 18 percent of world FDI flows over the 1985–90 period, and close to 35 percent of world FDI flows over the 1991–95 period.

High-income countries are generally eager to promote economic development in low-income parts of the world. With that goal (and others) in mind, they often provide special fiscal incentives for their own firms to do business in developing countries. This paper examines the effect of the most common of these incentives, the provision of "tax sparing" credits.

"Tax sparing" is a practice designed to promote the effectiveness of local tax incentives for foreign investment. Developing countries are often willing to provide foreign investors significant fiscal incentives in order to encourage FDI and thereby stimulate local economic growth. Popular incentives include lengthy tax holidays, expensing or other generous tax treatment of new investment expenditures, and other tax reductions, as well as providing roads, worker training, and other public inputs at below-market prices. Tax incentives have the ability to stimulate foreign investment effectively and efficiently. Home-country tax systems may, however, reduce—or in some cases completely remove—incentives created by host-country tax abatements through corresponding increases in home-country tax burdens.

As an example, a multinational firm headquartered in a home country (such as the United States or Japan) that operates a residence-based worldwide tax system and grants foreign tax credits may find that tax reductions offered as investment incentives by host countries are exactly offset by higher home-country taxes. The reason is that host-country tax reductions imply that the firm can claim fewer foreign tax credits against home-country tax obligations.

In reaction to this possibility, many governments provide tax sparing credits for investments in developing countries. Tax sparing is the practice by which capital-exporting countries amend their taxation of foreign source income to allow firms to retain the advantages of tax reductions provided by host countries. Specifically, tax sparing often takes the form of allowing firms to claim foreign tax credits against home-country tax liabilities for taxes that *would* have been paid to foreign governments, in the absence of special abatements, on income from investments in certain developing countries. Since foreign tax credits are then based on tax obligations calculated without regard to taxes actually paid, any special tax breaks offered by host-country governments enhance the after-tax profitability of foreign investors and are not simply offset by higher home-country taxes.

The practice of granting tax sparing credits is controversial, coming under fire from critics who claim that tax sparing credits are ineffective in encouraging greater investment in developing countries.[2] The purpose of this paper is to evaluate this claim. Specifically, the paper compares patterns of Japanese and U.S. FDI over the same time period. Japan permits

2. See, e.g., the arguments advanced in OECD (1998).

its firms to claim tax sparing credits for investments in certain developing countries, while the United States does not. Holding other considerations constant, it follows that, to the extent that tax sparing is effective, Japanese firms will exhibit greater willingness than U.S. firms to invest in developing countries. In addition, Japanese firms are more likely than U.S. firms to receive special tax breaks from countries with whom Japan has tax sparing agreements.

The results indicate that tax sparing is effective in stimulating FDI. Japanese firms locate a much higher fraction of their foreign investment in countries with whom Japan has tax sparing agreements than do U.S. firms. Furthermore, host governments appear to grant Japanese firms significant tax reductions that are not available to their U.S. counterparts. All other things being equal, tax sparing agreements are associated with 140–240 percent higher FDI levels and 23 percent lower tax rates on FDI.

Since Japan does not randomly assign tax sparing agreements to developing countries, one interpretation of the FDI evidence is that low-income countries with whom Japan has significant economic relations due to geographic proximity or cultural connections are those with whom Japan, in turn, decides to sign tax sparing agreements. In order to evaluate this interpretation, the regressions are rerun using, as an instrument for Japanese tax sparing, the existence of a tax sparing agreement between the United Kingdom and the country in question. The United Kingdom has a tax system very similar to Japan's and is likewise a major capital exporter that grants tax sparing for investments in a large number of developing countries—but the United Kingdom's geographical and cultural connections differ from Japan's. The results obtained using U.K. tax sparing agreements as instruments for Japanese tax sparing agreements are very similar to those generated by the ordinary least squares (OLS) regressions that take Japanese tax sparing to be exogenous.

These results are consistent with a growing body of recent evidence that tax systems influence the volume and location of FDI. Much of this evidence concerns the activity of U.S. firms, or of foreign firms investing in the United States, so it is useful to compare the behavior of U.S. firms to that of firms from a country, such as Japan, that has an otherwise similar tax system that differs in one important respect (tax sparing). The results are particularly impressive in light of the fact that host countries with whom Japan has tax sparing agreements face incentives to substitute tax incentives for nontax investment incentives they would otherwise offer Japanese firms. Since nontax investment incentives are difficult to verify and impossible to quantify, they are omitted from the regressions; so, to the degree that such incentives influence investment patterns, there is likely to be a bias against finding an important effect of tax sparing on the volume of FDI.

Section 2.2 of the paper reviews the tax treatment of foreign investment income and evidence of the impact of taxation on FDI patterns. Section 2.3 presents a model of the effect of tax sparing on FDI when host governments provide tax and nontax inducements to foreign investors. Section 2.3 also describes the data used in the empirical analysis. Section 2.4 presents the regression results. Section 2.5 is the conclusion.

## 2.2    Taxation and Foreign Direct Investment

In order to appreciate the likely effect of Japanese willingness (and U.S. reluctance) to grant tax sparing for investments in developing countries, it is useful first to review important aspects of the Japanese and U.S. systems of taxing foreign source income.[3] This review is greatly simplified by the strong similarities between the two tax systems. This section considers the likely implications of tax sparing given existing evidence of the effect of taxation on the volume and location of FDI.

### 2.2.1    Japanese and U.S. Taxation of FDI

Both Japan and the United States tax income on a residence basis, meaning that corporations and individuals owe taxes to their home governments on all of their worldwide incomes, whether earned at home or abroad. In order to avoid subjecting multinationals to double taxation, Japan and the United States permit firms to claim foreign tax credits for income taxes (and related taxes) paid to foreign governments.[4] The U.S. corporate tax rate is currently 35 percent. Under the foreign tax credit system, a U.S. corporation that earns $100 in a foreign country with a 15 percent tax rate pays a tax of $15 to the foreign government and $20 to the U.S. government, since its U.S. corporate tax liability of $35 (35 percent of $100) is reduced to $20 by the foreign tax credit of $15.

*Tax Deferral*

Under both Japanese and U.S. law, firms must pay taxes to home governments on their worldwide incomes, with the exception that a certain category of foreign income is temporarily excluded from home-country taxation. The excluded category is the unrepatriated portion of the profits earned by foreign subsidiaries; taxpayers are permitted to defer any home-country tax liability on those profits until they are paid as dividends to

---

3. Portions of the following brief description of U.S. law are excerpted from Hines (1991, 1997) and Hines and Hubbard (1995).
4. Japan and the United States are not alone in taxing the worldwide income of their resident companies while permitting firms to claim foreign tax credits. Other countries with such systems include Greece, Italy, Norway, and the United Kingdom. Under Japanese and U.S. law, firms may claim foreign tax credits for taxes paid by foreign affiliates of which they own at least 10 percent, and only those taxes that qualify as income taxes are creditable.

parent firms resident in Japan or the United States.[5] This deferral is available only on the active business profits of foreign affiliates that are separately incorporated as subsidiaries in foreign countries. The profits of unincorporated foreign businesses, such as those of Japanese or U.S. branch banks in other countries, are taxed immediately by their home governments.

To illustrate deferral, consider the case of a foreign subsidiary of a U.S. firm that earns $200 in a foreign country without corporate taxes. This subsidiary might remit $50 in dividends to its parent U.S. company, using the remaining $150 to reinvest in its own, foreign, operations. The U.S. parent firm must then pay U.S. taxes on the $50 of dividends it receives, but is not required to pay U.S. taxes on any part of the $150 that the subsidiary earns abroad and does not remit to its parent company. If, however, the subsidiary were to pay a dividend of $150 the following year, the firm would then be required to pay U.S. tax on that amount. Japanese, and to a greater extent, American, laws restrict the ability of firms to avoid home-country taxes by delaying the repatriation of lightly taxed foreign earnings. American laws do so by recharacterizing income from passive investments, conduit income, and funds reinvested in home countries as "deemed distributed" and therefore immediately taxable by home governments. Japanese laws do so with rules restricting the ability of subsidiaries to defer home taxation of profits earned in foreign tax havens.

*Excess Foreign Tax Credits*

The Japanese and U.S. governments permit firms to claim foreign tax credits, doing so with the understanding that these policies reduce tax collections on any given amount of foreign source income. The foreign tax credit is intended to reduce the problems created by international double taxation, since, in the absence of some kind of correction, the combined burdens of host-country and home-country taxation might effectively prohibit most international business transactions. Consequently, governments design their foreign tax credit systems to prevent firms from using foreign tax credits to reduce home-country tax liabilities that arise from profits earned *within* home countries.

There are limits on the foreign tax credits that Japanese and U.S. firms may claim; a firm's foreign tax credit limit equals the home-country tax liability generated by its foreign source income. For example, with a U.S. tax rate of 35 percent, an American firm with $200 in foreign income faces a foreign tax credit limit of $70 (35 percent of $200). If the firm paid foreign income taxes of less than $70, then the firm would be entitled to claim

5. Deferral of home-country taxation of the unrepatriated profits of foreign subsidiaries is a common feature of systems that tax foreign incomes. Other countries that permit this kind of deferral include Canada, Denmark, France, Germany, Norway, Pakistan, and the United Kingdom.

foreign tax credits for all of its foreign taxes paid. If, however, the firm paid $95 in foreign taxes, it would be permitted to claim no more than $70 in foreign tax credits.

Firms described by this second case, in which foreign tax payments exceed the foreign tax credit limit, are said to have "excess foreign tax credits"; the excess foreign tax credits represent the portion of foreign tax payments exceeding home-country tax liabilities generated by foreign incomes. Firms described by the first case, in which foreign tax payments are smaller than the foreign tax credit limit, are said to have "deficit foreign tax credits." Under Japanese and U.S. law, firms may use excess foreign tax credits in one year to reduce their tax obligations in other years. Japanese firms are allowed to apply any excess foreign tax credits against their Japanese tax obligations in the three previous years or in any of the following three years; American firms are allowed to apply any excess foreign tax credits against U.S. tax obligations in the two previous years or in any of the following five years. Foreign tax credits are not adjusted for inflation when applied against tax obligations in other years.

In practice, the calculation of the foreign tax credit limit entails many complications not reviewed here. One is that Japanese and U.S. laws require firms to use all of their worldwide foreign incomes to calculate foreign tax credit limits. Firms then have excess foreign tax credits if their worldwide foreign income tax payments exceed this limit.[6] This procedure is known as "worldwide averaging."

*Tax Sparing*

The term "tax sparing" denotes the practice of amending home-country taxation in a way that permits investors to receive the full benefits of tax reductions by host countries. Many high-income capital-exporting countries, including Australia, Canada, France, Germany, Italy, Japan, the Netherlands, Norway, Sweden, Switzerland, and the United Kingdom, offer one form or another of tax sparing for investments in certain developing countries.[7] In the cases of Japan and the United Kingdom, who have tax systems very similar to that of the United States, tax sparing typically takes the form of permitting firms to claim foreign tax credits for foreign

---

6. Not all countries that grant foreign tax credits use worldwide averaging. For example, the United Kingdom instead requires its firms to calculate foreign tax credits on an activity-by-activity basis. The United States at one time required firms to calculate separate foreign tax credit limits for each country to whom taxes were paid; the current system of worldwide averaging was introduced in the mid-1970s.

7. For a survey of tax sparing practices, see OECD (1998). As the OECD report notes, tax sparing is an issue for countries that routinely exempt most foreign income from taxation, since certain categories of passive foreign income are generally not exempt from home-country taxation. Furthermore, countries that ordinarily exempt foreign income from taxation usually apply antiavoidance regimes that subject foreign income to taxation (while granting foreign tax credits) if the foreign income is very lightly taxed by host governments.

taxes that would be paid in the absence of special tax abatements. As a result, the benefits of any host-country tax abatements are not offset by reductions in the foreign tax credits that investors can claim against home-country tax liabilities. This consideration is important to the extent that firms have deficit foreign tax credits and would incur significant costs in deferring repatriation of foreign profits to years in which there would be no associated home-country tax liability.[8]

Japan and the United Kingdom grant tax sparing credits through the terms of bilateral treaties with low-income countries. The Japanese government explains that it grants such credits in order to maintain the ability of developing countries to use fiscal incentives to attract Japanese FDI.[9]

The United States has been unwilling to grant tax sparing in any of its bilateral tax treaties, though the issue has arisen on numerous occasions. The most visible episode took place in 1957, when the United States signed a treaty with Pakistan providing that the United States would grant tax sparing credits for American investments in Pakistan. At the time, Pakistan granted tax concessions to qualifying enterprises making new investments in certain industries. Under the terms of the treaty, American investors in Pakistan would be entitled to claim foreign tax credits for the taxes they would have paid to Pakistan absent the special concessions granted by the Pakistani law.

U.S. tax treaties are not legally binding unless and until ratified by the U.S. Senate. After extensive hearings and deliberations, and amid considerable controversy,[10] the U.S. Senate ratified the Pakistan treaty, but in so doing struck from the treaty its tax sparing provision. In subsequent treaties over the following forty-three years the United States has been unwilling to provide tax sparing for investments in any country.[11] In opposing

8. See Hartman (1985), Sinn (1993), and Hines (1994) for analyses of the incentives created by foreign tax credits and deferral of home-country taxation. For evidence of the effect of home-country taxation on dividend repatriations, see Hines and Hubbard (1990), Altshuler and Newlon (1993), and Altshuler, Newlon, and Randolph (1995).

9. "Many developing countries have introduced various tax incentives in order to attract investment from abroad. Without the tax-sparing credit system, even if such tax incentive exempts Japanese investors from tax in a foreign country, they are taxed on worldwide income in Japan and the spared amount will only be transferred from the treasury of the developing country to that of Japan through smaller foreign tax credits allowed in Japan. The result is that no tax benefits remain in the hands of the investors. Therefore, the tax-sparing credit system does not annul the effect of tax incentives adopted by developing countries" (Japanese Ministry of Finance 1996, 122).

10. See U.S. Senate (1957). For samples of the ensuing controversy, see Crockett (1958) and Surrey (1958).

11. As Tillinghast (1996) notes, the Senate persists in rejecting not only treaties with tax sparing provisions but also those with creative alternatives. The signed, but unratified, 1967 Brazil-U.S. treaty contained a clause granting U.S. investors an investment tax credit, for investments in Brazil, that would be used to reduce U.S. tax liabilities on foreign source income. A similar type of investment tax credit was then available for domestic investments in the United States. The Senate refused to ratify the treaty with the investment tax credit provision. American intransigence concerning tax sparing is further illustrated by the fact

ratification of the Pakistan treaty, Surrey (1958) argued that provision of tax sparing for investments in Pakistan would pressure the United States to provide tax sparing in all of its treaties with developing countries,[12] and that such concessions are unwise and excessively costly. Furthermore, the Pakistan treaty raised fears of encouraging FDI at the expense of investment in the United States.

### 2.2.2   Effect of Taxation on FDI

During the deliberations over Senate ratification of the Pakistan treaty, Stanley Surrey (1958) could confidently assert that there was no reliable evidence that tax-based incentives, such as those created by tax sparing provisions, were likely to influence the pattern of FDI. That is an appropriate summary of the quantitative literature as it existed at the time. Now, more than forty years later, there is a considerable body of evidence, much of it recent, that documents a sizable effect of tax policies on the location and volume of FDI. Consequently, it is reasonable to expect tax sparing provisions to encourage direct investment and to affect host-country policies toward foreign investors.

Evidence of the effect of taxation on FDI comes in a variety of forms. Time series studies generally find FDI levels to respond positively to available after-tax rates of return,[13] and cross-sectional studies of the location of outbound investment and the incentives facing different investors report consistently large effects of taxes.[14] There is additional evidence of the ability of parent companies to adjust the financing of their foreign affiliates and the transfer prices used in transactions between related parties in response to tax differences, which may contribute to the appeal of locating FDI in low-tax locations.[15] While this evidence varies in quality and in persuasiveness, taken as a whole it suggests that tax sparing is likely to influence significantly the location and experience of FDI.

### 2.3   Tax Sparing and Foreign Direct Investment

This section analyzes the effect of tax sparing on incentives for host governments to provide tax abatements, and nontax investment incentives,

---

that, of the twenty OECD members with tax treaties with China, the United States is alone in not granting tax sparing credits (Li 1995).

12. True to this prediction, subsequent diplomatic notes with several developing countries (including China, India, and Thailand) bind the United States to provide tax sparing credits for investments in those countries if it ever grants tax sparing for investments anywhere else.

13. See, e.g., Hartman (1984), Boskin and Gale (1987), Newlon (1987), Young (1988), Slemrod (1990), and Swenson (1994).

14. See Grubert and Mutti (1991), Harris (1993), Hines and Rice (1994), Hines (1996), Devereux and Griffith (1998), and Desai and Hines (1999).

15. See Hines (1997, 1999) for interpretive surveys of this evidence and of the FDI literature.

to foreign investors. This is followed by a review of the available data concerning foreign direct investment by Japanese and U.S. firms.

### 2.3.1 Behavior of Host Governments

Tax sparing agreements encourage FDI if foreign investors receive special tax abatements from host governments that would otherwise be offset by home-country taxes. For the same reason, host governments are considerably more likely to offer special tax abatements to foreign investors if their home governments grant tax sparing. In turn, tax abatements reduce the value of attracting additional FDI, and thereby make host governments somewhat less willing to provide nontax inducements for FDI. This section analyzes a simple model that formalizes these notions.

Consider the behavior of a government that maximizes $\Psi$, defined as

$$(1) \qquad \Psi \equiv B(I) + \tau Q(I,G) - cG,$$

in which $I$ denotes the level of inbound FDI and $Q(I, G)$ is local profitability of that investment. Inbound FDI is taxed at rate $\tau$, so $\tau Q(I, G)$ is the local government's tax revenue from FDI. $B(I)$ denotes the nontax benefits of FDI to the local economy, measured in tax revenue equivalent units. $G$ is the level of public services provided by local governments to enhance a country's attractiveness to foreign investors, and $c$ is the per-unit cost of providing such services.[16]

The level of foreign investment is a function of various country characteristics and two variables under the government's control: the tax rate, $\tau$, and the level of public services, $G$. Investment can be written as $I(\tau^*, G)$, in which $\tau^*$ is the combined host- and home-country effective rate of profit taxation, itself a function of $\tau$. The first-order conditions characterizing interior solutions to the maximization of $\Psi$ over the choices of $\tau$ and $G$ are

$$(2) \qquad \left[ B'(I) + \tau \frac{\partial Q}{\partial I} \right] \frac{\partial I}{\partial \tau^*} \frac{\partial \tau^*}{\partial \tau} = -Q(I,G),$$

$$(3) \qquad \left[ B'(I) + \tau \frac{\partial Q}{\partial I} \right] \frac{\partial I}{\partial G} = c - \tau \frac{\partial Q}{\partial G}.$$

Since $\tau^*$ is the combined level of home- and host-country taxation, it can be represented as

$$(4) \qquad \tau^* = \tau + \gamma[\tau^h - \tau(1 - \alpha) - \tau^f \alpha],$$

---

16. It is important that $c$ is the net cost of providing public services to attract FDI. For example, a government-provided road might simultaneously enhance the productivity of foreign capital and offer valuable services to local travelers. In such a case, $c$ is appropriately calculated as the cost of the road net of the monetary benefits of enhanced local travel (the numeraire taken to be the value of tax revenue).

in which $\tau^h$ is the home-country tax rate and $\tau^f$ is the foreign tax rate in the absence of special abatements. The parameter $\gamma$ reflects the importance of home-country taxation: $\gamma = 0$ if firms are effectively exempt from home-country taxation (either because they have excess foreign tax credits or because they have opportunities for costless and indefinite deferral), while $\gamma = 1$ if firms pay home-country taxes on any differences between domestic and foreign tax rates. In a sample of U.S. multinational firms, the average value of $\gamma$ is likely to be strictly bounded by 0 and 1. The parameter $\alpha$ denotes tax sparing; $\alpha = 1$ if the home country grants tax sparing, and $\alpha = 0$ if not.

Differentiating equation (4),

(5)
$$\frac{\partial \tau^*}{\partial \tau} = 1 - \gamma(1 - \alpha),$$

which reflects that tax sparing is relevant only insofar as the home country taxes foreign profits.

Equation (5) illuminates the effect of tax sparing on tax rate choices by host governments, because taking tax sparing to be a continuous rather than a discrete event, equation (5) implies that $(\partial^2\tau^*)/(\partial\tau\partial\alpha) = \gamma$. Tax sparing increases the sensitivity of total tax burdens to host-country tax rates. This, in turn, implies that tax sparing is likely to encourage host countries to offer foreign investors special tax reductions. From equation (2), it is clear that, absent a large effect of tax sparing on investment (ignoring any induced changes in $\tau$), tax sparing must be associated with reduced home-country tax rates. Consider, for example, the case in which a host government does not offer any special tax abatements and the home government suddenly grants tax sparing. If $\tau$ does not change, then tax sparing has no effect on $I$, because tax sparing credits are available only for special tax reductions. But as long as $\gamma > 0$, the introduction of tax sparing raises the value of $\partial\tau^*/\partial\tau$, so if equation (2) characterizes the host government's taxation of foreign investors prior to the introduction of tax sparing, it cannot continue to do so once the home government grants tax sparing—unless $\tau$ falls.

Tax-sparing induced lower rates of home-country taxation are likely to be accompanied by reduced provision of government services valued by foreign investors. Lower rates of $\tau$ reduce the size of the bracketed term on the left side of equation (3) and increase the size of the expression on the right side of that equation, thereby implying that $\partial I/\partial G$ must rise in response. Since, under normal circumstances, $\partial I/\partial G$ is a decreasing function of $G$, it follows that tax sparing is associated with lower levels of government spending. Tax sparing encourages host governments to reduce $\tau$, thereby lowering the value to host governments of any additional $I$ triggered by higher levels of $G$. Put differently, tax sparing encourages host governments to substitute tax for nontax investment incentives.

## 2.3.2   Data

The model implies that tax sparing encourages FDI in two ways: by reducing home-country taxation of foreign source income, and by encouraging host governments to offer special tax abatements to foreign investors. Existing Japanese and U.S. data are sufficient (if just barely) to test the investment and tax rate implications of the model. To a certain degree, the investment incentives created by tax sparing agreements will be offset by a tendency to substitute tax for nontax methods of encouraging investment by multinational firms based in countries granting tax sparing. However, because the willingness of many capital-exporting countries to grant tax sparing also encourages host countries to increase their default corporate tax rates, there are likely to be large differences between the tax rates paid by Japanese and U.S. firms, and significant differences in their investment patterns as a result.

The United Nations (1993) reports accumulated stocks of outbound FDI by Japanese and U.S. firms. Stock figures are denominated in U.S. dollars, and are distinguished by location for a large sample of countries. Foreign direct investment stocks consist of accumulated debt and equity investment from parent companies plus reinvested profits of foreign affiliates. Japanese and U.S. FDI stocks are book figures, which makes them sensitive to inflation and therefore no better than proxies for market values of FDI. Japanese and U.S. shares of total FDI stocks are, in principle, comparable, but since the estimation sample excludes FDI in Japan and the United States, mean values of Japanese and U.S. FDI will differ in a systematic way.[17] Data on GDP are taken from the Summers-Heston database (Summers and Heston 1991). Table 2.1 presents means and standard deviations of variables used in the regressions.

Data on the foreign activities of U.S. firms are collected by the U.S. Department of Commerce Bureau of Economic Analysis (BEA), which performs periodic benchmark surveys of the foreign operations of U.S. multinational corporations.[18] U.S. Department of Commerce (1992) contains income and balance sheet information for 1989 for foreign affiliates owned at least 10 percent by U.S. parents. The BEA reports aggregate figures for countries in which there is substantial U.S. investment; to protect the confidentiality of survey respondents, BEA suppresses information for coun-

17. In 1990, 42 percent of the Japanese FDI stock was located in the United States, while 5 percent of the U.S. FDI stock was located in Japan. By omitting data on FDI in Japan and the United States from the sample, the mean share of U.S. FDI is certain to exceed the mean share of Japanese FDI.

18. American firms with foreign affiliates and assets exceeding $3 million are obliged to respond to the BEA survey; BEA estimates that its survey respondents have 99.6 percent of the foreign assets of U.S. firms. The regression variables are constructed from BEA data on the activities of nonbank affiliates of nonbank parent firms. The BEA data are the basis of FDI studies by Grubert and Mutti (1991), Hines and Rice (1994), and Desai and Hines (1999), from which some of the following descriptive material is drawn.

Table 2.1          Means and Standard Deviations of Regression Variables

| Variable | Mean | Standard Deviation | N |
|---|---|---|---|
| *A. FDI Sample (Tables 2.3, 2.5)* | | | |
| Japan FDI share minus U.S. FDI share | −0.005269 | 0.023243 | 67 |
| Tax sparing | 0.22388 | 0.41999 | 67 |
| ln(GDP) | 18.0559 | 1.6787 | 67 |
| Tax sparing × ln(GDP) | 3.9464 | 7.7661 | 67 |
| *B. Tax Rate Sample (Table 2.7)* | | | |
| Japan tax rate minus U.S. tax rate | 0.08548 | 0.22381 | 18 |
| Tax sparing | 0.44444 | 0.51131 | 18 |
| ln(GDP) | 19.7114 | 1.0179 | 18 |
| Tax sparing × ln(GDP) | 7.5464 | 9.7638 | 18 |
| *C. Equity Investment Sample (Tables 2.9, 2.10)* | | | |
| Japan equity share minus U.S. equity share | −0.002896 | 0.021906 | 19 |
| Tax sparing | 0.42105 | 0.50726 | 19 |
| ln(GDP) | 19.6060 | 1.0907 | 19 |
| Tax sparing × ln(GDP) | 7.1492 | 9.6454 | 19 |

*Note:* The table presents means and standard deviations of variables used in the regressions. Foreign direct investment shares are ratios of FDI stocks in 1990 to total stocks of outbound FDI by source countries. Tax rates are ratios of income taxes paid in 1989 to total pretax income. Equity investment shares are ratios of stocks of paid-in equity in 1989 to total foreign equity investment stocks of source countries. "Tax sparing" is a dummy variable that equals 1 if Japan grants tax sparing and 0 otherwise.

tries in which one or two U.S. firms represent large fractions of total U.S. investment.

The BEA reports amounts of paid-in affiliate equity, as well as the pretax incomes and income tax payments of U.S. firms. It is therefore possible to construct an average income tax rate that equals the ratio of income taxes paid by local affiliates of U.S. firms to their local pretax incomes. Such a calculation is based on aggregates, and may therefore overstate tax rates by including information on affiliates with tax losses. Nevertheless, it is a reliable indicator of the use of tax preferences such as special deductions, depreciation rules, carryforwards and carrybacks, tax holidays, and nonstandard income concepts.

Data on the foreign business activities of Japanese firms come from annual surveys conducted by the Japanese Ministry of International Trade and Industry (MITI), which cover foreign operations in which parent firms hold at least 10 percent ownership stakes. Firms are not obliged to respond to these surveys, and while most do, the response rate is far from 100 percent.[19] Responses to the 1989 survey, tabulated in MITI (1991), constitute the Japanese data used in the empirical work.

19. For example, in the 1991 survey, MITI sent questionnaires to 3,368 companies, of which 1,789 responded. While Japanese firms with extensive foreign operations are perhaps

The MITI reports aggregate information for Japanese affiliates in order to preserve the confidentiality of survey respondents, but it distinguishes some items by location of affiliate and industry of parent company. The MITI data include information on the paid-in equity of parent Japanese firms, the "ordinary income" of affiliates, and affiliates' after-tax profits. The Japanese translation of "paid-in equity" is "capital stock," but this balance sheet entry excludes retained earnings and is therefore comparable to the American notion of paid-in equity.

"Ordinary income" is a Japanese accounting concept that equals the difference between income items (such as net sales revenue and capital income) and expense items (including interest charges and depreciation). "After-tax profits" equal "ordinary income" plus net extraordinary gains, plus net disposition of special reserves, minus corporate taxes. It is possible, therefore, to use the difference between ordinary income and after-tax profits as an indicator of the corporate tax burden facing Japanese affiliates, though this entails ignoring the (typically small) differences introduced by extraordinary gains and the disposition of special reserves.[20] More likely to be problematic are systematic differences between Japanese and U.S. accounting conventions, making levels of Japanese and U.S. tax burdens (thereby calculated) not exactly comparable. Consequently, the empirical work focuses on differences between average tax rates paid by Japanese firms in countries with whom Japan does and does not have tax sparing agreements, contrasting these with differences in tax rates paid by U.S. firms.

## 2.4    Evidence from U.S. and Japanese Firms

This section evaluates evidence of the impact of tax sparing agreements appearing in differences between the location and performance of foreign investment by U.S. and Japanese firms.

### 2.4.1    FDI in a Large Cross Section

Japanese investors exhibit a pronounced tendency to locate FDI in countries with whom Japan has tax sparing agreements. Table 2.2 presents a simple comparison of Japanese and U.S. investment patterns. Of the sixty-seven receiving countries for whom FDI data are available, Japan has tax sparing agreements with fourteen. The Japanese share of FDI located in a country is defined to be $(FDI_i/FDI_{tot})$, in which $FDI_i$ is the stock

---

more likely than others to respond to the MITI questionnaire, there is no way of verifying this directly.

20. The calculations constrain tax rates facing Japanese and U.S. firms to lie between 0 and 100 percent. Calculated tax rates omit consideration of taxes other than income taxes, since firms are eligible to claim foreign tax credits only for income taxes paid to foreign governments.

Table 2.2             FDI Shares

|                           | Japan  | United States |
|---------------------------|--------|---------------|
| Tax sparing ($N = 14$)    |        |               |
|   Median (%)     | 0.601  | 0.358         |
|   Mean           | 0.942  | 0.715         |
|   Standard deviation | 1.06   | 0.988         |
| No tax sparing ($N = 53$) |        |               |
|   Median (%)     | 0.0219 | 0.124         |
|   Mean           | 0.604  | 1.38          |
|   Standard deviation | 1.54   | 3.29          |

*Note:* The table presents medians, means, and standard deviations of Japanese and U.S. FDI shares in two groups of countries in 1990: those with whom Japan has tax sparing agreements (fourteen countries), and those with whom Japan does not have tax sparing agreements (fifty-three countries). Entries are percentages. Foreign direct investment shares are ratios of FDI stocks in 1990 to total stocks of outbound FDI by source countries. Median FDI shares are observations with median values in each cell.

of Japanese FDI located in country i in 1990, and $FDI_{tot}$ is the stock of Japanese FDI located in all countries in 1990. American FDI shares for 1990 are defined analogously. The median Japanese FDI share in the fourteen countries with whom Japan has tax sparing agreements is 0.60 percent and the mean Japanese FDI share is 0.94 percent, both of which exceed the median (0.36 percent) and mean (0.72 percent) U.S. FDI shares in the same countries.

It is useful to confirm that these differences are not merely functions of Japanese and U.S. investment patterns in countries excluded from the sample (particularly the United States and Japan), so the second row of table 2.2 presents investment share information for the fifty-three sample countries with whom Japan does not have tax sparing agreements. Investment patterns in these countries differ markedly from those with whom Japan has tax sparing agreements. The median Japanese FDI share in this subsample is 0.02 percent and the mean share is 0.64 percent, while the U.S. FDI share has a median of 0.12 percent and a mean of 1.38 percent.

Figure 2.1 illustrates the comparison between Japanese and U.S. investment patterns. The black bars in the figure represent mean shares of Japanese investment, and the white bars mean shares of U.S. investment. The two bars on the left describe investment shares in countries with whom Japan does not have tax sparing agreements, whereas the two bars on the right describe investment shares in countries with whom Japan does have tax sparing agreements.

These differences can be compared in a straightforward way in a regression context. The first column of table 2.3 presents estimated coefficients from regressing differences between Japanese and U.S. FDI shares in each of the sample countries on a constant term and a dummy variable that

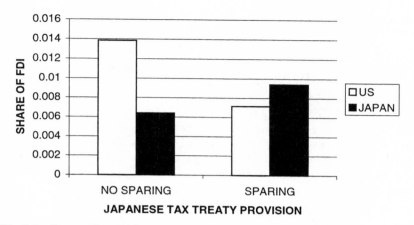

**Fig. 2.1   Tax sparing and FDI**

*Note:* The figure presents mean FDI shares of U.S. and Japanese firms. Foreign direct investment shares are ratios of FDI stocks in 1990 to total stocks of outbound FDI by source countries. White bars depict average FDI shares of U.S. firms, and black bars depict average FDI shares of Japanese firms. The two bars on the left describe FDI shares in countries with whom Japan does not have tax sparing agreements, whereas the two bars on the right describe FDI shares in countries with whom Japan does have tax sparing agreements.

**Table 2.3          FDI Shares and Tax Sparing**

| | Dependent Variable: Japanese FDI Share Minus U.S. FDI Share | | |
|---|---|---|---|
| | (1) | (2) | (3) |
| Constant | −0.007445 | 0.097620 | 0.097485 |
| | (0.003538) | (0.037801) | (0.037076) |
| Tax sparing | 0.009719 | 0.016805 | |
| | (0.004517) | (0.006756) | |
| ln(GDP) | | −0.005907 | −0.005894 |
| | | (0.002266) | (0.002220) |
| Tax sparing × ln(GDP) | | | 0.0009296 |
| | | | (0.0003494) |
| $R^2$ | 0.031 | 0.196 | 0.201 |
| $N$ | 67 | 67 | 67 |

*Note:* The dependent variable is the difference between Japanese and U.S. shares of their respective total FDI stocks in 1990. "Tax sparing" is a dummy variable that equals 1 if Japan grants tax sparing and 0 otherwise. The table presents estimated coefficients from OLS regressions; heteroskedasticity-consistent standard errors are in parentheses.

equals 1 if Japan has a tax sparing agreement, and equals 0 otherwise. The estimated coefficient on the dummy variable, 0.0097, indicates that differences between Japanese and U.S. FDI shares are roughly 1 percent higher in countries with whom Japan has tax sparing agreements than they are in other countries. The regression reported in column (2) of table 2.3 indicates that the effect of tax sparing on Japanese U.S. FDI share differences rises with the inclusion of ln(GDP) as an explanatory variable, the estimated coefficient on the dummy variable implying that Japanese FDI shares are roughly 1.7 percent higher in countries with whom Japan has tax sparing agreements. The third column of table 2.3 reports the results of a regression specification in which the tax sparing dummy variable is interacted with ln(GDP); again, tax sparing is associated in a significant way with higher FDI levels. Evaluated at the mean of ln(GDP), the coefficient implies that tax sparing agreements coincide with 1.7 percent higher Japanese FDI shares. Since the Japanese FDI share has a sample mean of 0.71 percent, effects in the range of 0.97–1.7 percent correspond to FDI that is 1.4–2.4 times greater than what it would have been in the absence of tax sparing.

Japan does not grant tax sparing on a random basis, thereby raising the possibility that the observed correlation between FDI and tax sparing reflects the influence of variables omitted from the FDI equation. Countries with whom Japan has close economic or cultural ties are likely to receive unusually large fractions of Japanese FDI and might also be countries with whom Japan is inclined to conclude tax sparing agreements. Given the arbitrariness of most methods of identifying the closeness of bilateral relations with Japan, it can be difficult to distinguish the effect of tax sparing on Japanese FDI from the effect of other connections that are correlated with the presence of tax sparing agreements.

An alternative method is to use tax sparing agreements between the United Kingdom and various developing countries as instruments for tax sparing agreements that involve Japan. The United Kingdom is a major capital exporter, has a tax system that resembles Japan's, and is similarly inclined to include tax sparing provisions in its bilateral treaties with developing countries. The advantage of using U.K. tax sparing provisions as proxies for Japanese provisions is that the United Kingdom has economic and cultural ties that differ from Japan's, and U.K. tax treaty patterns are therefore less likely to be influenced by important variables that are omitted from the Japanese FDI equation. Table 2.4 presents information on the countries with whom Japan and the United Kingdom had tax sparing arrangements as of 1990. Both countries exhibit a tendency to offer tax sparing for investments in major developing countries, but there are some differences between their country coverages.

Table 2.5 presents instrumental variables (IV) estimates of the FDI equations reported in table 2.2, with a 0–1 dummy variable indicating the

**Table 2.4**     **Tax Sparing Agreements with Japan and the United Kingdom**

| Country | Japan | United Kingdom | Country | Japan | United Kingdom |
|---|---|---|---|---|---|
| Argentina | No | No[a] | Malaysia[b] | SP | SP |
| Australia[b] | No | No | Mauritania | No | No |
| Austria | No | No | Mauritius | No | SP |
| Bangladesh | SP | SP | Mexico[b] | No[a] | No[a] |
| Bolivia | No | No | Morocco | No | SP |
| Brazil[b] | SP | No | Netherlands[b] | No | No |
| Cameroon | No | No | New Zealand[c] | No | No |
| Canada[b] | No | No | Nigeria | No | SP |
| Chile | No | No | Norway | No | No |
| China[b] | SP | SP | Pakistan | SP | SP |
| Colombia | No | No | Panama | No | No |
| Costa Rica | No | No | Papua New Guinea | No | SP |
| Cyprus | No | SP | Paraguay | No | No |
| Denmark | No | No | Peru | No | No |
| Dominican Republic | No | No | Philippines[b] | SP | No |
| Ecuador | No | No | Poland | No | No |
| Egypt | No | SP | Portugal | No | SP |
| Finland | No | No | Senegal | No | No |
| France[b] | No | No | Singapore[b] | SP | SP |
| Gabon | No | No | South Africa | No | No |
| West Germany[b] | No | No | Spain[b] | SP | SP |
| Ghana | No | SP | Sri Lanka | SP | SP |
| Greece | No | No | Sweden | No | No |
| Guyana | No | No[a] | Switzerland[b] | No | No |
| Hong Kong[b] | No | n.a. | Thailand | SP | SP |
| India | SP | SP | Trinidad & Tobago | No | SP |
| Indonesia[b] | SP | SP | Tunisia | No | SP |
| Iran | No | No | Turkey | No[a] | SP |
| Ireland | SP | No | United Kingdom[b] | No | n.a. |
| Israel | No | SP | Uruguay | No | No |
| Italy[b] | No | No | Venezuela | No | No[a] |
| Jamaica | No | SP | Zambia | SP | SP |
| Kenya | No | SP | Zimbabwe | No | No |
| Korea, Republic of[b] | SP | SP | | | |

*Note:* The table consists of the sixty-seven countries for whom FDI and GDP data are available for 1990. Entries in the first column indicate whether Japan grants tax sparing in 1990, and in the second column, whether the United Kingdom does so. SP = tax sparing; No = no tax sparing; n.a. = not applicable (governments do not have treaties with themselves).

[a]Denotes countries with tax sparing agreements subsequent to 1990.

[b]Denotes observations included in the eighteen- and nineteen-country samples analyzed in tables 2.6–2.10.

[c]Denotes the observation (New Zealand) included in the nineteen-country sample analyzed in tables 2.9 and 2.10.

**Table 2.5**         **FDI Shares and Tax Sparing, IV Specification**

|  | Dependent Variable: Japanese FDI Share Minus U.S. FDI Share | | |
|---|---|---|---|
|  | (1) | (2) | (3) |
| Constant | −0.012186 | 0.112725 | 0.116498 |
|  | (0.005503) | (0.040895) | (0.041754) |
| Tax sparing | 0.030895 | 0.030150 |  |
|  | (0.013881) | (0.012128) |  |
| ln(GDP) |  | −0.006909 | −0.0071516 |
|  |  | (0.002482) | (0.0025396) |
| Tax sparing × ln(GDP) |  |  | (0.0018653 |
|  |  |  | (0.0007268) |
| $N$ | 67 | 67 | 67 |

*Note:* The dependent variable is the difference between Japanese and U.S. shares of their respective total FDI stocks in 1990. "Tax sparing" is a dummy variable that equals 1 if Japan grants tax sparing and 0 otherwise. The table presents estimated coefficients from instrumental variables regressions in which U.K. tax sparing agreements are used as instruments for Japanese tax sparing agreements. Heteroskedasticity-consistent standard errors are in parentheses.

presence of a U.K. tax sparing agreement serving as an instrument for Japanese tax sparing agreements. (The first stage equations of these IV estimates are specified as linear probability models.) The results are somewhat more dramatic than those reported in Table 2.3: the estimated effect of Japanese tax sparing remains significant, and is now on the order of 3 percent differences in FDI shares.

### 2.4.2   Tax Sparing and Tax Rates

The model analyzed and described in section 2.3 implies that foreign investors are likely to receive fiscal inducements in the form of reduced taxes in situations in which home countries grant tax sparing credits. This section compares the experiences of Japanese and U.S. firms in order to test this implication of the model.

Table 2.6 distinguishes the average tax rates faced by Japanese and U.S. firms in sample countries with whom Japan has tax sparing agreements and those with whom Japan does not have tax sparing agreements. Aggregate tax burdens are quite consistent with the model's implications. In the seven countries in the sample with whom Japan has tax sparing agreements, Japanese firms face average tax rates of 28 percent, as compared with 32 percent for U.S. firms. Sample medians differ more widely: The average Japanese tax rate in the median country is 23 percent, while the average U.S. tax rate in the median country is 39 percent.

Comparison of the average foreign tax burdens of U.S. and Japanese firms can be highly problematic due both to differences in their tax treat-

**Table 2.6**     **Tax Rates**

|  | Japan | United States |
|---|---|---|
| Tax sparing ($N = 7$) | | |
| Median (%) | 22.5 | 38.5 |
| Mean | 27.7 | 32.2 |
| Standard deviation | 2.02 | 18.9 |
| No tax sparing ($N = 11$) | | |
| Median (%) | 52.6 | 35.8 |
| Mean | 48.3 | 29.4 |
| Standard deviation | 26.5 | 12.2 |

*Note:* The table presents medians, means, and standard deviations of Japanese and U.S. average tax rates in two groups of countries in 1989: those with whom Japan has tax sparing agreements (seven countries), and those with whom Japan does not have tax sparing agreements (eleven countries). Entries are percentages. Tax rates are ratios of income taxes paid in 1989 to total pretax income. Median tax rates are observations with median values in each cell.

ments by host governments and to differences in national accounting conventions. The most useful way to frame the tax rate information reported in the first row of table 2.6 is to contrast it with evidence of average tax rates faced by U.S. and Japanese firms in other countries. The second row of table 2.6 reports this information, which suggests that, in countries with whom Japan does not have tax sparing agreements, Japanese firms report significantly higher average tax rates than do U.S. firms. The average foreign tax rate faced by Japanese firms in sample countries with whom Japan does not have a tax sparing agreement is 48 percent, while the corresponding average tax rate faced by U.S. firms is 29 percent. Median tax rates are 53 percent and 36 percent, respectively. These data suggest that some combination of national accounting practices, differences in the ways that foreign affiliates are financed, and other business practices that enable firms to avoid local taxes, tend to elevate the calculated tax rates faced by Japanese firms compared to their American counterparts. These differences make more striking the evidence of lower tax rates faced by Japanese firms in countries with whom Japan has tax sparing agreements.

Figure 2.2 presents these differences graphically. The black bars in the figure represent average tax rates paid by Japanese firms, and the white bars average tax rates paid by U.S. firms. The two left-most bars describe tax rates in countries with whom Japan does not have tax sparing agreements, whereas the two right-most bars describe tax rates in countries with whom Japan does have tax sparing agreements.

Table 2.7 presents estimates of the effect of tax sparing on average tax rate differences. The OLS estimates in column (1) confirm that the differences apparent in table 2.6 are statistically significant: A tax sparing agreement with Japan is associated with Japanese tax rates that are 23 percent lower than those faced by U.S. firms. Although the small sample

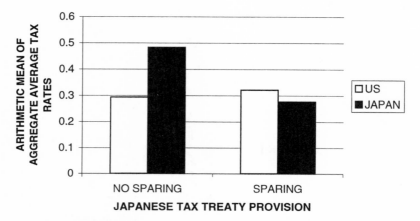

**Fig. 2.2   Average tax rates**

*Note:* The figure presents average tax rates paid by U.S. and Japanese firms. Tax rates are ratios of income taxes paid in 1989 to total pretax income. White bars depict average tax rates paid by U.S. firms, and black bars depict average tax rates paid by Japanese firms. The two bars on the left describe tax rates in countries with whom Japan does not have tax sparing agreements, whereas the two bars on the right describe tax rates in countries with whom Japan does have tax sparing agreements.

**Table 2.7           Tax Rates and Tax Sparing**

| | Dependent Variable: Japanese Tax Rate Minus U.S. Tax Rate | | | |
| --- | --- | --- | --- | --- |
| | OLS | OLS | IV | IV |
| Constant | 0.18962 | −0.43658 | 0.14474 | −0.71477 |
| | 0.05954 | (0.86044) | (0.07305) | (0.73381) |
| Tax sparing | −0.23430 | −0.22076 | −0.13332 | −0.11314 |
| | (0.09320) | (0.09608) | (0.11885) | (0.11744) |
| ln(GDP) | | 0.03146 | | 0.04315 |
| | | (0.04330) | | (0.03781) |
| $R^2$ | 0.287 | 0.306 | | |
| $N$ | 18 | 18 | 18 | 18 |

*Note:* The dependent variable is the difference between host-country tax rates facing Japanese and U.S. firms in 1989. Tax rates are ratios of income taxes paid in 1989 to total pretax income. "Tax sparing" is a dummy variable that equals 1 if Japan grants tax sparing and 0 otherwise. The first two columns present estimated coefficients from OLS regressions. The third and fourth columns present estimated coefficients from IV regressions in which U.K. tax sparing agreements are used as instruments for Japanese tax sparing agreements. Heteroskedasticity-consistent standard errors are in parentheses.

size (only eighteen observations) is unfortunate, it is worth bearing in mind that these eighteen countries receive 66 percent of Japanese FDI not bound for the United States. Inclusion of GDP as a regressor changes the results very little, as the results reported in column (2) indicate. Using the existence of a tax sparing agreement with the United Kingdom as an instrument for Japanese tax sparing reduces both the size and the statistical significance of the estimated effect of tax sparing, as indicated by the instrumental variables (IV) results reported in columns (3) and (4). Though the estimates continue to imply a large (13 percent) effect of tax sparing on tax rate differences between Japanese and U.S. firms, this difference is no longer significant in the IV regressions. At least in part, this is the product of using an IV procedure on such a small sample.

### 2.4.3   Tax Sparing and Equity Investments

From the evidence reported in section 2.4.1 it is clear that Japanese firms are more inclined than are U.S. firms to locate FDI in countries with whom Japan has tax sparing agreements. Foreign direct investment equals equity and debt flows from parent firms plus the reinvested profits of local affiliates. Tax sparing agreements will, therefore, encourage Japanese FDI even if the agreements affect only the reinvested profits of Japanese affiliates. Suppose that affiliates routinely reinvest a certain fraction of their after-tax profits; if tax sparing agreements prompt host governments to reduce local taxes, then affiliates' after-tax profits will rise and so will the retained earnings component of FDI. Consequently, the observed correlation between tax sparing agreements and FDI does not necessarily imply that tax sparing encourages equity investments. Because the determinants of equity capital flows are of independent interest, and because host countries are understandably eager to attract such flows, it is useful to consider the determinants of U.S.-Japanese differences in equity investments. In addition, the equity data come in a disaggregated form that distinguishes investments by industry of affiliate. As with the tax rate information, however, the data are available for only a rather small sample of countries.

Table 2.8 presents data on U.S. and Japanese shares of equity capital located in the nineteen sample countries for which such data are available.

**Table 2.8**          **Equity Investment Shares**

|  | Japan | United States |
|---|---|---|
| Tax sparing ($N = 7$) | | |
| Median (%) | 2.65 | 0.401 |
| Mean | 2.55 | 0.978 |
| Standard deviation | 1.27 | 1.32 |
| No tax sparing ($N = 12$) | | |
| Median (%) | 0.743 | 2.48 |
| Mean | 1.50 | 3.14 |
| Standard deviation | 1.54 | 2.70 |

*Note:* The table presents medians, means, and standard deviations of Japanese and U.S. shares of equity investment in two groups of countries in 1989: those with whom Japan has tax sparing agreements (seven countries), and those with whom Japan does not have tax sparing agreements (twelve countries). Entries are percentages. Equity investment shares are ratios of stocks of paid-in equity in 1989 to total foreign equity investment stocks of source countries. Median investment shares are observations with median values in each cell.

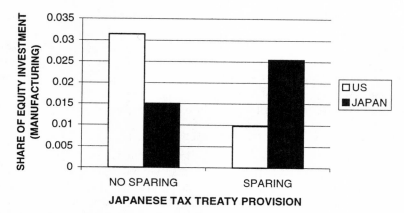

**Fig. 2.3   Tax sparing and equity investment**

*Note:* The figure presents mean equity investment shares of U.S. and Japanese firms in manufacturing industries. Equity investment shares are ratios of stocks of paid-in equity in 1989 to total foreign equity investment stocks of source countries. White bars depict average equity investment shares of U.S. firms, and black bars depict average equity investment shares of Japanese firms. The two bars on the left describe equity investment shares in countries with whom Japan does not have tax sparing agreements, whereas the two bars on the right describe equity investment shares in countries with whom Japan does have tax sparing agreements.

Data apply to firms in manufacturing industries only.[21] Japanese firms locate an average of 2.6 percent of their foreign equity in the seven sample countries with whom Japan has tax sparing agreements, and 1.5 percent in the twelve countries without Japanese tax sparing agreements. By comparison, U.S. firms locate an average of 1 percent of their foreign equity in tax sparing countries and 3.1 percent in those with whom Japan does not have tax sparing agreements. Similarly signed and somewhat more dramatic differences appear between median equity investments of Japanese and U.S. firms. Figure 2.3 depicts the mean equity investment shares of Japanese (black bars) and U.S. (white bars) firms in countries with and without Japanese tax sparing agreements.

Table 2.9 analyzes these data in a regression context. In the regression reported in column (1), tax sparing is associated with a 3.2 percent difference between Japanese and U.S. shares of investment in the form of equity capital. The estimated effect of tax sparing is 3.1 percent when ln(GDP) is included as a regressor (as reported in column [2]), as it is when tax sparing is interacted with ln(GDP) (as reported in column [3]), and its effect evaluated at the mean value of ln(GDP). Evaluated at the mean Jap-

21. The sample is restricted to manufacturing industries in order to enhance the comparability of figures for Japanese and U.S. firms and to increase the available sample size. The results reported in tables 2.8–2.10 are very similar to those obtained using data on firms in all industries.

Table 2.9          **Equity Investment Shares and Tax Sparing**

| | Dependent Variable: Japanese Equity Investment Share Minus U.S. Equity Investment Share | | |
|---|---|---|---|
| | (1) | (2) | (3) |
| Constant | −0.016399 | 0.108494 | 0.115843 |
| | (0.004706) | (0.047536) | (0.044455) |
| Tax sparing | 0.032069 | 0.030605 | |
| | (0.006924) | (0.006639) | |
| ln(GDP) | | −0.006339 | −0.006616 |
| | | (0.002411) | (0.002286) |
| Tax sparing × ln(GDP) | | | 0.001534 |
| | | | (0.000368) |
| $R^2$ | 0.551 | 0.650 | 0.606 |
| $N$ | 19 | 19 | 19 |

*Note:* The dependent variable is the difference between Japanese and U.S. equity investment shares in manufacturing industries in 1989. "Tax sparing" is a dummy variable that equals 1 if Japan grants tax sparing and 0 otherwise. The table presents estimated coefficients from OLS regressions; heteroskedasticity-consistent standard errors are in parentheses.

anese equity investment share of 1.9 percent, a 3.1 percent difference implies that tax sparing is associated with Japanese equity investments that are 1.6 times greater than they would have been in the absence of tax sparing.

Table 2.10 presents the results of IV regressions in which tax sparing agreements with the United Kingdom serve as instruments for Japanese tax sparing agreements. The results are quite similar to those reported in table 2.9, with the difference that the estimated effect of tax sparing on equity investment rises (e.g., to 4.1 percent in the regression reported in column [1]), and the estimated standard errors are somewhat larger as well.

Industry-level data on Japanese and U.S. equity investments are, in principle, available for numerous two-digit industries, but various omissions make it impossible to obtain even modest sample sizes for any but six manufacturing industries. The six two-digit industries for which it is possible to make meaningful comparisons of Japanese and U.S. equity investment shares are food products, chemicals, metal products, nonelectrical machinery, electric and electronic equipment, and transportation equipment. Table 2.11 presents results of six regressions in which differences between Japanese and U.S. equity investment shares are regressed on constants and a dummy variable indicating the presence of a Japanese tax sparing agreement. All of the estimated coefficients on the tax sparing dummy variable are positive; in three cases (chemicals, metal products, and electric and electronic equipment), they are significant at the 95 percent confidence level, and in two others (food products and transportation equipment), at the 90 percent confidence level.

**Table 2.10**  **Equity Investment Shares and Tax Sparing, IV Specification**

| | Dependent Variable: Japanese Equity Investment Share Minus U.S. Equity Investment Share | | |
|---|---|---|---|
| | (1) | (2) | (3) |
| Constant | −0.019994 | 0.096699 | 0.091997 |
| | (0.005629) | (0.059393) | (0.078644) |
| Tax sparing | 0.040606 | 0.039028 | |
| | (0.008303) | (0.008551) | |
| ln(GDP) | | −0.005918 | −0.0057752 |
| | | (0.002958) | (0.0039112) |
| Tax sparing × ln(GDP) | | | 0.0025648 |
| | | | (0.0007048) |
| N | 19 | 19 | 19 |

*Note:* The dependent variable is the difference between Japanese and U.S. equity investment shares in manufacturing industries in 1989. "Tax sparing" is a dummy variable that equals 1 if Japan grants tax sparing and 0 otherwise. The table presents estimated coefficients from instrumental variables regressions in which U.K. tax sparing agreements are used as instruments for Japanese tax sparing agreements. Heteroskedasticity-consistent standard errors are in parentheses.


**Table 2.11**  **Tax Sparing and Equity Investment by Industry**

| Industry | Dependent Variable: Japanese Equity Investment Share Minus U.S. Equity Investment Share | | | |
|---|---|---|---|---|
| | Constant | Tax Sparing | $R^2$ | N |
| Food products | −0.046152 | 0.060704 | 0.337 | 10 |
| | (0.021636) | (0.027808) | | |
| Chemicals | −0.027949 | 0.059861 | 0.577 | 15 |
| | (0.009784) | (0.014118) | | |
| Metal products | −0.028922 | 0.071336 | 0.337 | 14 |
| | (0.015063) | (0.029844) | | |
| Nonelectric machinery | −0.008548 | 0.002025 | 0.002 | 11 |
| | (0.009247) | (0.010235) | | |
| Electric equipment | −0.035529 | 0.049279 | 0.739 | 8 |
| | (0.009245) | (0.011971) | | |
| Transportation equipment | −0.000949 | 0.018457 | 0.224 | 11 |
| | (0.007879) | (0.010084) | | |

*Note:* The dependent variables are differences between Japanese and U.S. equity investment shares in each of the six indicated two-digit manufacturing industries in 1989. "Tax Sparing" is a dummy variable that equals 1 if Japan grants tax sparing and 0 otherwise. The table presents estimated coefficients from OLS regressions; heteroskedasticity-consistent standard errors are in parentheses.

While these results are, of course, consistent with all of the other available evidence of the effect of tax sparing on investment, the very small sample sizes make their interpretation for any particular industry quite difficult. What the results reported in table 2.11 do is to clarify that the tax sparing evidence available from aggregate data do not reflect obvious industrial differences between Japanese and U.S. investment patterns. Table 2.12 presents the results of industry-level regressions in which U.K. tax sparing agreements are used as instruments for Japanese tax sparing agreements. The estimated effects of tax sparing on equity investment are very similar to those reported in table 2.11.

### 2.4.4  Implications

The regression results indicate that tax sparing agreements have sizable effects on the location and volume of FDI, and on the tax rates faced by foreign investors. These two effects are of course related, since host-country tax reductions encourage FDI, and host governments grant tax abatements in anticipation of attracting additional FDI. Estimates available in the literature (e.g., Hines and Rice 1994) suggest that tax rate reductions of 23 percent should stimulate roughly 80 percent greater FDI; but these estimates are based on the behavior of U.S. firms that are not entitled to claim tax sparing credits for host-country tax reductions. Tax

**Table 2.12**  **Tax Sparing and Equity Investment by Industry, IV Specification**

| Industry | Dependent Variable: Japanese Equity Investment Share Minus U.S. Equity Investment Share | | |
|---|---|---|---|
| | Constant | Tax Sparing | $N$ |
| Food products | −0.043827 | 0.054889 | 10 |
| | (0.024629) | (0.048381) | |
| Chemicals | −0.028804 | 0.061465 | 15 |
| | (0.011315) | (0.019402) | |
| Metal products | −0.021615 | 0.045763 | 14 |
| | (0.018839) | (0.023065) | |
| Nonelectric machinery | −0.008548 | 0.002025 | 11 |
| | (0.009247) | (0.010235) | |
| Electric equipment | −0.035529 | 0.049279 | 8 |
| | (0.009245) | (0.011971) | |
| Transportation equipment | −0.002761 | 0.023440 | 11 |
| | (0.008232) | (0.011714) | |

*Note:* The dependent variables are differences between Japanese and U.S. equity investment shares in each of the six indicated two-digit manufacturing industries in 1989. "Tax Sparing" is a dummy variable that equals 1 if Japan grants tax sparing and 0 otherwise. The table presents estimated coefficients from instrumental variables regressions in which U.K. tax sparing agreements are used as instruments for Japanese tax sparing agreements. Heteroskedasticity-consistent standard errors are in parentheses.

sparing increases, possibly manyfold, the sensitivity of FDI to host-country taxes. Consequently, the finding that tax sparing is associated with 140–240 percent greater FDI, or roughly double the effect that would have been predicted on the basis of tax rate differences and in the absence of tax sparing credits, is quite consistent with the earlier literature.

### 2.5  Conclusion

Most high-income capital-exporting countries, including Japan, provide tax sparing for investments in developing countries. The United States steadfastly refuses to do so, and Japanese and U.S. FDI experiences differ as a consequence. Japanese firms are significantly more likely than U.S. firms to concentrate their outbound FDI, and its equity component, in countries with whom Japan has tax sparing agreements. Host-government policies are also affected: Japanese firms are taxed at lower rates than are U.S. firms in countries with whom Japan has tax sparing agreements. These differences persist when tax sparing agreements with the United Kingdom are used as instruments for Japanese tax sparing agreements.

The argument that tax sparing is unlikely to influence FDI patterns is inconsistent with this evidence and with a larger literature that documents the effect of taxation on the activities of multinational firms. There is a more basic question, which this paper does not directly address, of the desirability of encouraging FDI in this way. In order to answer this question, it is necessary to evaluate not only the likely effects of tax sparing on levels of FDI and the policies of host governments, but also the effects of tax sparing on tax compliance and tax complexity, its impact on ongoing treaty negotiations, the effect of outbound FDI on domestic economic performance, and the desirability of enacting major tax provisions through treaties rather than tax legislation. For more than forty years, the U.S. Senate has held that these considerations (and possibly others) imply that it is not in the interest of the United States to grant tax sparing in any of its treaties. In practice, this position appears to be partly responsible for the relatively modest levels of American investment in developing countries.

## References

Altshuler, Rosanne, and T. Scott Newlon. 1993. The effects of U.S. tax policy on the income repatriation patterns of U.S. multinational corporations. In *Studies in international taxation,* ed. Alberto Giovannini, R. Glenn Hubbard, and Joel Slemrod, 77–115. Chicago: University of Chicago Press.
Altshuler, Rosanne, T. Scott Newlon, and William C. Randolph. 1995. Do repatri-

ation taxes matter? Evidence from the tax returns of U.S. multinationals. In *The effects of taxation on multinational corporations,* ed. Martin Feldstein, James R. Hines Jr., and R. Glenn Hubbard, 253–72. Chicago: University of Chicago Press.

Boskin, Michael, and William G. Gale. 1987. New results on the effects of tax policy on the international location of investment. In *The effects of taxation on capital accumulation,* ed. Martin Feldstein, 201–19. Chicago: University of Chicago Press.

Calvo, Guillermo A., Leonardo Leiderman, and Carmen M. Reinhart. 1996. Inflows of capital to developing countries. *Journal of Economic Perspectives* 10 (2): 123–39.

Crockett, Joseph P. 1958. "Tax sparing": A legend finally reaches print. *National Tax Journal* 11 (2): 146–55.

Desai, Mihir A., and James R. Hines Jr. 1999. "Basket" cases: Tax incentives and international joint venture participation by American multinational firms. *Journal of Public Economics* 71 (3): 379–402.

Devereux, Michael P., and Rachel Griffith. 1998. Taxes and the location of production: Evidence from a panel of US multinationals. *Journal of Public Economics* 68 (3): 335–67.

Grubert, Harry, and John Mutti. 1991. Taxes, tariffs and transfer pricing in multinational corporate decision making. *Review of Economics and Statistics* 73 (2): 285–93.

Harris, David G. 1993. The impact of U.S. tax law revision on multinational corporations' capital location and income-shifting decisions. *Journal of Accounting Research* 31 (Suppl.): 111–40.

Hartman, David G. 1984. Tax policy and foreign direct investment in the United States. *National Tax Journal* 37 (4): 475–87.

———. 1985. Tax policy and foreign direct investment. *Journal of Public Economics* 26 (1): 107–21.

Hines, James R., Jr. 1991. The flight paths of migratory corporations. *Journal of Accounting, Auditing, and Finance* 6 (4): 447–79.

———. 1994. Credit and deferral as international investment incentives. *Journal of Public Economics* 55 (2): 323–47.

———. 1996. Altered states: Taxes and the location of foreign direct investment in America. *American Economic Review* 86 (5): 1076–94.

———. 1997. Tax policy and the activities of multinational corporations. In *Fiscal policy: Lessons from economic research,* ed. Alan J. Auerbach, 401–45. Cambridge, Mass.: MIT Press.

———. 1999. Lessons from behavioral responses to international taxation. *National Tax Journal* 52 (2): 305–22.

Hines, James R., Jr., and R. Glenn Hubbard. 1990. Coming home to America: Dividend repatriations by U.S. multinationals. In *Taxation in the global economy,* ed. Assaf Razin and Joel Slemrod, 161–200. Chicago: University of Chicago Press.

———. 1995. Appendix. In *Taxing multinational corporations,* ed. Martin Feldstein, James R. Hines Jr., and R. Glenn Hubbard, 103–6. Chicago: University of Chicago Press.

Hines, James R., Jr., and Eric M. Rice. 1994. Fiscal paradise: Foreign tax havens and American business. *Quarterly Journal of Economics* 109 (1): 149–82.

Japanese Ministry of Finance. Tax Bureau. 1996. *An outline of Japanese taxes, 1996.* Tokyo: Japanese Ministry of Finance.

Japanese Ministry of International Trade and Industry (MITI). Industrial Policy Bureau, Multinational Firm Division. 1991. *Kaigai toshi tokei soran* (Compendium of foreign investment statistics). Tokyo: Ministry of Finance Printing Office.

Li, Jinyan. 1995. China's tax treaties and their impact on foreign investment. *Tax Notes International* 10 (23): 1891–1911.

Newlon, Timothy Scott. 1987. *Tax policy and the multinational firm's financial policy and investment decisions.* Ph.D. diss. Princeton University.

Organization for Economic Cooperation and Development (OECD). 1998. *Tax sparing: A reconsideration.* Paris: OECD.

Sinn, Hans-Werner. 1993. Taxation and the birth of foreign subsidiaries. In *Trade, welfare and economic policies: Essays in honor of Murray C. Kemp,* ed. Horst Herberg and Ngo Van Long, 325–52. Ann Arbor: University of Michigan Press.

Slemrod, Joel. 1990. Tax effects of foreign direct investment in the United States: Evidence from a cross-country comparison. In *Taxation in the global economy,* ed. Assaf Razin and Joel Slemrod, 79–117. Chicago: University of Chicago Press.

Summers, Robert, and Alan Heston. 1991. The Penn world table (mark 5): An expanded set of international comparisons. *Quarterly Journal of Economics* 106 (2): 327–68.

Surrey, Stanley S. 1958. The Pakistan tax treaty and "tax sparing." *National Tax Journal* 11 (2): 156–67.

Swenson, Deborah L. 1994. The impact of U.S. tax reform on foreign direct investment in the United States. *Journal of Public Economics* 54 (2): 243–66.

Tillinghast, David R. 1996. U.S. tax treaty issues. *Tax Notes International* 13 (8): 625–40.

United Nations. 1993. *World investment directory 1992: Foreign direct investment, legal framework and corporate data.* Vol. 3. *Developed countries.* New York: United Nations.

United Nations. 1997. *World investment report 1997: Transnational corporations, market structure, and competition policy.* New York: United Nations.

U.S. Department of Commerce. Bureau of Economic Analysis. 1992. *U.S. direct investment abroad: 1989 benchmark survey, final results.* Washington, D.C.: GPO.

U.S. Senate Committee on Foreign Relations. 1957. *Double taxation convention with Pakistan: Hearings before the Senate Committee on Foreign Relations.* 85th Cong., 1st sess. Washington, D.C.: GPO.

Young, Kan H. 1988. The effects of taxes and rates of return on foreign direct investment into the United States. *National Tax Journal* 41 (1): 109–21.

# Comment     Timothy J. Goodspeed

Developing countries need to attract capital to grow. The importance of evaluating how developing countries can attract long-term foreign capital has always been important, but the question has become particularly relevant in light of the recent rapid outflows of short-term capital and the resulting volatility in capital markets in countries such as Mexico and South Korea. As we have witnessed, turmoil in global capital markets

Timothy J. Goodspeed is associate professor of economics at Hunter College and the City University of New York Graduate Center.

affects the welfare of both developed and developing countries. Tax sparing is one fiscal tool that developed countries have at their disposal to help developing countries attract capital.

Developing countries consider a tax sparing provision to be an important element of tax treaties with developed country treaty partners that practice worldwide taxation and give a foreign tax credit. For, without a tax sparing provision, a developing country that tries to attract foreign investment by offering a reduced tax rate for a period of time (a tax holiday) will find that its policy is ineffective and simply transfers tax revenue to the developed country treaty partner. This is because a multinational based in the developed country that repatriates (or is deemed to repatriate) income from a subsidiary in the developing country (and that finds itself in a deficit foreign tax credit position) will owe tax to the developed country in the amount of the difference between the (reduced) taxes paid to the developing country and the taxes that would have been owed to the developed country had the income been earned there. Under a tax sparing provision, credit is normally calculated at the higher statutory rate rather than at the reduced rate of the tax holiday. The multinational is, in effect, given credit for taxes it did not actually pay, thereby preserving the intended incentive of the tax holiday.

The paper by James R. Hines Jr. addresses whether tax sparing is effective in attracting capital to developing countries. As readers of the literature in international taxation have come to expect from the author, he once again brings clever and impressive economic analysis to bear on an important but neglected aspect of international taxation. For U.S. policy makers, his empirical results may be surprising and somewhat disconcerting. As he indicates, the United States has historically refused to approve tax treaties that contain tax sparing provisions. While this is partly due to general tax principles, it also derives from the perception that tax sparing is ineffective in helping developing countries attract capital. If tax sparing is ineffective in stimulating new investment, it may simply provide a windfall to old capital. Hines finds that this perception is incorrect; he finds that tax sparing is effective in stimulating investment, including new equity investment, in developing countries. The study constitutes an important advance in our understanding of the effect of tax sparing on investment activities.

Hines goes about his task by comparing outbound investment patterns and foreign average tax rates of companies based in two countries, Japan and the United States, that both use a foreign tax credit system. Japan tends to grant tax sparing to developing countries while the United States does not. The evidence is presented in three parts. First, Hines examines whether the share of Japanese FDI in country. A relative to the share of U.S. FDI in country A depends on whether country A has a tax sparing agreement with Japan. Second, he examines whether the average tax rate faced by Japanese companies investing in country A relative to the average tax rate faced by American companies investing in country A depends on whether Japan has a tax sparing agreement with country A. Third, Hines tries to ascertain whether investment that is induced by tax sparing agreements is new equity investment or simply higher after-tax earnings resulting from, for instance, a tax holiday, that is reinvested.

The first part of the evidence presented uses United Nations data on FDI by Japanese and U.S. multinationals in sixty-seven countries. A dummy variable is used to indicate whether a country has a tax sparing agreement with Japan; Hines finds that the existence of a tax sparing agreement (controlling for GDP differences) has a positive and significant effect on the share of Japanese relative to U.S. investment. The second and third parts of the evidence presented use data on investment activities of Japanese multinationals published by the Japanese Ministry of International Trade and Industry (MITI) to construct average tax rates and measure new equity investment of Japanese multinationals in eighteen countries. Corresponding variables for U.S. multinationals are constructed from data compiled by the Bureau of Economic Analysis (BEA). Hines finds that tax sparing is negatively and significantly associated with the difference between Japanese and U.S. tax rates in a country. He also finds that tax sparing is positively and significantly related to the difference between Japanese and U.S. equity investment shares. It is easy to criticize the regressions that use the MITI data for the small number of observations, but one must recognize that obtaining the Japanese data at all (and understanding Japanese accounting, not to mention the linguistic interpretations of accounting concepts) is a difficult problem that the author had to overcome. The use of this untapped data constitutes a valuable addition to our knowledge.

The biggest problem that Hines faces (and he recognizes this) is that there are many factors besides tax sparing that influence the difference in investment shares of U.S. and Japanese companies. In analyzing trade patterns, it is particularly important to note the proximity and historical ties of trading partners. What this means in the case of U.S. versus Japanese investment patterns is that one is likely to find a greater share of Japanese investment going to Asian trading partners. As it happens, many Japanese tax sparing agreements are with countries in Asia. The problem, then, is that one may find a positive correlation between countries with tax sparing agreements with Japan and Japan's share of investment relative to the U.S. share that is due to natural trading patterns rather than to tax sparing agreements.

This applies equally to the results on tax rates. Tax sparing can lead to lower tax rates for Japanese companies either directly or because of tax competition among similar countries. One possible reason for observing lower Japanese tax rates in the tax sparing countries is that these countries are in competition with other Asian countries. Again, since Japanese tax sparing agreements tend to be with Asian countries, it is not easy to separate out the effect that results from tax sparing and the effect that results from tax competition among Asian countries for Japanese investment.

One natural correction for this is to include a dummy variable for Asian countries, possibly augmented by more sophisticated spatial econometric techniques. This is difficult, however, because few non-Asian countries in Hines's sample have a tax sparing agreement with Japan. (The countries in this category are Brazil and Spain in the small sample; the UN data add Zambia and Ireland to the list.) Hines comes up with a clever alternative. He attempts to circumvent the problem by using the countries with which the United Kingdom has a tax sparing agreement as an instrument for a country that has a tax sparing agreement with Japan. The United Kingdom tends to have tax sparing agreements with most of the countries with Japanese tax sparing agreements (Ireland being one notable exception), and in addition, the United Kingdom has tax sparing agreements with several other African, Caribbean, and European countries. The instrumental variable approach tends to support the conclusion that tax sparing agreements are associated with higher Japanese relative to American shares of FDI.

A second factor apart from tax sparing that might influence the difference in investment shares of U.S. and Japanese companies is different laws in the two countries. For instance, although both the United States and Japan calculate the foreign tax credit on a worldwide basis (as Hines points out), the way in which the credit is calculated differs. The United States calculates its foreign tax credit limit using "baskets" to try to divide highly taxed and lowly taxed income. Japan, on the other hand, does not, and uses some other rules (described in Ault 1997) to try to limit averaging of foreign taxes. If it is easier for Japanese companies to average foreign taxes, there could be a greater incentive for Japanese companies to generate income in a low-tax country, thereby offsetting taxes paid in a high-tax country. This could lead to a high response of investment from tax sparing by Japan that would not be replicated by a U.S. tax sparing agreement. The tax sparing dummy could be partially picking up the difference between laws in the United States and those in Japan.

A third factor that might be influencing investment patterns are public good levels. Hines includes public expenditures as well as taxes in his theoretical model, and his inclusion of GDP as an explanatory factor may partly proxy for general demand for public goods. However, some disaggregation of demand for public goods may be called for if some countries provide more in the way of public goods that are valued by businesses. To the extent that U.S. and Japanese investment patterns are similar across industries, this should not matter much, because any bias introduced will be the same for both countries. However, it could matter if one country's

FDI is skewed more toward industries that use public goods valued more intensively by businesses.

Finally, I would like to bring up some issues not directly addressed in the study that are important in determining whether tax sparing is desirable. First, there are many methods of encouraging capital accumulation and growth in developing countries. Tax sparing is but one method, and its advantages and disadvantages should be compared to those of other methods of encouraging investment. For example, what are the advantages and disadvantages of using tax sparing rather than direct aid to encourage investment? One problem with tax sparing is that it provides an incentive for a profitable company only. New start-up ventures that anticipate initial losses will have little additional incentive because there is no advantage for those who have no tax liability. Another problem with tax sparing is that it may encourage transfer pricing abuses. Hines reports that Japanese companies tend to report tax rates that are higher than for American companies in countries without a tax sparing agreement. Yet the data of Grubert, Goodspeed, and Swenson (1993) (GGS) indicate low rates of return (taxable income divided by assets) earned by Japanese companies in the United States. This raises the possibility that Japanese companies could be using transfer prices to funnel income earned in the United States through tax sparing countries. Since GGS find that at least half of the low taxes paid by Japanese companies in the United States can be explained by reasons other than transfer pricing, such pricing strategies may not be overly abusive; nevertheless, transfer pricing problems need to be evaluated in judging the efficacy of tax sparing. Direct aid avoids the possible transfer pricing problems of tax sparing, but has problems of its own, such as the need to set up a bureaucracy to administer grants and the lack of private market determination of which projects are financed.

A second issue that is important to understand that is not addressed in Hines's study is how tax sparing affects the timing of repatriation decisions. Suppose developing country A decides to offer a tax holiday; further suppose that the United States, for instance, changes its tax treaty with country A to allow tax sparing. Without the tax sparing provision, the reduced tax rate will be valuable only if income is not repatriated. With the tax sparing provision, income can be repatriated without further taxation. Hence, a U.S. multinational may have an incentive to repatriate income more rapidly than it would have otherwise. Such a reaction on the part of the U.S. multinational could lead to greater volatility in capital markets, rather than less.

All this is not meant to take away from the important contribution of the paper, which is the first serious effort to measure the effect of tax sparing on investment decisions. Moreover, the paper rather ingeniously gets the most out of the data by using an instrumental variables approach to address one of the problems just outlined—that of Japanese trade patterns with Asian countries apart from tax sparing provisions. Still, the data limitations lead one to conclude that the results of this paper are suggestive, but do not yet provide a definitive answer to the question of whether and by how much tax sparing affects investment activities. This, in turn, suggests that there remain a number of interesting ways in which future studies could advance research on tax sparing. Such studies will need to work with a somewhat broader data set. With such a data set, recent techniques developed using spatial econometric methods or fixed effects models could be implemented. Such studies would be a valuable addition, and could provide more assurance to policy makers who remain skeptical about the value of tax sparing.

### References

Ault, Hugh. 1997. *Comparative income taxation: A structural analysis.* Boston: Kluwer Law International.

Grubert, Harry, Timothy J. Goodspeed, and Deborah Swenson. 1993. Explaining the low taxable income of foreign-controlled companies in the United States. In *Studies in international taxation,* ed. Alberto Giovannini, R. Glenn Hubbard, and Joel Slemrod, 237–70. Chicago: University of Chicago Press.

# Does Corruption Relieve Foreign Investors of the Burden of Taxes and Capital Controls?

Shang-Jin Wei

## 3.1 Introduction

This paper studies the effects of several irritants to foreign direct investment, including taxes, capital controls, and corruption. Moreover, it investigates whether corruption provides international investors relief from the taxes and capital controls they face in host countries.

A large number of excellent papers study the effect of taxation on international direct investment (e.g., Altshuler, Grubert, and Newlon [chap. 1 in this volume], and papers in Feldstein, Hines, and Hubbard 1995). Corruption has recently attracted attention not only from academics but also from international financial institutions, as exemplified by the IMF's decision to condition its loans to Kenya on the latter's effort to reduce corruption. Using data on outward investment from the United States, Hines (1995) found that American firms invest less in more corrupt host countries, which he interpreted as the effect of the U.S. Foreign Corrupt Practices Act. Using a sample of bilateral investment from fourteen major source countries to forty-five host countries, Wei (1997, 2000) found that all major source countries invest less in more corrupt countries. Later, Hines (1996) found that capital controls have a statistically significant and

Shang-Jin Wei is associate professor of public policy at Harvard University's Kennedy School of Government and a faculty research fellow of the National Bureau of Economic Research. During 1999–2000, he serves as an advisor at the World Bank on anticorruption and international capital flow issues.

The author thanks Jim Hines for providing intellectual stimulation on this project; Bernie Yeung, Joel Slemrod, and other conference participants for very helpful comments; and Jung-shik Kim and Greg Dorchak for very efficient research and editorial assistance. The views in the paper are the author's and may not be shared by any organization that he is or has been associated with.

negative effect on inward foreign investment. These papers have studied the effects of corruption and capital controls in isolation, but not in an integrated framework.

Furthermore, a separate strand in the literature (e.g., Leff 1964; Huntington 1968; Lui 1985) sees virtue in corruption. In particular, in an environment with excessive tax, severe capital control, or numerous licensing requirements, bribery allows firms to circumvent these otherwise suffocating regulatory burdens. Therefore, holding the level of tax and capital controls constant, more bribes may lead to more foreign (and domestic) investment. This argument may be characterized as a theory of "efficient grease payments." On the other hand, if regulatory burdens are endogenously chosen by the bureaucrats solely to extract rents, one may see more regulatory burdens in countries with more corruption (see Kaufmann and Wei 1999 for a formal model and some firm-level evidence). Therefore, whether corruption in a host country with high tax rates and severe capital controls is responsible for more or less foreign investment is an open question, the answer to which depends on the degree to which taxes and capital controls are erected and maintained for rent-seeking purposes. Earlier papers have not investigated possible interactions between corruption and taxation, and between corruption and capital controls. This paper tries to fill that void.

Using data over a large number of source-host pairs, this study quantifies the importance of a number of economic and noneconomic factors that may affect international direct investment. It compares these effects with those of corporate income taxation whenever possible. Most importantly, it examines whether bribery in countries with high tax rates and severe capital controls tends to encourage inward foreign direct investment.

The paper is organized as follows. Section 3.2 describes the data set. Section 3.3 discusses the statistical analyses and interpretations. Section 3.4 concludes.

## 3.2  Data

### 3.2.1  Bilateral International Direct Investment

The dependent variable is (a transformation of) bilateral stocks of foreign investment in 1991 from fourteen major source countries to forty-five host countries. The list of source countries includes the seven largest (in terms of outward direct investment) in the world: the United States, Japan, Germany, the United Kingdom, France, Canada, and Italy. The number of the host countries in the sample is constrained by the joint availability of data on tax rates, corruption levels, and capital controls. The data come from the OECD database on international direct investment (OECD 1991).

### 3.2.2   Tax

The host countries' tax rates are 1989 values. It is worth noting that tax rates do not change very much over the 1989–91 period. The actual measure is the smaller of two numbers (whenever both are available): the statutory marginal tax rate on foreign corporations as reported by Price Waterhouse (1990), or the actual average tax rate paid by the foreign subsidiaries of U.S. firms in that country. The data on twenty-eight of the host countries are taken from Desai and Hines (1996, app. 2). The rest are obtained using the Price Waterhouse source with the able assistance of Mihir Desai.

### 3.2.3   Corruption

The empirical work in the paper utilizes two measures of corruption. The first is the Business International (BI) index, which is based on surveys from 1980 to 1983, and ranks countries from one to ten according to "the degree to which business transactions involve corruption or questionable payments." The data were provided by Paolo Mauro and were used in his 1995 paper on corruption and economic growth. The second source is the index composed by Transparency International (TI), an agency dedicated to fighting corruption worldwide. The TI index (available at http://www. transparency.de/) is an average of ten surveys by different agencies over a number of years. It has an advantage and a disadvantage relative to the BI index. On the one hand, assuming measurement errors in different surveys are independent, the averaging process of the TI index may produce smaller measurement errors in the end. On the other hand, different surveys cover different sets of countries and may use different criteria, so the ratings on different countries in the TI index may be less comparable. Fortunately, the two indexes are highly correlated (with a correlation coefficient of 0.88). Which index to use makes no qualitative difference for subsequent discussions; hence, later sections will report results with the BI index only.

In both original sources, the indexes are defined so that a high number means low corruption. To avoid awkwardness in interpretation, I have rescaled them so that a large number means more corruption.

### 3.2.4   Capital Controls

There are two capital control measures. The first is a survey-based measure from Business International, collected from 1980 to 1983. In the original survey, a higher number (say, ten) meant less restriction on capital account. I have rescaled the numbers so that a higher number means more restrictions. This measure is supposed to be on a one-to-ten scale, although, in the sample, the minimum and maximum are one and eight, respectively. This measure is used in Hines (1996). The second measure is a dummy based on IMF's *Exchange Arrangements and Exchange Restrictions.* The two measures have a correlation coefficient of 0.46. This paper reports the results using only the BI measure.

### 3.2.5    Other Data

The GDP data come from the IMF's *International Financial Statistics* database. In a few cases in which GDP data are not available, GNP data are used instead.

The bilateral distance data measure the "greater circle distance" between the economic centers in source-host pairs. The dummy variable measure of linguistic ties takes the value of 1 if the source and host share a common language (either English, French, Spanish, German, Arabic, Chinese, Japanese, Portuguese, or Italian) and 0 otherwise. Both data are taken from Frankel, Stein, and Wei (1995).

Four additional potential irritants to foreign investment are (1) restrictions on foreign firms' access to domestic capital markets, (2) restrictions on their abilities to set up joint ventures with domestic firms, (3) restrictions on their abilities to bid on public sector projects, and (4) restrictions on their corporate control rights. The paper uses four binary measures (dummies) for the four irritants; they are all survey responses of subjective perceptions from the *Global Competitiveness Report* (World Economic Forum 1997).

Table 3.1 reports summary statistics on some of the key variables. The average corruption level (BI index) is 3.70 (on a one-to-ten scale); the average degree of capital control (BI index) is 3.31 (on a one-to-ten scale); and the average tax rate in the sample is 34 percent.

### 3.3    Statistical Analyses

One could run an ordinary least squares (OLS) specification of the following sort:

$$\ln(\text{FDI}_{ij}) = X_{ij}\beta + u_{ij},$$

where $\text{FDI}_{ij}$ is the stock of foreign investment from source country $i$ to host country $j$, and $X$ is a vector of regressors, including the host country's GDP in logarithm and the distance between the source and host countries in logarithm. Experience indicates that, in analogy to the gravity specification on trade flows, the logarithmic transformation on both sides of the equation (of the dependent variable and of most of the regressors), called double-log linear specification, produces the best functional fit.

Many host countries receive no direct investment from some source countries. A serious drawback of the double-log linear specification is that observations of zero FDI are dropped by this specification. It is natural

**Table 3.1**  Summary Statistics

| | Mean | Standard Deviation | Minimum | Maximum | Skewness | Kurtosis | N |
|---|---|---|---|---|---|---|---|
| Corruption | | | | | | | |
| BI index | 3.70 | 2.49 | 1 | 10 | 0.75 | -0.20 | 45 |
| TI index | 4.55 | 2.63 | 1 | 10 | 0.42 | -1.02 | 42 |
| Tax | 0.34 | 0.12 | 0.02 | 0.55 | -0.69 | 0.42 | 45 |
| Capital account restrictions | | | | | | | |
| BI index | 3.31 | 2.06 | 1 | 8 | 0.75 | -0.49 | 44 |
| IMF index | 0.64 | 0.48 | 0 | 1 | -0.61 | -1.64 | 42 |
| Political stability | 7.93 | 1.17 | 5 | 10 | -0.56 | -0.31 | 45 |
| Red tape | 4.34 | 2.30 | 1 | 9 | 0.15 | -1.05 | 45 |

Pairwise Correlation Matrix ($N = 40$)

| | C(BI) | C(TI) | Tax | KA-res(BI) | KA-res(IMF) | Stability |
|---|---|---|---|---|---|---|
| Corruption(BI) | 1 | | | | | |
| Corruption(TI) | 0.88 | 1 | | | | |
| Tax | 0.20 | 0.28 | 1 | | | |
| KA-res(BI) | 0.47 | 0.48 | 0.42 | 1 | | |
| KA-res(IMF) | 0.23 | 0.22 | 0.18 | 0.46 | 1 | |
| Political stability | -0.69 | -0.65 | -0.11 | -0.46 | -0.28 | 1 |
| Red tape | 0.88 | 0.85 | 0.33 | 0.59 | 0.27 | -0.63 |

*Note:* Corruption (BI index) = 11 − original BI index score. Corruption (TI index) = 10 − original TI index score. Capital controls (BI index) = 11 − original BI index score. Red tape = 11 − original BI index.

to think of using a Tobit specification to replace the OLS; but the problem there is that the simple Tobit specification conflicts with the double-log transformation, as log of zero is not defined. To deal with this problem, I employ the following specification in this paper:

$$\ln(\text{FDI}_{ij} + A) = X\beta + u_{ij} \quad \text{if } X\beta + u_{ij} > \ln(A)$$

$$= \ln(A) \quad \text{if } X\beta + u_{ij} \leq \ln(A),$$

where $A$ is a threshold parameter to be estimated, $u$ is an independently and identically distributed (i.i.d.) normal variate with mean zero and variance $\sigma^2$. In this specification, if $X\beta + u$ exceeds a threshold value, $\ln(A)$, source country $i$ accumulates a positive stock of investment in host country $j$; otherwise, the realized foreign investment is zero (and the desired level could be negative).

This framework is modified in subsequent implementation to become a quasi–fixed effects specification: There are source-country dummies, but no host-country dummies. The source-country dummies are intended to capture source country–specific differences in the stock of bilateral direct investment. Such differences include the sizes and levels of development of the source countries, and possibly different definitions of outward direct investment used by different source countries (under the assumption that the FDI amount under one definition is proportional to the amount under another definition plus an i.i.d. random error). Host country dummies are not included because there are no reliable measures of year-to-year variations in corruption and capital controls, which are key variables for this paper.

### 3.3.1  Empirical Results: Continuous Measures

To get some idea of the quantitative importance of corruption levels and tax rates, I have implemented a very simple specification. The two key regressors are tax rate and average corruption level (BI index). In addition, the estimating equation includes source-country dummies, host-country GDP in logarithm, distance between the source and host countries in logarithm, and a dummy indicating whether the source and host countries share a common language. The last two regressors are motivated by recent emphasis on the importance of networks in trade and investment, as in the work of Rauch (1996).

Table 3.2 presents the basic results. In column (1), which has the most parsimonious specification, both tax rate and corruption measure have negative and statistically significant coefficients. A one-step increase in corruption rating has the same negative effect on FDI as an increase in the tax rate by 4.69 percentage points ($0.09/[0.01 \times 1.92] = 4.69$). For instance, an increase in corruption level from that of Singapore (with a BI corruption rating of 1) to that of Colombia (with a BI corruption rat-

**Table 3.2**  Tax, Capital Control, Corruption and FDI (modified Tobit, with continuously measured corruption and capital controls)

|  | Dependent Variable: Log(stock of FDI from $i$ to $j$ in 1991 $+ A$)[a] | | | | |
|---|---|---|---|---|---|
|  | (1) | (2) | (3) | (4) | (5) |
| Tax rate | −1.92* | −1.62* | −1.16# | −0.74## | −0.60 |
|  | (0.47) | (0.46) | (0.70) | (0.47) | (0.78) |
| Corruption(BI index)[b] | −0.09* | −0.05* | −0.07 | −0.12* | −0.11# |
|  | (0.02) | (0.02) | (0.06) | (0.04) | (0.05) |
| Capital control(BI index)[b] |  | −0.14* | −0.13* | −0.23* | −0.22* |
|  |  | (0.03) | (0.03) | (0.07) | (0.07) |
| Corruption × tax rate |  |  | 0.05 |  | −0.044 |
|  |  |  | (0.18) |  | (0.200) |
| Corruption × capital control |  |  |  | 0.021* | 0.020* |
|  |  |  |  | (0.010) | (0.010) |
| log(GDP$_j$) | 0.54* | 0.50* | 0.49* | 0.46* | 0.45* |
|  | (0.10) | (0.10) | (0.09) | (0.09) | (0.09) |
| log(Distance$_{ij}$) | −0.28* | −0.30* | −0.29* | −0.29* | −0.29* |
|  | (0.06) | (0.06) | (0.06) | (0.06) | (0.06) |
| Linguistic tie | 0.70* | 0.70* | 0.67* | 0.66* | 0.64* |
|  | (0.28) | (0.28) | (0.27) | (0.27) | (0.26) |
| Constant | 1.6E+4* | 1.6E+4* | 1.6E+4* | 1.6E+4* | 1.6E+4* |
|  | (3.0) | (4.4) | (2.6) | (2.8) | (2.4) |
| $A$ | 6.3E+9* | 6.2E+9* | 6.4E+9* | 6.4E+9* | 6.6E+9* |
|  | (6.4E+6) | (2.2E+7) | (5.2E+6) | (9.0E+6) | (2.3E+6) |

(*continued*)

**Table 3.2** (continued)

| | (1) | (2) | (3) | (4) | (5) |
|---|---|---|---|---|---|
| | | | Dependent Variable: Log(stock of FDI from $i$ to $j$ in 1991 + $A$)[a] | | |
| $\sigma$ | 1.16* | 1.15* | 1.11* | 1.12* | 1.10* |
| | (0.18) | (0.18) | (0.17) | (0.18) | (0.17) |
| Source dummies? | yes | yes | yes | yes | yes |
| $N$ | 545 | 545 | 545 | 545 | 545 |
| Log likelihood | 1,789.32 | 1,792.20 | 1,802.13 | 1,802.92 | 1,808.24 |

*Note:* Eicker-White standard errors that are computed from analytic first and second derivatives are in parentheses. All reported coefficients and standard errors have been multiplied by $10^3$.

[a] Each column represents the result of a regression that is based on the following modified Tobit specification: $\ln(\text{FDI}_{ij} + A) = X\beta + u_{ij}$ if $X\beta + u_{ij} > \ln(A)$; $\ln(\text{FDI}_{ij} + A) = \ln(A)$ if $X\beta + u_{ij} \le \ln(A)$, where $A$ is a threshold parameter to be estimated and $u$ is an i.i.d. normal variate with mean zero and variance $\sigma^2$.

[b] "Corruption" and "Capital control" equal to 11 minus the corresponding BI indexes, so that larger numbers mean more corruption or more capital controls.

*Significantly different from zero at the 5 percent level.

#Significantly different from zero at the 10 percent level.

##Significantly different from zero at the 15 percent level.

ing of 6.5) is equivalent to raising the tax rate by 25.8 percentage points ([6.5 − 1] × 4.69 = 25.8). Similarly, an increase in the average corruption level from that of Singapore to that of Mexico (with a BI corruption rating of 7.25) is equivalent to raising the tax rate by 29.3 percentage points ([7.25 − 1] × 4.69 = 29.3).

We note that all three control variables have statistically significant coefficients and sensible signs. A host country with a larger GDP attracts more FDI than otherwise. A host country that is closer to the source country either geographically or linguistically (or that is historically related to the source country) also attracts more inward investment than otherwise.

A measure of severity of capital controls (by the BI index) is added in column (2). This variable has a negative sign and is statistically different from zero. Because countries that impose capital controls and those that have high taxes tend to be correlated (with a correlation coefficient of 0.40, according to table 3.1), the coefficient on the tax variable declines a bit (from −1.92 to −1.62) but remains statistically significant. Taking the point estimates literally, a one-step increase in the severity of capital controls is equivalent to raising the marginal tax rate by 13.2 percentage points (= 0.14/[0.01 × 1.62]). An increase in the severity of capital controls from the Singapore level (BI index value of 1) to the Philippines level (BI index level of 4) is equivalent to raising the marginal tax rate by 39.6 percent.

So far, we have considered the effects of tax, corruption, and capital control in isolation. Again, a popular (and previously untested) argument is that bribes can sometimes function as "grease payments," helping firms by effectively reducing tax burden or evading capital controls. If the grease payment effect works in reality, then the same level of tax should be a lesser hindrance to foreign investment in countries with greater possibility of bribing officials.

Alternatively, the grease payment argument may have no merit. Kaufmann and Wei (1999) argue that regulatory burdens, such as those imposed by taxes and capital controls, may well be endogenous, implemented by corruption-prone officials in order to extract bribes. In other words, bribes might reduce taxes only in a partial equilibrium story in which the tax rate is predetermined. In a general equilibrium, however, taxes may in fact be higher in corrupt countries so that firms there do not end up paying less in taxes (or facing less severe capital controls).

We now check this possibility. We first add a new term to the regression, "Corruption × tax rate." The efficient grease theory implies that the coefficient on this interactive term should be positive. Column (3) of table 3.2 reports the regression with the new interactive term, "Corruption × tax rate." As it happens, the corresponding coefficient does not differ from zero statistically (though it is positive); hence, there is no statistical support for the grease payment argument; foreign investors' sensitivity to host tax rate does not seem to diminish as the host country gets more corrupt.

The efficient grease argument is equally applicable to capital controls, so that one may ask: Does greater corruption in a host country make the same degree of capital controls more tolerable to foreign investors? To investigate this question, we augment the specification in column (2) with a different interactive term, "Corruption × capital control." The result is reported as column (4) of table 3.2. The coefficient turns out to be positive and statistically significant. This means literally that the sensitivity of FDI to the severity of capital controls is indeed less for more corrupt host countries. This seems to support the grease payment hypothesis as applied to capital controls.

On the other hand, this result does not imply that foreign investors would necessarily invest more in a more corrupt host country. Consider two host countries with identical capital controls (say, capital control indexes = 4, approximately the mean in the sample, of which the Philippines and Ecuador would be examples). If country A is more corrupt than country B (say, the corruption indexes are 9 and 7, respectively), the net effect of this increment in corruption on FDI is still negative, because $(9 - 7) \times (-0.12) + (9 - 7) \times 4 \times 0.021 = -0.072$.

### 3.3.2  Empirics: Binary Measures of Corruption and Capital Controls

In the previous subsection, we measure capital controls and corruption on a one-to-ten scale. Because these measures come from surveys of respondents' impressions, small measurement errors can easily change the ranking of host countries. In this subsection, we eliminate the overly fine gradation of the capital control and corruption measures by constructing corresponding binary measures. Specifically, we define D(corruption) as a dummy that takes the value of 1 if the corruption index exceeds 6, and the value of 0 otherwise. Similarly, we define D(cap-control) to be a dummy for countries whose capital control index exceeds 6.[1]

Table 3.3 replicates all the regressions in table 3.2, after replacing the ten-step measures of corruption and capital controls by their binary counterparts. In columns (1) and (2), tax, corruption, and capital control individually still have a negative and statistically significant effect on inward foreign investment. Other things being equal, foreign investors invest less in a country with higher tax, more corruption, or more severe capital controls.

The last three columns show the interactions between corruption and tax rates, and between corruption and capital controls. In column (3), where only the former interaction is shown, the coefficient on the regressor "D(corruption) × tax rate" is negative. As in the regressions reported in table 3.2, this finding is contrary to the hypothesis that grease payments make taxes less irritating to investors. In column (4), where the interaction term "D(corruption) × D(cap-control)" is added alone, the coefficient on

---

1. Other threshold values (5 and 7) were tried and did not make a qualitative difference for the subsequent discussion.

**Table 3.3  Binary Measures of Corruption and Capital Controls (modified Tobit)**

| | Dependent Variable: Log(stock of FDI from $i$ to $j$ in 1991 + $A$) | | | | |
| --- | --- | --- | --- | --- | --- |
| | (1) | (2) | (3) | (4) | (5) |
| Tax rate | −2.12* | −1.01* | −0.95* | −0.91* | −0.84* |
| | (0.43) | (0.39) | (0.40) | (0.39) | (0.40) |
| D(corruption) | −0.30* | −0.20* | 0.33 | −0.37* | 0.13 |
| | (0.11) | (0.10) | (0.65) | (0.18) | (0.06) |
| D(cap-control) | | −0.13* | −0.14* | −0.14* | −0.14* |
| | | (0.03) | (0.03) | (0.03) | (0.03) |
| D(corruption) × tax rate | | | −1.61 | | −1.45 |
| | | | (2.65) | | (1.86) |
| D(corruption) × D(cap-control) | | | | 0.044 | 0.041 |
| | | | | (0.044) | (0.042) |
| log(GDP$_j$) | 0.51* | 0.44* | 0.43* | 0.42* | 0.41* |
| | (0.09) | (0.08) | (0.08) | (0.08) | (0.08) |
| log(distance$_{ij}$) | −0.26* | −0.27* | −0.26* | −0.26* | −0.25* |
| | (0.05) | (0.05) | (0.05) | (0.05) | (0.05) |
| Linguistic tie | 0.65* | 0.61* | 0.61* | 0.59* | 0.58* |
| | (0.25) | (0.28) | (0.24) | (0.23) | (0.23) |
| Constant | 1.6E+4* | 1.6E+4* | 1.6E+4* | 1.6E+4* | 1.6E+4* |
| | (3.6) | (4.4) | (4.9) | (2.4) | (2.1) |
| $A$ | 7.1E+9* | 7.3E+9* | 7.4E+9* | 7.5E+9* | 7.7E+9* |
| | (1.9E+7) | (0.6E+7) | (3.3E+7) | (6.3E+6) | (2.1E+6) |
| $\sigma$ | 1.01* | 0.99* | 0.97* | 0.97* | 0.94* |
| | (0.16) | (0.16) | (0.15) | (0.15) | (0.15) |
| Source dummies? | yes | yes | yes | yes | yes |
| $N$ | 545 | 545 | 545 | 545 | 545 |
| Log likelihood | 1,829.38 | 1,847.23 | 1,849.34 | 1,854.82 | 1,859.62 |

*Note:* See footnotes to table 3.2. D(corruption) and D(cap-control) are dummies for host countries that are highly corrupt, or with severe capital account restrictions, respectively. D(corruption) = 1 if BI corruption index > 6, and 0 otherwise. D(cap-control) = 1 if BI capital control index > 6, and 0 otherwise.

the term is positive but not statistically different from zero at the 10 percent level. In fact, even if one takes the point estimate as given, the estimates suggest that investors will unambiguously invest less in a more corrupt country whether that country has tight or loose capital controls. This differs from the earlier observation in table 3.2, that bribes may reduce the negative effect of capital controls on foreign investment. In other words, the earlier observation is not robust. In column (5), both interactive terms are put together in the regression. The result is essentially the same as before; there is no statistically significant support for the grease payment argument on either the effect of tax or on that of capital controls.

### 3.3.3 Additional Controls

To check for robustness with regard to our inference on the validity of the grease payment argument, I add some further control variables. The results are reported in table 3.4.

The first column of table 3.4 adds a measure of political stability in the host countries. Not surprisingly, more stable regimes attract more investment. Note that our conclusions on the interactions between corruption and tax, and between corruption and capital controls, remain true; there is no support for the grease payment argument.

The second column adds a measure of red tape or bureaucracy in the host countries. While the new variable has a negative sign, as would be consistent with one's intuition, it is not different from zero statistically.

The last column adds average hourly wage in host countries' manufacturing sectors as well as a dummy for OECD host countries. Because the wage data are available for a smaller number of countries, this change cuts down the sample size considerably. As it turns out, the OECD dummy is positive and significant: All else being equal, OECD hosts attract more FDI. The wage variable has a negative and significant coefficient; countries with lower labor costs also attract more FDI. Controlling for these effects, there is still no support for the validity of the grease payment hypothesis.

Subsequent regressions experiment with adding (1) foreign firms' access to domestic capital markets, (2) foreign firms' ability to set up joint ventures with domestic firms, (3) foreign firms' ability to bid on public sector projects, and (4) foreign firms' ability to exert corporate control rights. The four dummies are all survey responses of subjective perceptions from the 1997 *Global Competitiveness Report* (World Economic Forum 1997). As it happens, the four dummies are highly correlated. If all four are put into the regression, none has a coefficient statistically different from zero. Moreover, the earlier conclusions regarding the effects on FDI of tax rates, corruption levels, and capital controls, as well as their interactions, remain the same. If we add only one of the four dummies, say, foreign firms' access to domestic capital markets, this variable does have a statistically significant coefficient. Greater restrictions on access to domestic capital lead to less foreign investment. (The regression results are not reported.)

**Table 3.4**    **More Robustness Checks (modified Tobit, binary measures of corruption and capital controls)**

| | Dependent Variable: Log(stock of FDI from $i$ to $j$ in 1991 + $A$) | | |
|---|---|---|---|
| | (1) | (2) | (3) |
| Tax rate | −0.77# | −0.74# | −1.07* |
| | (0.40) | (0.41) | (0.45) |
| D(corruption) | 0.76 | 0.74 | 1.11# |
| | (0.70) | (0.69) | (0.07) |
| D(cap-control) | −0.13* | −0.12* | −0.11* |
| | (0.03) | (0.03) | (0.04) |
| D(corruption) × tax rate | −3.00## | −2.89 | −3.63# |
| | (2.07) | (2.03) | (1.96) |
| D(corruption) × D(cap-control) | 0.056 | 0.053 | 0.044 |
| | (0.043) | (0.043) | (0.046) |
| Political stability | 0.10* | 0.09# | 0.12* |
| | (0.05) | (0.06) | (0.06) |
| Red tape | | −0.01 | −0.07# |
| | | (0.03) | (0.04) |
| OECD dummy | | | 0.37* |
| | | | (0.13) |
| log(wage$_j$) | | | −0.24* |
| | | | (0.08) |
| log(GDP$_j$) | 0.41* | 0.40* | 0.40* |
| | (0.08) | (0.08) | (0.08) |
| log(distance$_{ij}$) | −0.25* | −0.25* | −0.25* |
| | (0.05) | (0.05) | (0.06) |
| Linguistic tie | 0.60* | 0.56* | 0.59* |
| | (0.23) | (0.28) | (0.22) |
| Constant | 1.6E+4* | 1.6E+4* | 1.6E+4* |
| | (2.5) | (2.5) | (2.3) |
| $A$ | 7.6E+9* | 7.7E+9* | 8.5E+9* |
| | (5.7E+6) | (6.2E+6) | (4.5E+6) |
| $\sigma$ | 0.96* | 0.94* | 0.91* |
| | (0.15) | (0.15) | (0.15) |
| Source dummies? | yes | yes | yes |
| $N$ | 545 | 545 | 450 |
| Log likelihood | 1,860.02 | 1,867.71 | 1,627.73 |

*Note:* See the notes to tables 3.2 and 3.3. "Red tape" equal to 11 minus the corresponding BI index, so that larger numbers mean more red tape.

## 3.4    Concluding Remarks

This paper investigates the effects of corruption, tax rates, and capital on the ability of host countries to attract foreign direct investment. It reaches two main conclusions. First, in isolation, each of the three factors has a negative effect on inward investment: Countries with higher tax rates, or more corruption, or more restrictions on capital account transactions, attract less foreign investment, all other things being equal.

Second, the three factors could interact with each other and produce a complicated aggregate effect. In particular, it is sometimes argued that corruption may allow firms to evade excessive taxation and severe capital account restrictions (the grease payment argument) and thereby actually encourage investment. In the data, there is no support for the view that taxation has a smaller negative effect on foreign investment in a more corrupt host country. With regard to capital controls, there is some support for the view that corruption may reduce the burden of severe capital controls when a ten-step measure of the control is used. However, this result is not robust to the use of dummy variables to separate high corruption from low corruption, and severe capital controls from mild capital controls. Hence, the data do not support the efficient grease payments argument.

In short, the evidence indicates that taxes and capital controls hinder foreign investment. Bureaucratic corruption adds rather than relieves the burdens that they impose.

# References

Desai, Mihir, and James R. Hines Jr. 1996. "Basket" cases: International joint ventures after the Tax Reform Act of 1986. NBER Working Paper no. 5755. Cambridge, Mass.: National Bureau of Economic Research, September.

Feldstein, Marin, James R. Hines Jr., and R. Glenn Hubbard. 1995. *The effects of taxation on multinational corporations.* Chicago: University of Chicago Press.

Frankel, Jeffrey, Ernesto Stein, and Shang-Jin Wei. 1995. Trading blocs and the Americas: The natural, the unnatural, and the super-natural. *Journal of Development Economics* 47 (June): 61–95.

Hines, James R., Jr. 1995. Forbidden payment: Foreign bribery and American business after 1977. NBER Working Paper no. 5266. Cambridge, Mass.: National Bureau of Economic Research, September.

———. 1996. Capital controls and foreign direct investment.

Huntington, Samuel P. 1968. *Political order in changing societies.* New Haven: Yale University Press.

Kaufmann, Daniel, and Shang-Jin Wei. 1999. Does "grease money" speed up the wheels of commerce? NBER Working Paper no. 7093. Cambridge, Mass.: National Bureau of Economic Research, April.

Leff, Nathaniel H. 1964. Economic development through bureaucratic corruption. *American Behavior Scientist* 8 (2): 8–14.

Lui, Francis. 1985. A equilibrium queuing model of bribery. *Journal of Political Economy* 93 (4): 760–81.

Mauro, Paolo. 1995. Corruption and growth. *Quarterly Journal of Economics* 110: 681–712.

Organization for Economic Cooperation and Development (OECD). 1991. *International direct investment statistics yearbook.* Paris: OECD.

Price Waterhouse. 1990. *Information guide,* for various countries. New York: Price Waterhouse.

Rauch, James. 1996. Networks versus markets in international trade. NBER Working Paper no. 5617. Cambridge, Mass.: National Bureau of Economic Research, June.

Wei, Shang-Jin. 1997. Why is corruption so much more taxing than tax? Arbitrariness Kills. NBER Working Paper no. 6255. Cambridge, Mass.: National Bureau of Economic Research, November.

———. 2000. How taxing is corruption on international investors? *Review of Economics and Statistics* 82 (1): 1–11.

World Economic Forum. 1997. *Global competitiveness report*. Geneva, Switzerland: World Economic Forum.

# Comment    Bernard Yeung

The objective of this paper is to determine whether taxes, capital controls, and corruption discourage inward foreign direct investment. More importantly, the paper attempts to check whether corruption will serve as a "grease payment" that mitigates the negative effect of tax and capital controls in attracting foreign direct investment. The main results are that taxes, capital controls, and corruption all discourage inward foreign direct investment and that the grease payment effect is absent.

In my opinion, the empirical attempt is timely and important. Economics is an applied science; we need solid empirical results to back up our theories and thus to strengthen our understanding of the world. The research design in the paper is rather clever—it will allow the data to speak up if corruption has a grease payment effect. Praise to the author.

The empirical results in the paper are appealing. As an economist trained in North America, I am biased against corruption and genuinely would hope that the results are as credible as they can be. Therefore, I would like to point out some needed data improvements to make the results more credible.

The dependent variable is 1991 inward foreign direct investment from fourteen countries (including the largest industrialized countries, in terms of outward direct investment) to forty-five countries and is obtained from an OECD database. Different countries have different definitions for foreign direct investment. For example, the United States uses 10 percent ownership for both inward and outward foreign direct investment, whereas Japan uses 25–50 percent for inward and 10 percent for outward. Hence, what is counted as inward foreign direct investment in one country may not be counted as such in another. To the extent that countries with more capital controls have a higher ownership requirement to classify inward

Bernard Yeung is the Abraham Krasnoff Professor of Global Business at New York University's Stern School of Business.

investment as "direct," a systematic bias may exist in the data. I have a hunch that this bias may not be empirically important. Still, it would be useful to check how the OECD data are compiled and whether the above problem exists in a material manner.

The independent variables have more problems. Let me start with the tax variable. In the paper, the tax variable is defined as the lower of two numbers: "the statutory marginal tax rate on foreign corporations as reported by Price Waterhouse (1990), or the actual average tax rate paid by the foreign subsidiaries of U.S. firms in that country." Actual tax paid is an endogenous variable likely affected by corruption. Apparently, the author believes that American firms are mostly honest and that they follow tax codes strictly, so that their tax rates are representative of the actual tax rates. Some would have doubts. One wonders why the author does not use the Price Waterhouse reported rates only.

The capital control data are based on 1980–83 surveys. Capital controls changed quite a bit from 1983 to 1991. In particular, many Asian countries relaxed their capital controls and rolled out a red carpet for foreign investment. The historical survey data would not be irrelevant as long as foreign direct investment behavior did not change much in the eighties. However, to the extent that foreign direct investment surged in the eighties, the author should find a set of survey data closer to 1991. Similarly, although corruption likely changes less rapidly than capital controls, it would be nice to have more current corruption data.

The most interesting result of the paper is that a grease payment effect does not exist. The grease payment effect is that companies can bribe government officers to reduce the damage of taxes and capital controls on their businesses. As a consequence, taxes and capital controls have less negative effect in attracting foreign direct investment. The cross terms between "corruption" and "tax" and between "corruption" and "capital control" are supposed to capture that—that the presence of a grease payment effect will lead to positive and significant cross terms. Note that the design suggests that the corruption survey data should capture only "government corruption." The corruption survey data used capture something more general: "the degree to which business transactions involve corruption or questionable payments." While the more general survey data are likely highly correlated with "government corruption," the more precise survey variable is known to exist.

Overall, this paper attempts to show empirical evidence of the idea that taxes, capital controls, and corruption discourage foreign direct investment and that the grease payment effect does not exist. The results are intuitively believable. I doubt the suggested data improvements would change the results. Rather, they should strengthen their credibility.

# Transaction Type and the Effect of Taxes on the Distribution of Foreign Direct Investment in the United States

Deborah L. Swenson

## 4.1 Introduction

This paper studies how the tax responsiveness of foreign direct investment (FDI) differs across investment types. Most analyses of foreign investment rely on aggregate data such as flow of funds, the volume of new enterprises in the United States, or the operations of foreign subsidiaries in the United States.[1] While these data provide a comprehensive description of overall investment activities, they are less informative if one wishes to analyze individual firm decisions.

There are at least two reasons that treatment of firm issues is warranted in the analysis of the tax effects on the distribution of foreign investment. To begin, we know that any set of tax rules may lead to different consequences for firms that are in different positions. For example, it is well known that tax changes are likely to have different effects on old and new capital. In the context of this paper, these differences might reveal themselves in different effects for new plants versus mergers and acquisitions. To the extent that firms located in some countries are more likely to perform acquisitions than greenfield investment, apparent country differences in

Deborah L. Swenson is associate professor of economics at the University of California, Davis, and a faculty research fellow of the National Bureau of Economic Research.

The author thanks the Institute for Global Cooperation and Conflict and Institute for Governmental Affairs at UC Davis for research support. Carissa Perez provided outstanding research assistance. All remaining errors are the author's.

1. These are exemplified by U.S. Department of the Treasury flow of funds data, and by annual Bureau of Economic Analysis (BEA) articles in the *Survey of Current Business* and BEA surveys of foreign investment activities of foreign affiliates in the United States or of U.S. affiliates abroad.

tax responsiveness will reflect these countries' investment compositions as well as the structure of the tax reform itself.[2]

We might also expect that investors pursuing acquisitions or joint ventures would place a higher value on the nontax attributes of prospective investment choices than would foreign investors involved in greenfield investment. When a foreign firm decides to make a U.S. acquisition and selects an acquisition target, that firm has decided that it is cheaper and faster to acquire the U.S. target's intangible assets than to develop these assets internally. While the firm might prefer to locate in a state that has lower taxes, its choice will be constrained by the location and availability of appropriate targets. As a result, taxes are less likely to change such a firm's decisions, unless the tax costs are extraordinarily large relative to the nontax advantages offered by a particular target. In addition, these taxes may not impose severe costs on the foreign acquirer because the taxes should be capitalized, reducing the ultimate acquisition price of the target firm.

The second reason we might expect different types of investments to respond more or less vigorously to tax differentials is that various investment transactions will be subject to differing degrees of investment persistence. Investment persistence is the tendency of firms to select locations that have already been selected by their predecessors in the industry, and it may be driven by either agglomeration externalities or specific factor endowments. If agglomeration economies are present, new investors benefit from externalities gained from operation within close proximity to other firms in the same industry. In support of these arguments, Head, Ries, and Swenson (1999, 1995) demonstrate that Japanese investors prefer to locate in states that have been selected previously by U.S. or other Japanese firms in their respective industries. This analysis finds that the tendency toward agglomeration or investment persistence is more generally observable in the behavior of all foreign investors.

It is also likely that investment persistence derives from the cost structure of multinational activity. In the context of exports, Roberts and Tybout (1995) demonstrate how previous firm decisions can predispose firms toward continuation of prior activity.[3] Since new investors are not constrained by prior firm decisions, they should be more responsive to tax differentials than are firms that have established earlier operations in the

2. In a similar vein, Auerbach and Hassett (1993) show that a country's response to TRA 1986 depends on compositional issues, such as the fraction of acquisitions in the country's foreign investment. They argue that distinctions that classify investors into residential versus territorial categories are called into question by evidence that the relative importance of manufacturing investment increased for both territorial and residential investors after TRA 1986.

3. See Markusen (1995) for a survey of multinational firms' decision making. Markusen and Venables (1996) provide simulations that illustrate the potency of these effects.

United States. As a result, I expect that states with higher taxes may, ceteris paribus, attract fewer new investments.

The practical implication of agglomeration economies and other rigidities in investment decisions is that past decisions will affect current foreign investors' responsiveness to taxes. A state that offers few agglomeration benefits to prospective investors may not be attractive even if it offers a lower tax rate. Although I do not focus on investment persistence in this study, I believe it is a phenomenon for which one must control if one is to measure tax effects accurately. To implement controls for investment persistence I introduce variables that describe the industry similarities of states in the eyes of the prospective investor.[4]

This study utilizes individual firm investment transactions data. The information that is especially important to this study is the classification of transaction type—merger/acquisition, plant expansion, new plant, joint venture, or equity increase—as well as information on the industry of investment. The presence of these industry classifications (in conjunction with data from the U.S. Bureau of the Census) allows me to examine the potency of tax effects across investment types.

Other work on the tax responsiveness of inbound investment flows to the United States has yielded mixed results, though the studies that identify the dampening effects of taxes on investment tend to provide more precise tax measures.[5] I find that transaction type is another dimension that should be considered by researchers in creating more precise measures. High state taxes are associated with inhibited levels of new plant or plant expansion. In contrast, even after one controls for state characteristics and industry-specific agglomeration economies, it appears that the level of foreign merger and acquisition activity is positively correlated with high state taxes. I discover that a portion of the cross-country heterogeneity in tax responsiveness can be attributed to national differences in the composition of investment flows, especially whether investors from a particular country have engaged more in greenfield investments than mergers and acquisitions.

The paper proceeds as follows. Section 4.2 develops a simple model of investment to motivate the importance of taxes and agglomeration mea-

---

4. Other studies have implemented the investment choice as a sequential decision framework in which the investor chooses a region first, then selects a state from that region in the second stage. This framework lends itself to nested-logit estimation. I choose to condition on investment persistence terms instead, because they allow for greater flexibility in the determination of relevant state choices by industry.

5. Hines (1996b), Bartik (1991), and Wasylenko (1991) provide comprehensive reviews of the evidence. In general, more powerful tax effects are found by studies that look at smaller jurisdictions (such as metropolitan areas), as compared with interstate or international distributions of investment. Greater effects also tend to emerge in studies that tailor the tax terms to the particular industry of investment or to investor characteristics, as in Papke (1991).

sures, and to provide a background for the later econometric specification. Section 4.3 describes the construction of the data set and provides some details regarding country differences in foreign investment activities. Econometric tests of the investment model are performed in section 4.4, which is followed by concluding comments in section 4.5.

## 4.2 Research Design

### 4.2.1 General Framework

I choose a flexible estimation framework that is based on the assumption that foreign firms have decided to invest in the United States, and that each will select that U.S. state for which its rise in incremental profits is the greatest. This approach can be estimated by conditional logit models developed by McFadden (1974).[6] Both the firm's activities and the industrial composition of each prospective state affect the firm's decisions regarding current investments. Although we can't observe profits directly, we can use information on firms' actual investment choices to draw inferences about the effects of various state characteristics.

Suppose that, in general, the incremental after-tax profit a firm earns on a current investment placed in state $s$ can be represented as

$$(1) \qquad \Pi_s = \pi(v_s, p) * (1 - \tau_s).$$

The reduced-form profit function represents the additional operating profit the firm will generate if it chooses state $s$.[7] The function includes arguments for input costs $v$, and taxes $\tau$, both of which are unique to the recipient states. The effects of state-specific factors or agglomeration economies are captured in the input costs $v$ because these externalities reduce input costs. Two possible agglomeration externalities would include a well-developed supplier network or a pool of highly specialized labor. Because the extent of these externalities rises as a state gains a high concentration of firms in a particular industry, one would expect a state's attractiveness to increase as its concentration of relevant firms increases. A difference between investment persistence based on agglomeration economies and investment persistence driven by industry-specific factors is that specific

6. Work on investment that adopts this approach was initially performed by Carlton (1983) and Bartik (1985). Bartik (1991) surveys work in this area.

7. I abstract from the issue of formula apportionment. Because it is difficult to attribute profits precisely to particular states, states instead define taxable income as some share of the firm's national income, with the share imputed through formula apportionment. Typically, the share calculations are based on a weighting scheme that includes the firm's capital, wages, and sales in a state relative to its capital, wages, and sales nationally. See Gordon and Wilson (1986) for a discussion of the implications of formula apportionment, or Klassen and Shackelford (1997) for empirical evidence regarding the effects of formula apportionment on state revenues as related to state tax rates.

factors may face ultimate congestion, whereas agglomeration externalities may grow indefinitely with industry size. In principle, it might be possible to disentangle investment incentives based on agglomeration economies from investment persistence driven by factor-specific endowments.[8] However, this would require one to use a sufficiently long time series, and could be tested only if it were possible to assume that industry factor demands were not changed over time by underlying influences such as technical change. For the purposes of this paper, I term the propensity of firms to cluster *agglomeration,* but I remain agnostic on its source. The primary benefit of controlling for agglomeration effects or investment persistence is that it provides a flexible method for characterizing the states an investor might select, rather than assuming that all states are equally substitutable a priori, or imposing an arbitrary structure for investor substitution among states.

Another element of the firm's profit function is the price of the firm's output *p.* However, I assume that the final goods price is the same regardless of the investment location selected, because there is no reason to believe that the value of a product depends on the state in which it is produced. As a result, though price influences the level of profits, it will not exert any effect on the relative attractiveness of one state compared with the others, and does not need to be included in the econometric specification.

Under this set of conditions, if the gain in operating profits exceeds the fixed cost of investing in the new operations, the firm will place its investment in the state that yields the greatest profits. As long as the component of the profit function that is attributable to agglomeration economies is separable from the component of the profit function attributable to other factors, the profitability of state $s$ to investor $i$ can be represented as

$$\Gamma_{is} = \delta_s + \beta_{us} * \ln(\text{Est-US}_{is}) + \beta_f * \ln(\text{Est-For}_{is}) + \gamma \ln(1 - \tau_s) + \varepsilon_s.$$

In this formulation, the attractiveness of state $s$ to the representative investor is captured by $\delta_s$. The Est-US and Est-For terms capture agglomeration economies by measuring the counts, at the time of $i$'s investment decision, of U.S. and foreign establishments in state $s$, which are in the same industry as firm $i$.

The probability that state $s$ yields the highest profits to investor $i$ is given by the logit expression

$$\Pr(is) = \frac{\exp(\Gamma_{is})}{\sum_{s \in S} \exp(\Gamma_{is})}.$$

---

8. One would also need to characterize how firms form their expectations, unless one can assume that current agglomeration economies are a sufficient statistic for the future path.

I use maximum likelihood techniques, based on these probabilities, to estimate the tax, investment persistence, and state fixed effects.

### 4.2.2  Tax Issues

The reduced-form profit function in equation (1) displays the after-tax profits a foreign firm will earn in the United States before it repatriates its funds to the parent firm for distribution to its owners or shareholders. As a result, the amount of money that the firm has available for ultimate distribution depends, in part, on how the parent firm's home country treats taxes already paid in host-country locations such as the United States.

The notable distinction to consider here is whether the parent firm is taxed by its home taxing authority on a territorial or residential basis. Firms such as those from France or Germany that are taxed on a territorial basis are not taxed on their foreign earnings. As a result, equation (1) provides a fairly accurate view of their net of tax earnings.

In contrast, firms headquartered in residential tax countries are liable for taxes in their home countries for all earnings, both domestic and foreign. At the same time, these firms are usually given a credit for taxes already paid on their foreign earnings. The firm is left with a home tax liability that is based on the residual difference between its assessed home tax bill and any taxes deemed paid on its foreign income. One can not determine a priori whether a firm will pay additional tax to its home taxing authority. However, firms of residential origin are likely to owe home taxes if the rate of home taxation exceeds the amount of taxes paid in the United States and if the foreign firm is in an excess limit position.[9]

The consequence of this tax distinction is that foreign firms of territorial origin should be especially sensitive to state tax differences, since any additional taxes levied will diminish their profits one for one. In contrast, firms of residential origin may not be affected by differences in state taxation if the assessed tax burdens they face at home exceed the amount of taxes they pay in the United States. However, if firms of residential origin are in an excess credit position, then they should respond to interstate tax differentials in a fashion that is similar to that of territorial investors, since their profits are diminished by U.S. state taxes in an equivalent manner. As shown in Hines (1996a), the territorial/residential distinction implies that territorial investors should respond to interstate tax differentials more vigorously than would residential investors.

---

9. For the late 1980s and early 1990s this would imply that U.K. firms should be more responsive to U.S. taxes than were Japanese firms, as the rate of corporate taxation was lower in Britain than in Japan.

## 4.3   Data

### 4.3.1   Foreign Investment Transactions

The foreign investments analyzed in this paper are collected from the publication "Foreign Direct Investment in the United States."[10] The data define foreign investment to be any transaction for which a foreign firm has the direct or indirect ownership of 10 percent or more of the voting securities of an incorporated business enterprise, or an equivalent interest in an unincorporated business. The roster of firms analyzed in this study includes all manufacturing sector foreign investments conducted between 1984 and 1994.[11]

The interesting feature of these data is that they not only record the state of the investment, the nationality of the investor, and the four-digit Standard Industrial Classification (SIC) of the industry in which the investment is placed, but that they also distinguish the type of investment. There are six categories: New Plant, Plant Expansion, Merger and Acquisition, Joint Venture, Equity Increase, and Other. The final category (Other) represents investments that do not fit neatly into one of the previous categories, and/or transactions the designations of which are precluded by a lack of information. The data on transaction type are used to create a set of interaction terms, which are used to test for variation in tax response across transaction type.

Table 4.1 presents an overview of the data. Of the full 3,212-observation sample, the most frequently represented transaction is Mergers and Acquisitions. This is followed by New Plant and, more distantly, by Plant Expansion activities, Other transactions, Joint Ventures, and Equity Increases. The low number of equity increase observations may reflect reporting differences, because it is possible that physical investments are more accurately observed than are financial decisions. Nonetheless, underreporting of this category should not bias the estimation of coefficients, because the conditional logit framework is based on the observation of individual decisions. Though the equity increase variables may be estimated with less precision, the magnitude of their effects will not be biased unless there is some systematic difference between the universe of equity increases and the subset that appears in the data set.

---

10. The International Trade Administration of the U.S. Department of Commerce is responsible for this data collection. This data collection effort was initiated by Executive Order no. 11,858, dated 7 May 1975, by which the Secretary of Commerce is responsible for "the obtainment, consolidation, and analysis of information on foreign direct investment in the United States."

11. This paper considers the same data source that is the basis of the study by Ondrich and Wasylenko (1993). However, since their work focuses only on the new plants built between 1978 and 1987, they cannot address the tax responsiveness of other investment types.

**Table 4.1**   Foreign Investment in Manufacturing Industries: Country Distribution by Investment Type, 1984–94

| | Full Sample | New Plant | Plant Expansion | Merger & Acquisition | Joint Venture | Equity Increase | Other |
|---|---|---|---|---|---|---|---|
| | | | | Number of Transactions | | | |
| *All investments* | 3,212 | 703 | 436 | 1,328 | 275 | 150 | 320 |
| *Primary investors* | | | | | | | |
| Australia | 42 | 5 | 0 | 31 | 1 | 1 | 4 |
| Belgium | 21 | 5 | 4 | 10 | 1 | 0 | 1 |
| Canada | 242 | 39 | 17 | 142 | 5 | 14 | 25 |
| France | 157 | 19 | 11 | 87 | 15 | 11 | 14 |
| Germany | 296 | 71 | 54 | 114 | 15 | 14 | 27 |
| Japan | 1,545 | 458 | 280 | 368 | 196 | 61 | 182 |
| Netherlands | 80 | 12 | 10 | 45 | 5 | 2 | 6 |
| Sweden | 77 | 8 | 4 | 47 | 9 | 2 | 6 |
| United Kingdom | 432 | 28 | 26 | 322 | 9 | 18 | 28 |

*Note:* The Primary Investors category includes the nine most frequent investor nations from the full data set, which includes forty-six investor countries.

Although forty-six countries are responsible for the transactions included in the data set, many of their investors conducted only a handful of transactions each. Table 4.1 provides a view of the composition of investment types for the most frequent investors in the United States. What is striking is the heterogeneity in investment activities. As has been remarked elsewhere, Japan more than other countries was engaged in new plant, plant expansion, and joint venture activities. Although Japanese investors completed a number of large acquisitions that captured news headlines, they engaged in acquisition activity less frequently than the average country. Germany was the other large investor that was more heavily involved in new plant and plant expansion activity than in acquisitions. In contrast, firms from the United Kingdom, France, and Sweden were most frequently involved with acquisitions. If tax effects differ across transaction types, then cross-country differences in investment composition could cause researchers to attribute cross-country heterogeneity in tax responses incorrectly to country differences, rather than to differences in transaction prevalence.[12]

### 4.3.2   Investment Persistence and Agglomeration

In order to measure investment persistence, or agglomeration, I use establishment counts that are collected from the U.S. Bureau of the Census in Darney (1992, 1996). The variable Est-US$_{s,t}$ provides the count of firms in state $s$ in the same four-digit SIC industry as the prospective investor in year $t$. Unlike the investment data, which are collected on an annual basis, the establishment census is conducted only every five years. The most recent counts were performed in 1982, 1987, and 1992. As a result, the independent variables that describe establishment activity must be attached to recent year counts.[13] For this study, transactions completed between 1984 and 1986 were attached to the 1982 industry establishment counts; transactions occurring between 1987 and 1991 were attached to the 1987 counts; and the transactions of 1992 to 1994 were attached to the 1992 counts.

In Head, Ries, and Swenson (1999, 1995) it is apparent that Japanese firms respond not only to overall establishment counts but also to counts of Japanese establishments. To capture both the foreign element and the overall pattern, I use the 1974–83 rosters of my transactions data to create Est-For$_{is}$. This variable counts the number of foreign firms located in a

---

12. I assume that cross-country differences are not driving firms' decisions regarding the type of transaction to perform.

13. It would be possible to create an interpolated series that would allow the variable "Est" to evolve over time. However, the use of an arbitrary assignment scheme would introduce measurement error. Another possibility would be to allow "Est" to grow in the intervening years according to some metric, such as state income. However, this scheme is also problematic, because state income or other measures that could be used to apportion the changes may influence investment on their own.

Table 4.2                Sample Distribution of Est-US$_{is}$ and Est-For$_{is}$

|  | Est-US$_{is}$ | Est-For$_{is}$ |
|---|---|---|
| Range | 0–4034 | 0–72 |
| Mean | 26 | 3.4 |
| Median | 4 | 1 |
| 25th percentile | 0 | 0 |
| 75th Percentile | 20 | 3 |

U.S. state $s$, in the same two-digit industry as the investor, at the time of the foreign investor's decision. I use two-digit counts for this variable for two reasons. First, unlike the Census data, which includes thousands of firms, the foreign rosters have far fewer observations. If I apportion these observations across the fifty states and into 461 four-digit SIC categories, the data are very thin, and almost every count observation is zero. More importantly, there is reason to believe that foreign firms may be attracted to states based on the foreign concentration of similar two-digit industry firms. These foreign firms may be choosing the states because they have upstream or downstream linkages to these prior investors; or, if the prior investors provide information, as suggested by Casella and Rauch (1997), then informational clarity may cause the firms to choose the attractive states for which there is an established track record.

An interesting aspect of these investment variables is their distribution. As table 4.2 shows, the investment counts are highly skewed: whereas some states have a large number of establishments, states in the 25th percentile of any particular industry have no establishments whatsoever, domestic or foreign.

### 4.3.3    Fiscal Variables

I measure state taxes by corporate tax rates. These corporate tax rates were collected from publications of the National Association of State Development Agencies (1986, 1991) and supplemented by tax charts from the Advisory Commission on Intergovernmental Relations. Across the sample period, state tax rates on corporate income ranged from 0 to 12 percent. In all years of the data analysis, the average state tax rate was between 6 and 7 percent. This provides the false impression that state taxes changed very little. However, while the average state tax rate changed little, the average conceals the fact many changed their tax rates in both the positive and the negative direction.

## 4.4    Estimation Results

The primary goal of my analysis is to determine the tax responsiveness of different types of investment in light of investor-specific factors that may predispose investors to choose particular states. I begin with an estimation that considers the importance of investor type, then broaden the analysis to consider cross-country differences in tax responsiveness and how these differences relate to transaction type.

The first column of table 4.3 provides a baseline regression that constrains tax effects to be uniform for all transaction types. The coefficient implies that higher taxes reduce the probability that a particular state will be picked by foreign investors. Because I am analyzing transactions data, this describes the effect of taxes on the frequency of investment, as opposed to investment volumes. The regression also includes state fixed effects and two measures of previous industry activity. Although I do not report the individual state fixed effects, they are highly significant, which implies that certain states have characteristics that cause them to be relatively more attractive to all investors.

I also find that both measures of industry activity, my investment persistence variables, are positive and highly significant. These coefficients imply that investors are attracted to states with a high concentration of other firms in their same four-digit industries, and that their propensities to invest in these states is further enhanced if there is a concentration of similar-industry investors of foreign origin. I interpret this as evidence that agglomeration spillovers, or industry-specific factors, are strong determinants of a firm's location decision. The fact that the concentration of foreign investors provides further information implies that information channels opened by the actions of other foreign investors enhance the attractiveness of a state above and beyond the attractiveness indicated by the mostly domestic distribution of firms.

In the second column of table 4.3 I continue to work with the full sample, but I now allow the tax coefficients to differ for exemption or territorial investors, as opposed to residential or worldwide investors.[14] These results are presented in the second column of table 4.3. Contrary to the predictions, the results indicate that the probability of a state's selection by territorial investors is not statistically related to interstate tax differences. In contrast, I find that higher taxes reduce the probability that a state will be selected by investors of residential origin. An $F$-test reveals that the difference in the coefficients for territorial versus residential investors is statistically significant. This finding contradicts the prediction that territorial investors would be more likely than residential investors to avoid high-tax states. However, this finding may be affected by the choice of dependent variable. I am observing investment location decisions, rather than the volume of investments. Although the territorial investors may not

---

14. In this analysis the designation "territorial" encompasses the investments of firms from Australia, Canada, France, Germany, and Switzerland, whereas the designation "residential" applies to the investments of Japan and the United Kingdom.

**Table 4.3**    **Conditional Logit Regressions of Foreign Investment by State, 1984–94**

| | All | All | New Plant | Plant Expansion | Merger & Acquisition | Joint Venture | Equity Increase | Other |
|---|---|---|---|---|---|---|---|---|
| $\ln(1-t_s)$ | 1.6229 | | | | | | | |
| | (.5550) | | | | | | | |
| *Taxpayer type* | | | | | | | | |
| $\mathrm{Terr}*\ln(1-t_s)$ | | -.6049 | 2.9649 | 9.8037 | -3.4094 | -6.4065 | 3.7289 | -5.2798 |
| | | (1.2904) | (2.8025) | (3.3218) | (1.9291) | (6.4930) | (6.4833) | (4.8337) |
| $\mathrm{Res}*\ln(1-t_s)$ | | 2.8974 | 5.6468 | 4.9810 | -2.1044 | -.9473 | 8.5883 | 5.0755 |
| | | (.6836) | (1.3310) | (1.6946) | (1.2609) | (3.6812) | (1.9821) | (2.2072) |
| $F$-test | | 5.92 | .076 | 1.69 | .34 | .55 | .52 | 3.97 |
| (Res = Terr) | | 0.015 | .385 | .193 | .563 | .457 | .472 | .046 |
| *Investment persistence* | | | | | | | | |
| $\ln(\text{Est-US}_{is})$ | .7825 | .7828 | .6615 | .7741 | .9096 | .8194 | .8241 | .6065 |
| | (.0226) | (.0226) | (.0424) | (.0586) | (.0383) | (.1104) | (.0771) | (.0735) |
| $\ln(\text{Est-For}_{is})$ | .3181 | .3183 | .1350 | .1248 | .3322 | .4683 | .2640 | .7025 |
| | (.0251) | (.0249) | (.0518) | (.0668) | (.0396) | (.1203) | (.0851) | (.0819) |
| $N$ | 127,800 | 127,800 | 30,050 | 18,850 | 48,800 | 11,300 | 5,400 | 13,300 |
| Number of choosers | 2,556 | 2,556 | 601 | 377 | 976 | 226 | 180 | 266 |
| Log likelihood | -8088.2 | -8085.1 | -2064.5 | -1255.4 | -2843.1 | -739.1 | -307.6 | -770.1 |

*Note:* Standard errors in parentheses. For each investment in the sample, the dependent variable codes the recipient state as 1, and all other states as 0. State taxes are measured by $(1-t_s)$, or 1 minus the state rate of taxation. The $F$-test examines the equality of the tax coefficients for residential and territorial investors, who are represented by the dummy variables Res and Terr. The first line reports the test statistic, and the second line reports the $p$-value for the test. Est-US$_{is}$ is the count of similar-industry establishments in the state, and Est-For$_{is}$ is the count of similar-industry foreign investments in the state. Regressions include state fixed effects.

avoid high-tax states altogether, they may place smaller investments in those locations.[15]

I consider the possibility that the distinction between worldwide and territorial investors became more powerful after the implementation of Public Law 99-514, the U.S. Tax Reform Act of 1986 (TRA 1986). Because the full sample covers 1984–94, the early observations predate the implementation of TRA 1986. To see whether the choice of sample period influences my results, I restricted the analysis to investments that occurred after the reform, and repeated the previous regression analysis. However, I do not report these results because the change in time frame does not alter the basic finding.

The last six columns of table 4.3 investigate how the tax responses of residential and territorial investors differ across investment categories. I repeat the previous regression specification, but now restrict the analysis to subsamples of the data that are defined by transaction type. I find that one cannot reject the hypothesis that residential and territorial investors exhibit similar tax responses for new plant, plant expansion, merger, joint venture, and equity increase decisions. All foreign investors performing new plant, plant expansion, or equity increase decisions, regardless of home tax system, appear to be dissuaded from selecting states with higher taxes. In contrast, foreign firms of all origins appear more likely to select higher tax states when they are engaged in mergers and acquisitions or in joint venture activity.

All else being equal, we might expect that tax considerations would inhibit the acquisition of targets located in high-tax states. However, Scholes and Wolfson (1992) demonstrate that there may be a tax clientele effect for foreign investors from worldwide tax countries. If the foreign firms are less adversely affected by high taxes, they may then place a higher value on these targets located in high-tax states.[16] Collins, Kemsley, and Shackelford (1993) provide evidence that contradicts this notion. They investigated the postacquisition performance of a number of firms purchased by Japanese and U.K. investors after 1986. They find that, at most, only 59 percent of the acquisitions satisfied the conditions that are necessary for the Scholes and Wolfson hypothesis to hold. More important, they find that the most optimistic prediction of tax benefits accruing to these residential purchasers is minuscule when compared with the acquisition prices they paid to purchase their U.S. targets. Barring highly optimistic and unrealistic expectations on the part of these acquirers, the results suggest that nontax

---

15. Hines (1996a) provides evidence on the volume-versus-frequency question. His work finds that taxes exert a larger effect on shares of plant, property, and equipment value attracted to states than they do on the distribution of foreign affiliates as measured by affiliate counts.

16. If the marginal buyers are U.S. firms, and foreign firms have better tax treatment, then they would be predisposed to the selection of these targets.

factors dominated tax considerations in these foreign acquisitions. One last surprise in table 4.3 is that the positive association between taxes and acquisitions exists for both territorial and residential investors.

The only disjoint finding in table 4.3 appears in the category "Other." Territorial investors appear to be attracted to higher tax states, whereas residential investors are repelled by higher taxes. The difference in these coefficients is statistically significant. Nonetheless, because the category "Other" contains transactions that were difficult to categorize, I do not place much weight on this finding. The important result of table 4.3 is that foreign residential and territorial investors seem to respond to interstate tax differences in a similar fashion, once one controls for investment type.

In table 4.4 I return to estimates that involve the full sample, but that allow for variation in the tax responsiveness across investment types. In column (2) of table 4.4, I include interaction terms that allow the tax responsiveness of investors to vary across the six types of investment. As I found with the subsamples in table 4.3, foreign investors' new plant, plant expansion, and joint venture activities appear to be repelled by states with higher taxes. At the same time, the probability that a foreign investor will perform an acquisition in a state is positively correlated with tax rates. I also find a positive correlation for the Equity Increase and Other categories, but neither of these effects is statistically significant. Because the Other category is imprecisely defined, I exclude all transactions labelled "other" from my next regression, which is displayed in column (3) of table 4.4. However, the tax coefficients change only modestly, leaving the essential result unchanged.

Finally, in column (4) of table 4.4, I include both the investor-type interaction terms and the transaction-type interaction terms for the four types of transactions that were precisely estimated. I find that the results for the four transaction types are qualitatively similar to the earlier regressions. The only difference is that the statistical significance of the acquisition variable is diminished markedly. At the same time, the residential and territorial variables do not enter the specification in a significant fashion. These results seem to imply that distinguishing investments by transaction type provides more predictive insight when considering tax effects than does the distinction of residential versus exemption investor type.

As a result, I move away from the residential versus territorial distinction, and perform estimations in table 4.5 that allows the tax responsiveness of investment to differ freely across countries. In columns (1) and (2), I consider the full sample first, then a subsample of frequent investors. Column (2) indicates, for example, that only three countries demonstrated a tax responsiveness that was significantly different from zero. Japanese and Belgian investors appear to have avoided high-tax states, whereas the probability of investment for U.K. investors was positively correlated with tax rates. As before, the regressions include fixed effects, and investment

Table 4.4    **Conditional Logit Regressions of Foreign Investment by State, 1984–1994**

|  | (1) | (2) | (3) | (4) |
|---|---|---|---|---|
| *Taxpayer type* | | | | |
| Terr$*\ln(1-t_s)$ | −.7652 | | | −3.0451 |
|  | (1.2958) | | | (2.0145) |
| Res$*\ln(1-t_s)$ | 2.7485 | | | 1.1780 |
|  | (.6896) | | | (1.6851) |
| *Transaction type* | | | | |
| NP$*\ln(1-t_s)$ | | 6.5130 | 6.2555 | 8.0356 |
|  | | (1.1716) | (1.1751) | (2.0110) |
| PE$*\ln(1-t_s)$ | | 6.9670 | 6.7249 | 8.5039 |
|  | | (1.4732) | (1.4777) | (2.2016) |
| MA$*\ln(1-t_s)$ | | −3.9668 | −4.3677 | −2.2443 |
|  | | (1.0611) | (1.0655) | (1.9392) |
| JV$*\ln(1-t_s)$ | | 8.2263 | 7.9892 | 9.5683 |
|  | | (1.8612) | (1.8666) | (2.4855) |
| EI$*\ln(1-t_s)$ | | −4.4710 | −4.8322 | |
|  | | (3.1641) | (3.1725) | |
| OT$*\ln(1-t_s)$ | | −0.5347 | | |
|  | | (1.9384) | | |
| *Investment persistence* | | | | |
| $\ln(\text{Est-US}_{is})$ | .7733 | .7689 | .7849 | .7692 |
|  | (.0251) | (.0251) | (.0263) | (.0251) |
| $\ln(\text{Est-For}_{is})$ | .3074 | .2991 | .2537 | .2988 |
|  | (.0281) | (.0280) | (.0295) | (.0280) |
| $N$ | 127,800 | 127,800 | 114,500 | 127,800 |
| Number of choosers | 2,556 | 2,556 | 2,290 | 2,556 |
| Log likelihood | −8085.1 | −8049.3 | −7264.13 | −8049.1 |

*Note:* Standard errors in parentheses. For each investment in the sample, the dependent variable codes the recipient state as 1, and all other states as 0. State taxes are measured by $(1-t_s)$, or 1 minus the state rate of taxation. Res and Terr are dummy variables that represent residential and territorial investors. The tax variable is interacted with the following transaction types: NP = New Plant, PE = Plant Expansion, MA = Merger and Acquisition, JV = Joint Venture, EI = Equity Increase, and OT = Other. Est-US$_{is}$ is the count of similar-industry establishments in the state, and Est-For$_{is}$ is the count of similar-industry foreign investments in the state. Specification includes unreported state fixed effects.

count variables that measure the propensity towards investment persistence. These variables continue to display high significance, with the investment persistence variables implying that the interstate distribution of foreign investment is highly correlated with the domestic and foreign distribution of economic activity in the same industry.

In the specifications for columns (3) and (4), I augment the specification from columns (1) and (2) with tax interaction terms based on investment type. Again, I choose to include only those terms that were significant before: new plant, plant expansion, and merger and acquisition. Column (4) is the analogue of column (2). I find that the positive correlation I found earlier for the United Kingdom disappears when the investment-type interaction terms are added. At the same time, the magnitude and signifi-

**Table 4.5**     **Conditional Logit Regressions of Foreign Investment by State, 1984–1994**

|  | (1) | (2) | (3) | (4) |
|---|---|---|---|---|
| $\ln(1-t_s)$ | −1.8341 | | −.8701 | |
| | (1.7687) | | (2.0310) | |
| *Country effects* | | | | |
| UK*$\ln(1-t_s)$ | −1.3933 | −3.3725 | .6118 | −.0891 |
| | (2.3417) | (1.5622) | (2.3766) | (2.0015) |
| JA*$\ln(1-t_s)$ | 6.2367 | 4.3053 | 3.8987 | 3.2737 |
| | (1.9088) | (.7570) | (1.9466) | (1.2308) |
| FR*$\ln(1-t_s)$ | −1.5500 | −3.5118 | −.9453 | −1.6497 |
| | (3.0943) | (2.5565) | (3.1165) | (2.7691) |
| GE*$\ln(1-t_s)$ | 2.1288 | .1918 | .7150 | .1135 |
| | (2.4951) | (1.7789) | (2.5244) | (2.0968) |
| CA*$\ln(1-t_s)$ | .7577 | −1.2021 | 1.4465 | .7658 |
| | (2.6571) | (2.004) | (2.6797) | (2.3059) |
| NL*$\ln(1-t_s)$ | 4.4488 | 2.5011 | 4.7711 | 4.1261 |
| | (3.6972) | (3.2613) | (3.7240) | (3.4691) |
| AS*$\ln(1-t_s)$ | −3.294 | −5.2674 | −1.2406 | −1.9542 |
| | (5.2953) | (5.0040) | (5.3386) | (5.1817) |
| BE*$\ln(1-t_s)$ | 24.2665 | 22.4178 | 23.8237 | 23.3171 |
| | (6.3180) | (6.1461) | (6.4116) | (6.2794) |
| SW*$\ln(1-t_s)$ | 2.3058 | .3712 | 3.5667 | 2.8777 |
| | (3.8390) | (3.4200) | (3.8647) | (3.6038) |
| *Transaction types* | | | | |
| NP*$\ln(1-t_s)$ | | | 4.9889 | 4.5010 |
| | | | (1.5405) | (1.6092) |
| PE*$\ln(1-t_s)$ | | | 5.1002 | 4.4718 |
| | | | (1.7578) | (1.8923) |
| MA*$\ln(1-t_s)$ | | | −5.2352 | −5.5501 |
| | | | (1.4767) | (1.5633) |
| *Investment persistence* | | | | |
| $\ln(\text{Est-US}_{is})$ | .7826 | .7770 | .7788 | .7738 |
| | (.0226) | (.0238) | (.0226) | (.0238) |
| $\ln(\text{Est-For}_{is})$ | .3135 | .3051 | .3102 | .3013 |
| | (.0251) | (.0265) | (.0251) | (.0264) |
| $N$ | 160,600 | 144,550 | 160,600 | 144,550 |
| Number of choosers | 3,232 | 2,891 | 3,232 | 2,891 |
| Log likelihood | −10075.9 | −9111.9 | −10045.4 | −9085.9 |

*Note:* Standard errors in parentheses. For each investment in the sample, the dependent variable codes the recipient state as 1, and all other states as 0. State taxes are measured by $(1-t_s)$, or 1 minus the state rate of taxation. Res and Terr are dummy variables that represent residential and territorial investors. The tax variable is interacted with country- and transaction-type dummies. The dummy variables for nations are UK = United Kingdom, JA = Japan, FR = France, GE = Germany, CA = Canada, NL = Netherlands, AS = Australia, BE = Belgium, SW = Sweden. The dummy variables for transaction type are: NP = New Plant, PE = Plant Expansion, and MA = Merger and Acquisition. Specification includes unreported state fixed effects.

| Table 4.6 | **Estimated Transaction Elasticities** |
|---|---|

| *Tax* | |
|---|---|
| Overall | −0.108 |
| New plant | −0.110 |
| Plant expansion | −0.069 |
| Merger and acquisition | 0.065 |
| Joint venture | −0.052 |
| *Investment persistence* | |
| U.S. establishments | 1.196 |
| Foreign establishments | 0.258 |

*Note:* Overall tax elasticity is based on first column coefficient in table 4.3. Disaggregated tax elasticities are based on the fourth column estimates of table 4.4.

cance of the Japanese interaction term fall. Again, these results suggest that many of the perceived differences in the cross-country responsiveness to taxes reflect the *composition* of these countries' investments, rather than cross-country heterogeneity in the avoidance of high-tax states.

At the same time, the continued strength of the Japan effect is noteworthy. Japan taxes its investors on a residential basis, and is thought to have a higher rate of taxation than that of the United States. As a result, because we would predict that the level of U.S. taxes would affect merely the residual payments Japanese firms make to the Japanese government (but not the overall taxes paid by Japanese firms), we would not expect Japanese firms to be so strongly deterred by taxes.

### 4.4.1   Interpretation of Results

To provide an economic interpretation of my results I present elasticities in table 4.6 that are based on prior regressions. If I consider differential transaction effects, as measured by column (4) of table 4.4, the estimates imply that a 1 percent increase in a state's taxes would cause 0.11 percent fewer new plants to locate within their borders. The state would also attract 0.069 percent fewer plant expansions. On the mergers and acquisitions side, the increase in taxes would be associated with a 0.065 percent increase.

While these responses are precisely estimated, they are all relatively small, which may imply that firms are not likely to be dissuaded strongly from locating in states with higher taxes, because they may have a number of nontax reasons for selecting the states they prefer. At the same time, these firms may decide to minimize the capital and payroll expenses they place in the high-tax states, as these will boost the shares of their incomes that are taxable in the high-tax states.

To put the tax elasticities in perspective, I also calculated elasticities for the agglomeration or investment persistence variables. I learned that a 1 percent increase in the U.S. establishment variable is associated with a rise of slightly more than 1 percent in a state's probability of selection. At the same time, a 1 percent rise in the foreign investment persistence variable is correlated with a 0.25 percent rise in a state's probability of selection.

## 4.5 Conclusion

This paper provides evidence on the effect of taxes on foreign investment in the United States between 1984 and 1994. The results suggest that analyses of aggregate data obscure some distinctive effects of taxes on foreign investment. In particular, I demonstrate that states with higher taxes attract fewer new plants or plant expansions; however, foreign acquisitions are not similarly deterred. If one instead analyzes the data delineating investments by investor type (exemption versus foreign tax credit), the results are influenced by the composition of these investors' transaction activities.

Work in international economics, such as Wheeler and Mody (1992) or Brainard (1997), has used fairly simple descriptions of taxes, and has found that the distribution of outbound U.S. investment is, at best, weakly correlated with cross-country tax differences. This analysis suggests that the failure to find significant tax effects may instead reflect problems introduced by aggregation. On a country basis, I find very few significant tax effects. In contrast, the effects that are attributed to transaction type appear to be fairly uniform across investors. As a result, although tax effects may be present and distinct across transaction type, the importance of these tax effects may be lost when one analyzes data aggregated at the country level.

In sum, much of what is interpreted as cross-country heterogeneity in tax response is actually determined by the cross-country heterogeneity in the *composition* of investment.

## References

Advisory Commission Intergovernmental Relations. Available at http://www. library.unt.edu/gpo/ACIR/Default.html
Auerbach, Alan J., and Kevin Hassett. 1993. Taxation and foreign direct investment in the United States: A reconsideration of the evidence. In *Studies in international taxation,* ed. Alberto Giovannini, R. Glenn Hubbard, and Joel Slemrod, 119–44. Chicago: University of Chicago Press.
Bartik, Timothy J. 1985. Business location decisions in the United States: Estimates of the effects of unionization, taxes and other characteristics of states. *Journal of Business and Economic Statistics* 8 (1): 14–22.
———. 1991. *Who benefits from state and local economic development policies?* Kalamazoo, Mich.: W. E. Upjohn Institute.
Brainard, Lael S. 1997. An empirical assessment of the proximity-concentration

tradeoff between multinational sales and trade. *American Economic Review* 87 (4): 520–44.

Carlton, Dennis W. 1983. The location and employment choices of new firms: An econometric model with discrete and continuous endogenous variables. *Review of Economics and Statistics* 65 (3): 440–49.

Casella, Alessandra, and James E. Rauch. 1997. Anonymous market and group ties in international trade. NBER Working Paper no. 6186. Cambridge, Mass.: National Bureau of Economic Research, September.

Collins, Julie H., Deen Kemsley, and Douglas A. Shackelford. 1993. Taxes and foreign acquisitions in the United States. University of North Carolina, Kenan-Flagler School of Business, Working Paper.

Coughlin, Cletus C., Joseph V. Terza, and Vachira Arromdee. 1991. State characteristics and the location of foreign direct investment within the United States. *Review of Economics and Statistics* 68 (4): 675–83.

Darney, Arsen J., ed. 1992. *Manufacturing USA: Industry analyses, statistics and leading companies* (2nd ed.). Detroit: Gale Research.

Darney, Arsen J., ed. 1996. *Manufacturing USA: Industry analyses, statistics and leading companies* (5th ed.). Detroit: Gale.

David, Paul A., and Joshua L. Rosenbloom. 1990. Marshallian factor market externalities and the dynamics of industrial location. *Journal of Urban Economics* 28 (3): 349–70.

Gordon, Roger, and John D. Wilson. 1986. An examination of multijurisdictional corporate income taxation under formula apportionment. *Econometrica* 54 (6): 1357–73.

Head, C. Keith, John C. Ries, and Deborah L. Swenson. 1999. Attracting foreign manufacturing: Investment promotion and agglomeration economies. *Regional Science and Urban Economics* 29 (2): 197–218.

———. 1995. Agglomeration benefits and location choice: Evidence from Japanese manufacturing investment in the United States. *Journal of International Economics* 38 (3/4): 223–47.

Hines, James R., Jr. 1996a. Altered states: Taxes and the location of foreign direct investment in America. *American Economic Review,* 86 (5): 1076–94.

———. 1996b. Tax policy and the activities of multinational corporations. NBER Working Paper no. 5589. Cambridge, Mass.: National Bureau of Economic Research, May.

Klassen, Kenneth J., and Douglas A. Shackelford. 1997. State and provincial corporate tax planning: Income shifting and sales apportionment factor management. University of North Carolina, Chapel Hill, Kenan-Flagler School of Business, Working Paper (June).

Markusen, James R. 1995. The boundaries of multinational enterprises and the theory of international trade. *Journal of Economic Perspectives* 9 (2): 169–89.

Markusen, James R., and Anthony J. Venables. 1996. The theory of endowment, intra-industry, and multinational trade. NBER Working Paper no. 5529. Cambridge, Mass.: National Bureau of Economic Research, April.

McFadden, Daniel. 1974. Conditional logit analysis of qualitative choice behavior. In *Frontiers in econometrics,* ed. P. Zaermbka, 104–42. New York: Academic Press.

National Association of State Development Agencies. 1986. *Directory of incentives for business investment and development in the United States: A state-by-state guide* (new and rev. 2nd ed.). Washington, D.C.: Urban Institute Press.

National Association of State Development Agencies. 1991. *Directory of incentives for business investment and development in the United States: A state-by-state guide* (3rd ed.). Washington, D.C.: Urban Institute Press.

Ondrich, Jan, and Michael Wasylenko. 1993. *Foreign direct investment in the United States: Issues, magnitudes, and the location choice of new manufacturing plants.* Kalamazoo, Mich.: W. E. Upjohn Institute.

Papke, Leslie E. 1991. Interstate business tax differentials and new firm location. *Journal of Public Economics* 45 (1): 47–68.

Roberts, Mark, and James Tybout. 1995. An empirical model of sunk costs and the decision to export. World Bank Policy Research Working Paper no. 1436. Washington, D.C.: World Bank.

Scholes, Myron S., and Mark A. Wolfson. 1992. *Taxes and business strategy: A planning approach.* Englewood Cliffs, N.J.: Prentice Hall.

Swenson, Deborah L. 1994. The impact of U.S. tax reform on foreign direct investment in the United States. *Journal of Public Economics* 54 (2): 243–66.

Wasylenko, Michael. 1991. Empirical evidence on interregional business location decisions and the role of fiscal incentives in economic development. In *Industry location and public policy,* ed. Henry W. Herzon Jr. and Alan M. Schottmann, 13–30. Knoxville, Tenn.: University of Tennessee Press.

Wheeler, David, and Ashoka Mody. 1992. International investment location decisions: The case of U.S. firms. *Journal of International Economics* 33:57–76.

# Comment    William C. Randolph

There has been substantial interest among economists in behavior underlying the growth of inbound U.S. FDI since the early 1980s. Given the major changes in U.S. federal tax laws during the early and middle 1980s, especially the Tax Reform Act of 1986, a number of researchers have asked how those tax changes influenced inbound investment.

Most of the researchers have used aggregate time series data. Such studies suggest that the tax changes played a significant role in determining the levels of inbound FDI. For example, studies by Scholes and Wolfson (1992) and Swenson (1994) focused on the importance of tax clientele effects whereby multinational based in countries that exempt active foreign source income from tax (territorial systems) should value U.S. investments differently than multinationals based in countries that tax all foreign source income but allow a foreign tax credit (worldwide systems).

Of course, such time series studies have well-known potential limitations. It is often very difficult to identify tax effects separately from the effects of other intertemporal changes—for example, in relative factor input prices, exchange rates, expected rates of return, and so forth. There is always a nagging possibility that the estimated time series effect of tax changes is a spurious indicator of time trends in other important omitted variables.

William C. Randolph is an economist and director of international taxation in the Office of Tax Analysis of the U.S. Department of the Treasury.

The views expressed in this comment are those of the author and do not necessarily represent the views of the U.S. Department of the Treasury.

Another related line of empirical research has focused on cross-sectional interstate variation of inbound FDI and its relation to interstate variation of tax rates. A notable recent example is the study by Hines (1996). In this line of research, the main econometric challenge is to identify the effects of interstate variation of taxes separately from the effects of interstate variation of public services, factor prices, transportation costs, and the like. Hines (1996) identifies the tax effects separately from those other factors by recognizing that interstate variation in tax rates should influence the location of U.S. inbound FDI by multinationals based in countries with territorial systems by more than the location of investment by multinationals based in countries with worldwide tax systems.

Auerbach and Hassett (1993) have demonstrated cause for concern about studies of inbound FDI because the empirical studies group modes of investment together, without regard to whether the "investment" takes the form of, for example, the acquisition of an existing business or the establishment of a new enterprise. They show that, theoretically, taxes can have different effects on investment, depending on the mode of investment. If so, results of aggregate studies that group the investment modes together would be meaningful only under special conditions.

In this new paper, Deborah Swenson studies the determinants of inbound foreign direct investment by examining microdata on inbound transactions. The data and her model have important features that allow her to pull together different possible information sources to identify the effect of taxes, and to distinguish among the effects of taxes on different modes of investment. The data provide a richness of information on variation in the choice of investment mode and tax rates over time (1984–94), on variation across the states, and on variation in the tax treatment of foreign source income by the countries where the foreign multinationals are based.

This is an area of empirical research in which there has been considerable interest. It has attracted some first-rate analysis by first-rate researchers, all of whom have made use of relatively scant data. It is therefore admirable that Swenson has been able to provide new insight based on data that have gone previously untapped for this purpose.

Swenson uses a logit model to characterize the choice, by a foreign-based multinational corporation, of a U.S. state in which to locate an investment transaction (the basic unit of observation in her data). Because the data span eleven years, they can be thought of as a time series of repeated cross sections. Because state tax rates varied over the time period, by different amounts in different states, she is able to study the effect of taxes while implicitly controlling for all fixed state differences that would potentially affect inbound investment in the same fashion in all years. She also includes measures to capture the possible effects of agglomeration economies on the location of investment.

To study whether it is important to distinguish among investment modes, the author first estimates the parameters of a pooled regression. She then estimates separate regressions for investments in new plants, plant expansion, mergers and acquisitions, joint ventures, equity increases, and other modes. From the pooled regression, she finds that higher taxes appear to discourage inbound investment transactions by multinationals based in countries with worldwide tax systems. However, taxes do not appear to influence the investment decisions by multinationals based in countries with territorial tax systems. This pair of results, as discussed by the author, is contrary to the economic prediction that local taxes should actually have a larger effect on investment location decisions by multinationals based in territorial countries.

A partial resolution of this unexpected result is apparently provided by the results of separate regressions for different modes of investment. For the separate regressions, tax effects have the predicted signs, overall, for investments in new plants, plant expansion, and equity increases, although only the plant expansion regression estimates are consistent with the prediction that taxes should have a larger effect for multinationals based in territorial countries. State taxes do not appear to have any effect on the likelihood that a multinational enters into a joint venture. For mergers and acquisitions, however, increased state tax rates appear to increase the likelihood that an investment transaction occurs, regardless of the type of home-country tax system. Based on these results for separate investment types, it is reasonable to conclude that the estimation results for the regression are not meaningful when investment types are pooled.

Although this aggregation result is well motivated because, in theory, taxes should affect the cost of capital differently for different modes of investment and differentially situated investors, as shown, for example, by Auerbach and Hassett (1993), the results for the individual regressions are still too peculiar to provide convincing evidence that the differences in the estimated tax effects are really driven by differences in changes in the cost of capital. The central theoretical prediction—that is, that taxes should have a larger effect on investment location decisions by multinationals based in territorial countries—is consistent with the separate regression results for plant expansions only. For investments in the form of new plants and equity increases, taxes actually have the larger effect on multinationals from countries with worldwide systems. For investments in the form of mergers and acquisitions, the tax effect even has the wrong sign. It is possible that the sign reversal results from the type of clientele effect examined by Scholes and Wolfson (1992) and Swenson (1994), but that effect would cause taxes to be positively correlated with acquisitions only when the foreign multinational is based in a country with a worldwide system. In these estimation results, however, not only is the sign the same for both groups of multinationals, but it is larger for multinationals based in territorial countries.

These unexpected estimation results may be explained by a data limitation. As discussed by the author, the data on investment transactions are only qualitative. They don't measure the sizes of investments. It might be true that the number of inbound acquisitions is negatively correlated with the total value of acquisitions in a state, although it is hard to imagine why this would be true.

A more likely source of the unexpected results is the lack of control in the regressions for time series aspects of the data. I'm not familiar with the time pattern of inbound investment transaction counts, but inbound FDI in the United States was highly time trended and apparently highly nonstationary during parts of the time period covered by the data examined by Swenson. Moreover, such time patterns differed by type of investment transaction and by location of the home countries of foreign-based multinationals. It is likely that the same patterns were also reflected in transaction counts.

In Swenson's regressions, the tax effects are identified mainly by the fact that state tax rates change over time in different ways in different states. In fact, the tax rate is the only right-hand side variable that changes independently over time. The tax rate coefficients could thus be biased by the omission from the regressions of any time varying factor, such as economic growth, that influenced inbound FDI location decisions. Further, there is no reason to expect this omitted time series bias to be the same for all investment modes, which might explain why only some of the estimation results are anomalous.

Because this study is focused mainly on the effect of taxes, as a solution it may be sufficient to simply control for possible omitted time series by including time trends, measures of growth at the state level, or time dummy variables. Although time dummy variables could not be included for each state, they could be included at either the national level or at a regional level to control for regional differences in time patterns of investment activity.

Swenson's analysis in this paper is a useful contribution to our understanding of investment location decisions. It represents a first step taken with new data and provides important potential for future research. Because the data provide alternative sources of identification for tax effects, they can be used to examine the validity and importance of identifying assumptions made in previous research on inbound FDI. Further, if taxes have different effects on different types of investment transactions, it is also reasonable to expect that taxes should influence the choice of transaction type, a choice that Swenson's paper treats as being exogenous.

I've enjoyed reading and thinking about this paper. I've learned a lot and look forward to future installments.

## References

Auerbach, Alan J., and Kevin Hassett. 1993. Taxation and foreign direct investment in the United States: A reconsideration of the evidence. In *Studies in international taxation,* ed. Alberto Giovannini, R. Glenn Hubbard, and Joel Slemrod, 119–44. Chicago: University of Chicago Press.

Hines, James R., Jr. 1996. Altered states: Taxes and the location of foreign direct investment in America. *American Economic Review* 86 (5): 1076–94.

Scholes, Myron S., and Mark A. Wolfson. 1992. *Taxes and business strategy: A planning approach.* Englewood Cliffs, NJ: Prentice Hall.

Swenson, Deborah L. 1994. The impact of U.S. tax reform on foreign direct investment in the United States. *Journal of Public Economics* 54 (2): 243–66.

# Tax Planning by Companies and Tax Competition by Governments
## Is There Evidence of Changes in Behavior?

Harry Grubert

## 5.1 Introduction

Many claims have been made in recent years, both by the popular media and by prominent economists, that we are living in a period of more aggressive tax planning by multinational corporations (MNCs) and more intense tax competition by governments (Tanzi 1996). The source of such claims is globalization brought on by the relaxation of controls on trade and capital and by the revolution in communications. This paper examines the extent to which the evidence supports these claims. The emphasis is on the period from 1984 to 1992, for which the available U.S. Department of the Treasury firm-level files can be used, supplemented by published data for the years after 1992. In addition to the firm-level data, changes in average effective tax rates in sixty countries are used to examine the responses of governments to the new global environment.

Various areas of MNC and government behavior are examined. One is the effective tax rates that MNCs pay to host governments. Have some U.S. companies been able to obtain larger than average tax concessions through tax planning? In addition to the question of the tax *rate* is that of the tax *base* to which the effective rate applies. Have U.S.-based MNCs been able to shift larger amounts of income to low-tax locations? Is more company debt put on the books of high-tax affiliates? Have U.S. subsidiar-

Harry Grubert is an economist in the Office of Tax Analysis of the U.S. Department of the Treasury.

Special thanks are due to Donald Rousslang, Rosanne Altshuler, Joel Slemrod, and Jim Hines for helpful comments; and to Gordon Wilson and Paul Dobbins for assembling the data files. Nothing in this paper should be construed as reflecting the views and policy of the U.S. Department of the Treasury.

ies abroad paid out more royalties to their parents because their parents expect to have excess credits that can shield the royalties from U.S. tax?

Turning to the behavior of governments, did the pattern of declines in effective tax rates suggest increased tax competition? Was there a significant convergence in effective tax rates? Were there disproportionate declines in more homogeneous regions, such as the European Economic Community (EEC), where tax competition might be expected to be more intense? Did governments grant greater concessions to new companies or to internationally mobile industries, such as electronics and finance?

The possibility that MNCs have managed to lower their foreign tax rates through tax planning or that governments have increased their concessions to MNCs is suggested by Grubert, Randolph, and Rousslang (1996), who found that the average foreign tax rate on the repatriated income of U.S. parent companies declined from 36 percent in 1984 to 25 percent in 1992. The decline was attributable primarily to a reduction in host-country effective tax rates. The increased importance of royalties at the expense of dividends also played a role. The country-by-country changes in effective tax rates reported by U.S. companies are generally larger than one might expect from published reports of tax reforms or available estimates of changes in Hall-Jorgenson marginal effective tax rates. One question, therefore, is the extent to which company tax planning may have contributed to this large fall in the burden of taxation abroad. Another question is whether countries gave preferences to certain kinds of industries or companies.

A way of evaluating any company role in falling effective tax rates is to attempt to identify those companies that might be expected to take advantage of the changed international environment. There are at least two alternative hypotheses, however, for which companies might make the greatest effort to lower their foreign tax burdens. One is based on the incentive to reduce excess foreign tax credits. For some companies, incentives for lowering foreign tax burdens were greatly increased by the Tax Reform Act of 1986 (P.L. 99-514). The Tax Reform Act of 1986 (TRA 1986) reduced the U.S. corporate tax rate from 46 to 34 percent. Companies with overall average foreign tax rates on net repatriated income higher than 34 percent (not just those with rates higher than 46 percent) would now have excess credits. Companies that, as a result, might now expect to be permanently in excess credit would have a much greater incentive to reduce foreign tax rates than would companies whose average foreign tax rates were already lower than 34 percent in 1984. In addition, the companies with overall foreign tax rates initially higher than 46 percent would attempt to take advantage of new opportunities for reducing foreign taxes.

The alternative hypothesis is basically the mirror image of the first one. If a company had a low overall foreign tax rate in 1984, one explanation is that its operations were mobile. It might be expected to have achieved the largest declines in its effective tax rates in any given location after 1984 if countries began to compete for its locations more aggressively. For example, the company might threaten to leave if it were not granted special concessions. Another possibility is that the parent company had a low overall foreign tax rate in 1984 because it was innovative in tax planning. Globalization might give the parent new opportunities to use its experience to lower its tax rates even further. In either case, the company would gain not in the form of lower taxes no longer useful as credits, but in the form of lower foreign taxes on income it retained abroad.

Although it is convenient to distinguish between the behavior of governments and the behavior of companies, it is frequently impossible to identify the source of a tax differential, which is presumably brought about in a mutual process. If a government lowers its tax rate by the same amount to all entrants, that lowering can fairly be regarded as a country response. If a company shifts income because of a difference in statutory tax rates, the shift can be referred to as a company response. Other cases are more ambiguous, however. If companies with initially low average worldwide tax rates succeed in achieving even larger reductions, they may have been able to do so because of either their innovations in tax planning or their being able to get even greater concessions from governments because they are mobile.

The evidence provides some signs of changes in behavior by companies. Parent companies with low overall foreign tax rates in 1984 did enjoy significantly greater declines in effective tax rates in a given location than did the average U.S. parent. Accordingly, the aggressive-or-mobile-parent hypothesis dominates the excess-credit hypothesis, although anticipated excess credits seem to have played a role in the switch from dividends to royalties. Income shifting from high-tax to low-tax locations also seems to have become more aggressive, judging by the differential in the pretax return on assets for a given difference in statutory tax rates. However, the allocation of debt between high and low statutory tax countries was very stable. In both 1984 and 1992, leverage is strongly influenced by local tax rates but the equations are virtually identical in both years.

The evidence of increased tax competition at the country level is also mixed. Effective tax rates fell on average but there was a wide diversity of behavior among countries. The concessions enjoyed by newly investing companies compared to mature companies were about the same in 1992 as in 1984. The gap between the effective tax rate on finance affiliates and manufacturing subsidiaries widened only slightly, if at all. More mobile manufacturing industries, such as electronics, did not enjoy greater tax reductions. Tax rates did not fall more in homogeneous areas with low trade barriers, such as the EEC. Furthermore, countries did not aggressively attempt to attract tax bases, as opposed to real activities, by disproportionately lowering statutory tax rates compared to effective rates. Indeed, statutory tax rates fell less than effective rates in absolute terms even though they were much higher to start with.

That said, there are significant signs of heightened tax competition by governments. The smaller, poorer, and more open countries lowered their tax rates the most. They might be expected to be most affected by the increased mobility of capital. Also, the implications for foreign governments of the apparent increased tax sensitivity of real U.S. investment found by Altshuler, Grubert, and Newlon (chap. 1 in this volume) suggest that tax competition may explain the large fall in effective tax rates that took place. What if governments set tax rates on U.S. companies only in order to maximize revenue? Using the Altshuler-Grubert-Newlon elasticity (with respect to $(1 - t)$) of 1.53 in 1984 and 2.77 in 1992, we find that the simple revenue-maximizing tax rate on inbound U.S. investment in manufacturing decreased from 39.5 percent to 26.5 percent.[1] This is only slightly larger than the mean change in average effective tax rates that actually occurred, and the levels match pretty closely as well.

What are the implications of this mixed picture? Why is there not a more consistent pattern of reactions to globalization? Perhaps "globalization" has not been occurring as fast as supposed. Indeed, U.S. Department of Commerce evidence indicates that interaffiliate transactions have not increased in relative importance since 1977. The gross product of U.S. manufacturing affiliates abroad grew at about the same rate as U.S. manufacturing from 1982 to 1994. It may be that the new incentives for tax planning created by TRA 1986 were not very significant to start with because of the opportunities for deferral that had always existed; or it may be that the incentives were diluted by governments' reducing effective tax rates on their own largely for domestic purposes.

Recent accounts of the growing importance of tax planning and tax competition may also overlook the weapons that governments have at their disposals to resist the erosion of their tax bases. Countries have become more aware of potential transfer pricing abuses and have introduced new regulations. Many home governments have either introduced new or strengthened existing controlled foreign corporation (CFC) rules that reduce the benefits of using tax havens for passive and other income. Indeed, the expanded current U.S. taxation of financial CFCs mandated by TRA 1986 may be one reason finance affiliates did not obtain greater tax benefits from host governments.

Furthermore, governments may be able to do much more on their own. Evidence at the end of this paper suggests that perhaps the U.S. CFC rules, which are probably the most restrictive of those of the major industrialized

---

1. This is based on countries' assuming that the pretax rate of return will remain the same as the tax rate is lowered.

countries, may not go far enough. A substantial amount of tax haven income seems to escape current U.S. tax.

Turning to methodology, the results call into question the common use of a parent company's excess credit position as an exogenous variable in studies of MNC behavior. Companies are not be born high-tax or low-tax, nor are they assigned randomly to these categories. If a company has managed to arrange a low-average effective tax rate on its foreign operations, it might be that its behavior is systematically different from that of its U.S. counterparts.

The plan of the paper is as follows: Section 5.2 reviews the incentives for tax planning by U.S. multinational companies and how these may have changed as a result of TRA 1986. It also summarizes recent data on the extent of globalization. Section 5.3 describes the data used in the empirical analysis. Because a company's expectations about its excess credit position may be important in its tax-planning strategy, section 5.4 begins the empirical analysis by evaluating alternative predictors of a company's future excess credit status. The results are used as building blocks in the subsequent sections. Section 5.5 presents the basic empirical results of the relationship between an MNC's overall worldwide tax rate in 1984 and the change in the tax burden on its operations in each country from 1984 to 1992. Each parent company's operations in a given location in 1984 and 1992 are linked to see which type of company obtained the largest tax reductions. Sections 5.6 and 5.7 use parallel regressions at the CFC level for 1984 and 1992. Section 5.6 examines CFC effective tax rates to see if countries have given greater tax concessions to new, more mobile operations. Section 5.7 compares income-shifting behavior in 1984 and 1992 to see if reported CFC profitability has become more sensitive to local tax rates. It also determines whether more debt is being placed in high-tax CFCs, because this is one of the ways in which taxable income can be shifted in the worldwide company. Section 5.8 examines the relationship between excess credit expectations and the change in royalties received by the parent to determine whether companies that expected to be in excess credit received more royalties from their affiliates. Section 5.9 switches the focus from the company level to the country level to determine which countries cut their tax rates on U.S. companies the most. The object is to see if we can identify patterns consistent with increased tax competition. Section 5.10 reviews CFC rules that eliminate the benefits of using tax havens.

## 5.2 The Changed Incentives for Lowering Foreign Taxes

### 5.2.1 The Effect of the Tax Reform Act of 1986

The TRA 1986 made several changes affecting companies' tax planning incentives: (1) Most importantly, it lowered the statutory U.S. tax rate to

34 percent from 46 percent. Accordingly, any company whose foreign tax rate on distributed income would have been between 46 and 34 percent had an increased incentive to lower foreign taxes because, on the margin, foreign taxes had no value as credits. (2) Companies were required to allocate more U.S. expenses, particularly interest, to foreign source income for the purpose of calculating the foreign tax-credit limitation. This would tend to drive some companies into excess credit and increase the excess credits of those already over the threshold. (3) The tightening-up of the antiabuse rules in subpart F of the U.S. Internal Revenue Code, providing for the current taxation of "passive" and other tainted CFC income, reduced the benefits of tax planning. The *de minimis* threshold for the amount of tainted income that would trigger current U.S. tax was lowered substantially. In addition, the "active banking" exception for passive income was eliminated. Prior to TRA 1986, an "active" financial operation abroad was not subject to current U.S. tax on investment income such as interest.

If a company starts to have excess credits because of the lowering of the U.S. corporate rate, it obviously has an incentive to reduce its foreign taxes as long as it does not increase U.S. taxable income. A lower foreign tax burden can be achieved in various ways. The company may attempt to negotiate or otherwise arrange lower effective rates in its locations abroad. It could increase the amount of income it has in low-tax locations, either by shifting the location of real activity or by shifting the location of income. Altshuler, Grubert, and Newlon in this volume examine the change in the tax sensitivity of real investment. This paper focuses on planning that lowers effective tax rates or shifts income.

It is necessary, however, to be more precise about the changed incentives for income shifting. Because of the opportunities for deferring income in low-tax locations, the change in incentives for some types of income shifting may not have been great when TRA 1986 caused a company to move from excess limit to excess credit. If the parent is in excess limit, income can be shifted from a high-tax foreign country to a low-tax location where repatriation to the United States can be deferred. The only offset to the tax savings in the high-tax country, compared to a company with excess credits, would be the additional credits that distributions from a high-tax country could generate to the extent that its effective tax rate was above the U.S. rate.[2] If a company is pushed into excess credit by the reduction in the U.S. tax rate, the value of low-tax income will increase only to the extent of the present value of the U.S. taxes that would have been paid

---

2. Even these might not all be currently used as credits against U.S. tax because CFCs do not generally distribute all of the income. Furthermore, a country may have a high statutory tax rate, which determines the value of shifting income on the margin, but a low average effective rate, which would result in a positive repatriation tax if income is repatriated. (See Grubert 1998.)

formerly, when the low-tax income was repatriated. (As I explain later on, the company can get a further benefit if it can bring the low-tax income home as a royalty because it is deductible abroad and exempt in the United States.) The net change resulting from TRA 1986 may be small if most of the low-tax income had been retained abroad and the tax rate in the high-tax country was not far above the U.S. rate, creating few spillover tax credits.

Turning to the incentives for shifting income in or out of the United States: When a parent company is in excess limit, shifting income from the United States to a low-tax location where the income is deferred can be very profitable. On the other hand, shifting income from a high statutory tax country to the United States in the excess limit case is useful only if all of the foreign income would not have been distributed. If all high-tax income is distributed, any savings in foreign tax are simply offset by lower foreign tax credits in the United States.

If the parent is in excess credit, the value of shifting income out of the United States to a low-tax country increases only to the extent of the elimination of any residual tax on eventual dividends. The value of shifting income *out* of a high-tax foreign country *to* the United States depends on whether the higher payment by the foreign affiliate to its parent is foreign or U.S. source. If it is U.S. source—for example, a payment for U.S. services—the benefit of shifting from a foreign country to the United States is simply $t_F - t_{US}$ where $t_F$ is the foreign statutory tax rate and $t_{US}$ is the U.S. tax rate. Any subsequent repatriations of foreign income are irrelevant because they neither trigger U.S. tax nor generate useful excess credits.

However, increased royalties, which are foreign source, could become much more profitable when the parent is in excess credit. When the parent company did not have excess credits, the value of an extra royalty paid by a foreign affiliate depended on the difference between the foreign statutory tax rate, at which the royalty is deducted, and the domestic tax rate, at which it is included in income. Furthermore, even that margin of benefit for paying royalties from a high-tax country would disappear if the income was distributed as a dividend and produced excess credits. If the parent is now in excess credit, the benefits of an increased royalty payment is fully the saving in foreign tax (less any withholding tax, which is typically small), because the royalty, being foreign source, would be exempt from U.S. tax. The U.S. tax rate on the royalty is lowered not to 34 percent but, effectively, to 0.

The benefits of shifting debt from the United States abroad and from high-tax to low-tax countries can be summarized briefly. Reallocating debt within the worldwide corporation is one way in which net income can be shifted, but interest allocations to foreign income by the parent add a further consideration. If the parent has to make interest allocations, it has the added bonus of shifting debt abroad if it is in excess credit because parent interest expense is not fully deductible against U.S. tax. (See Altshuler and

Mintz 1995.) Thus, TRA 1986 may have increased the incentive to shift debt abroad.

To summarize, for firms that move to an excess credit position due to TRA 1986, the incentive to shift income from high- to low-tax jurisdictions may not be greatly altered; the incentive to shift income into the United States is greatly enhanced if the payment is foreign source (e.g., a royalty); and the incentive to shift debt from the United States is increased.

### 5.2.2    Globalization

A company's strategy for shifting income and using tax-saving strategies is a function of (1) the differing tax rates in the countries in which they operate, (2) the opportunities for implementing tax-saving strategies provided by their operations, and, (3) the antiabuse and penalty provisions that governments can use to thwart various tax-planning devices. The previous section outlined how TRA 1986 changed the benefits of various tax-minimizing strategies for a given set of international tax systems.

Commentators who stress globalization presumably emphasize the second factor. Multinational operations around the world, it is said, are now more closely linked, providing greater opportunities to reduce taxes. In fact, the evidence does not point to the growing importance of intrafirm trade. A recent report by the U.S. Department of Commerce, examining transactions from 1977 through 1994, concludes that "The shares of intrafirm trade in U.S. exports and imports of goods have changed very little" (U.S. Department of Commerce 1997a). Also, intrafirm trade has not increased as a percentage of foreign affiliates' total trade. Another Department of Commerce study found that the real gross product of U.S. manufacturing affiliates grew from 1982 to 1994 at about the rate of host-country industrial production over the period. In addition, the real product of U.S. manufacturing affiliates abroad increased less than the gross product of manufacturing industries in the United States (U.S. Department of Commerce 1997b).

Moreover, discussions of tax competition often downplay the third factor, the fact that governments can respond to companies' attempts to exploit differences in tax rates. Many have adopted CFC rules that subject interest, dividends, and royalties received to current home-country tax. (See OECD 1996.) For example, the United Kingdom's CFC legislation was enacted in 1984, partly in response to the abolition of exchange controls in 1979. The New Zealand CFC regime became effective in 1988 and the Australian legislation became effective in 1990. The U.S. subpart F rules go farther than most in that they subject related-party sales routed through a low-tax affiliate to current tax. However, some countries' CFC provisions even go so far as to eliminate tax deferral for all investment in low-tax countries. Many governments have implemented a new round of more stringent and explicit transfer pricing guidelines. In addition, some governments have attempted to reduce the opportunities for portfolio investors to accumulate passive income tax-free abroad by adopting rules similar to the passive foreign investment company (PFIC) legislation in the United States. The Australian and New Zealand FIF (foreign investment fund) regimes are examples.

### 5.3 Data Sources

The principal data source is made up of the linked corporate tax files of large (assets greater than $250 million in 1984 and $500 million in 1992) U.S. MNCs in 1984 and 1992. The files comprise Form 1120, the basic corporate tax return; Form 1118, on which foreign tax credits are claimed; and Form 5471, giving information on the sales, income, and assets of each CFC. Companies were included in the empirical work only if they filed corporate tax returns in each of the two years analyzed. (Firms might disappear from the file because of mergers and acquisitions, among other reasons.) In addition, each had to have filed either Form 5471 or Form 1118 in each year. (An MNC might not file Form 1118 in a given year if it had worldwide losses or could not claim a foreign tax credit for other reasons.) Parents whose principal business was finance were excluded because of their special nature and the particular tax rules (for insurance reserves, for example) that apply to them. Information on company R&D was taken from Standard & Poors Compustat Services.

The average effective tax rates used in the empirical work, either for a given CFC or for the country average, are based on the foreign taxes paid and net income reported on Form 5471. The net income measure is earnings and profits (E&P), which is defined in the Internal Revenue Code and is an attempt to approximate "true" net equity income. It is *not* local host-country taxable income, which can reflect various investment incentives. Finally, country statutory tax rates were taken from the Price Waterhouse guides for 1984 and 1992.

Hall-Jorgenson-King-Fullerton (HJKF) marginal effective tax rates are not available for the sixty-country sample used in the paper. Besides, the average effective tax rates used here have some advantages over HJKF rates, which usually reflect only a few basic features of business taxation— namely, the statutory tax rate, tax depreciation rates, and investment tax credits. The HJKF rates also overlook many important features of the tax system, such as the capitalization of expenses rules that were very important in TRA 1986. The HJKF marginal tax rates also do not capture special incentives offered to companies in "not fully transparent" systems, which may be important in the context of this paper.[3]

---

3. Chennels and Griffith (1997) have estimated HJKF rates for ten countries over the period. The country-by-country changes they report do not seem consistent with the changes we compute from the U.S. Department of the Treasury files.

Table 5.1          Predictors of 1992 Credit Position (dependent variable is foreign tax rate on net repatriated income in 1992)

|  | (1) | (2) | (3) | (4) |
|---|---|---|---|---|
| Foreign tax rate on distributed income in 1984[a] | .329 |  |  | .304 |
|  | (4.76) |  |  | (3.01) |
| (Limitation − foreign taxes)/parent assets |  | −.009 |  | −.005 |
|  |  | (4.64) |  | (2.08) |
| Computed average tax rate on foreign operations in 1984[b] |  |  | .153 | .133 |
|  |  |  | (.60) | (.58) |
| Foreign tax rate on dividends in 1984 |  |  |  | −.069 |
|  |  |  |  | (.78) |
| Adjusted $R^2$ | .125 | .120 | −.01 | .184 |

*Note:* $N = 152$. Sample is large nonfinancial parents who claimed a foreign tax credit in both 1984 and 1992. Numbers in parentheses are $t$-values.
[a] Foreign tax rate on net distributed income is the ratio of total foreign taxes paid on distributed income to total net foreign distributed income. All calculations are for the "general" or "other" baskets only.
[b] This is calculated from all the income and foreign taxes paid as reported by foreign corporations controlled by the parent. It therefore includes the income (and associated taxes) that is not repatriated.

## 5.4    The Persistence of Excess Credit Positions?

The discussion in the previous section of the relationship between excess credit positions and the incentives to reduce both total foreign taxes paid and foreign tax rates assumed that companies' positions were completely predictable. Yet a company's excess credit in any one year, 1984 for example, reflects its repatriation decisions in that year and may be subject to various transitory influences. This section, therefore, attempts to determine which measure derived from a company's 1984 reports is the best predictor of the foreign tax rate on its repatriated income in the general basket in 1992. This may help us identify the companies whose incentives may have changed.

The dependent variable in table 5.1 is the foreign tax rate on repatriated income in 1992 in the general or "active" basket, which seems a convenient measure of the company's 1992 credit status.[4] (Simply using a variable indicating whether the company is in excess credit yields similar results.) The subsample is made up of those companies in the original sample that claimed a foreign tax credit in both 1984 and 1992. The alternative predictors based on 1984 information were

1. The foreign tax rate on net distributed income in 1984.
2. The 1984 foreign tax rate on dividends only. This may be a better indicator of permanent excess credit status because it is less sensitive to yearly changes in the mix of foreign income.

4. The U.S. limitation on foreign tax credits is calculated for each type of "basket" of foreign income. The intent is to isolate active income, which tends to bear relatively high foreign taxes, from lightly taxed income, such as passive interest.

3. The difference between the tentative U.S. tax on the foreign income and total foreign tax paid, divided by total parent assets. This scaling is used to express the significance of any excess credit (or limit) level. If repatriations are small in any year, they may not be good indicators of future excess credit status.

4. The synthetic average tax rate on foreign activity computed from the location of each company's foreign capital and host-country tax rates. It is the potential average foreign tax rate on a company's foreign operations, regardless of whether the income is repatriated, and is computed from the location of its real assets abroad as reported by its CFCs in 1984 and the average effective tax rate in each location. The country average tax rate is used to filter out the noise in rates for specific companies in any year. Also, the CFC's own rate would not exist if it were making losses in that year.

Table 5.1 indicates that foreign tax credit status in 1984 and 1992 are correlated, although the persistence may not be quantitatively very impressive. The company's foreign tax rate on net distributed income in 1984, used in column (1), turns out to be the best predictor of the comparable tax rate in 1992. Column (2) indicates that the absolute deficit in credits in relation to parent size performs almost as well, and it is still significant in the last column when all measures are included in the regression. Column (3) shows that the measure intended to reflect permanent excess credit status unfortunately has little predictive power.[5] The foreign tax, or "gross up," rate on dividends added in column (4) also does not contribute much information. The straightforward overall foreign tax rate on repatriated net income seems to be more useful because it reflects all the various components of foreign income and is computed after all deductions to foreign income, which may be significant for some companies. (Even though some 1984 indicators did not seem useful in predicting the 1992 position, they will nevertheless be used as possible predictors of changes in behavior.)

### 5.5    Change in Country Tax Rates by Company

The question is: Why did some companies in a given location have larger declines in effective tax rates on net income than others? Is it because of expected foreign tax credits that may have affected their incentives for using tax planning devices or attempting to negotiate lower rates? Were some industries favored over others, as might be the case if countries are competing to attract more mobile industries? Or was it simply that companies with unusually high effective tax rates in 1984 had a tendency to return to the mean?

Accordingly, in this section, a parent U.S. company's operations in a

---

5. One reason may be that there isn't much variation in the measure across companies. The standard deviation in the computed foreign tax rate is only about 5 percent.

given country in 1984 are linked with its operations in 1992. In each year, all CFCs owned by a given parent in a location are first aggregated. Because the change in country tax rates is the focus, a company-country observation is used only if the company has CFCs in the country in both years. In addition, it has to be possible to compute a tax rate in each year, so E&P before tax must be positive in both years.

In table 5.2, each parent company-country combination for which data are available is a separate observation. The dependent variable is a company's effective tax rate (ETR) in the country in 1984 minus its effective tax rate in 1992—that is, the reduction of the tax rate in percentage points. A larger fall from 1984 to 1992 is, therefore, a larger positive number. The independent variables are (1) the change in the *average* effective tax rate in the country for all U.S. manufacturing affiliates, (2) the discrepancy between the company's 1984 effective tax rate and the country average in 1984, to capture the possibility of a tendency to return to the country average, (3) a dummy variable for parents in electronics and computers, and (4) various measures of the company's actual or potential excess credit status in 1984. Electronics and computer companies are chosen because they seem to be very responsive to local tax rates (see Grubert and Mutti 1997).

Table 5.2 indicates that a higher parent overall foreign tax rate in 1984 is associated with a *smaller* decline in the company's tax rate in a country compared to the average country decline, not a higher one as the increased incentives for planning by companies in an excess credit position might lead one to expect. In column (1), the third independent variable (the parent's overall foreign tax rate on repatriated income in 1984) tests the hypotheses on which companies had the largest reductions in foreign tax burdens. It has a significant *negative* coefficient, so that companies with higher overall foreign taxes in 1984 obtained smaller declines in foreign tax burdens. The first independent variable (the average change in the effective tax rate on manufacturing in the country) shows that, not surprisingly, it is an important determinant of the change in the company's tax rate. The second independent variable (the difference between a company's tax rate in the country in 1984 and the country average) indicates a strong regression to the mean. Finally, the coefficient for the electronics and computers dummy is negative and smaller than its standard error, indicating that the industries that appear to be mobile did not receive unusually large reductions in their tax burdens.

The succeeding columns, which use alternative measures of the parent company's excess credit status in 1984, present a picture similar to that in the first column. Column (2) recognizes that companies with permanently very high foreign tax rates in 1984 already had a strong incentive to reduce the burdens of their foreign taxes because they were in excess credit even at a U.S. rate of 46 percent. The foreign tax rate on repatriated income is divided into three intervals, a rate higher than 0.46, a rate between 0.46

**Table 5.2**    **Which Companies Obtained the Largest Tax Reductions? Change in Company Country Effective Tax Rates**

| Independent Variables | Dependent Variable: ETR 1984 − ETR 1992 | | | | |
| --- | --- | --- | --- | --- | --- |
| | (1) | (2) | (3) | (4) | (5) |
| Change in country average effective tax rate in manufacturing | .824 (16.71) | .823 (16.98) | .826 (16.70) | .819 (16.50) | 1.16 (10.31) |
| Company rate in 1984 − average country rate in 1984 | .874 (35.94) | .875 (35.88) | .880 (35.69) | .869 (35.56) | .874 (35.95) |
| Parent foreign tax rate on distributed income in 1984[a] | −.128 (3.63) | | | | |
| Electronics and computers | −.011 (.85) | −.088 (.60) | | | |
| Rate on repatriated income > .46 | | −.042 (3.52) | | | |
| Rate on distributed income .46–.34 | | −.020 (1.57) | | | |
| Foreign tax rate on dividends in 1984 | | | −.107 (2.80) | | |
| Computed average tax rate on foreign operations in 1984[a] | | | | .051 (.59) | |
| Tax rate on distributed income * change in country average | | | | | −.833 (3.40) |
| Adjusted $R^2$ | .543 | .542 | .541 | .538 | .543 |

*Note:* $N$ = 1,154. ETR = effective tax rate. All of an MNC's CFCs in a country are aggregated. Observations are used only if company has CFCs in a given location in both years. Each company-country combination is a separate observation. Country average effective tax rates are computed from total CFC earnings and foreign taxes paid in a location. Only CFCs with positive earnings are included in country average. Numbers in parentheses are $t$-values.

[a] Definition same as in table 5.1.

and 0.34, and a rate lower than 0.34. There is not much evidence of a nonlinear effect, and higher overall foreign tax rates in 1984 are still associated with smaller declines in the country for the company. Both columns (1) and (2) indicate that the average tax rate on repatriated income has a quantitatively large effect on country tax reductions. For example, the −0.128 coefficient in column (1) means that a 1 standard deviation increase in the 1984 tax rate on distributed income resulted in a 1.8 percentage point reduction in the local tax rate.

Column (3) uses the 1984 foreign tax rate on dividends as the measure of excess credit positions. It also has a significant negative, not positive, coefficient, which is consistent with the results in the first two columns. In column (4), the computed measure of the average foreign tax rate on foreign activity, based on the location of CFC assets and average tax rate in the country, again has little explanatory power. Column (5) interacts the tax rate on repatriated income in 1984 with the change in country average tax rates on the grounds that planning might be most important when country tax rates are falling. The coefficient is negative again, indicating that companies with high overall foreign tax rates in 1984 obtained smaller reductions in effective tax rates.

These results support the interpretation that parent companies are not born high-tax or low-tax, nor are they randomly assigned to high- or low-tax countries. A low parent average tax rate in 1984 presumably indicates that the parent had mobile activities or was engaged in aggressive tax planning. These were the companies that enjoyed larger than average declines in foreign tax rates in the countries in which they were located. Their larger than average reduction in foreign tax rates may indicate their continued aggressive tax planning; it may also indicate their ability to negotiate lower tax rates because of the potential mobility of their operations. Companies whose 1984 overall foreign tax rate would lead them to expect excess credits as a result of TRA 1986 were not the ones who lowered their foreign tax burdens the most.

### 5.6    Tax Rates at the CFC Level

This section examines CFC tax rates in 1984 and 1992 to see if country behavior has changed. For example, have governments made greater concessions to attract finance affiliates? The observations in this section and the next are on individual CFCs, in contrast to those of the previous section in which all of a parent's CFCs in a given location were aggregated. Some data of interest are CFC specific, such as business activity and date of incorporation. Furthermore, CFCs in 1984 and 1992 are not linked. Rather, we use parallel regressions for each year, although the sample is restricted only to parents on the corporate tax files in both years. It is also necessary that data on the parent's foreign tax credit status in 1984 be available. Finally, CFCs with less than $10 million in assets are excluded because of the likely noise in small operations. Also, larger CFCs tend to receive more careful editing when the data file is assembled.

Before proceeding to the parallel regressions for tax rates in 1984 and 1992 in this section, and to debt and income shifting in the next section, it might be appropriate to consider what a change in behavior means. For example, what if finance affiliates retain the same 5 percentage point tax advantage over manufacturing affiliates? The average tax rate on manufacturing fell substantially, but is a finance affiliate's increased *relative* advantage important? Does it indicate that countries are competing more aggressively for finance companies? Companies are presumably interested in the after-tax rate of return in a given location. A reduction of 5 percentage points will have the same absolute effect on after-tax rates of return whatever the initial level of tax rates. This absolute change may be relevant if a location has to overcome a certain absolute cost disadvantage. Furthermore, if tax rates fall generally in all countries, a 5 percentage point advantage for finance will result in a smaller percentage advantage in after-tax rates of return for finance than it did when tax rates were higher. In any case, the attractive power of a 5 percentage point discount has not increased.

However, when we come to income shifting in the next section, relative comparisons may be in order. We will see that, consistent with earlier studies, income tends to be shifted to locations with low statutory tax rates. Average rates of return abroad may, however, change over time, and in that case it might be appropriate to assume that, with unchanged incentives and opportunities, a given percentage point difference in statutory tax rates would result in the same amount of relative income shifting in the two years, because tax officials' responses might be guided by relative differences in return. If the probability of penalties depends on relative differences in returns and the amount of the penalty is proportional to the current return, a given difference in statutory tax rates would seem to result in a given amount of relative income shifting over time.

Table 5.3 reports on the parallel regressions for CFCs' effective foreign tax rates in 1984 and 1992. The effective tax rate is again defined as the ratio of foreign tax paid to E&P, the measure of net equity income. The independent variables are the country average effective tax rate in manufacturing, two age categories based on the CFCs' dates of incorporation, and a dummy variable for CFCs in finance. (Note that only nonfinancial parents are in our sample, but they may have finance CFCs for various reasons.)

The 1984 regression in the first row of table 5.3 indicates that CFCs incorporated relatively recently have significantly lower tax rates than the country average. Investment incentives such as accelerated depreciation and tax holidays tend to benefit recently incorporated companies. Finance affiliates have a tax rate more than 6 percentage points lower, holding the country effective tax rate on manufacturing constant.

The second row shows that the regression for CFC tax rates in 1992 is virtually identical to the 1984 regression. Recently incorporated companies get about the same benefits as in 1984. The tax advantage obtained by finance subsidiaries is about the same. The last row of table 5.3 includes the parent's foreign tax rate on repatriated income in 1984. The coefficient is consistent with the finding in the previous section that companies with high overall foreign tax rates in 1984 did not obtain greater country reductions in tax rates by 1992.

Greater tax competition by governments is not apparent in this CFC-level data. Newly incorporated companies did not receive greater tax concessions in 1992 than they did in 1984. Operations that appear to be highly mobile, such as finance, always have lower tax rates than the average, but this differential does not seem to be much larger in 1992 than in 1984.

**Table 5.3**   Did Governments Increase Concessions to New and Mobile Operations? CFC Effective Tax Rates in 1984 and 1992

| Year | Country Average ETR in 1984 Manufacturing | Country Average ETR in 1992 Manufacturing | Age < 5 Years | Age 5–15 Years | Finance | Parent Foreign Tax Rate on Repatriated Income in 1984 | Adjusted $R^2$ |
|---|---|---|---|---|---|---|---|
| 1984 | .694 (17.08) | | −.050 (2.70) | −.045 (3.75) | −.062 (2.84) | | .177 |
| 1992 | | .668 (17.12) | −.054 (3.89) | −.040 (3.98) | −.077 (4.31) | | .139 |
| 1992 | | .664 (17.04) | −.052 (3.71) | −.038 (3.77) | −.075 (4.22) | .092 (3.01) | .142 |

*Note:* Dependent variable is foreign tax/earning and profits for CFC. $N$ = 1,854 CFCs in 1984. $N$ = 2,334 CFCs in 1992. Each CFC is a separate observation. Unlike in table 5.2, all of a parent's CFCs in a country are not aggregated, and 1984 and 1992 are not linked. Only CFCs with positive earnings are used. CFCs with assets less than $10 million are excluded. Numbers in parentheses are $t$-values.

## 5.7    Have Income Shifting and the Allocation of Debt Become More Sensitive to Taxes?

Table 5.4 moves on to the analysis of income shifting from high-tax to low-tax countries. The incentives, on the margin, to shift income into or out of a jurisdiction depend on its statutory tax rate. However, there is an issue as to what measure of income—pretax profits or after-tax profits— is the best indicator of the extent of income shifting. Pretax profits seem to be the most reliable, robust measure because there may be market forces that tend to equate pretax rates of return. For example, the Samuelson-Lerner theorem on factor price equalization is in terms of pretax factor returns. If there is a tendency for the equalization of pretax rates of return, then a comparison of *after-tax* returns will automatically find lower profits in high-tax countries without any income shifting.

Accordingly, table 5.4 uses the ratio of pretax profits to total assets as the profitability measure. (We will note the results for after-tax returns after the discussion of table 5.4.) Columns (1) and (3) have parallel regressions for 1984 and 1992 pretax income with the relevant year's statutory tax rate, the age dummies, and the finance dummy as independent variables. The statutory tax rate coefficient is negative in each case and statistically significant. The 1992 coefficient is almost twice the 1984 coefficient in absolute value and the mean return is lower in 1992, suggesting both a relative and an absolute increase in income shifting for a given statutory tax rate differential.

Columns (2) and (5), which add the effective tax rate as well as the statutory tax rate to the 1984 and 1992 regressions, indicate that the role of the effective tax rate (or the information it provides) also seems to have changed. In 1984, a higher effective tax rate increased pretax profits, holding the statutory tax rate constant. This might be expected in that a higher local effective tax rate raises pretax profits for all firms apart from any impact of income shifting. In 1992, however, the effective tax rate in column (5) has a negative coefficient. Indeed, in column (6), when the effective tax rate is used alone as the exclusive tax variable, its coefficient is very close to the statutory tax rate coefficient in size and significance. (In contrast, the comparable effective tax rate coefficient for 1984, not shown in the table, is small and statistically insignificant.)

This change in the role of the local effective tax rate in income shifting may be attributable to the changing behavior of countries and companies. One possibility is that some host countries grant companies special statutory tax rates, in the form of tax holidays and the like, that are not apparent in published descriptions of their tax regimes. These kinds of concessions, however, would be reflected in the effective tax rate reported by CFCs in that location. Another possibility is that companies lower their applicable statutory tax rates on their own through tax planning. This

**Table 5.4**     Is More Income Being Shifted to Low-Tax Locations?

| Year | 1984 (1) | 1984 (2) | 1992 (3) | 1992 (4) | 1992 (5) | 1992 (6) |
|---|---|---|---|---|---|---|
| 1984 statutory tax rate | -.086 (3.10) | -.156 (3.64) | | | | |
| 1992 statutory tax rate | | | -.166 (6.23) | | | |
| 1984 average effective tax rate | | | | -.176 (4.82) | -.123 (3.01) | |
| 1992 average effective tax rate | | .104 (2.14) | | | -.067 (1.39) | -.112 (5.30) |
| Age < 5 years | -.018 (1.31) | -.016 (1.18) | -.051 (5.08) | -.051 (5.04) | -.052 (5.10) | -.060 (6.09) |
| Age 5–15 years | -.004 (.46) | -.003 (.34) | -.020 (2.52) | -.020 (2.50) | -.020 (2.54) | -.020 (2.58) |
| Finance | -.070 (3.95) | -.068 (3.83) | -.045 (3.05) | -.045 (3.05) | -.046 (3.09) | -.039 (2.75) |
| Parent foreign tax rate on repatriated income in 1984 statutory tax rate | | | | .025 (.40) | | |
| Mean of dependent variable | .123 | .123 | .109 | .109 | .109 | .109 |

*Note:* Dependent variable is the ratio of pretax profits to total assets. $N = 2,157$ in 1984. $N = 3,210$ in 1992. Includes all CFCs of nonfinancial parents, including those with losses. Numbers in parentheses are *t*-values.

might be the case if they use hybrid companies (to be described in more detail shortly), in which a CFC in a high-tax location owns a tax-haven downstream operation that is a corporation from the high-tax host country's point of view, but is a branch—and therefore consolidated with its upstream owner—from the U.S. tax system's point of view. The CFC and its tax haven operation, to which the CFC can shift income untaxed by the high-tax country would appear as a single CFC in our data.

Column (4) of table 5.4 interacts the country statutory tax rate with the parent's 1984 overall foreign tax rate. High-tax companies in 1984 would have had the greatest incentive to shift income out of high-tax countries because of the greater likelihood that they would be in excess credit. The variable, however, has no explanatory power. The parent's current 1992 excess credit status, not shown in the table, also has no explanatory power.

Regressions (not shown) in which the ratio of *after-tax* income to assets is used as the profitability measure show that, in these as well, the 1992 coefficient for the statutory tax rate is much larger in absolute value than the 1984 coefficient: $-0.187$ versus $-0.115$. Here, however, the results are somewhat more difficult to interpret because average after-tax returns were higher in 1992 than in 1984, and some increase in the amount of income shifting for a given statutory tax rate differential might have been expected.

Turning to the allocation of debt in the MNC, table 5.5 has parallel regressions for CFC debt in 1984 and 1992. The principal incentive to allocate enterprise debt is indicated again by the country statutory tax rate. (Some shifting of debt may contribute to the income shifting in table 5.4 because profitability is expressed in relation to total assets, not to equity.) As expected, CFCs in high statutory tax countries have much more debt in both 1984 and 1992. The mean level of debt abroad is higher in 1992, which might be expected from the incentives to shift debt abroad created by the interest allocation rules, but the coefficient for the statutory tax rate in 1992 is virtually the same as in 1984. As before, the parents' 1984 credit status in the third row has no explanatory power for 1992 debt.[6]

The analysis of pretax rates of return in this section seems to indicate that companies engaged in greater income shifting from high-tax to low-tax countries in 1992 than they did in 1984. Globalization may have increased the opportunities for, and lowered the costs of, shifting income to low-tax locations. It is difficult to detect any evidence that expected excess credits played a role.[7]

6. The 1992 coefficient for the statutory tax rate is very close to the coefficient reported by Altshuler and Grubert (1997) in an equation with other tax variables, such as the withholding tax rate on interest.

7. If, as Grubert, Randolph, and Rousslang (1996) report, companies' excess credit positions have in general returned to their 1984 level, their marginal incentive for income shifting would remain the same; but if income shifting had contributed to this elimination of prospective excess credits, one should nevertheless see proportionately greater income in low-tax countries compared to the distribution of income in 1984.

**Table 5.5  Is More Debt Being Placed in High Tax Subsidiaries? Regressions for CFC Debt in 1984 and 1992**

| Year | Statutory Tax Rate in 1984 | Statutory Tax Rate in 1992 | Age < 5 Years | Age 5–15 Years | Finance | Parent Foreign Tax Rate on Repatriated Income * Statutory Tax Rate | Mean of Dependent Variable |
|---|---|---|---|---|---|---|---|
| 1984 | .378 (10.11) | | .091 (4.77) | .028 (2.25) | .060 (2.52) | | .501 |
| 1992 | | .388 (10.78) | .056 (4.02) | .020 (1.85) | .061 (3.09) | | .556 |
| 1992 | | .397 (7.97) | .056 (4.00) | .020 (1.84) | .061 (3.08) | −.023 (.27) | .556 |

*Note:* Dependent variable is ratio of debt to total assets. $N = 2,503$ in 1984. $N = 3,048$ in 1992. Debt includes all liabilities, including accounts payable. Numbers in parentheses are *t*-values.

Table 5.6          **Did Expectations about Excess Credits Affect Royalty Payments?**
                   **The Change in the Ratio of Royalties to Sales from 1984 to 1992**
                   **(parent level)**

|                                                      | (1)     | (2)     |
| ---------------------------------------------------- | ------- | ------- |
| R&D/sales in 1984                                    | .1152   | .0002   |
|                                                      | (4.03)  | (.01)   |
| Foreign tax rate on repatriated income in 1984       | .0042   |         |
|                                                      | (.78)   |         |
| Foreign tax rate * R&D                               |         | .316    |
|                                                      |         | (2.12)  |
| Adjusted $R^2$                                       | .054    | .069    |
| Mean of dependent variable                           | .0054   | .0054   |

*Note:* $N = 256$. Numbers in parentheses are *t*-values.

## 5.8   The Shift to Royalties and Excess Credit Positions

Grubert, Randolph, and Rousslang (1996) noted that one contributor to the reduction in the foreign tax rate on distributed income in 1992 was the shift from dividends to royalties. The previous discussion showed the potentially large benefits from switching to royalties if the parent is in an excess credit position; this section indicates that the shift to royalties is one area in which expectations of excess credits seem to have been significant.

Table 5.6 presents regressions for the changing importance of royalties to the parent company from 1984 to 1992. In each year, royalties received by the parent, which tend to be mainly foreign, are first scaled by dividing by the parent's sales. The dependent variable is the change in this ratio of royalties to sales from 1984 to 1992.

In the first regression, the independent variables are the parent's R&D as a percentage of sales in 1984 and the indicator of its future credit position, its foreign tax rate on repatriated income in 1984. Research and development has a positive and significant effect but the coefficient for the 1984 foreign tax rate is not significant. In the second regression, when the 1984 foreign tax rate is interacted with R&D, the interaction term is significant and the coefficient of the R&D term by itself virtually disappears. The equation also has more explanatory power. Companies that performed more R&D had a greater opportunity to increase royalties, and, of these, the ones that would have expected to have greater excess credits took advantage of the opportunity.

## 5.9   Changes in Tax Rates by Country:
## Who Cut Their Tax Rates the Most?

This section moves from the firm-level data and reviews the changes in effective and statutory tax rates in sixty countries from 1984 to 1992. As

**Table 5.7**                    **Tax Rates in 1984 and 1994: Manufacturing (sixty countries)**

|  | Average Effective Rate | | Statutory Tax Rate | |
|---|---|---|---|---|
|  | Mean | Standard Deviation | Mean | Standard Deviation |
| 1984 | .329 | .141 | .412 | .146 |
| 1992 | .230 | .114 | .334 | .121 |
| 1984 minus 1992 | .100 | .113 | .077 | .083 |

*Note:* Effective tax rates are total foreign tax paid divided by total pretax E&P in a location. Only CFCs with positive earnings are included in totals.

described earlier, the effective tax rates are based on information returns filed by U.S. CFCs. The effective rates apply to manufacturing CFCs only, and where there is a specific statutory tax rate for manufacturing, it is the one that is used.

Table 5.7 gives the mean effective and statutory tax rates in the sixty-country sample in 1984 and 1992. Consistent with Grubert, Randolph, and Rousslang (1996), the table shows that the mean average effective tax rate fell by almost 10 percentage points between 1984 and 1992. However, there was no notable convergence in tax rates; the standard deviation in effective rates fell only modestly and increased in relation to the mean. (In fact, the standard deviation of the effective tax rates in 1980, not shown on the table, was virtually the same as in 1992 even though the mean was more than 8 percentage points higher.) The last row of the table indicates that there was a wide diversity in tax changes from 1984 to 1992. Table 5.7 also shows that statutory tax rates fell substantially, but by less than effective rates did. There was also no convergence of statutory rates. The diversity in behavior among countries may indicate that the system has not yet settled down to a new equilibrium. The regressions in the next table do indicate that, not surprisingly, high-tax countries tended to cut their tax rates the most. Still, a greater convergence of tax rates would be a more convincing sign of increased tax competition.

Table 5.8 presents simple regressions for the changes in effective and statutory tax rates. (The variables are the 1984 rate minus the 1992 rate, so a reduction is positive.) In the first regression, the dependent variables are the effective tax rate in 1984 and the regional dummies. As already noted, the high-tax countries in 1984 lowered their effective tax rates the most[8]—but these tax reductions may have been for purely domestic reasons. Does the pattern suggest tax competition? The regional dummies show that, if anything, taxes fell less in the EEC than the average even though one might expect that the integration of the European economies

8. There was no disproportionate reduction at the high end. When a squared 1984 effective tax rate term is introduced (not shown on the table), it is not close to being significant.

Table 5.8     Which Countries Cut Their Taxes on U.S. Businesses the Most? Change in Tax Rate Regressions (sixty countries)

| | Dependent Variable | | | | | |
| --- | --- | --- | --- | --- | --- | --- |
| | Change in Effective Tax Rate (1984 ETR − 1992 ETR) | | | | Change in Statutory Tax Rate (1984 STR − 1992 STR) | |
| Independent Variable | (1) | (2) | (3) | (4) | (5) | (6) |
| Effective tax rates in 1984 | .48 (5.43) | | | | | |
| EEC | −.021 (.65) | | | | −.015 (.59) | |
| Latin America | .024 (.78) | | | | .033 (1.37) | |
| Asia | −.06 (1.75) | | | | −.021 (.82) | |
| Change in statutory rates | | | .54 (3.32) | | | |
| Statutory effective tax rate in 1984 − effective tax rate in 1984 | | | | .90 (6.20) | | .19 (2.11) |
| Statutory tax rate in 1984 | | | | −.66 (5.75) | .35 (5.38) | .26 (3.89) |
| Population less than 15 million | | .063 (2.83) | | | | |
| Open trade regime | | .074 (2.29) | | | | |
| GDP per capita less than $4,000 | | .085 (2.67) | | | | |
| Constant term | −.048 (1.17) | −.193 (4.25) | .058 (3.12) | .084 (5.41) | −.068 (2.05) | −.045 (1.69) |
| Adjusted $R^2$ | .41 | .48 | .15 | .45 | .32 | .33 |

*Note:* Numbers in parentheses are *t*-values.

would encourage tax competition. (Regional effects are also weak in the statutory tax rate regression in column [5].)

The second regression, however, indicates that effective tax rates fell much more in small, open, poor economies (see Grubert and Mutti 1997 for the measure of openness).[9] The small countries may be the ones that feel that greatest impact of more mobile capital flows. Countries with open regimes are the ones that would be engaged in tax competition. Investments in low-income countries with relatively cheap, unskilled labor may be the kind that is most sensitive to cost differentials. Low-income countries may also be most susceptible to tax planning or demands for concessions by MNCs. This second regression reveals a pattern that strongly suggests an international motivation for corporate tax reductions.

The third regression examines the correlation between changes in statutory tax rates and effective tax rates. If changes in effective tax rates on U.S. companies are completely explained by changes in local statutory tax rates, no room would be left for special concessions to MNCs or MNC tax planning. Column (3) in table 5.8 indicates that the change in effective tax rates is correlated with the change in local statutory tax rates, but the correlation is not very high. However, the addition of the 1984 discrepancy between the statutory tax rate and the effective tax rate in column (4) greatly increases the explanatory power of the change in statutory tax rates. One reason for adding the statutory versus effective rate discrepancy is that it may capture noise in the 1984 effective tax rate. A temporarily low effective tax rate in 1984 would be associated with a smaller fall in observed effective tax rates from 1984 to 1992 for any change in statutory rates. Another interpretation is that a large discrepancy between statutory and effective tax rates creates the conditions for "base broadening," in which statutory tax rates are lowered but average effective rates are not. In any case, the coefficient close to 1 for the change in statutory tax rates in column (4) suggests that governments were an important source of the observed reduction in effective tax rates. Nevertheless, the large positive constant term leaves open the possibility of a substantial contribution by company planning or special concessions to MNCs.[10]

The base-broadening interpretation for the statutory-effective rate difference receives some support in the regression for the change in statutory tax rates in the last column. The 1984 discrepancy between statutory and effective tax rates has a significant positive coefficient. For any given initial statutory tax rate, a country with an effective tax rate that is much

9. Grubert and Mutti (1997) use four categories of international restrictions, or the absence thereof, based on World Bank listings. The two categories with the lowest restrictions are in the open category in table 5.8.

10. This possibility is consistent with a change in statutory tax regression (not shown) in which two of the variables that were significant in explaining changes in effective tax rates in column (2), for open and poor countries, are *not* significant for statutory rates.

lower than its statutory tax rate decreased its statutory rate by a greater amount so that it could be more in line with its effective rate.

As noted in the introduction, the increased tax sensitivity of investment found by Altshuler, Grubert, and Newlon (chap. 1, this volume) seems generally consistent with the large mean decline in effective tax rates under the assumption that host governments simply maximize revenue from inbound U.S. investment. This is presented only as an illustrative exercise, and it raises the question as to why all governments do not converge on the mean. Presumably different governments weigh considerations other than revenue from U.S. companies differently. Some, for example, may put greater emphasis on the external benefits of inbound investment, whereas others may be concerned about revenue losses from their domestic corporate sector.

Some of the results in this section do suggest increased tax competition. The large drop in average tax rates is consistent with the increased mobility of capital. The small, open, low-income economies that might be expected to gain the most from lower tax rates did cut their taxes the most. Still, there was no convergence of tax rates and other signs of tax competition that might have been expected did not materialize. For example, effective tax rates in the EEC did not fall more than the average even though tax competition might be expected to be intense in this group of homogeneous integrated economies.

### 5.10  Tax Haven Income and the Antiabuse Rules

Countries can defend themselves against some attempts to move their tax bases offshore. In particular, the subpart F rules in the Internal Revenue Code subject interest, dividends, royalties, and other investment income received by controlled foreign corporations in the United States to current U.S. tax. In addition to eliminating deferral for passive income, the subpart F rules also tax income from the sales routed through a CFC for ultimate consumption in a third country. The current U.S. tax on passive and foreign base sales income acts as a backstop to the transfer pricing rules.

These antiabuse rules would appear to eliminate the benefits of using a low-tax country unless the source of the income is from manufacturing located there or from goods and services provided to the local population. But how effective are the antiabuse rules? As a test, we can see how much CFC income in low-tax countries with very tiny populations and virtually no manufacturing is actually subject to current U.S. tax. Take some low-tax countries in the Caribbean as an example. Controlled foreign corporations incorporated in the three most popular locations in the Caribbean report that currently-taxed subpart F income in 1992 was less than 50 percent of their total after-tax E&P in 1992. Apparently, the subpart F rules are not fully effective in achieving their objectives.

The evidence suggests that U.S. companies are using "hybrids" in these locations—that is, the low-tax CFC has an entity in another, high-tax, country that is a branch according to U.S. law but an incorporated subsidiary under the high-tax country's law. The high-tax entity can, therefore, pay royalties and interest to the low-tax CFCs that are deductible in the high-tax country but are not subject to current U.S. tax. The CFC and its branch are regarded as one consolidated corporation from the U.S. point of view. That these branches are being used is suggested by the fact that the Caribbean CFCs report paying tax equal to 11 percent of pretax income, which is much more than they could conceivably be paying to the countries in which they are incorporated.

### 5.11  Summary and Conclusions

There are some signs that governments and companies have responded to the integrating world. Small, open, and low-income countries have cut their effective tax rates on corporations the most. They might be expected to be the ones that are most affected by increased capital mobility. Companies with a low overall foreign tax rate on repatriated income in 1984 were able to achieve larger than average tax cuts in the countries in which they were operating. This may reflect their increased bargaining power because they are more mobile or because they have increased opportunities to exploit their skills at tax planning. More income is being shifted to low-tax locations.

Much of the evidence, however, points to stability. The sensitivity of the location of company debt in response to local statutory tax rates has not changed. Governments have not given greater inducements to new investors, nor to mobile businesses such as finance. Tax rates did not fall by a greater amount in homogeneous free-trade areas, such as the EEC, and there was little convergence of effective or statutory tax rates.

If there is a new international environment, both governments and tax payers can respond. Governments can respond by lowering their tax rates, but they can also respond by making resident companies less susceptible to the attraction of low tax rates. More stringent CFC rules and more comprehensive transfer pricing guidelines are two examples. If the opportunities and incentives for tax-minimizing strategies have increased, these may have been largely offset by changes in government policies.

## References

Altshuler, Rosanne, and Harry Grubert. 2000. Repatriation taxes, repatriation strategies and multinational financial policy. Paper presented at Seminar, Trans-Atlantic Public Economics. 22–24 May 2000, Gerzensee, Switzerland.

Altshuler, Rosanne, and Jack Mintz. 1995. U.S. interest allocation rules: Effects and policy. *International Tax and Public Finance* 2 (1): 7–35.

Chennels, Lucy, and Rachel Griffith. 1997. *Taxing profits in a changing world.* London: Institute for Fiscal Studies.

Grubert, Harry. 1998. Taxes and the division of foreign operating income among royalties, interest, dividends and earnings. *Journal of Public Economics* 68: 269–90.

Grubert, Harry, and John Mutti. Forthcoming. Do taxes influence where U.S. corporations invest? *National Tax Journal.*

Grubert, Harry, William Randolph, and Donald Rousslang. 1996. Country and multinational company responses to the Tax Reform Act of 1986. *National Tax Journal* 49 (3): 341–58.

Organization for Economic Cooperation and Development. 1996. *Controlled foreign company legislation.* Paris: OECD.

Price Waterhouse. 1984. *Corporate taxes: A worldwide summary.* New York: Price Waterhouse Center for Transnational Taxation.

———. 1992. Corporate taxes: A worldwide summary. New York: Price Waterhouse.

Standard & Poors Compustat Service. Available at http://garnet.acns.fsu.edu/~ppeters/fin6842/exer/compu.html

Tanzi, Vito. 1996. Globalization, tax competition and the future of tax systems. International Monetary Fund Working Paper no. WP/96/141.

U.S. Department of Commerce. 1997a. U.S. intrafirm trade in goods, by William J. Zeile. *Survey of Current Business* 77 (2): 23–38.

U.S. Department of Commerce. 1997b. Real gross product of U.S. companies' majority-owned foreign affiliates in manufacturing, by Raymond J. Mataloni. *Survey of Current Business* 77 (4): 8–17.

# Comment    Joel Slemrod

In this paper Harry Grubert assembles a wide range of evidence that sheds light on the important changes in U.S. foreign direct investment (FDI) since 1984. This evidence speaks to one of the most important public finance issues of the twenty-first century—the impact of globalization on the ability of countries to effectively tax the income of corporations and capital income more generally. A strength of the paper—that it is wide ranging—is also the source of its weakness—that it is a bit unfocused. A more descriptive title should really be something like: "Some Facts That May or May Not be Related to How the Tax Environment of U.S. Multinational Companies Changed Between 1984 and 1992." In the absence of a set of testable hypotheses derived from a structural model, or any model, the language of the paper is necessarily very guarded. There are many, many phrases such as "probably suggests," "may reflect," "may have been largely offset," and so on. In spite of this limitation, the paper offers a

Joel Slemrod is the Paul W. McCracken Collegiate Professor of Business Economics and Public Policy and director of the Office of Tax Policy Research at the University of Michigan, and a research associate of National Bureau of Economic Research.

feast of fascinating trends and relationships that are worth chewing on and trying to digest. No one working in this field could fail to be stimulated by it.

A recurring methodological issue is that, over the period under consideration, two things happened: a general globalization of economic affairs, and the passage of the Tax Reform Act of 1986 (TRA 1986). Do the changes we observe between 1984 and 1992 reflect the first, or the second, or a little of both? Would international business experts ignore TRA 1986, and interpret all changes as evidence of globalization? We know that most tax folks look at what happened over this period and presume that it's all due to TRA 1986. This question is reminiscent of the debate over the so-called difference-in-differences approach used to examine the responsiveness of high-income individuals to the tax cut in TRA 1986, and the tax increase of 1993. Is it really acceptable to ignore nontax changes occurring over this period? How can we reliably disentangle the two? How can we hope to do it without a model?

One of the important contributions of this paper is its marshaling of provocative facts. Here's one: The average foreign tax rate of U.S. multinational corporations (MNCs) fell from 36 percent in 1984 to 25 percent in 1992, a truly startling decline. Was this due to increased tax competition among governments, or increased tax planning by the corporations (maybe due to TRA 1986), or a little of both?

Table 5.8 in the paper suggests that the decline in countries' statutory rates could explain as much as four-fifths of the story; but it only suggests that. One problem is that the tax averages are, as far as I can tell, simple averages of all sixty host countries. Surely it would be informative to look at a weighted average. In fact, why not do the following? Start with the 1984 data on the pattern of U.S. MNC investments abroad. Then presume that, for each host country, the percentage reduction in average rates is equal to that of the statutory rate. Assume no behavioral change. How close does that get you to the pattern of company-by-company average tax rates (ATRs) observed in 1992? Alternatively, one could assign the country-wide average changes in ATR to each firm, assume no behavioral response, and examine what kinds of firms differ from that pattern. What I'm seeking is a better way to distinguish the "countries changed, firms were passive" story from "U.S. tax law changed, companies reacted" story.

Table 5.8 also reveals that the standard deviation of both the average tax rates and the statutory rates fell. (Wouldn't some kind of weighting be appropriate here, too?) Grubert concludes that the drop is not particularly large, and does not suggest intense competition for tax bases. To evaluate this claim, it would be very helpful to bring in some theoretical structure. A good start would be Roger Gordon and Jeffrey MacKie-Mason's (1995) theory that open economies would like to have no distorting source-based taxes, but to pay a cost in domestic income shifting if their corporate rate diverges too much from the rate on labor income. This raises the question of whether corporate statutory rates have moved in tandem with individual rates.

Table 5.9 goes beyond country averages to simple regressions explaining changes in tax rates. The regressions provide strong evidence of "regression toward the mean." For example, other things being equal, if a country had a tax rate of 0.5 in 1984, it would be 0.44 in 1992; if it was 0.2 in 1984, it would be 0.28 by 1992. This seems to me to be evidence of competition. However, the fact that there were lower reductions in the European Economic Community (EEC), for given 1984 tax rates, makes Grubert skeptical of the tax competition explanation, given that the pace of economic integration in Europe probably exceeded the pace elsewhere. In the absence of a model, however, it's not obvious why one should focus on this piece of evidence or another. Another bit of suggestive evidence is that governments lowered their statutory rates when they were far out of line with their effective rates. These facts are stimulating but, to my taste, less valuable than if they followed a careful discussion of exactly what would and what would not be evidence of tax competition, precisely defined.

The most fascinating aspect of this paper is the investigation of which MNCs' average tax rates fell from 1984 to 1992. Grubert lays out two (not necessarily mutually exclusive) hypotheses: (1) that TRA 1986 put more companies into an excess foreign tax credit position, forcing them to take more notice of host-country taxes and to flee high-rate countries, and (2) that more mobile (and therefore low-tax) companies took more advantage of opportunities, so that already low-rate tax companies found ways to do even more effective tax planning. Table 5.2 shows that, company by company, the tax rates of those companies with low ATRs in 1984 went down more than the tax rates of companies with high ATRs in 1984. This reflects badly on the first explanation, but it is not clear that it is consistent with the second: Why hadn't the "mobile" companies already taken full advantage of this mobility by 1984? One way to learn more about this question would be to hold constant the 1984 country tax rates in 1992, and look at the actual shift in company behavior—where the company is located, where income is earned. How close does that get us to the actual 1992 pattern of taxes paid?

I don't have the space to comment on all the evidence this paper unearths, and all the analyses it provides. There are a series of fascinating questions posed, and a broad range of evidence presented. One pervasive puzzle remains, though. Why, if the tax elasticity of FDI is 3, as work by Altshuler, Grubert, and Newlon in this volume and by Hines and Rice (1994) suggests, are corporate tax collections as high as they are? To answer that question, one needs to model both the country and firm optimization problems. As I suggested previously, for the country problem, one must consider the interaction between the domestic and foreign tax situations. For the firm, one needs a model of the joint decisions of where to locate real operations and the income-shifting opportunities that the real operations offer.

In the absence of structural models of these decisions, empirical analysis inevitably will be unable to answer certain critical questions, such as (1) If a country wants to increase inward FDI, should it do so by lowering its statutory rate, or by offering investment tax credits? (I strongly suspect that, for a given average tax rate, or even marginal effective tax rate, these two policies will not have the same effect.) And (2) What will be the effect on revenue of alternative tax changes?

I don't mean to imply that constructing a structural model of firm and country decisions that considers both the real investment and income-shifting margins is an easy task. It will certainly be hampered by imperfect data and tenuous identification conditions. I do, nevertheless, believe it is the appropriate path for future research. Grubert and I have made a small step in this direction (Grubert and Slemrod 1998) by modeling how the tax system affects U.S. corporations' investment and income shifting to Puerto Rico. Creating a multicountry model will be a much more difficult task.

Estimating such a structural model is an ambitious agenda, to be sure, but is one for which Harry Grubert and his collaborators has paved the way with their painstaking and thoughtful analyses of the influence of taxes on MNC behavior. I expect that he and they will be in the forefront of the next wave of research that continues to sort out how taxes influence our world of apparently ever-increasing economic integration.

### References

Gordon, Roger H., and Jeffrey K. MacKie-Mason. 1995. Why is there corporate taxation in a small open economy? The role of transfer pricing and income shifting. In *The effects of taxation on multinational corporations,* ed. Martin Feldstein, James R. Hines Jr., and R. Glenn Hubbard, 67–94. Chicago: University of Chicago Press.

Grubert, Harry, and Joel Slemrod. 1998. Tax effects on investment and income shifting to Puerto Rico. *Review of Economics and Statistics* 80 (3): 363–73.

Hines, James R., Jr., and Eric M. Rice. 1994. Fiscal paradise: Foreign tax havens and American business. *Quarterly Journal of Economics* 109:149–82.

# 6

## Valuing Deferral
## The Effect of Permanently
## Reinvested Foreign Earnings
## on Stock Prices

Julie H. Collins, John R. M. Hand,
and Douglas A. Shackelford

## 6.1 Introduction

In this paper we describe the international tax deferral benefits that firms communicate through their financial statements and investigate the U.S. capital market's valuation of these benefits. United States companies that operate in low–tax rate foreign jurisdictions and reinvest their foreign earned income abroad can garner large tax savings. If a U.S. MNC faces, on average, foreign tax rates in excess of the U.S. statutory rate (i.e., the MNC is in an excess foreign tax credit position), low–tax rate foreign earnings can be selectively repatriated with high-tax foreign earnings and generate zero repatriation tax liability. If a U.S. multinational faces, on average, foreign tax rates below the U.S. statutory rate (i.e., the MNC is in an excess limit position), the imposition of any residual U.S. tax (and of foreign withholding taxes) generally is deferred until the low–tax rate foreign income is repatriated to the United States. The benefit of this residual U.S. tax (and foreign withholding tax) deferral, however, is recognized in consolidated financial statement income and retained earnings only if management represents that the repatriation of the foreign income will be

Julie H. Collins is the Ernst & Young Distinguished Professor of Accounting and senior associate dean at the Kenan-Flagler Business School, University of North Carolina, and a research associate of the National Bureau of Economic Research. John R. M. Hand is professor and chair of accounting at the Kenan-Flagler Business School, University of North Carolina. Douglas A. Shackelford is the Arthur Andersen Distinguished Tax Scholar, professor of accounting, and associate dean of the Master of Accounting program at the Kenan-Flagler Business School, University of North Carolina, and a research associate of the National Bureau of Economic Research.

The authors thank Kevin Hassett, James Hines, Deen Kemsley, conference participants, and an anonymous reviewer for many helpful comments on an earlier draft of this paper.

postponed indefinitely (Accounting Principles Board [APB] Opinion no. 23, 1972). In such cases, the foreign earnings are designated as permanently reinvested foreign earnings (PRE), and any potential tax expense associated with repatriation is not recognized.

PRE tax deferral benefits (as a result of the unrecognized, and previously undisclosed, potential repatriation tax liability) have been recognized in financial statements for almost twenty-five years.[1] Beginning with fiscal year 1993, firms also are required to disclose an estimate of the unrecognized deferred U.S. income and foreign withholding tax liabilities associated with PRE (an amount denoted as TAX). That is, under SFAS no. 109, U.S. MNCs must in their income tax footnotes provide their undiscounted estimate of the taxes that would arise if PRE were repatriated, or else state that it is not practicable to determine such an estimate. The objectives of this paper are to describe the magnitudes and assess the capital market's valuation of disclosed PRE and TAX.

Financial statements are a key vehicle through which management can choose to inform investors of the firm's major tax-planning activities. However, publicly available financial statements may not provide investors with finely tuned or unambiguous tax-planning signals for at least two reasons. First, a tension exists between management's conflicting desires to provide value-relevant information to investors and to keep competitors and tax authorities uninformed. Numerous tax directors and professionals have indicated in private conversations that income tax footnotes required in public financial statements are often deliberately written to disguise the firm's tax-planning strategies. Second, the accounting guidance for reflecting international tax deferral savings in financial statement income is sufficiently open-ended and nebulous as to create an adverse selection problem. Investors may be unable to distinguish between (1) companies that designate earnings as PRE because they have substantial tax savings created by long-term deferral strategies, and (2) companies that designate earnings as PRE because they wish to report lower income tax expense and therefore higher financial statement net income.

We examine all publicly traded U.S. companies that disclose PRE in the income tax footnotes of their fiscal 1993 financial statements. Statement for Financial Accounting Standard (SFAS) no. 109 mandates that a firm disclose in its income tax footnote the amount of its PRE if it is material (i.e., deemed to be substantial enough to affect statement-users' inferences). We categorize our sample into four tax-liability reporting groups by what they disclose in the same income tax footnote about the magnitudes of TAX, the unrecognized deferred U.S. income and foreign withholding tax liabilities associated with PRE. The groups are (1) TAX is

---

1. Although disclosure was not formally required until 1993 by SFAS no. 109, many firms disclosed the cumulative amount of PRE (if material) in footnotes in earlier years.

positive ($n = 60$); (2) TAX is zero, insignificant, or substantially offset by foreign tax credits ($n = 79$); (3) TAX is "not practicable to estimate" ($n = 89$); and (4) no information is provided about TAX ($n = 112$).

We find that 340 companies, or 8.9 percent of all companies included in the National Automated Accounting Retrieval System (NAARS), report PRE in fiscal 1993. PRE ranges from 0 to $8.1 billion (reported by Exxon). Median PRE is $40 million, 7.5 percent of the market value of common equity. Median non-PRE retained earnings (RE) is $90 million, 18.5 percent of the market value of equity. Median proportion of PRE to total retained earnings is 31 percent.

Of our sample, 18 percent (sixty firms) report a positive unrecognized deferred tax liability associated with PRE. Presumably, companies with positive TAX are in excess limit foreign tax credit positions. For those firms, the median TAX is $13 million and 0.9 percent of the market value of equity, and the median ratio of TAX to PRE is 23 percent. Consistent with reporting positive TAX and facing excess foreign tax limits, these companies appear to have more extensive operations in low-tax foreign jurisdictions than do the other companies in the sample. Their median foreign effective tax rate is 28 percent, as compared to their median domestic effective tax rate of 32 percent. Of the four groups, they alone have a positive mean or median difference between domestic and foreign effective tax rates.

Our market valuation regressions provide preliminary evidence that the equity market views managers' representations of the potential tax liabilities associated with PRE as credible. We find that the market negatively values the unrecognized deferred tax liability disclosed with PRE. Thus, while the tax law allows this repatriation tax liability to be deferred, that liability appears to be capitalized currently in stock prices. These initial results are consistent with the inability of firms with potentially positive repatriation taxes to convince investors of the permanence of their tax savings from investments in low-tax countries. Potentially, this market capitalization of repatriation taxes diminishes the attractiveness for firms in excess limits to invest in and shift income to tax havens. Our results also are consistent with zero tax capitalization for those firms not reporting a positive repatriation tax liability associated with PRE. This implies that these firms credibly signal to the market that they face no repatriation taxes.

## 6.2 Background

Although the U.S. government taxes U.S. companies on their worldwide incomes, foreign subsidiaries are not included in the U.S. consolidated tax return. Active earnings generated by foreign subsidiaries are not taxed in the United States until cash is repatriated to the U.S. parent. Upon repatriation, foreign source earnings are taxed at the U.S. tax rate ($t_{US}$), subject to a credit for foreign taxes paid (which is limited to the amount of U.S. taxes that would have been owed on the income had it been U.S. source). As a result, a U.S. MNC facing an average foreign tax rate $(t_F)$ less than $t_{US}$ delays paying the residual U.S. tax $(t_{US} - t_F)$ until foreign earnings are repatriated to the United States. On the other hand, when a U.S. MNC with $t_F > t_{US}$ repatriates foreign earnings, it neither faces a residual U.S. tax liability nor receives full credit for prior foreign taxes paid.

In contrast to federal tax laws, U.S. accounting standards require companies to file consolidated financial statements in which the total current earnings of their foreign subsidiaries are recognized, regardless of whether they have been repatriated to the U.S. parent. In addition, firms must reduce current-period foreign earnings by an estimate of the total current and future foreign and U.S. taxes payable on them.[2] Consequently, the income tax expense reported in the income statement includes an estimated charge for future withholding and residual U.S. taxes (after adjusting for foreign tax credits) that will arise from the future repatriation of current earnings of foreign subsidiaries. The charge is not discounted—that is, it does not reflect the anticipated timing of the estimated future withholding and residual U.S. taxes.

The first key to our study is that U.S. accounting standards permit one exception to this comprehensive income tax treatment. If a firm indicates that its unrepatriated foreign earnings are permanently reinvested abroad, then no income tax expense for estimated future U.S. and withholding taxes is required. According to APB no. 23, paragraph 12 (and echoed in SFAS no. 109, paragraph 31a):

> The presumption that all undistributed earnings will be transferred to the parent company may be overcome, and no income taxes should be accrued by the parent company, if sufficient evidence shows that the subsidiary has invested or will invest the undistributed earnings indefinitely or that the earnings will be remitted in a tax-free liquidation. A parent company should have evidence of specific plans for reinvestment of undistributed earnings of a subsidiary, which demonstrate that remit-

2. APB Opinion no. 23, paragraph 10 (1972), indicates that it is generally presumed that all undistributed earnings of a foreign subsidiary will be transferred to the parent company. Accordingly, the undistributed current-period earnings of a foreign subsidiary are included in current-period consolidated accounting income and are accounted for as a timing difference (i.e., earnings are recognized for accounting and tax purposes at different times). Income tax expense recognized in the consolidated income statement that is attributable to timing differences is accrued currently. To quote APB no. 23 directly, "Problems in measuring and recognizing the tax effect of a timing difference do not justify ignoring income taxes related to the timing difference. Income taxes of the parent applicable to a timing difference in undistributed earnings of a subsidiary are necessarily based on estimates and assumptions. For example, the tax effect may be determined by assuming that unremitted earnings were distributed in the current period and that the parent company received the benefit of all available tax-planning alternatives and available tax credits and deductions" (paragraph 10).

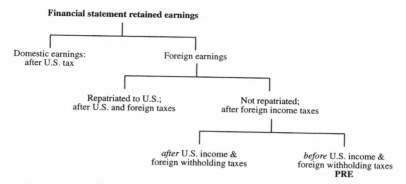

**Fig. 6.1    Financial statement retained earnings**

*Note:* A key distinction between U.S. GAAP and U.S. MNC taxation is that GAAP requires firms to record financial reporting tax expense against current and/or cumulative pretax foreign earnings that are not yet repatriated, *unless* the earnings are deemed to be permanently reinvested (PRE). However, no U.S. taxes are actually paid until repatriation occurs.

tance of the earnings will be postponed indefinitely. Experience of the companies and definite future programs of operations and remittances are examples of the types of evidence required to substantiate the parent company's representation of indefinite postponement of remittances from a subsidiary.

The results of this accounting guidance are reflected in the partitions of retained earnings illustrated in figure 6.1. Domestic earnings and repatriated foreign earnings are fully tax-affected. Unrepatriated foreign earnings are after foreign income taxes, but may be before (i.e., PRE) or after future repatriation taxes (i.e., foreign withholding and domestic income taxes).[3]

APB no. 23 anticipates the imprecision in designating foreign earnings as permanently reinvested by elaborating on the proper accounting treatment for situations in which circumstances change and it becomes apparent that some or all of the undistributed earnings that were previously considered permanently reinvested now will be remitted in the foreseeable future. In such cases, companies are instructed to accrue, as an expense of the current period, income taxes that are attributable to the anticipated remittance. The reverse accounting treatment is required whenever it becomes apparent that unremitted earnings that previously were not classified as currently reinvested (i.e., estimated taxes were provided) now will

3. An employee of a large U.S. MNC privately indicated to us that "postponed indefinitely" is interpreted by his/her company as "will not be remitted in the foreseeable future," where foreseeable future is defined as one year or less. This individual also indicated that a U.S. MNC anticipating repatriation of foreign earnings at little to no tax cost may designate such earnings as permanently reinvested to inform investors of a potential future tax liability that currently is estimated as zero.

not be remitted in the foreseeable future. Here companies must reduce their current tax expense by undoing some of the prior accrual.

The imprecision in classifying foreign earnings as PRE, combined with the potentially large effects on net income arising from changes in classification, may create an adverse selection problem for investors. Investors may be unable to distinguish between (1) companies that designate earnings as PRE because they have substantial tax savings created by long-term deferral of their residual U.S. and foreign withholding taxes, and (2) companies that designate earnings as PRE because they wish to report lower income tax expense and therefore higher financial statement net income. This is because managers may manipulate current net income up or down by whether they classify unremitted current- and/or prior-period foreign earnings as PRE. For example, if a company earns $100 abroad and pays $20 in foreign taxes, it can increase its current net income by $15 ($100 $\times$ 35% $-$ $20) if it represents that the remittance to the United States of the cash created by the foreign earnings is indefinitely postponed. Alternatively, it could decrease current net income by $15 by representing that $100 of prior-period PRE, on which it had paid $20 in foreign taxes, is now likely to be remitted in the future.

SFAS no. 109, effective for fiscal years beginning after 15 December 1992, is the most recent guidance regarding accounting for income taxes. Despite the imprecision in classifying foreign earnings as PRE, SFAS no. 109 justifies retaining the exception to comprehensive recognition of deferred taxes for undistributed earnings of foreign subsidiaries that will be invested indefinitely because of the complexities involved in determining the size of the potential deferred tax liability. However, paragraph 44c of SFAS no. 109 adds a new disclosure requirement that is the second key to our study. Firms with material amounts of PRE are required to disclose an estimate of the amount of TAX associated with their PRE or state that it is not practicable to estimate it.

Firms' disclosures under this new requirement fall into one of the four tax-liability reporting groups outlined in the introduction:

1. TAX is positive.
2. TAX is zero, insignificant, or substantially offset by foreign tax credits.
3. TAX is "not practicable to estimate."
4. No information is provided about TAX.

Table 6.1 provides an example of the kind of disclosure shown by each group using actual excerpts from fiscal year 1993 income tax footnotes of our sample companies. In the tests described in section 6.3, we assign the value of zero to our measure of the deferred tax liability for every group, except the first.

**Table 6.1**                **Examples from 1993 Income Tax Footnotes**

| Company | TAX | Footnote Description |
|---|---|---|
| Monsanto | Positive | Income and remittance taxes have not been recorded on $500 million in undistributed earnings of subsidiaries, either because any taxes on dividends would be offset substantially by foreign tax credits or because Monsanto intends to reinvest those earnings indefinitely. The estimated U.S. income tax if such earnings were paid as dividends would be $82 million. |
| Exxon | Zero, insignificant, or substantially offset by foreign tax credits | The corporation had $8.1 billion of indefinitely reinvested, undistributed earnings from subsidiary companies outside the United States. Unrecognized deferred taxes on remittance of these funds are not expected to be material. |
| Deere & Co. | Not practicable to estimate | As of 31 October 1993 accumulated earnings in certain overseas subsidiaries and affiliates totaled $361 million, for which no provision for U.S. income taxes or foreign withholding taxes had been made because it is expected that such earnings will be reinvested overseas indefinitely. Determination of the amount of unrecognized deferred tax liability on these unremitted earnings is not practicable. |
| H. J. Heinz & Co. | No information provided | Undistributed earnings of foreign subsidiaries considered to be reinvested permanently amounted to $1.14 billion as of 27 April 1994. |

## 6.3  Methodology

We describe the characteristics of the firms in 1993 that report PRE in aggregate and by the type of associated TAX each reports. In addition, we use market valuation tests to determine the value relevance of PRE and TAX. We estimate the following regression for all sample firms:

$$(1) \qquad PRICE_i = \beta_0 + \beta_1 DNI_i + \beta_2 FNI_i + \beta_3 CS_i$$
$$+ \beta_4 RE_i + \beta_5 PRE_i + \beta_6 TAX_i + \varepsilon_i,$$

where on a per-share basis,

PRICE = market price of common equity at the end of fiscal 1993,
DNI = after-tax financial statement domestic income for fiscal 1993,
FNI = after-tax financial statement foreign income for fiscal 1993,
CS = total common equity less total retained earnings at the end of fiscal 1993,
RE = total retained earnings less PRE at the end of fiscal 1993,

PRE = permanently reinvested foreign earnings at the end of fiscal 1993, and

TAX = unrecognized deferred tax liability associated with PRE at the end of fiscal 1993 if positive (otherwise zero).

We scale dollar amounts by the number of common shares outstanding at the end of fiscal 1993 in order to mitigate the effects of heteroskedasticity that are present in the unscaled data. Our model relies on a standard valuation model in which price is regressed on net book value and net income (e.g., Ohlson 1995; Barth, Beaver, and Landsman 1998; Francis and Schipper 1999; Collins, Maydew, and Weiss 1997). This valuation approach, which relies exclusively on accounting numbers, is isomorphic to a discounted dividend model under two assumptions (Ohlson 1995). The first assumption is that there is "clean surplus" between balance sheet numbers at the beginning and end of a period and net income and dividends over that period. This essentially means that retained earnings at the end of the period equals retained earnings at the beginning of the period plus net income earned over the period less dividends declared during the period. This clean-surplus assumption permits dividends to be expressed in terms of accounting numbers. It also implies that price equals book value plus the discounted sum of future abnormal earnings. The second assumption is that future abnormal earnings follow a first-order autoregressive process. This implies that the discounted sum of future abnormal earnings can be expressed as a multiple of current net income.[4]

For our purposes, we decompose net book value into the CS, RE, and PRE components and include the unrecognized tax liability, TAX, to examine separately the market valuations of PRE (alone and relative to RE) and TAX. If the market perceives firms' disclosures regarding the TAX associated with PRE as credible and capitalizes this tax liability into current prices, then we expect the TAX coefficient will be negative. If the market does not perceive the tax liability signal as credible or does not capitalize the expense into current prices, then we expect the TAX coefficient will not differ from zero. Thus, our tests regarding the TAX coefficient are analogous to prior accounting studies investigating the market valuation of disclosed, but unrecognized, nontax liabilities (e.g., Landsman 1986 and Barth 1991 examining unrecorded pension liabilities). In addition, our tests are analogous to prior economics and accounting studies investigating the capitalization of unrecorded future investor tax liabilities into stock prices (e.g., Harris and Kemsley 1999; Harris, Hubbard, and Kemsley 2000), although we examine an unrecorded future tax liabil-

---

4. Models such as the one we express in equation (1) have sparked a resurgence of interest in "levels-based" valuation research in accounting. See Harris and Kemsley (1999) and Harris, Hubbard, and Kemsley (2000) for recent applications of this type of valuation model to address capitalization of shareholder taxes.

ity assessed at the parent-corporation level rather than the external-investor level.

We decompose after-tax net income into its domestic and foreign components to control, at least partially, for possible valuation differences due to the extent of a company's foreign operations. Collins, Kemsley, and Lang (1998) report that foreign earnings are valued differently, and generally at a higher level, than domestic earnings for their sample of manufacturing companies. In addition, Bodnar and Weintrop (1997) provide some evidence that greater opportunities for growth in foreign operations contributes to higher foreign than domestic earnings valuation.

## 6.4  Sample and Descriptive Statistics

We constructed our data set through a keyword search of the NAARS database, which contains the full-text annual reports of approximately 3,800 publicly traded companies.[5] We searched the file for fiscal 1993, the most recent year in which full data are available and the first year all firms were required to disclose PRE and TAX under SFAS no. 109. Fiscal 1993 encompasses fiscal year ends between 1 July 1993 and 30 June 1994. Our keyword search yielded 576 potential matches. Of these, 350 related to permanently reinvested foreign earnings, and the amount of PRE was specified.[6] A further ten companies were excluded because either the number of shares or their price per share was reported on Compustat as zero or negative, or their retained earnings or financial statement net income was zero. The final sample consists of 340 publicly traded U.S. MNCs that reported a positive amount of PRE at the end of fiscal 1993.

Our sample is listed by two-digit Standard Industrial Code (SIC) and tax-liability reporting group in appendix A. Of the sample, some 292 (86 percent) are in the manufacturing industry (one-digit SIC = 2 or 3). This is consistent with prior research demonstrating that the manufacturing industry comprises the vast majority of U.S. companies with significant foreign operations (Collins, Kemsley, and Lang 1998). The largest number of sample companies (57, or 17 percent) are in the nonelectrical machinery industry (SIC = 35). There are 46 companies (14 percent) in the chemicals industry (SIC = 28), and 34 companies (10 percent) in the electrical machinery industry (SIC = 36). A casual review detects no relation between industries and tax-liability reporting groups.

5. Our key-word search terms were "undistributed w/1 earnings," or "permanently w/1 earnings," or "indefinitely w/1 reinvest!," or "permanently w/1 reinvest!," or "unremitted w/1 earnings," or "retained earnings subsidiaries outside," or "remit! w/15 ((foreign sub!) or (non-US sub!) or international)."

6. Potential matches were not included in the final sample for the following reasons: (1) the match was unrelated to foreign earnings, (2) the firm was not a U.S. multinational, (3) no Center for Research in Security Prices IPERM was found for the firm, and (4) PRE was zero.

Panels A and B of table 6.2 report descriptive statistics for the full sample. In panel A, we highlight the median statistic because many of the underlying variables are highly skewed. Total assets of our sample firms range from $24 million to $185 billion, having a median of $767 million. Revenues range from $15 million to $98 billion, with a median of $887 million. The range of the market value of common equity is $7 million to $78 billion, with a median of $768 million. Median after-tax domestic and foreign financial statement net incomes are $10 million and $3 million, respectively. The median PRE is $40 million, and the median proportion of PRE to total retained earnings is 31 percent. Descriptive statistics for the less skewed per-share variables used in our regression analysis also are shown in panel B. The mean common stock price per share (PRICE) is $29.24, while mean PRE and RE per share are $2.66 and $6.28, respectively.

Panel A of table 6.3 provides descriptive statistics by tax-liability reporting groups. Companies that disclose no TAX information tend to be smaller than companies in the other three groups.[7] Median assets are $1,230 million (TAX > 0 group), $863 million (TAX = 0 group), $1,002 million (Not Practicable to Estimate group), and $370 (No TAX Information group), respectively. Similar patterns exist for revenues and the market value of equity. In terms of income, the TAX > 0 and Not Practicable groups both have median after-tax domestic income of $22 million. However, the TAX > 0 group has a median after-tax foreign income of $11 million, while that of the Not Practicable group is only $3 million. Median after-tax domestic and foreign income for the TAX = 0 group and the No TAX Information group are $9 million and $2 million, and $4 million and $1 million, respectively. Median PRE is $57 million (TAX > 0), $58 million (TAX = 0), $54 million (Not Practicable), and $29 million (No TAX Information). The mean (median) estimated deferred tax liability (TAX) associated with PRE reported by the TAX > 0 group is $55 million ($13 million). For the firms reporting positive deferred repatriation taxes, the mean (median) of TAX as a percentage of PRE is 0.23 (0.23).

Descriptive statistics for the regression variables are shown by tax-liability reporting group in panel B of table 6.3. The means of PRICE are $34 (TAX > 0), $28 (TAX = 0), $31 (Not Practicable), and $25 (No TAX Information). The means of PRE are $2.66, $2.67, $2.99, and $2.38, respectively.

We also computed the difference in domestic and foreign effective tax rates for those firms in each group that reported (1) zero or positive domestic and foreign tax expense and (2) positive domestic and foreign before-tax income. Effective tax rates greater than 1 were truncated to 1. On average,

---

7. Inferences are unaltered if we exclude firms that provide no TAX information from our tests.

**Table 6.2    Descriptive Statistics**

| | Mean | Standard Deviation | Minimum | 25% | Median | 75% | Maximum |
|---|---|---|---|---|---|---|---|
| | | *A. Variables in $ Millions* | | | | | |
| Assets | 5,243 | 17,152 | 24 | 212 | 767 | 3,049 | 184,835 |
| Revenues | 3,539 | 8,745 | 15 | 245 | 887 | 2,856 | 97,825 |
| Market value of equity | 3,335 | 7,947 | 7 | 183 | 768 | 2,868 | 78,401 |
| Domestic after-tax net income | 96 | 347 | −606 | −2 | 10 | 83 | 2,879 |
| Foreign after-tax net income | 38 | 234 | −2,049 | −1 | 3 | 24 | 1,481 |
| Residual common equity | 154 | 1,127 | −14,573 | 14 | 62 | 300 | 5,664 |
| All non-PRE retained earnings | 792 | 2,850 | −2,326 | 7 | 90 | 534 | 41,265 |
| PRE | 253 | 691 | 0 | 10 | 40 | 184 | 8,100 |
| Unrecognized deferred tax liability on PRE | 48 | 106 | 0 | 2 | 10 | 36 | 700 |
| | | *B. Variables on a $ per Share Basis* | | | | | |
| PRICE | 29.24 | 20.84 | 1.25 | 14.38 | 23.81 | 39.00 | 113.75 |
| DNI | 0.58 | 1.98 | −8.85 | −0.28 | 0.56 | 1.65 | 7.74 |
| FNI | 0.28 | 0.93 | −5.15 | −0.05 | 0.14 | 0.61 | 4.39 |
| CS | 4.08 | 6.25 | −17.83 | 1.02 | 3.39 | 7.03 | 36.73 |
| RE | 6.28 | 10.60 | −29.40 | 0.71 | 4.71 | 10.19 | 74.27 |
| PRE | 2.66 | 2.86 | 0.00 | 0.61 | 1.62 | 3.57 | 16.97 |
| TAX | 0.11 | 0.45 | 0 | 0 | 0 | 0 | 5.12 |

*Note:* Table reports descriptive statistics for the full sample of 340 publicly traded U.S. MNCs that reported a positive amount of PRE in fiscal 1993. PRICE is the market price of common equity at the end of fiscal 1993. DNI is after-tax financial statement domestic income for fiscal 1993. FNI is after-tax financial statement foreign income for fiscal 1993. CS is total common equity less total retained earnings at the end of fiscal 1993. RE is total retained earnings less PRE at the end of fiscal 1993. PRE is permanently reinvested foreign earnings at the end of fiscal 1993. TAX is the unrecognized deferred tax liability associated with PRE at the end of fiscal 1993. A value of zero is assigned to companies not reporting a positive TAX. All variables are scaled by common shares outstanding at the end of fiscal 1993.

**Table 6.3**    **Descriptive Statistics**

| | TAX > 0 (n = 60) | | TAX = 0 (n = 79) | | Not Practicable to Estimate (n = 89) | | No TAX Information (n = 112) | |
|---|---|---|---|---|---|---|---|---|
| | Mean | Median | Mean | Median | Mean | Median | Mean | Median |
| *A. Variables in $ Millions* | | | | | | | | |
| Assets | 11,862 | 1,230 | 4,894 | 863 | 4,804 | 1,002 | 2,290 | 370 |
| Revenues | 4,840 | 1,417 | 4,511 | 1,187 | 3,964 | 1,203 | 1,818 | 461 |
| Market value of equity | 4,634 | 1,290 | 4,039 | 1,002 | 3,748 | 896 | 1,812 | 535 |
| Domestic after-tax net income | 167 | 22 | 74 | 9 | 132 | 22 | 45 | 4 |
| Foreign after-tax net income | 84 | 11 | −14 | 2 | 67 | 3 | 27 | 1 |
| Residual common equity | 60 | 92 | 71 | 63 | 266 | 70 | 174 | 54 |
| All non-PRE retained earnings | 1,099 | 139 | 1,109 | 71 | 864 | 203 | 346 | 51 |
| PRE | 266 | 57 | 319 | 58 | 332 | 54 | 136 | 29 |
| Unrecognized deferred tax liability on PRE | 55 | 13 | 0 | 0 | 0 | 0 | 0 | 0 |
| *B. Variables on a $ per Share Basis* | | | | | | | | |
| PRICE | 34 | 33 | 28 | 24 | 31 | 25 | 25 | 20 |
| DNI | 0.92 | 0.85 | 0.35 | 0.54 | 0.94 | 0.87 | 0.27 | 0.29 |
| FNI | 0.44 | 0.29 | 0.24 | 0.12 | 0.34 | 0.15 | 0.16 | 0.12 |
| CS | 3.70 | 3.58 | 4.81 | 3.80 | 3.95 | 3.15 | 3.87 | 3.07 |
| RE | 7.34 | 5.30 | 4.87 | 4.37 | 7.52 | 6.46 | 5.72 | 3.62 |
| PRE | 2.66 | 1.64 | 2.67 | 1.37 | 2.99 | 2.05 | 2.38 | 1.56 |
| TAX | 0.62 | 0.31 | 0 | 0 | 0 | 0 | 0 | 0 |

*Note:* Table reports descriptive statistics for 340 publicly traded U.S. MNCs that reported a positive amount of PRE in fiscal 1993, by tax-liability reporting group. PRICE is the market price of common equity at the end of fiscal 1993. DNI is after-tax financial statement domestic income for fiscal 1993. FNI is after-tax financial statement foreign income for fiscal 1993. CS is total common equity less total retained earnings at the end of fiscal 1993. RE is total retained earnings less PRE at the end of fiscal 1993. PRE is permanently reinvested foreign earnings at the end of fiscal 1993. TAX is the unrecognized deferred tax liability associated with PRE at the end of fiscal 1993. A value of zero is assigned to companies not reporting a positive TAX. All variables are scaled by common shares outstanding at the end of fiscal 1993.

**Table 6.4**                **Pearson and Spearman Correlation Coefficients**

|        | PRICE | DNI | FNI | CS | RE | PRE | TAX |
|--------|-------|-----|-----|-----|-----|-----|-----|
| PRICE  |       | 0.41 | 0.31 | −0.15 | 0.61 | 0.39 | 0.06 |
| DNI    | 0.46  |      | 0.21 | −0.15 | 0.29 | −0.03 | −0.02 |
| FNI    | 0.35  | 0.26 |      | −0.09 | 0.12 | 0.30 | 0.11 |
| CS     | −0.11 | −0.15 | −0.12 |      | −0.47 | −0.11 | −0.09 |
| RE     | 0.59  | 0.49 | 0.17 | −0.45 |      | 0.28 | 0.09 |
| PRE    | 0.36  | 0.03 | 0.31 | −0.09 | 0.24 |      | 0.32 |
| TAX    | 0.15  | 0.06 | 0.11 | −0.01 | 0.07 | 0.06 |      |

*Note:* Pearson (Spearman) correlations of variables used in the cross-sectional valuation regressions are above (below) the diagonal. Correlations are for the full sample of 340 publicly traded U.S. MNCs that reported a positive amount of PRE in fiscal 1993. PRICE is the market price of common equity at the end of fiscal 1993. DNI is after-tax financial statement domestic income for fiscal 1993. FNI is after-tax financial statement foreign income for fiscal 1993. CS is total common equity less total retained earnings at the end of fiscal 1993. RE is total retained earnings less PRE at the end of fiscal 1993. PRE is permanently reinvested foreign earnings at the end of fiscal 1993. TAX is the unrecognized deferred tax liability associated with PRE at the end of fiscal 1993. A value of zero is assigned to companies not reporting a positive TAX. All variables are scaled by common shares outstanding at the end of fiscal 1993. Correlations in excess of 0.11 (0.15) in absolute magnitude are significant at $\alpha = 0.05$ (0.01).

the domestic effective tax rate exceeds the foreign effective tax rate only for companies reporting positive repatriation taxes. The mean domestic effective tax rate and foreign effective tax rate differences are 6.5 percent (TAX $> 0$), −18.6 percent (TAX $= 0$), −14.7 percent (Not Practicable), and −5.5 percent (No TAX Information). The correlation between the difference in domestic and foreign effective tax rates and TAX/PRE, where TAX equals zero for all companies other than TAX $> 0$, is 0.28 ($p < 0.001$). These results are consistent with the TAX $> 0$ companies' being in excess limit and provide some support for prior studies' use of foreign effective tax rates to approximate repatriation tax liabilities and foreign tax credit positions (e.g., Hines 1996; Collins, Kemsley, and Lang 1998).

Pearson and Spearman correlations between the regression variables are provided in table 6.4. The Pearson (Spearman) correlations between DNI and PRICE and between FNI and PRICE are 0.41 (0.46) and 0.31 (0.35), respectively. The Pearson (Spearman) correlations between RE and PRICE and between PRE and PRICE are 0.61 (0.59) and 0.39 (0.36), respectively. The Pearson (Spearman) correlations between DNI and FNI and between RE and PRE are 0.21 (0.26) and 0.28 (0.24), respectively.

## 6.5   Results

The results of estimating equation (1) are shown in column (1) of table 6.5.[8] The TAX coefficient is −3.19 (*t*-statistic = −1.75), which is margin-

8. Diagnostic tests indicate that the results reported in table 6.5 are unaffected by outliers, and the null hypothesis of correct model specification under White's (1980) test is never

**Table 6.5**          **Regression Coefficient Estimates**

| Variable | Full Sample (1) | TAX > 0 (2) | TAX = 0 (3) | Not Practicable to Estimate (4) | No TAX Information (5) |
|---|---|---|---|---|---|
| N | 340 | 60 | 79 | 89 | 112 |
| Intercept | 13.28 | 26.52 | 13.95 | 9.58 | 10.47 |
|  | (9.81) | (6.35) | (4.75) | (3.69) | (4.88) |
| DNI | 2.68 | 1.93 | 1.92 | 4.54 | 1.79 |
|  | (6.36) | (1.60) | (2.25) | (5.92) | (2.28) |
| FNI | 3.25 | 3.25 | 2.16 | 5.35 | 3.99 |
|  | (3.63) | (1.46) | (1.31) | (2.45) | (2.28) |
| CS | 0.59 | −0.17 | 0.48 | 0.68 | 0.79 |
|  | (4.20) | (−0.43) | (1.44) | (3.00) | (3.17) |
| RE | 1.06 | 0.81 | 0.99 | 1.10 | 1.14 |
|  | (12.02) | (3.33) | (4.47) | (5.14) | (9.52) |
| PRE | 1.80 | −0.23 | 2.31 | 1.52 | 1.80 |
|  | (5.78) | (−0.29) | (3.64) | (2.71) | (3.33) |
| TAX | −3.19 |  |  |  |  |
|  | (−1.75) |  |  |  |  |
| Adjusted $R^2$ | 0.54 | 0.35 | 0.49 | 0.63 | 0.59 |

*Note:* Table gives cross-sectional OLS (ordinary least squares) valuation regressions of stock price per share on disaggregations of the book value of common equity and financial statement net income. The full sample is the 340 publicly traded U.S. MNCs that reported a positive amount of PRE in fiscal 1993. Subsets are based on disclosures in income tax footnotes about TAX (the unrecognized deferred U.S. income and foreign withholding tax liabilities associated with PRE). Regression model: $PRICE_i = \beta_0 + \beta_1 DNI_i + \beta_2 FNI_i + \beta_3 CS_i + \beta_4 RE_i + \beta_5 PRE_i + \beta_6 TAX_i + \varepsilon_i$. PRICE is the market price of common equity at the end of fiscal 1993. DNI is after-tax financial statement domestic income for fiscal 1993. FNI is after-tax financial statement foreign income for fiscal 1993. CS is total common equity less total retained earnings at the end of fiscal 1993. RE is total retained earnings less PRE at the end of fiscal 1993. PRE is permanently reinvested foreign earnings at the end of fiscal 1993. TAX is the unrecognized deferred tax liability associated with PRE at the end of fiscal 1993. A value of zero is assigned to companies not reporting a positive TAX. All variables are scaled by common shares outstanding at the end of fiscal 1993.

ally significant ($p < 0.05$) using a one-tailed test. These results provide weak evidence consistent with the market capitalizing the deferred repatriation tax liability into current stock prices. The PRE coefficient is 1.80 and greater than the RE coefficient of 1.06 at the 0.05 level.[9] However, the

---

rejected at conventional levels. The regression coefficient estimates are unaltered materially if dummy variables depicting one-digit SIC codes are added to the regression; however, the *t*-statistic for TAX is reduced to −1.39. If the intercept is scaled by common shares outstanding, inferences are unaltered; however, the PRE coefficient increases to 3.24. No other coefficients change materially.

9. If higher levels of PRE signal greater foreign investment and future foreign earnings, then this finding is consistent with prior evidence of higher foreign (relative to domestic) earnings valuation (e.g., Bodnar and Weintrop, 1997; Collins, Kemsley, and Lang 1998). However, we are unable to discern to what extent, if any, RE represents repatriated foreign earnings or unrepatriated foreign earnings (which have not been, but could be, designated as PRE in the future) and the effect, if any, of such amounts on the relative magnitudes of

foreign earnings multiple of 3.25 is not significantly greater than the domestic earnings multiple of 2.68.[10]

A TAX coefficient of $-3.19$ implies that each dollar (per share) of reported unrecognized deferred tax liability reduces the per-share price by $3.19. This seems large on face value. However, TAX represents the unrecognized deferred tax liability associated with both current and prior foreign earnings that are designated as PRE, and thus is expected to reflect some combination of the earnings multiples reflected in the PRE and FNI coefficients. Thus, we compare the absolute value of the estimated TAX coefficient to both the PRE and FNI coefficients. Our tests reveal that the absolute value of the TAX coefficient is not significantly different from either the PRE or the FNI coefficients. The magnitude of the negative value that the market assigns per dollar of TAX is not significantly different from the magnitude of the positive value the market assigns per dollar of PRE or FNI. Thus, it appears that the market capitalizes TAX using earnings multiples similar to those applied to PRE and FNI.

The results of estimating equation (1) separately for each tax-liability reporting group also are shown in table 6.5, columns (2–5). The TAX $> 0$ firms' PRE coefficient in column (2) is $-0.23$ ($t$-statistic $= -0.29$). This PRE coefficient is significantly less than each of the other groups' PRE coefficients.[11]

The PRE coefficient for the TAX $= 0$ group is 2.31 ($t$-statistic $= 3.64$), for the Not Practicable group is 1.52 ($t$-statistic $= 2.71$), and for the No TAX Information group is 1.80 ($t$-statistic $= 3.33$). These coefficients are not significantly different from one another. For these three groups, which do not report a positive deferred tax liability, the market consistently values a dollar of PRE from 1.5 to 2 times more than a dollar of other fully

the PRE and RE coefficients. Nevertheless, we also explore the effect of PRE on parent-company dividend distributions to external shareholders by regressing dividends per share on the independent variables in equation (1). The coefficients ($t$-statistics) are as follows: Intercept 0.14 (2.92), DNI 0.08 (5.05), FNI 0.00 (0.08), CS $-0.00$ ($-0.92$), RE 0.03 (8.43), PRE 0.08 (6.95), TAX $-0.12$ ($-1.83$). To the extent that RE represents domestic retained earnings, the larger coefficient on PRE relative to RE is consistent with Hines's (1996) finding of parent company's dividend payout rates being three times higher for foreign profits than for domestic profits. The DNI and FNI coefficients, however, are inconsistent with higher foreign profit dividend payout rates.

10. We also estimate equation (1) combining PRE and TAX into a single independent variable, PRE-TAX. The PRE-TAX coefficient is 1.78 ($t$-statistic $= 5.73$). All other coefficients remain essentially the same as those in column (1) of table 6.5.

11. When TAX is added to the regression shown in column (2), the PRE coefficient is 3.01 ($t$-statistic $= 1.60$) and the TAX coefficient is $-11.09$ ($t$-statistic $= -1.89$). The remaining coefficients do not differ materially from those shown in column (2). The TAX coefficient of $-11.09$ is larger relative to the PRE and FNI coefficients than we would expect. We attribute some of the unusual magnitude simply to measurement error. In addition, it may be that the reporting of an estimated deferred tax liability other than zero causes investors to react as if the "true" liability is potentially larger.

tax-affected retained earnings. However, the difference between the PRE and RE coefficients is not statistically significant in any of the groups. The similarity across PRE coefficients for the firms not reporting a positive tax liability suggests that the market infers a zero repatriation tax liability for firms in all three groups. Consistent with the full sample estimates, the foreign earnings multiple is not significantly different from the domestic earnings multiple in any of the four tax-liability reporting groups.

## 6.6    Conclusion

This study provides initial evidence consistent with the current capitalization into stock prices of the unrecognized deferred tax liability associated with unrepatriated foreign earnings generated in low-tax jurisdictions. Such evidence implies that firms in excess limit positions receive little to no market reward for deferring material repatriation tax liabilities. Many tax directors and advisors have indicated in private conversations that publicly traded companies focus primarily on tax planning strategies that enhance stock prices. Thus, our results imply that the incentive for excess limit companies to structure complex tax planning schemes involving either tax havens or shifting income from the United States to low-tax foreign jurisdictions is potentially diminished. These results are consistent with Collins, Kemsley, and Lang's (1998) failure to detect shifting of income from the United States to low-tax foreign jurisdictions by U.S. MNCs in excess limit positions.

Besides documenting a potential disincentive for excess limit firms to reinvest in low-tax jurisdictions, the findings may provide preliminary input to the long-standing debates in the public finance literature regarding the capitalization of shareholder taxes. The negative coefficient on TAX is consistent with the market's anticipation of eventual remittance of unrecognized deferred repatriation taxes and capitalization of these costs into current stock prices. This result is also consistent with Hartman (1985), who indicates that timing is irrelevant for repatriations that generate a tax liability of $1 today and a tax liability of $1(1 + r)^n$ at time $n$. The results are also consistent with zero tax capitalization for firms anticipating no material future repatriation tax liabilities (all groups, except TAX > 0). In other words, share prices reflect cross-sectional variation in repatriation marginal tax rates as captured by the measures of TAX. The market appears to interpret that firms other than TAX > 0 are able to extract their foreign affiliate profits through non-costly dividends or some other tax-planning device, and that firms reporting TAX > 0 have exhausted their options to extract foreign profits without incurring tax cost and thus must use costly dividend payments to transfer profits to the United States.

An important distinction between this study and other recent findings of tax capitalization (e.g., Harris, Hubbard, and Kemsley 2000; Auerbach and Hassett 1997) is that this study investigates future intrafirm transfers (i.e., from subsidiary to parent, rather than from parent to external shareholders). Because this study evaluates future transfers involving a single shareholder transferee (the parent), we are able to incorporate more precise measures of future dividend taxes into our tests than are studies examining tax capitalization of external shareholder taxes.

Finally, future studies should consider the robustness of these preliminary findings by, for example, examining years subsequent to 1993 and/or employing event studies to evaluate the share-price response around the public announcement of PRE and TAX. Event studies could provide more powerful tests of the valuations of PRE and TAX and the capitalization of TAX in share prices. Unfortunately, the release of PRE and TAX in the annual 10-K filing coincides with the disclosure of voluminous information. As a result, structuring expectations models for PRE and TAX and isolating their respective price effects will be challenging.

# Appendix

**Table 6A.1    List of Sample Companies across Tax-Liability Reporting Groups and by SIC**

| SIC | Description | Tax$ > 0 (n = 60) | Tax$ = 0 (n = 79) | Not Practicable (n = 89) | No Tax Info (n = 112) |
|---|---|---|---|---|---|
| 10 | Metal mining | | | | Placer Dome Inc. |
| 13 | Oil and gas | | Triton Energy Corp.<br>BJ Services | Tuboscope Vetco | Maxus Energy Corp.<br>Rowan Companies |
| 14 | Mining, nonmetal | Nord Resources | | | |
| 15 | Construction, building | Morrison Knudsen | | | |
| 16 | Construction, nonbuilding | Fluor Corporation<br>Jacobs Engineering | | | Guy F Atkinson Co. |
| 17 | Construction, special trade | | | | C H Heist Corp.<br>Insituform Mid America |
| 20 | Food products | Brown Forman<br>Coca Cola Company<br>Philip Morris<br>William Wrigley Jr. Co. | General Mills<br>Campbell Soup | Pepsico Inc.<br>Tootsie Roll Ind.<br>McCormick & Co.<br>Pilgrims Pride | H J Heinz Co. |
| 22 | Textile | Unifi Inc. | | Interface Inc. | Chemfab Corp.<br>Albany International |
| 23 | Apparel | Farah Inc. | | | Kellwood Co.<br>Stage II Apparel |
| 25 | Furniture | | BE Aerospace<br>Interlake Corp.<br>Johnson Controls | Herman Miller Inc. | |

| Code | Industry | | | | |
|---|---|---|---|---|---|
| 26 | Paper products | John Wiley & Sons | International Paper<br>James River Corp.<br>Sonoco Products | Bemis Inc.<br>Bowater Inc.<br>Champion International<br>Federal Paper Board<br>Minnesota Mining<br>Weyerhauser Co.<br>Westvaco Corp. | Avery Dennison Corp.<br>Boise Cascade<br>Riverwood International<br>Scott Paper Co. |
| 27 | Printing | McGraw-Hill<br>Paxar Corp. | | American Greetings | Filtertek Inc. |
| 28 | Chemicals | Vigoro Corp.<br>Lawter International<br>Monsanto<br>Pfizer Inc. | Armor All Products<br>Block Drug Inc.<br>Helene Curtis Ind.<br>Abbott Labs<br>Bairnco Corp.<br>Ecobal Inc.<br>International Flavors<br>Marion Merrell Dow<br>Rhone Poulenc Rorer<br>Rohm & Haas Co.<br>Smith International<br>Witco Corp. | Learonal<br>Allergan Inc.<br>B F Goodrich<br>Dow Chemical<br>E I DuPont<br>Guardsman Products<br>Life Technologies<br>P P G Industries<br>Schering Plough Corp.<br>Stepan Chemical<br>Union Carbide<br>W R Grace & Co.<br>H B Fuller Co. | I M C Fertilizer Group<br>Mallinckrodt Group<br>Proctor & Gamble Co.<br>N C H Corp.<br>Forest Laboratories<br>Macdermid Inc.<br>Aloette Cosmetics<br>Betz Laboratories<br>Bristol Myers Squibb<br>Ferro Corp.<br>F M C Corp.<br>Hercules Inc.<br>Sherwin Williams<br>Wellman Inc.<br>Lilly Industries<br>Air Products<br>Syntex Corp. |
| 29 | Petroleum | Amerada Hess Corp.<br>Ultramar Corp. | Exxon Corp.<br>Mobil Corp.<br>Unocal Corp. | Amoco Corp.<br>Chevron Corp.<br>Murphy Oil Corp. | |

(continued)

**Table 6A.1**   (continued)

| SIC | Description | Tax$ > 0 (n = 60) | Tax$ = 0 (n = 79) | Not Practicable (n = 89) | No Tax Info (n = 112) |
|---|---|---|---|---|---|
| 30 | Rubber | Nike Inc.<br>Furon Co.<br>Armstrong World Industries | Illinois Tool Works | Reebok International | First Brands Corp. |
| 31 | Leather | Brown Group | | | |
| 32 | Stone, clay, glass | Owens Corning | | Corning Inc.<br>Manville Corp. | Donnelly Corp.<br>A P Green Industries<br>Devcon International<br>Lafarge Corp. |
| 33 | Primary metals | | Engelhard Corp.<br>Phelps Dodge Corp. | Aluminum Company<br>Asarco Inc. | Alcan Aluminum<br>Reynolds Metals<br>Talley Industries |
| 34 | Fabricated metals | Blount Inc. | B M C Industries<br>Eljer Industries<br>Hexcel Corp.<br>S P S Technologies | Watts Industries | American Consumer Products<br>Crown Cork & Seal<br>Eastern Co.<br>Robertson Ceco Corp.<br>Wahlco Environmental |
| 35 | Machinery, excluding electronic | Seagate Technology<br>3Com Corp.<br>Compaq Computer Corp.<br>Data Switch Corp.<br>Selas Corp. America<br>Storage Technology<br>York International | Baldwin Technology<br>Flow International<br>Maxtor Corp.<br>Joy Technologies<br>Black & Decker<br>Cray Research<br>Industrial Acoustics | Telxon Corp.<br>Chipcom Corp.<br>Clark Equipment<br>Genicom Corp.<br>Graham Corp.<br>Hein Werner<br>IMO Industries | Manitowoc Inc.<br>Silicon Graphics<br>Adaptec Inc<br>Bantec Inc.<br>Cincinnati Milacron<br>Conner Peripherals<br>International Totalizator |

**36  Machinery, electrical**

National Semiconductor
Exide Corp.
Unitrode Corp.
Advanced Micro Devices
Bel Fuse Inc.
C T S Corp.
Tellabs Inc.

Raychem Corp.
Burr Brown Corp.
Genlyte Group
Maytag Corp.
Standard Motor Prod.
Tekelec
Thomas Industries
Time Warner Inc.

Salem Corp.
Thermedics Inc.
Unisys Corp.
Binks Manufacturing
Harnischfeger Ind.
Hewlett Packard
Nordson Corp.
Baker Hughes Inc.

Monarch Machine Tool
Nacco Industries
Network Systems
Raymond Corp.
S P X Corp.
Westinghouse Electric
Deere & Co.
Data General
Q M S Incorporated
Standex Int'l.
Duracell Int'l.
Harris Corp.
Intervoice Inc.
Brite Voice Systems
General Signal
Texas Instruments

Oilgear Co.
Premark International
Scotsman Industries
Sundstrand Corp.
Applied Materials
Dresser Industries
Kulick & Soffa Ind.
Moog Incorporated
Robbins & Myers
Datapoint Corp
Integrated Device Technology
Mitel Corporation
Plantronics Inc.
Knogo Corporation
Aydin Corporation
Checkpoint Systems
Communications System
D S C Communications
Franklin Electric
Vishay Intertechnology
Microsemi Corporation
Read Rite Corporation

**37  Transportation equipment**

A O Smith Corp.
Textron Inc.

Varity Corp.
Arvin Industries
Federal Mogul Corp.
United Technologies
Navistar International

Champion Parts
Chrysler Corporation

Augat Incorporated
I T T Corporation
McDonnell Douglas Corp.
Tenneco Incorporated
Walbro Corporation

(continued)

Table 6A.1    (continued)

| SIC | Description | Tax$ > 0 (n = 60) | Tax$ = 0 (n = 79) | Not Practicable (n = 89) | No Tax Info (n = 112) |
|---|---|---|---|---|---|
| 38 | Measurement instruments | U S Surgical Corp. | Dionex Corp.<br>Medex Inc.<br>Bio Rad Laboratories<br>Snap On Tools<br>St Jude Medical<br>Optical Coating | Concord Camera<br>Cordis Corp.<br>Biomet Inc.<br>Medtronic Inc.<br>Honeywell Inc.<br>Polaroid Corp.<br>Stryker Corp.<br>Becton Dickinson & Co. | Respironics Incorporated<br>Autoclave Engineers<br>Sci Med Life Systems<br>Badger Meter Inc.<br>Beckman Instruments<br>Mine Safety Appliances<br>Measurex Corporation<br>Daniel Industries<br>Litton Industries |
| 39 | Miscellaneous manufacturing | W M S Industries<br>A T Cross Co.<br>Tyco Toys<br>W H Brady Co. | Mattel Inc. | Dixon Ticonderoga | BIC Corporation<br>Hasbro Incorporated<br>Galoob Lewis Toys Inc. |
| 40 | Railroad | | | | |
| 44 | Water transportation | Tidewater Inc.<br>Overseas Shipholding Group | | C S X Corp. | Orient Express Hotels |
| 47 | Transportation services | | | | Air Express International<br>Expeditors International<br>Harper Group<br>A E S Corporation |
| 49 | Electric/gas service | | Thermo Process Systems | | |
| 50 | Durable goods (wholesale) | | Handleman Co. | Crane Company<br>Fisher Scientific | |
| 51 | Nondurable goods (wholesale) | Sigma Aldrich | International Multifoods | Standard Commercial Corp.<br>Enron Corp. | Terra Industries |

| Code | Industry | | | |
|---|---|---|---|---|
| 53 | General merchandise | Sears Roebuck & Co. | | Petrie Stores |
| 54 | Food stores | Great Atlantic & Pacific | | |
| 56 | Apparel and accessory stores | Woolworth Corp. | | |
| 58 | Eating and drinking places | | McDonalds Corp. | Sizzler International |
| 59 | Miscellaneous retail | Toys R US<br>Jan Bell Marketing | | Viking Office Products |
| 60 | Banking | | Advance Ross Corp. | |
| 61 | Credit agencies | American Express<br>Beneficial Corp. | H P S C Inc. | Household Int'l. |
| 62 | Securities and commodities | Merrill Lynch<br>Salomon Inc. | Bear Stearns | Franklin Resources |
| 63 | Insurance | | Intercargo Corp. | |
| 64 | Insurance agents | Arthur J Gallagher & Co. | Alexander & Alexander | |
| 72 | Personal services | | H & R Block Inc. | Crawford & Company<br>Service Corp International |
| 73 | Business services | Autodesk Inc. | Manpower Inc.<br>Continuum Inc.<br>Filenet Corp.<br>Nashua Corp.<br>Volt Information<br>Boole & Babbage<br>Comdisco Inc. | Blythe Holdings<br>B M C Software<br>Borland International<br>Enterra Corporation<br>Shared Medical Systems<br>Sothebys Holdings |
| 78 | Motion pictures | | Paramount Communications | |
| 80 | Health services | | | National Medical Enterprise |
| 82 | Educational services | | Berlitz Int'l. | |
| 87 | Engineering and management services | Dun & Bradstreet | Krug Int'l.<br>Ceridian Corp. | |

# References

Auerbach, A., and K. Hassett. 1997. On the marginal source of investment funds. University of California working paper.

Barth, M. 1991. Relative measurement errors among alternative pension asset and liability measures. *The Accounting Review* 66 (July): 433–63.

Barth, M., W. Beaver, and W. Landsman. 1998. Relative valuation roles of equity book value and net income as a function of financial health. *Journal of Accounting and Economics* 25:1–34.

Bodnar, G., and J. Weintrop. 1997. The valuation of the foreign income of U.S. multinational firms: A growth opportunities perspective. *Journal of Accounting and Economics* 24 (December): 69–97.

Collins, D. W., E. L. Maydew, and I. S. Weiss. 1997. Changes in the value-relevance of earnings and book values over the past forty years. *Journal of Accounting and Economics* 24 (December): 39–67.

Collins, J., D. Kemsley, and M. Lang. 1998. Cross-jurisdictional income shifting and earnings valuation. *Journal of Accounting Research* 36 (2): 209–30.

Francis, J., and K. Schipper. 1999. Have financial statements lost their relevance? *Journal of Accounting Research* 37 (Autumn): 319–53.

Harris, T., and D. Kemsley. 1999. Dividends and capital gains taxation in firm valuation: New evidence. *Journal of Accounting Research* 37 (Autumn): 275–91.

Harris, T., G. Hubbard, and D. Kemsley. 2000. The share price effects of dividend taxes and tax imputation credits. *Journal of Public Economics,* forthcoming.

Hartman, D. 1985. Tax policy and foreign direct investment. *Journal of Public Economics* 29:107–21.

Hines, J. R. 1996. Dividends and profits: Some unsubtle foreign influences. *Journal of Finance* 51 (June): 661–89.

Landsman, W. 1986. An empirical investigation of pension fund property rights. *Accounting Review* 61 (October): 662–91.

Ohlson, J. 1995. Earnings, book values, and dividends in security valuation. *Contemporary Accounting Research* (11):661–88.

White, H. 1980. A heteroskedasticity-consistent covariance matrix estimator and a direct test for heteroskedasticity. *Econometrica* 48:817–83.

## Comment    Kevin Hassett

In "Valuing Deferral: The Effect of Permanently Reinvested Foreign Earnings on Stock Prices," Professors Collins, Hand, and Shackelford have made a very important positive contribution to both the accounting and economics literatures. Their careful description of the accounting rules concerning both permanently reinvested earnings (PRE) and the concomitant taxes avoided provides researchers with valuable new insights into the behavior of firms. Those who teach graduate public finance will be remiss if they do not immediately add this paper to their reading lists, as the new ground broken provides ample opportunity for future research.

Kevin Hassett is a resident scholar at the American Enterprise Institute.

Although the new facts presented in this paper are an important first step, the empirical analysis falls a bit short for two reasons. First, valuation models of the type estimated are really reduced-form regressions that are virtually impossible to interpret; thus, the evidence concerning the relative importance of the new variables is difficult to interpret as well. Second, by keeping the focus that they have, the authors have fallen just short of providing priceless new evidence concerning one of the most important unresolved issues in the economics of the firm. The paper that the authors did not write (at least not yet) may be an even more important contribution. I will address each of these points in turn.

**What Does Their Reported Regression Mean?**

About the only thing that we learn from the regressions reported is that the PRE distinction is not simply a meaningless ploy—it does seem to have some effect on value. It would be wrong to conclude more than that, however, because it is essentially impossible to interpret the coefficients in table 6.5.

In an important theoretical paper, Ohlson (1995) provides justification for regressing the market value of the firm on net book value and net income. While this approach has been widely adopted in the accounting literature, I believe it is of little value because it does not provide coefficients that have any meaning when applied to actual data.

It is hard to figure what the book value measures are capturing, because economic and accounting depreciation are so different, and more importantly, because the units are all messed up. The market value measure is in current dollars, but the book value variables are in mish-mash dollars, depending on the timing of the relevant earnings and transactions. Because each firm has its own timing, each firm has its own flavor of mishmash, and identifying things off the cross-sectional variation in mish-mash seems overly optimistic.

Ignoring that problem, the net income measures are meant to capture the present value of profits. If they do, their coefficients should be something like $1/(r - g)$, where $r$ is the firm-specific discount rate and $g$ is the firm-specific profit growth rate. Because these coefficients must vary both within firms and across firms for different source income depending on potentially country-specific $r$'s and $g$'s, it is hard to interpret what we learn from pooled regressions. The more likely case, however, is that the relationship between these earnings and future outcomes is nonlinear in an unknown fashion, and that any other current variable included in the regression may matter in a linear equation simply because it helps approximate the firm's discount rate or future earnings better than do current earnings all by their lonesome selves. These forces are clearly important in this context, because the flow variable coefficients are only a little larger than the coefficients on stocks, when a sensible back-of-the-envelope expectation might be that the coefficient are ten times as large. Moreover, the difficulty of interpreting these reduced-form regressions is apparent in the dividend regression presented in n. 9. Because PRE is a signal that money is not coming home, higher PRE should lower current dividends. Since the regression shows the opposite, however, one can only conclude that there is much more going on, and that PRE signals something not elsewhere controlled for.

Aside from the problem of mixing stocks and flows, the timing of the variables in these regressions is also unusual, to say the least. As the discussion of the theory makes clear, announcements are the events that provide the useful distinguishing characteristics. Because the left-hand side variable is the end-of-year market price, and the right-hand side variables are the accounting things for that year, we have the peculiar case that the information in the explanatory variables postdates the information in the dependent variable, because the accounting information is released a number of months after the end of the year.

## How Does the Evidence Provided Relate to Different Views of Dividend Taxation?

The authors mention some implications of their results regarding the new and old views in their conclusion. This section fleshes this out a little more, and discusses how the work might be extended to provide potentially priceless new information concerning the effects of dividend taxation.

### A Quick Review of the New and Old Views

The alternative views of the impact of dividend taxation on the firm relate to different assumptions concerning the sources and uses of funds.[1] According to the "old view," firms use equity issues to finance investment and distribute a fixed fraction of the proceeds as dividends. Under this view, an extra dollar of retained earnings is worth $1 to the shareholder because it substitutes for marginal equity funds obtained through a new share issue. That is, according to the old view, $q$ is always equal to 1.

It is instructive to stop for a minute and think about the equilibrating mechanisms that keep $q$ at 1 under the old view. Suppose the dividend tax rate were lowered. Shouldn't the value of the firm go up? No—according to the old view, $q$ is always 1, and does not depend on dividend taxes. In response to lower dividend taxes—which might initially drive up the value of its shares—the firm issues new shares and spends the proceeds on new capital, driving down the marginal earnings flow from capital until lower

---

1. These issues were first treated by King (1977), Auerbach (1979), and Bradford (1981).

earnings have exactly offset the benefits of the dividend tax decrease. Dividend taxes do not change value because they do change investment.

Under the new view, retained earnings provide the marginal equity funds, so the opportunity cost to the shareholder of new investment is reduced by the dividend taxes foregone, net of the increased tax burden on the capital gains induced by the accrual; $q$ is equal to $(1 - \theta)/(1 - c)$, where $\theta$ is the dividend tax rate and $c$ is the accrual equivalent capital gains tax rate. Thus the market value of the firm will respond to changes in dividend taxes. On the other hand, the decision to invest, which at the margin is equivalent to the decision to pay a dividend now as opposed to paying it at some point in the future, is unaffected by the dividend tax, because the same present value of dividend taxes will be paid regardless of the timing of the payment. So long as the tax rates do not change over time, dividend taxes are capitalized into the value of the firm, but do not affect investment.

Thus, under the new view, there is *no* equivalent equilibrating mechanism that responds when the dividend tax changes. The market value of the firm changes when dividend taxes change precisely because investment does not.

### What Is the Existing Empirical Evidence Concerning the Two Views?

Casual observation suggests that the old view has been adopted by most researchers as a strong prior, perhaps because the new view at times has counterintuitive implications. Although the latest evidence provides some support for the new view, the jury clearly is still out. One of the key differences between the two theories that has been exploited by empirical researchers has been between the theories' predictions concerning the impact of dividend taxation on investment. Poterba and Summers (1985) provide evidence supportive of the old view. One problem with this test, however, is that it depends on empirical investment equations that have very poor properties, making the power of such tests questionable. Recent papers more supportive of the new view include Harris, Hubbard, and Kemsley (1997) and Auerbach and Hassett (1997).

In the international tax arena, Hartman (1985) restated the new-view hypothesis as requiring that repatriation taxes do not affect the timing of repatriations. Altshuler, Newlon, and Randolph (1995) provide evidence supportive of the Hartman hypothesis.

### How Do These Views Inform Our Thinking about PRE and TAX?

The authors have presented us with two new variables to think about: PRE, which is the proportion of cumulative foreign earnings that is described as permanently reinvested abroad, and TAX, which is the company's estimate of how much tax it would pay if the money were repatriated immediately.

How should the market value of the firm respond to PRE and TAX announcements? It depends crucially on which view holds. Under the new view, an announcement of higher PRE is equivalent to an announcement that dividends will be lowered today to finance new investment. Absent any signaling effects, this is only a dividend-timing announcement, and should have no effect on market value. In an event study that focuses on changes, the coefficient on TAX should be zero as well, because the tax information should already be impounded in price. In regressions such as those reported in the paper, TAX should be fully capitalized into the value of the firm, so it should have a coefficient of $-1$ in a cross-sectional regression.

Under the old view, the effect depends on whether we think old-view adjustments occur instantaneously or that they take some time. If they occur instantaneously, then $q$ is always 1, and none of these variables will have an effect.[2] Running through the equilibrating mechanism, however, and allowing for some delayed adjustment, gives a different story. An announcement that PRE will be higher is the same as an old-view firm's declaring that it will lower its dividend payout rate. When this happens, the shareholder is made better off if dividend taxes are higher than capital gains taxes. In this case, a lower payout rate has an effect analogous to that of a lower dividend tax rate: $q$ increases above 1; firms issue shares and invest and drive it back to 1. So, allowing for adjustment costs (or some other impediment to instant adjustment), the old view would predict that an announcement of higher PRE would correspond to an increase in market value. TAX is a measure of how much the firm is saving shareholders by its new policy, so the TAX variable should be *positively* correlated with value.

Thus, the two views provide opposing predictions, and a well-designed test could shed significant light on which view is more relevant to U.S. MNCs. The theory makes it clear that the differential effect of the PRE and TAX variables should be strongest when firms make announcements of changes to these variables. In the future, the authors should attempt to identify the dates of these announcements, and should perform a simple event-study description of market value changes surrounding these announcements. This test will likely be biased against the new view because plausible signaling stories may explain announcement effects that look like old-view responses. The bias should affect PRE more than TAX, however, and a clear look at the TAX coefficients controlling for PRE could be the most powerful test performed to date.

2. This might seem to be an extreme view, but Fischer Black, while discussing an investment paper I presented at a conference once, stated that he had no idea why anyone would want to run $q$-regressions because $q$ is always 1, and any variation in $q$ was clearly the result of incompetent measurement on the part of the researcher.

## Conclusion

While I question the value of the regressions presented in table 6.5, there is no question that this paper provides a very important contribution to the literature. In addition to providing an interesting perspective on the accounting practices of firms, the authors have provided invaluable new information that can likely be used in the future to shed light on one of the more important unresolved issues in empirical public finance.

## References

Altshuler, R., S. Newlon, and W. Randolph. 1995. Do repatriation taxes matter? Evidence from the tax returns of U.S. multinationals. In *The effects of taxation on multinational corporations,* ed. M. Feldstein, J. Hines, and G. Hubbard 253–72. Chicago: University of Chicago Press.

Auerbach, A. 1979. Share valuation and corporate equity policy. *Journal of Public Economics* 11 (3): 291–305.

Auerbach, A., and K. Hassett. 1997. On the marginal source of investment funds. University of California working paper.

Bradford, D. 1981. The incidence and allocation effects of a tax on corporate distributions. *Journal of Public Economics* 15 (1): 1–22.

Harris, T., G. Hubbard, and D. Kemsley. 1997. Are dividend taxes and tax imputation credits capitalized in share values? Columbia University School of Business working paper.

Hartman, D. 1985. Tax policy and foreign direct investment. *Journal of Public Economics* 26 (1): 107–21.

King, M. 1977. *Public policy and the corporation.* London: Chapman and Hall.

Ohlson, J. 1995. Earnings, book values, and dividends in security valuation. *Contemporary Accounting Research* 11 (2): 661–88.

Poterba, J., and L. Summers. 1985. The economic effects of dividend taxation. In *Recent advances in corporate finance,* ed. E. Altman and M. Subrahmanyam, 227–84. Homewood, Ill.: Richard D. Irwin.

# 7

# The Impact of Transfer Pricing on Intrafirm Trade

Kimberly A. Clausing

## 7.1 Introduction

Multinational companies play a very large role in international trade. Not only is there a substantial amount of arm's-length trade between MNCs and unaffiliated buyers, but trade within MNCs is also quite considerable. For instance, in 1994, this intrafirm trade accounted for approximately 36 percent of U.S. exports and 43 percent of U.S. imports. These fractions vary somewhat from year to year, but intrafirm trade has been a similarly large share of international trade since 1977.[1]

Recently, researchers have devoted some attention to examining how intrafirm trade may be different from arm's-length trade.[2] One essential reason intrafirm trade may differ from nonintrafirm trade results from the fact that MNCs may alter their transactions in order to minimize worldwide tax burdens. It has long been recognized, for example, that firms may employ transfer pricing techniques that allow them to shift profits to low-tax locations, thus lowering their overall tax burdens. The empirical evidence indicates that such motivations are not just a theoretical possibility.

Using data on the operations of U.S. parent companies and their foreign affiliates, this paper examines the extent to which tax-minimizing behavior

Kimberly A. Clausing is assistant professor of economics at Reed College.

The author is grateful to James Hines, Deen Kemsley, Joel Slemrod, and other conference participants for many helpful comments.

1. The earliest year for which comparable data are available is 1977. See Zeile (1997) for additional information regarding trends in intrafirm trade.

2. For example, Rangan and Lawrence (1999) examine the response of U.S. MNCs to exchange rate fluctuations. In addition, a large literature (Blomström, Lipsey, and Kulchycky 1988; Lipsey and Weiss 1981, 1984; Grubert and Mutti 1991; Clausing 2000; etc.) considers the relationship between trade and multinational activity.

influences intrafirm trade patterns. The results indicate that taxes have a substantial influence on intrafirm trade flows. First, controlling for other factors that are likely to influence intrafirm trade balances, the data indicate that the United States has less favorable intrafirm trade balances with low-tax countries. This result is anticipated if U.S. sales to affiliates in low-tax countries are underpriced and U.S. purchases from affiliates in low-tax countries are overpriced. Second, additional evidence indicates that trade between U.S. affiliates in different foreign countries is also likely influenced by tax considerations. Sales by affiliates based in low-tax countries are greater than one would otherwise expect relative to sales by affiliates based in high-tax countries.

These results have several interesting implications. First, they indicate an important way in which intrafirm trade flows may indeed be different from international trade conducted at arm's length. Intrafirm trade flows are influenced by the tax minimization strategies of MNCs. Second, the results add evidence that transfer prices are influenced by tax considerations. Much of the previous literature has considered this question by focusing on firm profitabilities or tax liabilities; this paper shows how the actual transactions between countries are affected by transfer pricing strategies.

Section 7.2 will discuss the relationship between the tax minimization strategies of MNCs and intrafirm trade. It will review the previous theoretical and empirical literature in this area, and generate a simple model that demonstrates the relationship between taxes and intrafirm trade. Section 7.3 will consider the data on intrafirm trade between U.S. parents and their affiliates abroad, examining specifications that relate such intrafirm trade to the tax rates faced by affiliates in different countries. Section 7.4 considers the data on intrafirm trade between different foreign affiliates of U.S. firms, examining both the impact of transfer pricing on intrafirm trade and the potential impact of the subpart F provisions of U.S. tax law on intrafirm trade. Section 7.5 concludes.

## 7.2    The Impact of Tax Minimization Strategies on Intrafirm Trade

Multinational firms can typically lower their overall tax burdens by shifting profits toward low-tax countries and away from high-tax countries. Horst (1971) generated a simple model that shows how MNCs choose transfer prices in order to maximize their after-tax earnings. The model analyzes the choices of a monopolistic firm selling in two countries simultaneously. The firm's earnings are equal to its after-tax profits in the two countries plus a term that shows the impact of intrafirm trade. This generates a situation in which a firm chooses either the lowest or highest transfer price possible, depending on a comparison of the relative differential in tax rates between the importing and exporting countries with the tariff rate.

Eden (1985) and Diewert (1985) have demonstrated that such transfer pricing can affect intrafirm trade. Kant (1990, 1995) has elaborated on these insights, considering the likely impact of transfer pricing on intrafirm trade and government revenues. The 1990 model incorporates transfer pricing penalties and partial ownership. Transfer pricing penalties imply that there is a trade-off between the optimal transfer price and the probability of a penalty, leading to a solution in which the price is set closer to the arm's-length price than would be optimal from a profit perspective. Partial ownership implies that firms may be encouraged to shift profits home, ceteris paribus, because firms may own only a part of affiliates. Kant (1995) broadens the model to consider the impact of deferral of non-repatriated foreign profits on intrafirm trade, and finds that both deferral and partial ownership can lead to situations in which intrafirm trade is perverse, such that intrafirm exports originate in the country with the higher marginal cost.

Many empirical studies (such as Lall 1973; Jenkins and Wright 1975; Kopits 1976; Bernard and Weiner 1990; Grubert and Mutti 1991; Harris, Morck, Slemrod, and Yeung 1993; Hines and Rice 1994; and Collins, Kemsley, and Lang 1996) have estimated the magnitude of tax-induced transfer pricing. Due to data limitations, the evidence is necessarily indirect, but most studies indicate that transfer prices are likely to be influenced by tax considerations. Many studies focus on the profitability of affiliates in different countries. Jenkins and Wright (1975) examine the profitability of U.S. oil companies, finding that affiliates in low–tax rate countries are more profitable. Grubert and Mutti (1991) find that high taxes reduce after-tax profitabilities of local operations. Hines and Rice (1994) find even larger effects, suggesting that 1 percent tax rate differences are associated with 2.3 percent differences in before-tax profitability.

Collins, Kemsley, and Lang (1996) study the relationship between profit margins of U.S. MNCs and foreign tax rates, finding evidence of tax-motivated income shifting, particularly income shifting into the United States from high-tax countries. Harris et al. (1993) consider U.S. tax liabilities, finding that U.S. MNCs with tax haven affiliates have significantly lower tax liabilities than would otherwise be expected. Finally, Kemsley (1997) finds a positive relationship between a firm's propensity to serve (unaffiliated) customers by exporting (relative to foreign production) and the foreign tax rate, due to special export tax rules (IRC § 863[b]) that raise the tax incentive favoring exports.

If U.S. MNCs manipulate transfer prices in order to minimize worldwide tax burdens, then one may expect a country's tax rate to have an influence on the magnitudes of intrafirm trade flows between the United States and that country. For example, one method for shifting profits between countries is to underprice goods sold *to* affiliates in low-tax countries and overprice goods sold *by* affiliates in low-tax countries, following the opposite pattern for transactions with affiliates in high-tax countries. Such a strategy would suggest that intrafirm trade flows to (from) low-tax country affiliates should be low (high) relative to intrafirm trade flows to (from) high-tax country affiliates, ceteris paribus. On net, these tax considerations imply that U.S. intrafirm trade balances should be more favorable with high-tax countries than with low-tax countries.

Following Horst (1971) and Kant (1995), one can produce a simple model that generates this prediction. Consider an MNC with some degree of market power that is operating in two countries. It produces and sells in each country, and also exports part of its output from the home country (1) to the affiliate abroad (2).[3] For now, assume that the affiliate is fully owned.[4]

Profit functions for operations in the two countries are given by the following equations:

$$(1) \qquad \pi_1 = R_1(s_1) - C_1(s_1 + m) + pm,$$

$$(2) \qquad \pi_2 = R_2(s_2) - C_2(s_2 - m) - pm,$$

where $\pi_1$ is profit in the home country, which depends on revenues $R_1$ that are a function of sales $(s_1)$ and costs $(C_1)$ that are a function of production. Production includes both those goods sold at home and those sent to the affiliate abroad $(m)$. The output that is exported to the affiliates abroad is given the transfer price $p$.

Consider the case in which tax rates at home are greater than tax rates abroad $(t_1 > t_2)$ and deferral is allowed. Let $f$ represent the fraction of profits that are repatriated. The effective tax rate $(t^e)$ on income earned in the affiliate country is then

$$(3) \qquad t_2^e = t_2 + (t_1 - t_2)f.$$

The net profit function for the firm's global operations is

$$(4) \qquad \pi = (1 - t_1)\pi_1 + (1 - t_2^e)\pi_2.$$

To illustrate how the firm may choose a transfer price in order to maximize these net profits, consider the derivative of equation (4) with respect to the transfer price $p$.

$$(5) \qquad \pi_p = (1 - t_1)m - (1 - t_2^e)m$$

---

3. It is straightforward to extend this model to consider trade that originates in the affiliate country. One can also consider this trade to be in intermediate products without affecting the basic insights developed here.

4. The implications of relaxing this assumption are considered in Kant (1995) and briefly discussed later.

Substituting for $t_2^c$ using equation (3) and rearranging,

$$(6) \qquad \pi_p = -(t_1 - t_2)(1 - f)m.$$

So, if $t_1 > t_2$, the previous expression is negative, and the firm's net profits decrease with the transfer price. Thus, firms have an incentive to underprice goods sold to low-tax countries in order to shift profits to low-tax locations. Similarly, one can show that firms have an incentive to overprice goods sold to high-tax affiliates when $t_2 > t_1$.[5]

This analysis implies that firms will want to charge the lowest transfer price possible when $t_1 > t_2$. As Kant (1990) reminds us, however, two considerations may interfere with this motivation. First of all, a firm may be subject to penalties if its manipulation of transfer prices is too flagrant. If the probability of receiving a penalty increases as the transfer price is further from the arm's-length price, the firm will likely choose a transfer price that balances the gain from profit shifting with the possibility of a penalty.[6] Second, affiliates may not be wholly owned. This creates a second profit-shifting incentive, as a firm may choose to overprice shipments to affiliates to transfer profits to sources that are wholly owned and away from partially owned sources.[7]

The tax minimization incentives demonstrated previously generate similar predictions regarding intrafirm trade among different foreign affiliates of U.S. firms. One would expect, ceteris paribus, affiliates from low-tax countries to have higher sales to other foreign affiliates than do affiliates from high-tax countries. However, the incentives here are slightly more complicated. Under the subpart F provisions of U.S. tax law, U.S. firms are not eligible to defer taxation on unrepatriated foreign income that is derived from sales of goods between related parties where the goods are both manufactured outside the base country and sold for use outside the base country.[8] Basically, this provision implies that trade between foreign affiliates will be discouraged *if* such trade generates subpart F income and *if* affiliates find deferral a clear advantage. Affiliates that are located in low-tax countries are more likely to find deferral advantageous, ceteris paribus. Thus, subpart F acts as a second effect on trade between different foreign affiliates of U.S. firms that may act to offset the profit-shifting incentives discussed previously.

---

5. Note that these models implicitly assume that there is only one transfer price $p$; that is, firms keep just one set of books. Firms in reality may keep more than one set of books, using one set of prices to minimize tax liabilities and other sets of prices for other purposes, such as determining the relative performance of affiliates.

6. This consideration alters the degree of transfer price manipulation, but would not alter the desired direction of underpricing or overpricing.

7. While this consideration may influence the desired direction of transfer price changes, it also assumes that firms are free to manipulate transfer prices without the need to be responsive to the profits of their minority interests.

8. See Rapakko (1990) for a detailed description of these provisions.

### 7.3   Intrafirm Trade between U.S. Parents and Affiliates

Using data on intrafirm trade flows from the Bureau of Economic Analysis (BEA) surveys of U.S. direct investment abroad, this paper attempts to clarify the impact of tax-minimizing behavior on intrafirm trade flows. The analysis employs country-level data, because tax rates vary primarily by country (rather than by industry). It is possible to consider these relationships both across countries and over time because BEA surveys are available on an annual basis between 1982 and 1994. In this section, the analysis will focus on intrafirm trade flows between U.S. parents and their affiliates abroad, as illustrated in figure 7.1. In the following section, the analysis will turn to intrafirm trade between different foreign affiliates of U.S. firms.

The basic specification explains intrafirm trade flows as a function of tax rates and other exogenous variables that are likely to affect trade flows.

$$\text{Intrafirm Trade Balance}_{it} = \alpha + \beta_1 \text{Effective Tax Rate}_{it}$$
$$+ \beta_2 \text{Real Exchange Rate}_{it}$$
$$+ \beta_3 \text{Income Growth}_{it} + \beta_4 \text{ShareWh}_{it}$$
$$+ \beta_5 \text{ShareM}_{it} + \beta_6 \text{Trade Balance}_{it}$$
$$+ \beta_7 \text{Unaffiliated Trade Balance}_{it} + e_{it}$$

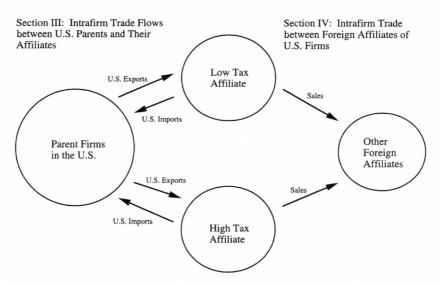

Section III:  Intrafirm Trade Flows between U.S. Parents and Their Affiliates

Section IV:  Intrafirm Trade between Foreign Affiliates of U.S. Firms

Low Tax Affiliate

U.S. Exports

U.S. Imports

Parent Firms in the U.S.

Other Foreign Affiliates

Sales

U.S. Exports

U.S. Imports

High Tax Affiliate

Sales

**Fig. 7.1   Two approaches to analyzing the relationship between transfer pricing and intrafirm trade**

**Table 7.1**          **Summary Statistics**

| Variable | $N$ | Mean | Standard Deviation |
|---|---|---|---|
| Intrafirm trade balance | 524 | .2627 | .4843 |
| Effective tax rate | 651 | .3450 | .2231 |
| Real exchange rate | 612 | 133.1 | 47.75 |
| Income growth | 605 | 3.395 | 4.091 |
| Share of sales in wholesale trade | 583 | .1976 | .1479 |
| Share of sales in manufacturing | 629 | .3841 | .2481 |
| Overall trade balance | 635 | −.0649 | .3200 |
| Unaffiliated trade balance | 561 | .2932 | .5291 |
| Sales to affiliates in other foreign countries | 589 | 2,530 | 5,149 |
| Sales to nonaffiliates in other foreign countries | 595 | 2,292 | 4,317 |
| Total sales | 651 | 19,171 | 35,543 |

*Note:* The data cover the period 1982–94. Fifty-eight countries are included. Each observation represents one country ($i$) and one year ($t$). "Intrafirm trade balance" is the amount of U.S. exports sent from parent firms to U.S. affiliates in country $i$ minus the amount of U.S. imports sent from U.S. affiliates in country $i$ to U.S. parents, relative to the total amount of trade between U.S. parents and their affiliates in country $i$. "Effective tax rate" is foreign income taxes paid relative to income. "Real exchange rate" is an index where 1980 = 100, calculated using nominal exchange rates and price indexes in the United States and country $i$. "Income growth" is the growth in real GDP for country $i$ in year $t$. "Share of sales in wholesale trade/manufacturing" are shares of total sales that are in wholesale trade/manufacturing. "Overall trade balance" is total U.S. exports to country $i$ minus total U.S. imports from country $i$, relative to total trade between the United States and country $i$ (excluding intrafirm trade between parents and affiliates in country $i$). "Unaffiliated trade balance" is U.S. exports by unaffiliated persons to affiliates in country $i$ minus U.S. imports sent from U.S. affiliates in country $i$ to unaffiliated persons in the United States, relative to the total trade between unaffiliated persons in the United States and affiliates in country $i$. "Sales to affiliates in other foreign countries" are sales by affiliates in country $i$ to affiliates in other foreign countries. "Sales to nonaffiliates in other foreign countries" are sales by affiliates in country $i$ to unaffiliated persons in other foreign countries. "Total sales" are the total sales in all locations by affiliates in country $i$. Real exchange rate and income growth data come from the International Monetary Fund's *International Financial Statistics* yearbooks. Overall trade data come from the U.S. International Trade Commission. All other data come from the Bureau of Economic Analysis annual surveys of *U.S. Direct Investment Abroad.*

Table 7.1 defines and summarizes the variables used in the analysis. The dependent variable is the intrafirm trade balance between the United States and the country hosting U.S. affiliates. The intrafirm trade balance is the amount of U.S. exports sent from parent firms to their affiliates abroad minus the amount of U.S. imports sent from affiliates to U.S. parents, relative to the total amount of trade between the U.S. parents and affiliates.

The tax rate variable used is an effective tax rate (ETR): foreign income taxes paid relative to income. Although using marginal tax rates is a theoretically superior alternative, the published marginal tax rates are an imperfect proxy for the actual tax rates firms face, because such rates do not account for the many subtleties (tax holidays, ad hoc arrangements, etc.) that determine the true tax treatment of firms.[9]

This basic specification offers a starting point for examining the influence of taxes on trade patterns between the United States and host countries. If host-country taxes are low, and firms systematically employ transfer pricing to shift profits to low-tax countries, one would expect U.S. intrafirm trade balances to be less favorable with such countries because intrafirm exports from the United States are underpriced and intrafirm imports into the United States are overpriced. Thus, if taxes affect trade patterns in the manner previously hypothesized, the expected sign of $\beta_1$ is positive.

The specification also includes other variables that are likely to affect intrafirm trade flows. These variables fall into three categories. First of all, I include two variables that reflect bilateral economic conditions: (1) the strength of the dollar relative to the affiliate country currency, measured by the real exchange rate between the two countries, and (2) the income growth of the affiliate country—one expects the United States to have more favorable trade balances when income growth abroad is relatively strong.[10]

In the second category, I include variables that reflect the character of affiliate operations in the host country. Countries where affiliate activities are primarily concentrated in wholesale trade may have substantially different trade patterns with the United States than do countries where affiliate activities are concentrated in manufacturing, finance, petroleum, or service industries. $ShareWh_{it}$ is the share of affiliate sales in country $i$ (and year $t$) that are in the wholesale trade industry; $ShareM_{it}$ is the share of affiliate sales that are in manufacturing industries. Dummy variables are also included in some specifications for countries that may have unique intrafirm trade relationships.[11]

In the third category I include other types of trade balances between the United States and the country in question. I include the total (excluding intrafirm trade) trade balance between the two countries, as a possible control for other factors that may influence the pattern of trade between the two countries. I also include the trade balance between affiliates abroad and nonaffiliated persons in the United States, as a possible control for characteristics of affiliates that may influence their trade with the United States.

Results are shown in table 7.2. The basic specification just described is

9. In addition, the average tax rates for this sample (of fifty-eight countries and thirteen years) are more readily available.

10. Most empirical studies of trade flows have utilized such variables because there are strong theoretical rationales for including them; see Deardorff (1998).

11. I include dummies for Japan and for the European countries as a group in some specifications.

Table 7.2        **Dependent Variable: Intrafirm Trade Balance**

| Independent Variables | (1) | (2) | (3) |
|---|---|---|---|
| Effective tax rate | .4353 | .5179 | .4226 |
| | (.0956) | (.0967) | (.1090) |
| Real exchange rate | .0013 | .0009 | .0011 |
| | (.0004) | (.0004) | (.0004) |
| Income growth | −.0058 | −.0090 | −.0095 |
| | (.0046) | (.0047) | (.0050) |
| Share of sales in wholesale trade | 1.179 | 1.506 | 1.236 |
| | (0.154) | (.141) | (0.167) |
| Share of sales in manufacturing | .1913 | .2496 | .2892 |
| | (.0830) | (.0832) | (.0873) |
| Overall trade balance | .8607 | .8367 | .8999 |
| | (.0644) | (.0649) | (.0685) |
| Unaffiliated trade balance | .0231 | .0566 | −.0201 |
| | (.0346) | (.0349) | (.0363) |
| European country dummy | .1660 | | .1445 |
| | (.0400) | | (.0416) |
| Japan dummy | .4292 | | .4385 |
| | (.1071) | | (.1060) |
| Constant | −.3580 | −.3548 | −.3392 |
| | (.0884) | (.0909) | (.0965) |
| $N$ | 449 | 449 | 397 |
| Adjusted $R^2$ | .425 | .392 | .447 |

*Note:* Standard errors are in parentheses. Columns (1) and (2) include all country/year pairs for which data are available. Column (3) excludes those countries defined as tax havens, where the effective tax rate is less than 10 percent. For variable definitions refer to table 7.1 note.

column (1). The coefficient on the effective tax rate variable indicates that an effective tax rate in the affiliate country 10 percentage points higher is associated with an intrafirm trade balance relative to country $i$ that is 4.4 percentage points greater. The fitted values from these regression results imply that the United States would have an intrafirm trade balance of 0.26 with a country that had an effective tax rate at the mean (0.33). Holding the other variables constant, the results suggest that the intrafirm trade balance with a country with an effective tax rate in the 10th percentile would be 0.14, whereas the intrafirm trade balance with a country with an effective tax rate in the 90th percentile would be 0.39.

Most of the other coefficients in the regression were approximately as expected. The real exchange rate coefficient indicates that as the dollar is stronger, intrafirm trade balances improve.[12] This contradicts one's expec-

12. When exchange rate lags were included, they were not statistically significant, nor did they improve the fit of the regression or noticeably change the other coefficients of interest. Therefore, they are not included for the results presented here.

tation that the U.S. trade balances should be more favorable when the dollar is depreciated. On the other hand, if intrafirm trade quantities are relatively fixed or slow to change, than intrafirm trade balances may actually improve in dollar terms when the dollar is appreciated, due to J-curve–type effects. Income growth abroad does not have a statistically discernible impact on intrafirm trade balances.

Both the share of sales in wholesale trade and the share of sales in manufacturing are positively associated with intrafirm trade balances, with the share of sales in wholesale trade having a particularly large effect. For instance, if affiliates in country $i$ have a 10 percent higher share of their total sales in wholesale trade, one can expect the United States to have intrafirm trade balances with country $i$ that are 12 percentage points greater. The United States tends to have more favorable intrafirm trade balances with European countries and Japan. Column (2) shows the same specification as column (1), excluding these dummy variables. This specification indicates that the inclusion of these variables does not affect most other coefficients in a statistically discernible fashion.

There is a strong and statistically significant positive relationship between the U.S. overall trade balance (excluding intrafirm trade) with a country and the intrafirm trade balance. This is perhaps due to common country-specific factors that affect both types of trade balances, including the relative savings/investment balance in the two countries.[13] The relationship between the intrafirm trade balance and the trade balance between affiliates in country $i$ and unaffiliated U.S. persons is not statistically significant.

Column (3) tests the basic specification, excluding countries that are defined as tax havens. For simplicity, I define tax havens to be those countries where the effective tax rate is less than 10 percent.[14] The results from this specification indicate that the tax effects shown are not dependent solely on those countries in the sample with the lowest tax rates.

However, it is the case that the tax sensitivity of intrafirm trade is driven by those countries in the sample whose effective tax rates are less than the U.S. tax rate. In particular, if one divides the sample into two groups of observations based on whether the effective tax rate is lower or higher than the U.S. marginal tax rate, one finds that the relationship between taxes and intrafirm trade is much more dramatic for the low-tax group. Results are shown in table 7.3.[15]

13. Countries that save more than they invest run global trade surpluses, whereas those that invest more than they save run deficits. These global deficits and surpluses are likely to influence levels of bilateral deficits and surpluses.

14. This definition follows that of Grubert and Mutti (1996).

15. One can also break down the sample to see if the tax effects remain the same for rich and poor countries. I broke down the sample into high-income countries (those with per capita incomes greater than $9,000) and other countries. The coefficients on the effective tax variable were statistically indistinguishable from each other in the two regressions.

I also tried specifications that looked at an inverse tax rate (equal to $1/(.1 + ETR)$, follow-

**Table 7.3**                **Dependent Variable: Intrafirm Trade Balance**

| Independent Variables | ETR < U.S. Rate (1) | ETR > U.S. Rate (2) |
|---|---|---|
| Effective tax rate | .8772 | −.0230 |
|  | (.1770) | (.2005) |
| Real exchange rate | .0028 | .0003 |
|  | (.0004) | (.0005) |
| Income growth | −.0027 | −.0049 |
|  | (.0053) | (.0076) |
| Share of sales in wholesale trade | .7163 | 1.657 |
|  | (.1849) | (.2758) |
| Share of sales in manufacturing | −.2042 | .2920 |
|  | (.1148) | (.1161) |
| Overall trade balance | .5776 | 1.107 |
|  | (.0762) | (.1068) |
| Unaffiliated trade balance | .0472 | −.1030 |
|  | (.0413) | (.0532) |
| European country dummy | .2689 | .0374 |
|  | (.0482) | (.0689) |
| Japan dummy |  | .4213 |
|  |  | (.1175) |
| Constant | −.4606 | −.0112 |
|  | (.1068) | (.1596) |
| N | 279 | 170 |
| Adjusted $R^2$ | .474 | .570 |

*Note:* Standard errors are in parentheses. The sample is divided into two subsets based on a comparison of the average effective tax rate (ETR) with the U.S. marginal tax rate. For variable definitions refer to table 7.1 note.

One advantage of considering these specifications in the context of a panel data set is that this allows a closer inspection of the influence of taxes on intrafirm trade both across countries and over time. It is also easier to consider how the relationships shown in the regressions of table 7.2 change due to particular events. One very important change that occurred during this time period was the Tax Reform Act of 1986 (TRA 1986). Many important changes in tax law affected MNCs at this time; perhaps the most important, TRA 1986 reduced the marginal corporate income tax rate from 46 to 34 percent. As Grubert, Randolph, and Rousslang (1996) point out, this was likely to increase the number of firms in excess credit position, giving firms a greater incentive to lower foreign taxes. These types of effects would indicate more income-shifting activity after 1986. However, Grubert, Randolph, and Rousslang note that the share of firms with excess credits did not increase post-1986. This could

ing Grubert and Mutti 1996) to test the hypothesis that there may be magnified sensitivity to low tax rates. In my specifications, however, I did not find that this variable improved the explanatory power of the regression, nor did it appear to be more statistically significant than the more conventional tax variable.

have been due to income shifting itself, but was also likely due to the fact that average foreign tax rates were falling during this time period, suggesting that there would be decreased incentives for income shifting.

Table 7.4 breaks down the sample into two time periods before and after TRA 1986. Although the 95 percent confidence interval for the effective tax rate variable coefficient overlaps, the point estimate for this coefficient is much higher in the earlier subperiod. This result may be due to the lesser dispersion of effective tax rates across countries in the later subperiod. In particular, the variation of the effective tax rate variable is smaller during the later time period. The mean of this variable is closer to the U.S. marginal tax rate during the later period as well.

Finally, the greater number of observations available using a panel of data improves the degrees of freedom, enabling more precise estimates of the coefficients. One might question, however, whether the overall tax effects are still discernible in individual cross sections. Table 7.5 shows estimates of the coefficients on the effective tax rate variable for the individual cross sections between 1982 and 1994. Of the thirteen years of cross sections, twelve of the coefficients on the effective tax rate variable are positive. Although only one of the coefficients is statistically significant at

**Table 7.4**    **Dependent Variable: Intrafirm Trade Balance**

| Independent Variables | 1986 and Before (1) | After 1986 (2) |
|---|---|---|
| Effective tax rate | .6977 | .3031 |
| | (.1652) | (.1204) |
| Real exchange rate | .0016 | .0007 |
| | (.0007) | (.0004) |
| Income growth | .0080 | −.0144 |
| | (.0074) | (.0059) |
| Share of sales in wholesale trade | 1.872 | .9053 |
| | (.0301) | (.1823) |
| Share of sales in manufacturing | .5378 | −.0103 |
| | (.1380) | (.1055) |
| Overall trade balance | .7945 | .8601 |
| | (.1122) | (.0813) |
| Unaffiliated trade balance | .0260 | .0431 |
| | (.0683) | (.0404) |
| European country dummy | .1365 | .1395 |
| | (.0661) | (.0507) |
| Japan dummy | .2841 | .4662 |
| | (.1714) | (.1357) |
| Constant | −.7863 | −.0762 |
| | (.1492) | (.1141) |
| $N$ | 157 | 292 |
| Adjusted $R^2$ | .501 | .408 |

*Note:* Standard errors are in parentheses. For variable definitions refer to table 7.1 note.

Table 7.5    **Tax Coefficient Estimates for Cross Sections, 1982–1994**

| Year | Coefficient on ETR | Significance Level (%) |
|------|--------------------|------------------------|
| 1982 | .6213 (.2897) | 87 |
| 1983 | .2059 (.5754) | 27 |
| 1984 | .8270 (.4903) | 89 |
| 1985 | .8558 (.4407) | 93 |
| 1986 | .9180 (.5760) | 87 |
| 1987 | .7900 (.4082) | 93 |
| 1988 | 1.118 (.380) | 99 |
| 1989 | .3835 (.2953) | 79 |
| 1990 | .5680 (.3322) | 90 |
| 1991 | .2469 (.5681) | 33 |
| 1992 | .4308 (.3193) | 81 |
| 1993 | −.0324 (.3305) | 7 |
| 1994 | .4276 (.3984) | 71 |

*Note:* The dependent variable is intrafirm trade balance. Standard errors are in parentheses.

a 95 percent confidence level, ten are statistically positive with greater than 70 percent confidence. These ten coefficients are estimated between 0.38 and 1.1, implying tax effects of a similar magnitude to those found in the panel regression.

## 7.4  Intrafirm Trade between Foreign Affiliates of U.S. Firms

Analyzing intrafirm trade patterns between different foreign affiliates of U.S. firms may be more complicated due to the combined influence of two effects: the incentive to shift profits to low-tax countries, and the incentive to avoid subpart F income in low-tax countries. Because the available trade data do not distinguish between the type of trade that triggers subpart F income and other trade, the influence of tax-minimizing incentives on intrafirm trade between foreign affiliates may be more difficult to isolate.

I consider a specification that explains sales from affiliates in a given host country to other foreign affiliates as a function of tax rates and other variables that are likely to affect these trade flows.

Sales to Affiliates in Other Countries$_{it}$

$$= \alpha + \beta_1 \text{Effective Tax Rate}_{it}$$

$$+ \beta_2 \text{Real Exchange Rate}_{it}$$

$$+ \beta_3 \text{ShareWh}_{it} + \beta_4 \text{ShareM}_{it} + \beta_5 \text{Sales}_{it}$$

$$+ \beta_6 \text{Sales to Nonaffiliates in Other Countries}_{it} + e_{it}$$

The dependent variable is the sales of affiliates in country $i$ (during year $t$) to affiliates in other foreign countries. This variable is no longer a trade balance because we do not have data on purchases of affiliates of a given host country from other foreign affiliates. (See fig. 7.1 for an illustration.) In addition, the data used are sales data rather than trade flows.[16] These data differ from trade data in several respects, the most important of which is that sales data include services as well as goods.[17]

In this regression, if income-shifting effects predominate, we would expect the coefficient $\beta_1$ to be negative, indicating that affiliates based in low-tax countries overprice their sales to affiliates in other countries in order to shift income to low-tax locations. If subpart F provisions are very important, on the other hand, one might expect sales to other foreign affiliates to be lower for affiliates based in low-tax countries because such affiliates would want to avoid generating subpart F income.

Many of the independent variables are defined as in the previous analysis. A few changes are noteworthy, however. First, it is no longer meaningful to include a variable measuring economic growth in country $i$ because we are trying to explain sales to foreign countries other than country $i$.[18] Second, the control variables are defined to be analogous to the dependent variable. In particular, total sales by affiliates in country $i$ (minus sales to other foreign affiliates) are included to proxy for influences that increase overall sales by affiliates in a given country. Sales to nonaffiliates in other

---

16. Trade data are not available. Also, trade data are calculated on a shipped basis, which usually requires firms to use shipping department invoices rather than accounting data.

17. One can take a similar approach to the previous specifications too, of course, in which case one would be explaining sales from affiliates in country $i$ to U.S. parents as a function of the standard independent variables, in addition to total sales by affiliates in country $i$ and sales by affiliates in country $i$ to nonaffiliates in the United States. Results from such a specification are shown in appendix table 7A.1. A tax rate 1 percentage point higher is associated with 0.36 percentage points fewer sales to the parent. (The elasticity of parent sales with respect to $(1 - \text{ETR})$ is 0.72; at the mean taxes/income ratio, this corresponds to an elasticity with respect to the ETR of $-0.36$.)

18. Dummy variables continue to be appropriate. For example, affiliates in European countries may be particularly likely to sell to affiliates in other countries due to their close geographical proximity to other European countries.

**Table 7.6**                 **Dependent Variable: Sales to Affiliates in Other Foreign Countries**

| Independent Variables | (1) | (2) | (3) |
|---|---|---|---|
| 1 − effective tax rate | 1.648 | .8934 | 1.870 |
| | (.286) | (.2987) | (.316) |
| Real exchange rate | −.0432 | −.1374 | .0704 |
| | (.1464) | (.1574) | (.1484) |
| 1 − share of sales in wholesale trade | .1859 | −1.608 | .4159 |
| | (.4268) | (.414) | (.4675) |
| 1 − share of sales in manufacturing | −1.507 | −2.185 | −1.353 |
| | (.259) | (.263) | (.278) |
| Total sales | .4569 | .3617 | .4374 |
| | (.0654) | (.0667) | (.0683) |
| Sales to nonaffiliates in other foreign countries | .4606 | .6403 | .4484 |
| | (.0507) | (.0480) | (.0526) |
| European country dummy | 1.126 | | 1.192 |
| | (.307) | | (.130) |
| Japan dummy | 1.286 | | 1.423 |
| | (.307) | | (.306) |
| Year | .0207 | .0119 | .0247 |
| | (.0126) | (.0137) | (.0130) |
| Constant | −2.288 | −2.288 | −3.268 |
| | (1.419) | (1.541) | (1.463) |
| $N$ | 480 | 480 | 421 |
| Adjusted $R^2$ | .789 | .751 | .794 |

*Note:* All variables are in natural logs with the exception of dummy variables and year. Standard errors are in parentheses. Columns (1) and (2) include all country/year pairs for which data are available. Column (3) excludes those countries defined as tax havens, where the effective tax rate is less than 10 percent. "Sales to affiliates in other foreign countries" are sales by affiliates in country $i$ to affiliates in other foreign countries. For other variable definitions refer to table 7.1 note.

foreign countries control for characteristics of host-country affiliates that may make them more likely to ship goods to other countries. Third, a specification in natural logs is considered. Because both the dependent variables and the control variables are no longer in percentage terms, such a specification makes the results easier to interpret.

Table 7.6 shows the results. In column (1), the coefficient on the effective tax variable suggests that a 1 percent increase in the effective tax rate in country $i$ is associated with a 0.82 percent reduction in sales to other foreign affiliates.[19] Sales to other foreign affiliates are positively related to the share of total sales in manufacturing in country $i$, the total sales of affiliates in country $i$ (excluding sales to other foreign affiliates), and the sales by affiliates in country $i$ to nonaffiliates in other foreign countries. Affiliates

19. The coefficient in the table indicates an elasticity of other country affiliated sales with respect to 1 − ETR of 1.65. At the mean ETR, this corresponds to an elasticity with respect to the ETR of −0.82.

based in Europe and Japan also sell more to other foreign affiliates. When these dummy variables are excluded in column (2), the point estimate of the coefficient on the effective tax rate is smaller and, as one might expect, the coefficient on the share of sales in wholesale trade becomes much more important and statistically significant.[20] Column (3) excludes from the sample those countries with effective tax rates less than 10 percent that are defined to be tax havens. Excluding tax havens has little effect on the results, so the demonstrated tax sensitivity is unlikely to be primarily a result of operations in very low tax countries.

There are several ways to interpret the tax coefficient results. It is possible that these results indicate tax-induced income shifting. Affiliates based in low-tax countries overprice their sales to other foreign affiliates in order to shift income from high-tax sources to low-tax sources. Although subpart F encourages affiliates in low-tax countries to avoid the type of sales to other affiliates that generates subpart F income, this influence is not apparent in the results, perhaps due to the fact that many types of trade do not generate subpart F income.

It is also possible that the tax coefficient result does not indicate tax-induced income shifting, but rather reflects the fact that low-tax locations are more attractive places to invest, and hence generate more trading activity of all types. One might hope that including the total level of sales in such countries as an independent variable would capture some of this influence, but it may not be adequate.

Another approach to this question would be to consider as a dependent variable the *share* of total sales that destined for affiliates in other countries. Figure 7.2 shows how total sales are typically divided between different destinations in the sample. If affiliates are attempting to shift income to low-tax locations, one would expect that affiliates in low-tax countries would see higher shares of their total sales going toward affiliates in other countries, relative to affiliates based in high-tax locations. Although there is no incentive to alter prices on local sales or sales to nonaffiliates, affiliates in low-tax countries have an incentive to overprice affiliate sales, whereas affiliates in high-tax countries have an incentive to underprice affiliate sales. Table 7.7 shows the results of these specifications. The estimates from column (1) indicate that an effective tax rate 1 percentage point higher in country *i* is associated with a 0.26 percentage point lower share of sales that are destined for affiliates in other foreign countries. Figure 7.3 shows a graphical representation of this negative relationship between the effective tax rate of the affiliate country and the share of total sales that is destined for affiliates in other countries.

20. Affiliates based in European countries have an average of 29 percent of their total sales in wholesale trade, and affiliates based in Japan have an average of 26 percent of their sales in wholesale trade. Affiliates based in other countries average only 14 percent of their total sales in wholesale trade.

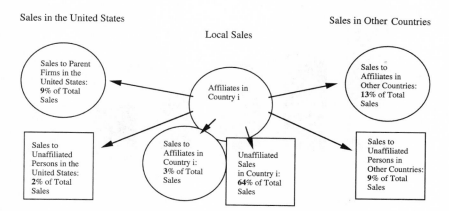

**Fig. 7.2**    **The distribution of total sales to affiliates and nonaffiliates in the United States, locally, and in other countries**

Table 7.7                    Equations Estimating the Share of Total Sales That Are to Affiliates

| Independent Variables | (1) | (2) | (3) |
|---|---|---|---|
| Effective tax rate | −.2603 | .0093 | −.3181 |
|  | (.0182) | (.0295) | (.0331) |
| Real exchange rate | .0001 | .0000 | −.0005 |
|  | (.0001) | (.0000) | (.0001) |
| Income growth | .0023 | .0017 | .0024 |
|  | (.0009) | (.0015) | (.0017) |
| Share of sales in wholesale trade | −.1807 | −.2333 | −.3281 |
|  | (.0302) | (.0501) | (.0555) |
| Share of sales in manufacturing | .0663 | −.1547 | .0010 |
|  | (.0163) | (.0262) | (.0297) |
| European country dummy | .1380 | −.0716 | .0615 |
|  | (.0078) | (.0130) | (.0141) |
| Japan dummy | .0587 | −.0716 | −.0188 |
|  | (.0212) | (.0353) | (.0383) |
| Constant | .1355 | .2230 | .4062 |
|  | (.0171) | (.0283) | (.0321) |
| $N$ | 477 | 484 | 467 |
| Adjusted $R^2$ | .536 | .210 | .231 |

*Note:* Dependent variables are shares of total sales to affiliates in other foreign countries (column [1]), to affiliates (parents) in the United States (column [2]), and to affiliates both in the United States and in other foreign countries (column [3]). Standard errors are in parentheses. For other variable definitions see table 7.1 note.

One would expect a similar relationship between tax rates and the share of sales destined for parents in the United States. Column (2) considers this hypothesis. However, the coefficient on the effective tax rate is not estimated precisely, and is statistically indistinguishable from zero. Column (3) looks at the relationship between effective tax rates in country $i$

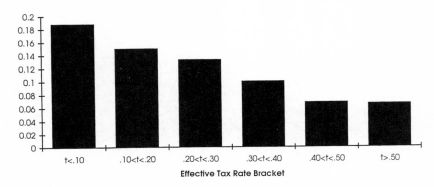

**Fig. 7.3    The share of total sales destined for affiliates in other countries**

and the combined share of sales to all other affiliates, both those in other foreign countries and parent firms in the United States. Here the coefficient on the effective tax rate implies that a 1 percentage point increase in the effective tax rate in country $i$ is associated with a 0.32 percentage point reduction in the share of sales to affiliates.[21]

These results provide evidence that the tax minimization strategies of MNCs may influence intrafirm trade. There is also a piece of indirect evidence regarding the effects of subpart F. Although concerns over triggering subpart F income do not appear to reduce sales from affiliates in low-tax countries to other affiliates, it is the case that affiliates operating in countries where a large share of sales are in wholesale trade have a lower share of sales to affiliates in other countries. Subpart F income is more likely when trade is in wholesale products, because subpart F income is generated only when trade between affiliates is in goods that are both manufactured outside the country of origin and sold for final use outside the country of origin. Thus, although subpart F may not substantially reduce most types of trade by affiliates in low-tax countries, it may reduce wholesale trade by such affiliates.

## 7.5    Conclusions

This paper studies the impact of tax-minimizing behavior on intrafirm trade patterns. Using data on the operations of U.S. parent companies and their foreign affiliates between 1982 and 1994, the paper examines the relationship between the effective tax rates faced by U.S. affiliates in different countries and intrafirm trade both between U.S. parents and their

21. Again, one can divide the sample into two subsets based on whether the ETR is lower or higher than the U.S. marginal tax rate. Results, shown in appendix tables 7A.2 and 7A.3 confirm the previous conclusion that the relationship between taxes and intrafirm trade is much stronger for low-tax countries.

affiliates abroad and between different foreign affiliates of U.S. firms. The results indicate a clear relationship between taxes and intrafirm trade flows.

First, controlling for other factors that are likely to influence intrafirm trade balances, the data indicate that the United States has less favorable intrafirm trade balances with low-tax countries. This result fits with the theoretical expectation that firms minimizing their worldwide tax burdens will underprice U.S. exports to affiliates in low-tax countries and overprice U.S. imports from affiliates in low-tax countries. An effective tax rate in the affiliate country 10 percentage points lower is associated with an intrafirm trade balance relative to that country that is 4.4 percentage points smaller.

Second, additional evidence indicates that trade between U.S. affiliates in different foreign countries is also likely influenced by tax considerations. Sales by affiliates based in low-tax countries to affiliates in other countries are greater than one would otherwise expect. In addition, the share of affiliates' total sales that are destined for other affiliates is negatively related to the effective tax rate of the affiliate country. These results, along with the previous ones, provide evidence that tax-minimizing motivations may be influencing intrafirm trade patterns.

These results have several noteworthy implications. First, they indicate an important way in which intrafirm trade may be different from international trade conducted at arm's length. Intrafirm trade flows are influenced by the tax minimization strategies of MNCs. As Kant (1995) demonstrates, this tax-minimizing behavior can lead to situations in which intrafirm trade is perverse, such that intrafirm exports originate in the country with the higher marginal cost.

Second, the results add more evidence to the body of literature that has measured the magnitude of tax-induced transfer pricing. Much of the previous literature has found evidence of transfer price manipulation by focusing on the relationship between the taxes faced by affiliates located in different countries and firm profitabilities or U.S. tax liabilities. This paper adds evidence showing a clear relationship between the taxes faced by affiliates abroad and their intrafirm trade transactions.

# Appendix

**Table 7A.1**          **Dependent Variable: Sales to U.S. Parents**

| Independent Variables | |
|---|---|
| 1-effective tax rate | .7224 |
| | (.2979) |
| 1-share of sales in wholesale trade | 2.700 |
| | (.495) |
| 1-share of sales in manufacturing | −1.598 |
| | (.273) |
| Total sales | 1.024 |
| | (.0672) |
| Sales to nonaffiliates in the United States | .1607 |
| | (.0425) |
| European country dummy | −.7818 |
| | (.1515) |
| Japan dummy | −.1392 |
| | (.3843) |
| Constant | −2.255 |
| | (.450) |
| N | 508 |
| Adjusted $R^2$ | .640 |

*Note:* Standard errors are in parentheses. "Sales to U.S. parents" are sales by affiliates in country $i$ to U.S. parent companies. "Sales to nonaffiliates in the United States are sales by affiliates in country $i$ to nonaffiliated persons in the United States. Other variables are defined as in table 7.1. All variables are in natural logs with the exception of dummy variables.

**Table 7A.2**          **Low Effective Tax Rate Sample**

| Independent Variables | (1) | (2) | (3) |
|---|---|---|---|
| Effective tax rate | −.4607 | −.1693 | −.6300 |
| | (.0405) | (.0419) | (.0600) |
| Real exchange rate | .0001 | −.0007 | −.0006 |
| | (.0001) | (.0001) | (.0002) |
| Income growth | .0021 | .0011 | .0027 |
| | (.0013) | (.0013) | (.0019) |
| Share of sales in wholesale trade | −.1933 | −.0452 | −.2388 |
| | (.0418) | (.0439) | (.0625) |
| Share of sales in manufacturing | .1127 | .0212 | .1371 |
| | (.0273) | (.0284) | (.0404) |
| European country dummy | .1540 | −.0990 | .0556 |
| | (.0113) | (.0117) | (.0167) |
| Constant | .1594 | .2575 | .4169 |
| | (.0237) | (.0252) | (.0362) |
| N | 293 | 293 | 288 |
| Adjusted $R^2$ | .545 | .379 | .362 |

*Note:* Dependent variables are shares of total sales to affiliates in other foreign countries (column [1]), to affiliates (parents) in the United States (column [2]), and to affiliates both in the United States and in other foreign countries (column [3]). Standard errors are in parentheses. Sample includes only those observations for which the effective tax rate is less than the U.S. marginal tax rate. For other variable definitions refer to table 7.1 note.

Table 7A.3            High Effective Tax Rate Sample

| Independent Variables | (1) | (2) | (3) |
|---|---|---|---|
| Effective tax rate | −.0342 | .0743 | .0054 |
| | (.0240) | (.0780) | (.0761) |
| Real exchange rate | .0001 | .0008 | −.0002 |
| | (.0001) | (.0002) | (.0003) |
| Income growth | .0021 | −.0028 | −.0014 |
| | (.0009) | (.0030) | (.0029) |
| Share of sales in wholesale trade | −.0901 | −.3678 | −.3951 |
| | (.0329) | (.1106) | (.1066) |
| Share of sales in manufacturing | .0483 | −.2280 | −.0622 |
| | (.0138) | (.0447) | (.0443) |
| European country dummy | .1046 | −.0436 | .0677 |
| | (.0081) | (.0278) | (.0259) |
| Japan dummy | .0320 | −.0099 | −.0050 |
| | (.0136) | (.0453) | (.0429) |
| Constant | .0247 | .1309 | .2448 |
| | (.0188) | (.0629) | (.0613) |
| N | 184 | 191 | 179 |
| Adjusted $R^2$ | .516 | .331 | .063 |

*Note:* Dependent variables are shares of total sales to affiliates in other foreign countries (column [1]), to affiliates (parents) in the United States (column [2]), and to affiliates both in the United States and in other foreign countries (column [3]). Standard errors are in parentheses. Sample includes only those observations for which the effective tax rate is greater than the U.S. marginal tax rate. For other variable definitions refer to table 7.1 note.

# References

Bernard, Jean-Thomas, and Weiner, Robert J. 1990. Multinational corporations, transfer prices, and taxes: Evidence from the U.S. petroleum industry. In *Taxation in the global economy,* ed. Assaf Razin and Joel Slemrod, 123–54. Chicago: University of Chicago Press.

Blomström, Magnus, Robert Lipsey, and Ksenia Kulchycky. 1988. U.S. and Swedish direct investment and exports. In *Trade policy issues and empirical analysis,* ed. Richard Baldwin, 259–97. Chicago: University of Chicago Press.

Bureau of Economic Analysis. 1982–1994. *U.S. direct investment abroad: Annual and benchmark surveys.* Washington, D.C.: U.S. Department of Commerce.

Clausing, Kimberly. 2000. Does multinational activity displace trade? *Economic Inquiry* 38 (2): 190–205.

Collins, Julie, Deen Kemsley, and Mark Lang. 1998. Cross-jurisdictional income shifting and earnings valuation. *Journal of Accounting Research* 36 (2): 209–30.

Deardorff, Alan V. 1998. Determinants of bilateral trade: Does gravity work in a neoclassical world? In *The realization of the world economy,* ed. Jeffrey A. Frankel, 3–31. Chicago: University of Chicago Press.

Diewert, W. Erwin. 1985. Transfer pricing and economic efficiency. In *Multinationals and transfer pricing,* ed. Lorraine Eden and Alan Rugman, 47–81. New York: St. Martin's Press.

Eden, Lorraine. 1985. The microeconomics of transfer pricing. In *Multinationals and transfer pricing,* ed. Lorraine Eden and Alan Rugman, 13–46. New York: St. Martin's Press.

Grubert, Harry, William C. Randolph, and Donald J. Rousslang. 1996. Country and multinational company responses to the Tax Reform Act of 1986. *National Tax Journal* 49 (3): 341–58.

Grubert, Harry, and John Mutti. 1996. Do taxes influence where U.S. corporations invest? U.S. Department of the Treasury. Mimeograph.

———. 1991. Taxes, tariffs and transfer pricing in multinational corporation decision making. *Review of Economics and Statistics* 17 (2): 285–93.

Harris, David, Randall Morck, Joel Slemrod, and Bernard Yeung. 1993. Income shifting in U.S. multinational corporations. In *Studies in international taxation,* ed. Alberto Giovannini, R. Glenn Hubbard, and Joel Slemrod, 277–302. Chicago: University of Chicago Press.

Hines, James R. 1997. Tax policy and the activities of multinational corporations. In *Fiscal policy: Lessons from economic research,* ed. Alan J. Auerbach, 401–45. Cambridge, Mass.: MIT Press.

Hines, James R., and Eric M. Rice. 1994. Fiscal paradise: Foreign tax havens and American business. *Quarterly Journal of Economics* 109 (1): 149–82.

Horst, Thomas. 1971. The theory of the multinational firm: Optimal behavior under different tariff and tax rates. *Journal of Political Economy* 79 (5): 1059–72.

International Monetary Fund. Various years. *International financial statistics yearbook.*

Jenkins, Glenn P., and Brian D. Wright. 1975. Taxation of income of multinational corporations: The case of the U.S. petroleum industry. *Review of Economics and Statistics* 57 (1): 1–11.

Kant, Chander. 1995. Minority ownership, deferral, perverse intrafirm trade and tariffs. *International Economic Journal* 9 (1): 19–37.

———. 1990. Multinational firms and government revenue. *Journal of Public Economics* 42 (2): 135–47.

Kemsley, Deen. 1998. The effect of taxes on production location. *Journal of Accounting Research* 36 (2): 321–41.

Kopits, George F. 1976. Intra-firm royalties crossing frontiers and transfer pricing behavior. *Economic Journal* 86 (344): 791–805.

Lall, Sanjaya. 1973. Transfer pricing by multinational manufacturing firms. *Oxford Bulletin of Economics and Statistics* 35 (3): 173–95.

Lipsey, Robert E., and Merle Yahr Weiss. 1984. Foreign production and exports of individual firms. *Review of Economics and Statistics* 66 (2): 304–08.

———. 1981. Foreign production and exports in manufacturing industries. *Review of Economics and Statistics* 63 (4): 488–94.

Rangan, Subramanian, and Robert Z. Lawrence. 1999. *A prism on globalization: Corporate responses to the dollar.* Washington: Brookings Institution Press.

Rapakko, Annamaria. 1990. *Base company taxation.* Boston: Deventer.

Zeile, William J. 1997. U.S. intrafirm trade in goods. *Survey of Current Business* 77 (2): 23–38.

## Comment     Deen Kemsley

In this study, Clausing provides evidence that corporate tax incentives materially influence intrafirm trade balances. In particular, she finds a posi-

Deen Kemsley is associate professor of accounting at Columbia University.

tive relation between U.S. MNCs' intrafirm trade balances (i.e., dollar-denominated exports less imports) and country-specific tax rates, which is consistent with the predicted effects of tax-induced transfer pricing. She also finds that patterns of sales among MNC affiliates in different foreign countries are consistent with tax-induced transfer pricing. Hence, Clausing extends the frontiers of empirical tax transfer pricing research to two new domains: trade balances and sales patterns among foreign affiliates.

This extension does not come without cost, for trade balances and sales patterns not only are functions of transfer pricing, but also are functions of international investment and production location decisions. As Clausing recognizes, it is difficult to distinguish between transfer pricing and investment location explanations for the empirical results, so she includes some controls for investment location. Nevertheless, future research is still required to distinguish between the two explanations, and to examine the relative magnitude of transfer pricing versus investment location effects.

My discussion of the paper proceeds as follows. I first analyze the relation between taxes and U.S.-foreign intrafirm trade balances. Next, I examine taxes and intrafirm trade among foreign affiliates of U.S. MNCs. Finally, I offer concluding remarks.

## Taxes and Intrafirm Trade between U.S. Parents and Affiliates

United States MNCs have a tax incentive to shift taxable income away from high-tax foreign affiliates to the United States, and to shift taxable income from the United States to low-tax affiliates. Using a variety of different approaches, several prior studies have provided evidence that U.S. firms pursue both of these income-shifting strategies (e.g., Grubert and Mutti 1991, Harris, Morck, Slemrod, and Yeung 1993, and Collins, Kemsley, and Lang 1998). As long recognized, however, the U.S. foreign tax credit system mitigates this income-shifting incentive for firms without enough credits to offset the entire U.S. tax on foreign source income. For example, if a deficit-credit firm shifts taxable income from the United States to a low-tax country, the firm must recapture the taxable income in the United States upon repatriation of the shifted profits. As a result, shifting income across jurisdictions often provides only temporary tax savings—but even temporary savings provide some incentive for firms to shift profits.[1]

---

1. Clausing accounts for repatriation policies in her income-shifting model by letting $f$ represent the fraction of profits repatriated to the United States. Because repatriation triggers the U.S. tax on the income of low-tax affiliates, income-shifting incentives decrease in $f$ and go to 0 when $f$ equals 1. In practice, firms' repatriation policies typically change over time, so $f$ is a complex function of several factors. For example, if firms eventually repatriate all foreign profits to the United States, and if the after-local-tax rates of return are the same in the foreign country as they are in the United States, then shifting income to the low-tax jurisdiction does not provide any net tax savings for a firm because the magnitude of the

One way to shift income across tax jurisdictions is to manipulate transfer prices. For example, a U.S. MNC selling goods to a low-tax foreign affiliate can shift taxable income away from the United States by undercharging the low-tax affiliate for the goods. Undercharging the affiliate for the goods would reduce reportable exports to the affiliate, decreasing the intrafirm trade balance. On the other hand, the firm would have an incentive to reduce taxable income for high-tax affiliates by overcharging them for goods, which would increase reportable exports and intrafirm trade balances. All else being equal, therefore, tax-induced transfer pricing is expected to result in a positive relation between intrafirm trade balances and country-specific tax rates. Consistent with this expectation, Clausing reports a positive estimated coefficient for the effective tax rate variable in table 7.2.

In addition to transfer pricing incentives, MNCs have a tax incentive to locate production facilities and other investment in low-tax countries. Grubert and Mutti (1996) provide evidence that firms respond to this incentive. Placing production in low-tax countries instead of the United States could reduce reportable exports to the affiliates relative to imports from the affiliates, decreasing intrafirm trade balances with the low-tax countries.[2] Similarly, MNCs have an incentive to shift production from high-tax countries to the United States, and U.S. export tax incentive rules magnify this incentive.[3] Kemsley (1998) provides evidence that firms respond to this tax incentive by exporting goods to high-tax countries, which would increase intrafirm trade balances. Like tax-induced transfer pricing, therefore, tax-induced investment location decisions generally are expected to result in a positive relation between intrafirm trade balances and country-specific tax rates.

A natural question, therefore, is whether the positive estimated coefficient for the effective tax rate (ETR) in table 7.2 captures transfer pricing effects, investment location effects, or both.[4] Here, Clausing provides some support for the transfer pricing interpretation by controlling for the "overall" and "unaffiliated" U.S. trade balances with each foreign country. After

---

eventual U.S. repatriation tax grows at the discount rate (Scholes and Wolfson 1992). Within Clausing's model, these strict assumptions would imply that $f$ equals 1 for deficit-credit firms, even if the current rate of repatriation is less than 1.

2. Placing production in low-tax countries could very well increase overall intrafirm activity with low-tax affiliates, both exports and imports. However, if the goods produced in low-tax countries are targeted for U.S. customers, imports from the low-tax affiliates typically would exceed exports to the affiliates.

3. Under IRC § 863(b), MNCs can treat half of their export profits as foreign source income. Hence export profits raise foreign tax credit limitations, allowing firms to use otherwise wasted excess foreign tax credits.

4. Unlike Grubert and Mutti (1996) and Kemsley (1998), Clausing uses each country's effective tax rate as an explanatory variable instead of using each country's marginal statutory tax rate. Both measures likely are subject to considerable measurement error, and it is not clear whether empirical results are sensitive to the choice of tax variable.

including these controls, the ETR coefficient reflects a unique relation between tax rates and *intrafirm* trade balances, which is where we expect to find transfer pricing effects. However, tax-induced production location decisions also may have an especially strong influence on intrafirm trade balances, as firms choose to produce goods in low-tax countries and ship the goods to sales affiliates in high-tax countries.[5] Hence it is unclear whether transfer pricing or investment location decisions drive the results presented in table 7.2.

Similarly, table 7.3 does not uniquely support transfer pricing effects, and it raises new questions. The evidence in this table indicates that the positive relation between ETRs and intrafirm trade balances is solely concentrated among countries with low tax rates. However, the tax incentive to shift taxable income away from high-tax countries to the United States increases in the foreign tax rate, and consistent with this incentive, Collins et al. (1998) provide evidence that firms shift a substantial amount of income to the United States. Indeed, the tax incentive to transfer price income from high-tax countries to the United States is less ambiguous than the incentive to shift income to low-tax countries, because firms must pay the difference between U.S. and low foreign tax rates upon repatriation of the shifted profits to the United States.[6] From a transfer pricing perspective, therefore, it is unclear why the estimated tax effect exists only among low-tax countries.

Table 7.4 indicates that tax effects were greater before 1988 than after this date. Again, it is difficult to interpret this finding in terms of tax incentives. Firms with excess foreign tax credits derive permanent tax savings from transfer pricing income to lower-taxed jurisdictions, whereas firms with deficit foreign tax credits only defer taxes until repatriation. The percentage of firms with excess foreign tax credits increased substantially when the United States reduced corporate tax rates with the Tax Reform Act of 1986, so tax transfer pricing (and investment location) incentives are greater in the latter period, not weaker as suggested by table 7.4.[7] On

5. Using firm-level evidence, Kemsley (1998) finds that tax incentives induce U.S. MNCs to increase exports to *unaffiliated* foreign customers (given data constraints, I do not examine the influence of taxes on intrafirm exports). This finding suggests that the relation between taxes and production location is not unique to intrafirm settings, which provides some support for a transfer pricing interpretation of Clausing's results. However, Clausing's unaffiliated trade balance control variable captures only exports from unaffiliated U.S. firms to the affiliates of U.S. MNCs, so it is an imperfect (but potentially helpful) control for the tax-induced exports from U.S. MNCs to unaffiliated entities captured by Kemsley.

6. The finding by Collins, Hand, and Shackelford (chap. 6, this volume) that investors capitalize future repatriation taxes into share prices further limits the incentive to shift taxable income to low-tax countries.

7. As Clausing points out, variation in the ETR variable is relatively small during the latter time period, which could contribute to the weak results. Outliers also could contribute to the weak results after 1988, for, as reported in table 7.5, the estimated ETR coefficient is positive in all years except 1993, and the study does not provide any sensitivity tests to determine whether outliers account for the negative coefficient in this year.

the other hand, many countries have implemented stronger tax rule restrictions against transfer price manipulation in recent years, which may contribute to the relatively weak results after 1988.

### Taxes and Intrafirm Trade among Foreign Affiliates

In a second set of tests, Clausing examines the hypothesis that sales among foreign affiliates are negatively related to the tax rates of the countries where the sales originate. That is, she examines whether low-tax foreign affiliates tend to sell more goods to high-tax affiliates than they buy from high-tax affiliates. Consistent with this hypothesis, she finds a negative relation (as reported in tables 7.6 and 7.7).

Again, it is difficult to distinguish between transfer pricing and investment location explanations for this result. On the one hand, transfer pricing income from high-tax affiliates to low-tax affiliates would increase (decrease) the reported sales of the low-tax (high-tax) affiliates. As Clausing notes, however, producing goods in low-tax countries and shipping the goods to high-tax affiliates also would result in high (low) reported sales for the low-tax (high-tax) affiliates. Therefore, she includes two control variables for the investment location explanation, sales to nonaffiliates in other countries and total sales. These variables may generally help control for tax-induced investment location decisions, but they are not specific enough to effectively rule out the possibility that firms are merely producing goods in low-tax countries for shipment to their high-tax affiliates.

### Conclusion

In summary, therefore, Clausing provides rather convincing evidence that taxes influence the intrafirm trade patterns of U.S. MNCs, but the evidence does not clearly distinguish between transfer pricing and investment location explanations for this finding. I do not believe this ambiguity detracts from the paper's central message that taxes influence trade balances. Instead, the paper has the potential to stimulate a substantial amount of future research in this area.

Key unanswered questions for future consideration include the following. What are the relative magnitudes of the influences of tax-induced transfer pricing versus tax-induced investment location strategies on intrafirm trade balances? What are the relative magnitudes of tax-induced income shifting into versus out of the United States? What are the firm- and industry-level determinants of firms' choices among various income shifting and investment location strategies? Have MNCs' preferred tax-planning strategies changed over time, and if so, why? I believe that answering these types of questions would provide us with a much more complete understanding of the links between taxes and multinational business practices than we can acquire by continuing to document different multinational tax strategies in isolation from each other.

## References

Collins, J., D. Kemsley, and M. Lang. 1998. Cross-jurisdictional income shifting and earnings valuation. *Journal of Accounting Research,* 36:209–30.

Grubert, H., and J. Mutti. 1996. Do taxes influence where U.S. corporations invest? Working Paper, 1996.

———. 1991. Taxes, tariffs, and transfer pricing in multinational corporation decision making. *Review of Economics and Statistics* 17 (2): 285–93.

Harris, D., R. Morck, J. Slemrod, and B. Yeung. 1993. Income shifting in U.S. multinational corporations. In *Studies in international taxation,* ed. A. Giovannini, R. G. Hubbard, and J. Slemrod. Chicago: University of Chicago Press.

Kemsley, D. 1998. The effect of taxes on production location. *Journal of Accounting Research,* 36:321–42.

Scholes, M., and M. Wolfson. 1992. *Taxes and business strategy: A planning approach.* Englewood Cliffs, N.J.: Prentice Hall.

# International Taxation and the Location of Inventive Activity

James R. Hines Jr. and Adam B. Jaffe

## 8.1 Introduction

Tax systems often encourage certain activities at the expense of others. Governments typically offer very attractive tax treatment to investments in research and development (R&D), because R&D is thought to be associated with large positive economic spillovers.[1] One of the factors contributing to the generosity of tax benefits for R&D is competition among governments to attract R&D-intensive investments by multinational corporations (MNCs). Because an MNC typically has the option of performing its R&D in any of several countries, the volume of its R&D activity in one country is likely to be affected by the attractiveness of opportunities elsewhere. In spite of the frequency with which R&D receives generous tax subsidies, and the widespread belief that these subsidies encourage the discovery and development of new technologies, very little of a quantitative nature is known about the impact of tax rules on the international location of innovative activity.

The purpose of this paper is to examine the effect of taxation on the distribution of inventive activity between the United States and foreign countries. The paper analyzes the effect of U.S. tax changes, particularly those introduced by the Tax Reform Act of 1986, on the international pattern of subsequent patenting by U.S. multinationals. Due to the spe-

James R. Hines Jr. is professor of business economics at the University of Michigan Business School and a research associate of the National Bureau of Economic Research. Adam B. Jaffe is chair of the Department of Economics at Brandeis University and a research associate of the National Bureau of Economic Research.

The authors thank Austin Nichols for excellent research assistance, Austan Goolsbee for helpful comments on an earlier draft, and the NBER for financial support.

1. Griliches (1992) surveys the econometric evidence of economic spillovers from innovative activity.

cifics of U.S. tax law, U.S. firms differ in the extent to which tax changes affect their after-tax costs of performing R&D in the United States. Firms also differ in the extent to which tax changes affect the returns to using the results of R&D performed in the United States to generate sales abroad. The same U.S. tax changes do not directly influence the return to R&D performed abroad by U.S. multinationals, so any induced international relocation of innovative activity in the years following tax changes reflect the ways in which domestic and foreign patenting activity are related.

There is extensive interest in understanding the role that MNCs play in transferring technologies across borders. There are two methods by which MNCs provide technology to the countries in which they invest. The first method is to develop new technologies locally, through R&D or other similar types of activity. The second method is to import technologies produced elsewhere.

The foreign affiliates of U.S. firms use both methods to bring technologies to the countries in which they invest, and there exists sufficient information to assess quantitatively the relative significance of each method. Direct information on the R&D activities of the foreign affiliates of U.S. firms is reported in surveys conducted by the U.S. Department of Commerce. Information on technology imports by these affiliates is considerably sketchier. One can, however, infer the approximate magnitude of technology imports from royalties paid by affiliates to U.S. parent firms and third parties in other countries, because royalty payments should, in principle, reflect the values of imported technologies.

Table 8.1 reports detailed information on the aggregate technology-related behavior of the foreign affiliates of U.S. firms in 1982, 1989, and 1994. It is noteworthy that affiliates paid more in royalties to their parent firms ($16.7 billion in 1994) than they spent on R&D ($11.9 billion in 1994), although, as the table indicates, there was extensive use of both methods of technology acquisition. The survey distinguishes two categories of R&D expenditure: R&D by affiliates for themselves and R&D by affiliates for others. R&D by affiliates for themselves constitutes roughly 80 percent of their total R&D expenditures.

In spite of extensive consideration in the literature of the role that MNCs play in facilitating international technology transfer,[2] there is very little in the way of quantitative evidence of the complementarity or substitutability of foreign and domestic technology. Hines (1995) offers evidence

---

2. See, for example, Teece (1976), Mansfield, Teece, and Romeo (1979), Mansfield and Romeo (1980), Davidson and McFetridge (1984), Lipsey, Blomström, and Kravis (1990), Zejan (1990), Blomström (1991), Wang and Blomström (1992), Blomström and Kokko (1995), and Ethier and Markusen (1996). These studies together consider the effect of a large number of variables on technology transfer and R&D activity, although they do not consider the potential complementarity of domestic and foreign innovation.

**Table 8.1**                **R&D and Royalty Activity of Foreign Affiliates of U.S. Multinationals**

|                                          | 1982  | 1989   | 1994   |
|------------------------------------------|-------|--------|--------|
| R&D expenditures of affiliates           |       |        |        |
| Total                                    | 3,851 | 7,922  | 11,877 |
| By affiliate for itself                  | 3,073 | 6,307  | 8,901  |
| By affiliate for others                  | 778   | 1,615  | 2,976  |
| Royalty receipts of affiliates           |       |        |        |
| Total                                    | 435   | 1,461  | 2,581  |
| From U.S. parents                        | 36    | 54     | 368    |
| From other foreign affiliates            | 193   | 656    | 1,096  |
| From unaffiliated Americans              | 26    | 97     | 387    |
| From unaffiliated foreigners             | 180   | 654    | 730    |
| Royalty payments by affiliates           |       |        |        |
| Total                                    | 4,308 | 12,472 | 22,039 |
| To U.S. parents                          | 3,663 | 9,839  | 16,744 |
| To other foreign affiliates              | 354   | 1,488  | 2,615  |
| To unaffiliated Americans                | 102   | 660    | 2,138  |
| To unaffiliated foreigners               | 189   | 485    | 543    |

*Note:* Amounts are in $ millions. Data cover majority-owned foreign affiliates of U.S. multinational firms.
*Source:* U.S. Department of Commerce (1985, 1992, 1996).

that domestic and foreign R&D are substitutes, but to the extent that firms establish foreign R&D to exploit the core competencies that they have developed at home by adapting the firms' technologies to foreign markets, we would expect that foreign and domestic R&D would be complementary. The evidence reported in Hines (1995) is based on an analysis of aggregate data concerning the R&D activities of U.S. multinationals abroad and the R&D activities of foreign investors in the United States. The purpose of the current investigation is to examine whether similar patterns appear at a firm level.

The empirical results in this paper suggest that foreign and domestic innovative activities are complements rather than substitutes. Specifically, firms with rising after-tax costs of performing R&D in the United States that is directed at generating technology for use abroad are those that exhibit the slowest growth of foreign patenting. This pattern is sensible if the willingness to undertake foreign R&D is a function of the propensity to perform related domestic R&D, and the latter is a function of domestic tax incentives. What the results indicate is that domestic tax incentives can significantly influence not only the rate of domestic innovation, but also the rate of foreign innovation by U.S. multinationals. Because complementarity is a symmetrical relationship, the results also imply that foreign tax incentives should influence the rate at which U.S. multinationals innovate in their domestic markets.

Evidence of the complementarity of innovative activity comes from an analysis of the behavior of a panel of U.S. multinationals over the 1982–1992 period. There were several important U.S. tax changes over this time period, notable among them the changes introduced by the Tax Reform Act of 1986 (TRA 1986). Using international patent data that specify the inventor's country of residence, it is possible to trace the effect of U.S. tax changes on subsequent patenting patterns, and thereby to identify any effects of U.S. tax changes on foreign innovative activity (as reflected by patents).

Section 8.2 of the paper reviews the U.S. tax treatment of foreign source income, with an emphasis on the tax treatment of R&D expenses and foreign royalty receipts. Section 8.3 presents a model of firm behavior and describes the data used in the empirical analysis. Section 8.4 presents the regression results and analyzes their implications. Section 8.5 is the conclusion.

## 8.2 Tax Incentives

The United States taxes income on a residence basis, meaning that U.S. corporations and individuals owe taxes to the U.S. government on all of their worldwide incomes.[3] The top U.S. corporate tax rate is now 35 percent. Because profits earned in foreign countries are usually taxed by host governments, U.S. law permits taxpayers to claim tax credits for foreign income taxes and related tax obligations, in order not to subject U.S. multinationals to double taxation. The foreign tax-credit mechanism implies that a U.S. corporation earning $100 in a foreign country with a 12 percent tax rate (and a foreign tax obligation of $12) pays only $23 to the U.S. government because its U.S. corporate tax liability of $35 (35 percent of $100) is reduced to $23 by the foreign tax credit of $12. The foreign tax credit is, however, limited to U.S. tax liability on foreign income; if, in the example, the foreign tax rate were 50 percent, then the firm would pay $50 to the foreign government but its U.S. foreign tax credit would be limited to $35. Thus, a U.S. firm receives full tax credits for its foreign taxes paid only when it is in a deficit credit position—that is, when its average foreign tax rate is less than its tax rate on domestic operations. A firm has excess credits if its available foreign tax credits exceed U.S. tax liability on its foreign income. Firms average together their taxable incomes and taxes paid in all of their foreign operations in calculating their foreign tax credits and the foreign tax credit limit.[4]

3. Portions of this brief description of U.S. law are excerpted from Hines (1991, 1994, 1997).

4. In order to qualify for the foreign tax credit, firms must own at least 10 percent of a foreign affiliate, and only those taxes that qualify as income taxes are creditable. Furthermore, income is broken into different functional baskets in the calculation of applicable credits and limits. Income earned and taxes paid in the conduct of most types of active foreign

Deferral of U.S. taxation of certain foreign earnings is another important feature of the U.S. international tax system. A U.S. parent firm is taxed on its subsidiaries' foreign income only when that income is repatriated to the parent corporation. This type of deferral is available only to foreign operations that are separately incorporated in foreign countries (subsidiaries of the parent) and not to consolidated (branch) operations. The U.S. government taxes branch profits as they are earned, just as it would profits earned within the United States.

The deferral of U.S. taxation may create incentives for firms with lightly taxed foreign earnings to delay repatriating dividends from their foreign subsidiaries.[5] This incentive arises in those cases in which firms expect never to repatriate their foreign earnings, or if they anticipate that future years will be more attractive for repatriation (either because domestic tax rates will be lower, or because future sources of foreign income will generate excess foreign tax credits that can be used to offset U.S. tax liability on the dividends).[6] It appears that, in practice, U.S. multinationals choose their dividend repatriations selectively, generally paying dividends out of their more heavily taxed foreign earnings first.[7] Consequently, the average tax rates that firms face on their foreign incomes need not exactly equal the average foreign tax rates faced by their branches and subsidiaries abroad.

Branch earnings and dividends from subsidiaries represent only two forms of foreign income for U.S. income tax purposes. Interest received from foreign sources also represents foreign income, although foreign interest receipts are often classified within their own "basket" and hence are not averaged with other income in calculating the foreign tax credit. Royalty income received from foreigners, including foreign affiliates of U.S. firms, is also foreign source income. Foreign governments often impose

business operations are grouped in one basket; petroleum industry income is grouped in a separate basket; and there are separate baskets for items such as passive income earned abroad. The basket distinctions imply that a firm might simultaneously have excess foreign tax credits in the petroleum basket (which is common because foreign tax rates on oil income are typically quite high) and deficit foreign tax credits in the active income basket. Such a firm would have to pay some U.S. tax on its active foreign income, even though it has excess foreign tax credits on its petroleum income.

5. The incentive to defer repatriation of lightly taxed subsidiary earnings is attenuated by the subpart F provisions, introduced into U.S. law in 1962, that treat a subsidiary's passive income, and income invested in U.S. property, as if it were distributed to its U.S. owners, thereby subjecting it to immediate U.S. taxation. The subpart F rules apply to controlled foreign corporations (CFCs), which are foreign corporations owned at least 50 percent by U.S. persons holding stakes of at least 10 percent each. CFCs that reinvest their foreign earnings in active businesses can continue to defer their U.S. tax liability on those earnings. See Hines and Rice (1994) and Scholes and Wolfson (1992) for the behavioral implications of these rules.

6. It is interesting to note that the deferral of U.S. tax liability does not itself create an incentive to delay paying dividends from foreign subsidiaries, because the U.S. tax must be paid eventually. See Hartman (1985).

7. See the evidence presented in Hines and Hubbard (1990), Altshuler and Newlon (1993), and Altshuler, Newlon, and Randolph (1995).

moderate taxes on dividend, interest, and royalty payments from foreign affiliates to their U.S. parent companies; these withholding[8] taxes are fully creditable against an American taxpayer's U.S. tax liability on foreign income.

Royalties received by U.S. parent firms for R&D used abroad represent taxable foreign source income of the U.S. firms. U.S. firms with deficit foreign tax credits must pay U.S. income tax on these royalty receipts, whereas firms with excess foreign tax credits can apply the excess credits against U.S. taxes due on the royalties, thereby eliminating the U.S. tax liability created by the royalty receipts.

Most of the world's governments impose withholding taxes on cross-border royalty payments from affiliates located within their countries. These royalty tax rates are frequently reduced according to the terms of bilateral tax treaties. For example, the United States imposes a 30 percent tax on royalties paid to foreign corporations, but this tax rate is often reduced, in some cases to zero, when recipients of royalty payments are located in countries with whom the United States has a tax treaty in force.

### 8.2.1   Interaction of R&D and Foreign Income Rules

U.S. firms with foreign income are generally not permitted to deduct all of their R&D expenditures in the United States against their domestic taxable incomes. Instead, the law provides for various methods of allocating R&D expenses between domestic and foreign income. The intention of the law is to retain the relatively generous treatment of R&D, but only for that part of a firm's R&D expenditures that is devoted to production for domestic markets. R&D-performing firms with foreign sales and foreign income are presumed to be doing at least some of their R&D to enhance their foreign profitability.

From the standpoint of taxpaying firms, the U.S. tax law's distinction between domestic and foreign R&D deductions is potentially quite important. If an R&D expense is deemed to be domestic, then it is deductible against the taxpayer's U.S. taxable income. Alternatively, if it is deemed to be foreign, then the R&D expense reduces foreign taxable income *for the purposes of U.S. income taxation only.* Foreign governments do not use U.S. methods of calculating R&D deductions, and generally do not permit U.S. firms to reduce their taxable incomes in foreign countries on the basis of R&D undertaken in the United States. Consequently, an R&D expense deduction allocated against foreign income is valuable to a U.S. firm only

---

8. Taxes on cross-border flows, such as dividends, interest, and royalties, are known as *withholding* taxes due to some of the niceties of their administration. Strictly speaking, these taxes represent obligations of the recipients and not of the payors; this arrangement permits immediate crediting of withholding taxes by recipients who are eligible to claim foreign tax credits. The taxes are called withholding taxes because the local payor is the withholding agent for the tax, and is therefore liable to ensure that the taxes are paid.

if the firm has deficit foreign tax credits. If the firm has deficit credits, then the firm pays some U.S. tax on its foreign income, and any additional dollar of R&D deduction allocated against foreign income reduces the firm's U.S. taxable income by a dollar. Hence, firms with deficit foreign tax credits are indifferent between allocating R&D expenses against foreign income and allocating them against domestic income.[9] In contrast, firms with excess foreign tax credits pay no U.S. tax on their foreign incomes, and therefore have no use for R&D deductions allocated against foreign income. Consequently, firms with excess foreign tax credits lose the value of any R&D deductions allocated against foreign income.

The tax law governing the allocation of R&D expenses was for years rather vague, but was codified by U.S. Treasury Regulation section 1.861-8 in 1977. The 1977 rules provide for several stages in allocating R&D expenditures for tax purposes. R&D in the United States that is undertaken to meet certain legal requirements (such as R&D devoted to meeting pollution standards) can be 100 percent allocated against domestic income. Firms that perform more than half of their (other-than-legally-required) R&D in the United States are permitted to allocate 30 percent of that R&D against U.S. income. The remaining 70 percent is then to be allocated between domestic and foreign sources on the basis of sales (including the sales of controlled foreign corporations [CFCs]). R&D is generally allocated according to activities within product lines (defined similarly to two-digit Standard Industrial Classification [SIC] codes), so that a corporation need not allocate part of its chemical R&D against foreign income simply because the electronics part of its business has foreign sales.

Several options are available to taxpayers who are unsatisfied with the outcome of the R&D allocation method just described. A firm is permitted to apportion more than 30 percent of its domestic R&D against U.S. income if it can establish that it is reasonable to expect the R&D so apportioned to have very limited application outside the country; the remaining portion of its R&D expenses are then allocated on the basis of sales. Alternatively, a firm is permitted to allocate its R&D on the basis of total foreign and domestic income (though without the 30 percent initial allocation to U.S. source), so that a firm with foreign operations that generate sales but not income (relative to domestic operations) might prefer the income allocation method. There is, however, a limit to the income allocation method: A firm is not permitted to reduce its foreign source R&D expense allocation to less than 50 percent of the allocation that would have been produced by the sales method (including the 30 percent initial apportionment).

9. This statement, along with much of the subsequent analysis, abstracts from the ability of firms to carry excess foreign tax credits backward two years and forward five years. Firms that can exploit carryforwards or carrybacks may (depending on specific circumstances) face intermediate incentives between those of deficit credit and excess credit firms.

The Economic Recovery Tax Act in 1981 changed these rules by permitting U.S. firms to allocate 100 percent of the expense of R&D performed in the United States against U.S. taxable income. This change was intended to be temporary (lasting two years), in order to offer strong R&D incentives while affording Congress the opportunity to rethink its R&D policy. At the end of that time, the U.S. Department of the Treasury produced a study (1983) concluding that the tax change offered a small R&D incentive to U.S. firms, and that it was desirable on that basis.[10] In 1984 and 1985 Congress extended the temporary change permitting 100 percent deductibility of U.S. R&D expenses against U.S. income, so these rules remained in place until the end of the 1986 tax year.

The Tax Reform Act of 1986 removed the 100 percent deductibility of U.S. R&D expenses, replacing it with a new (and again temporary) system of R&D expense allocation.[11] Under TRA 1986, 50 percent of U.S. R&D expense (other than R&D to meet regulations, which was 100 percent allocated to domestic source) was allocated to domestic source, with the remaining 50 percent allocated on the basis of sales or of income, at the taxpayer's choice. No limit was imposed on the degree to which allocation on the basis of gross income could reduce foreign allocation relative to the sales method. These rules, it turned out, were in effect only for 1987.

The Technical and Miscellaneous Revenue Act of 1988 changed the R&D expense allocation rules for the first part of 1988. For the first four months of the year, firms were permitted to allocate 64 percent of U.S. R&D expense against U.S. domestic income, with the remaining 36 percent allocated between foreign and domestic sources on the basis of either sales or income (at the taxpayer's choice). The 1988 Act further provided that if the 36 percent were allocated on the basis of income, then the R&D allocation against foreign income must equal at least 30 percent of the foreign allocation that would have been produced by the sales method. For the remaining eight months of the year, taxpayers were required to use the allocation method described in section 1.861-8 as of 1977 (and described previously).

The Omnibus Budget Reconciliation Act of 1989 again changed the R&D allocation rules, this time reintroducing the same rules that had applied for the first four months of 1988. The Omnibus Budget Reconciliation Act of 1990 and the Tax Extension Act of 1991 extended this treat-

10. The U.S. Department of the Treasury study (1983) based its conclusions on a range of assumed elasticities of R&D with respect to price changes; there was no attempt made to ascertain how firms responded to the changes introduced in 1981.

11. The Tax Reform Act of 1986 also introduced a number of other changes relevant to R&D investment decisions, including reducing the statutory corporate tax rate from 46 percent (the tax rate from 1979 to 1986) to 40 percent in 1987 and 34 percent for 1988 and subsequent years. The 1986 Act also removed a number of investment incentives, such as accelerated depreciation of capital assets and the investment tax credit for new equipment purchases.

ment of R&D expenses until a date that depends on a taxpayer's choice of fiscal year, but in no case later than 1 August 1992. Consequently, 64 percent of domestically performed R&D in 1989–1992 could be allocated against domestic income, with the remaining 36 percent allocated on the basis of either sales or income (although use of the income method could not reduce foreign source allocation to less than 30 percent of the foreign source allocation that would have been produced by the sales method).

The expiration of the R&D expense allocation legislation in the summer of 1992 motivated an extensive reconsideration of the issue of the appropriate tax treatment of R&D expenditures by MNCs. In June 1992, the U.S. Department of the Treasury temporarily suspended its section 1.861-8 allocation rules (the 1977 regulations), replacing them with an eighteen-month moratorium during which taxpayers could continue to use the system embodied in the legislation covering the years 1989–1992 (64 percent place-of-performance allocation, with the remaining deductions allocated on the basis of sales). The idea was that the Treasury would reexamine its section 1.861-8 regulations during the eighteen-month period. The rationale for the moratorium was "to provide taxpayers with transition relief and to minimize audit controversy and facilitate business planning during the conduct of the regulatory review."[12] Some contemporaneous observers noted that the extension of the R&D allocation rules through Treasury moratorium instead of Congressional legislation made the rules less costly from the standpoint of federal budget targets, because regulatory changes are exempt from the budget agreement limits. What role, if any, such considerations played in the decision to suspend the section 1.861-8 rules is not clear. In any case, the Treasury moratorium did not run its full course, being supplanted in 1993 by new legislation.

President Clinton's budget proposal of February 1993 recommended a major change in the allocation of R&D expenditures and the treatment of royalty receipts by U.S.-based MNCs. The president proposed that U.S. firms deduct 100 percent of their U.S. R&D expenditures against U.S. income, but that the same firms no longer be permitted to use foreign tax credits generated by their active foreign operations to reduce U.S. tax liabilities on royalty income from foreign sources. Instead, firms would be required to allocate foreign source royalty income to the passive basket in determining their foreign tax credit limits. The idea behind the change was to limit severely the ability of U.S. firms to use excess foreign tax credits to wipe out their U.S. tax liabilities on foreign source royalty income. Very few firms have excess foreign tax credits in the passive basket. Consequently, the overall effect of the proposal would have been to raise the deductions that firms with excess foreign tax credits receive for R&D performed in the United States, but to include—as income fully taxed by

---

12. U.S. Congress, Joint Committee on Taxation (1993, 55).

the United States—the royalties they receive from foreign sources. Congress chose not to include this proposal in the legislation passed in August 1993.

Instead, the Omnibus Budget Reconciliation Act of 1993 (OBRA 93) continued the pattern of allowing U.S.-based MNCs to deduct only a fraction of their U.S. R&D expenses against U.S. income, and, at the same time, permitted firms to use excess foreign tax credits to eliminate U.S. tax liabilities on foreign source royalty income. OBRA 93 permitted firms to allocate 50 percent of U.S.-based R&D expenses to domestic source, with the remaining 50 percent allocated between domestic and foreign source, based either on sales or on income, at the taxpayer's option (subject to the restriction that income-based allocation not reduce foreign source allocation to less than 30 percent of that produced by the sales method). The allocation rules under OBRA 93 were temporary, expiring one year after they took effect. As in earlier years, many observers attributed the temporary nature of the allocation rules to the mechanics of compliance with federal budget targets: If Congress were to pass permanent legislation covering the R&D allocation rules, then the cost, to the current-year budget, of any treatment more generous than the 1977 regulations, must include costs incurred in future years. By instead passing temporary legislation, Congress incurs budgetary costs only for the current year. Of course, budgetary costs need not bear any relation to the economic consequences of permanent legislation covering the allocation of R&D expenses.[13]

During 1995 the Treasury reconsidered the appropriateness of its 1977 R&D expense regulations. Based on newer analysis (U.S. Department of the Treasury 1995), the regulations were amended roughly along the lines of recent legislative developments. Specifically, the 1995 regulations permit firms to select one of two allocation methods: one in which firms allocate 50 percent of U.S.-based R&D expenses to domestic source, with the remaining 50 percent allocated between domestic and foreign source based on sales; and a second in which firms allocate 25 percent of U.S.-based R&D expenses to domestic source, with the remaining 75 percent allocated between domestic and foreign source based on gross income. Under these regulations, income-based allocation is not permitted to reduce foreign source allocation to less than 50 percent of that produced by the sales method. The new regulations amend the previous rules in certain, more minor, ways as well.[14] Owing to the expiration of the OBRA 93 R&D allo-

---

13. Some have strong feelings that permanent legislation creates a more predictable environment for businesses, thereby making the United States a more attractive location for R&D. Turro (1993, 436) quotes one tax practitioner, who describes Congress's decision to make the OBRA 93 R&D allocation rules temporary an "absurd tax policy decision."

14. Specifically, firms are required to make their elections permanent, so it is not possible to use the sales method in one year and the income method in the next. In addition, the new regulations specify that firms allocate R&D expenses based on three-digit SIC activities, rather than the two-digit SIC activities provided in the previous regulations.

cation rules, the 1995 Treasury regulations now govern the allocation of U.S. R&D expenses.[15]

## 8.3  Framework for Analysis

Changes in the U.S. tax treatment of R&D expenses affect some firms more than others, due to differences in excess foreign tax credit status and in the extent to which sales and income have foreign sources. Consequently, these changes can be used to identify differences between firms in costs of performing R&D in the United States in years before and after tax changes. The idea behind the empirical work that follows is to draw appropriate inferences from correlations between tax-driven cost changes and subsequent propensities to take out patents on the basis of U.S. and foreign research activities.

### 8.3.1  A Model

It is useful to distinguish three types of R&D undertaken by MNCs. The first type is R&D performed in the United States and intended to produce innovative output for the U.S. market. The second type is R&D performed in the United States and intended to generate foreign sales. The third type is R&D performed abroad. Tax incentives differ for each of these types, and as a result, the incentives that firms face to undertake R&D in domestic and foreign locations will differ. Of course, to a certain degree these distinctions may be more pronounced ex post than they are ex ante, because, in the early stages of industrial research, the location of ultimate sales may be more than a little bit uncertain. For the purpose of this analysis, firms are assumed to be able to distinguish the ultimate location of the uses of their innovative output at the time that they perform the initial R&D.

The R&D expense allocation rules imply that MNCs performing R&D in the United States are unable to deduct all of their R&D expenses in years after 1986. Instead, they can deduct a fraction $\alpha$ of such expenses, in which the value of $\alpha$ depends on the firm's foreign tax credit status, its ratio of foreign to domestic sales, and the tax rules in place at the time. U.S. tax rules in effect between 1981 and 1986 imply that $\alpha = 1$, whereas those in effect after 1986 imply that $1 \geq \alpha \geq 0$.

A U.S. firm that contemplates committing funds to an R&D project that is expected to generate innovative output, and therefore sales in the domestic market, maximizes

$$(1) \qquad \pi_i = Q(R_i, \theta_i)(1 - \tau) - R_i(1 - \alpha_i \tau),$$

15. It is noteworthy that the 1995 revisions to the R&D cost allocation regulations were not costly from the standpoint of federal budget targets because regulatory changes are not budgeted.

in which $\pi_i$ denotes firm $i$'s after-tax profits, $R_i$ is firm $i$'s expenditures on R&D, $Q(\cdot)$ is net sales generated by firm $i$'s R&D activity, $\alpha_i$ is the fraction of firm $i$'s R&D expenses that are deductible for tax purposes, and $\tau$ is the statutory tax rate. The variable $\theta_i$ is an unobservable parameter (assumed to be known to firms) that affects the productivity of firm $i$'s research activity and thereby influences its desired R&D spending. The function $Q(\cdot)$ is assumed to be twice continuously differentiable and concave in R. The first-order condition corresponding to an interior maximum of (1) is $\partial\pi_i/\partial R_i = 0$, which implies

$$(2) \qquad \frac{\partial Q(R_i, \theta_i)}{\partial R_i} = \frac{1 - \alpha_i\tau}{1 - \tau}.$$

Equation (2) expresses the simple point that reduced deductibility of domestic R&D expenses, which is captured by lower values of $\alpha_i$, are associated with higher required marginal products of R&D expenditures by profit-maximizing firms. Because the function $Q(\cdot)$ is assumed to exhibit decreasing returns to R, it follows that lower values of $\alpha_i$ reduce desired spending on R&D.

The incentives facing a U.S. multinational performing R&D in the United States for use abroad are potentially quite different. Returns to the innovating firm come in the form of foreign source royalties that are effectively untaxed by the United States if the firm has excess foreign tax credits, and that are fully taxed otherwise. Denoting firm $i$'s R&D undertaken for this purpose by $R_i^*$, and the relevant sales function by $Q^*(R_i^*, \theta_i)$,[16] the firm's profits from this source ($\pi_i^*$) equal

$$(3) \qquad \pi_i^* = Q^*(R_i^*, \theta_i)(1 - \beta_i\tau) - R_i^*(1 - \alpha_i\tau),$$

in which $\beta_i$ reflects the extent to which firm $i$'s foreign source royalties are taxed, so that $\beta_i = 0$ for firms with excess foreign tax credits and $\beta_i = 1$ for firms with deficit foreign tax credits.

The first-order condition corresponding to an interior maximum of (3) with respect to $R_i^*$ is $\partial\pi_i^*/\partial R_i^* = 0$, implying

$$(4) \qquad \frac{\partial Q^*(R_i^*, \theta_i)}{\partial R_i^*} = \frac{1 - \alpha_i\tau}{1 - \beta_i\tau}.$$

Equation (4) expresses in a simple way that the incentive to perform R&D in the United States for use abroad is a function of the deductibility of R&D expenses as well as of the tax treatment of foreign source royalty

16. Strictly speaking, it is necessary for the analysis that follows to include as an argument of the $Q^*(\cdot)$ function R&D undertaken by foreign affiliates; this argument is omitted, because including it complicates the notation without changing the interpretation of the results.

receipts. Assuming the $Q^*(\cdot)$ function to exhibit decreasing returns to $R^*$, it follows that the desired level of $R^*$ is an increasing function of $\alpha$ and a decreasing function of $\beta$.

The third type of R&D that MNCs undertake is foreign R&D. The foreign innovative activity of U.S. multinationals is a decreasing function of R&D performed in the United States and intended for foreign use ($R^*$) if foreign and domestic research are substitutes, and an increasing function of $R^*$ if they are complements.[17] Because $R_i^*$ is not directly observable, it is necessary to infer its value from the tax incentives that firm $i$ faces. This inference is greatly complicated by the likely importance of firm-specific technology shocks. Firms differ greatly in their abilities and willingness to patent new technologies, and these differences may change over time. It is convenient to introduce the variable $\phi_{it}$, which denotes a firm-specific shock to the patenting proclivity of firm $i$ in period $t$. The firm-specific shock $\phi_{it}$ differs from $\theta_{it}$, in that $\theta_{it}$ affects the marginal product of additional R&D spending, while $\phi_{it}$ affects the proclivity to obtain patents conditional on research activity.

It is helpful to define foreign and domestic patenting functions:

(5a) $$P_{it}^* = \psi^*(R_{it}^f, \phi_{it}),$$

(5b) $$P_{it} = \psi(R_{it}, \phi_{it}),$$

in which $R_{it}^f$ is the foreign R&D spending of firm $i$ in year $t$, $P_{it}^*$ is the number of foreign patents taken out by firm $i$ in year $t$, and $P_{it}$ is the corresponding number of domestic patents.[18]

From equation (4) it is clear that the after-tax cost of domestic R&D directed at producing sales in foreign markets is a function of the firm's domestic tax situation. The extent, therefore, to which these domestic tax considerations affect $R_{it}^f$ (and thereby affect $P_{it}^*$) depends on the complementarity or substitutability of foreign and domestic technology. The firm's derived demand for foreign R&D can be written

(6) $$R_{it}^f = g^* \left\{ \left[ \frac{(1 - \alpha_{it}\tau_t)}{(1 - \beta_{it}\tau_t)} \right], \theta_{it} \right\},$$

17. This discussion takes the returns to foreign R&D to be unaffected by domestic R&D intended for the domestic market. This is a reasonable assumption, given the very limited domestic use of technology produced by foreign affiliates, as reflected by royalty payments reported in table 8.1.

18. It is noteworthy that this specification assumes that any technology spillovers between domestic and foreign innovation are fully credited to proper sources and therefore reflected in royalty payments. The functional forms of equations (5a) and (5b) also require that patenting be affected only by R&D performed contemporaneously, a testable proposition examined in the next section.

in which the first argument of the $g*$ function is simply the after-tax cost of performing R&D at home to generate sales abroad, and other considerations, such as firm and economy characteristics in year $t$, are captured by $\theta_{it}$.

Combining equations (5a) and (6) yields a function that expresses foreign patenting as it is affected by the price of domestic R&D:

$$(7) \qquad P_{it}^* = h*\left\{\left[\frac{(1 - \alpha_{it}\tau_t)}{(1 - \beta_{it}\tau_t)}\right], \theta_{it}, \phi_{it}\right\}.$$

By a similar reasoning, the demand for domestic R&D directed at producing sales in the domestic market is a function of the implied after-tax cost indicated by equation (2):

$$(8) \qquad R_{it} = g\left\{\left[\frac{(1 - \alpha_{it}\tau_t)}{(1 - \tau_t)}\right], \theta_{it}\right\},$$

which, combined with equation (5b), implies

$$(9) \qquad P_{it} = h\left\{\left[\frac{(1 - \alpha_{it}\tau_t)}{(1 - \tau_t)}\right], \theta_{it}, \phi_{it}\right\},$$

in which the $h(\cdot)$ function expresses domestic patenting as a function of the price of domestic R&D as well as firm-specific shocks.

Linearizing the effect of $\theta$ and $\phi$ yields

$$(10) \qquad P_{it}^* = f*\left[\frac{(1 - \alpha_{it}\tau_t)}{(1 - \beta_{it}\tau_t)}\right] + c*(\theta_{it} + \phi_{it}),$$

and

$$(11) \qquad P_{it} = f\left[\frac{(1 - \alpha_{it}\tau_t)}{(1 - \tau_t)}\right] + c(\theta_{it} + \phi_{it}),$$

in which $c*$ and $c$ are constants that reflect the impact of firm-specific shocks on foreign and domestic patenting.

Combining equations (10) and (11), and taking first differences, yields

$$(12) \qquad P_{it}^* - P_{it-1}^* = \delta_{1it} - \left(\frac{c*}{c}\right)\delta_{2it} + \left(\frac{c*}{c}\right)(P_{it} - P_{it-1}),$$

$$\delta_{1it} \equiv f*\left[\frac{(1 - \alpha_{it}\tau_t)}{(1 - \beta_{it}\tau_t)}\right] - f*\left[\frac{(1 - \alpha_{it-1}\tau_{t-1})}{(1 - \beta_{it-1}\tau_{t-1})}\right],$$

$$\delta_{2it} \equiv f\left[\frac{(1 - \alpha_{it}\tau_t)}{(1 - \tau_t)}\right] - f\left[\frac{(1 - \alpha_{it-1}\tau_{t-1})}{(1 - \tau_{t-1})}\right].$$

Equation (12) expresses the change in foreign patenting as a function of three variables: the change in home-country tax incentives for home R&D directed at foreign markets, the change in tax incentives for home R&D directed at domestic markets, and the change in domestic patenting. Estimates of the propensity to develop foreign patents as a function of these variables implicitly estimate the degree of complementarity or substitutability of foreign and domestic R&D, because this connection is embedded in the $f^*(\cdot)$ function. It is this specification that provides the framework used in the empirical analysis.

### 8.3.2    Data

The empirical work that follows analyzes the behavior of publicly traded firms whose annual report information is collected by Standard and Poors Compustat Service. Starting from a universe of somewhat more than 7,500 companies, firms are included in the sample if they are multinationals incorporated in the United States, and if their reported foreign assets equal 1 percent or more of reported total assets for each year during 1986–1990. This criterion is satisfied by 422 firms.

Foreign tax rate information is central to the analysis, because the hypothesis that firms maximize after-tax profits implies that deficit foreign tax credit firms will react very differently than excess foreign tax credit firms to the changes introduced by TRA 1986. Compustat reports foreign pretax incomes and foreign taxes paid by the firms in the sample, from which it is possible to use simple division to obtain an estimate of effective foreign tax rates.[19] These average foreign tax rates for firms in 1985 form the basis of the tax calculations that follow. Data for 1985 are used because this was the last full year before passage of TRA 1986, which introduced incentives to relocate foreign operations and tax liabilities. Average foreign tax rates are truncated at 0 and 100 percent for purposes of this construction.

During the 1983–1986 period, U.S. tax law permitted U.S. firms to deduct 100 percent of their domestic R&D expenses against domestic taxable income. In the years after 1986, deductibility is based on excess foreign tax credit status and on shares of total sales in foreign markets. For the purposes of constructing regression variables, $\alpha_{it}$ is assigned a value of 1 for all firms until 1986. In the period after 1986, firms are assigned $\alpha_{it} = 1$ if the 1985 foreign average tax rate is below the (year $t$) U.S. statutory tax rate; otherwise $\alpha_{it} = [1 - 0.36$ (foreign sales fraction)], corresponding

19. Average foreign tax rates are used in place of actual foreign tax credit status (i.e., excess or deficit credit) for two reasons. The first is that actual foreign tax status is endogenous to a host of decision variables related to the financing, investment, repatriation, transfer pricing, and other activities of MNCs. Although average foreign tax rates are, by the same reasoning, also endogenous, the endogeneity problem is generally regarded to be more severe with excess foreign tax credit status than it is with average foreign tax rates. The second reason is that tax return data at the firm level are unavailable, so the actual foreign tax credit situations of firms in the sample cannot be determined.

to the expense allocation rules in place in 1991. Because the value of $\beta_{it}$ depends critically on foreign tax credit status about which only imprecise information is available, a more continuous tax specification is used in defining $\beta_{it}$: $\beta_{it}$ is defined to equal 1 minus the average foreign tax rate a firm faced in 1985.

To determine the international distribution of patenting, the 422 sample firms were matched to the database of U.S. patents created by NBER and Case Western Reserve University.[20] The NBER/CWRU database contains all patents granted by the U.S. government between 1963 and 1996. This database, based on the public patent records, identifies for every patent the inventors, the geographic location of the inventors, and a corporate assignee (if any) to whom the patent right is transferred by the inventor.[21] To use these data for the current purpose, it was necessary to identify all U.S. patents that were taken out by the sample firms or their affiliates, as well as the countries in which the patents originated.

The task of identifying the patents of the sample firms is complicated by two problems. First, the patent office does not utilize an external code or identifier that permits patenting assignees to be linked electronically to data such as provided by Compustat. Rather, assignees are indicated by name, and the spelling and punctuation of the names are not completely standardized—there may be patent records for "IBM" and others for "I.B.M." Secondly, and more fundamentally, companies choose the corporate entity to which the patent will be assigned, which could be a subsidiary or an affiliated company rather than the parent company. As described further in Hall, Jaffe, and Trajtenberg (2000), the NBER/CWRU database contains a match between the corporate assignees in the patent office data and Compustat firms; the match attempts to deal with both of these problems. First, spelling and punctuation variations were standardized by removing all spaces, punctuation, generic words (e.g., "Inc." and "Co.") and searching for apparent multiple versions of the same entities based on these compressed names. All potential matches of this sort were checked by hand to ensure that they were real. Second, approximately 30,000 subsidiaries and affiliates of the Compustat universe, as indicated in the 1998 *Who Owns Whom Directory of Corporate Affiliations* (Dun & Bradstreet Ltd. 1989), were matched to the patent database to identify patents taken out by these affiliates, and these affiliated patents were assigned to the parent companies for the purpose of this paper.

20. For more information on this database, see the description in Hall, Jaffe, and Trajtenberg (2000).
21. Patents must be taken out by the individual or individuals who created the invention. About three-fourths of all patents are assigned, at the time of the patent application, to an institution, typically the inventors' employer.
    The NBER/CWRU database contains additional information not used in this paper, including a technological classification of the patent and information about citations between patents. See Jaffe and Trajtenberg (1999) and Hall, Jaffe, and Trajtenberg (2000).

The geographic location of the patent is based on the location of the first inventor listed on the patent.[22] The inventor locations in the patent data are domestic residences (not citizenships or nationalities) of inventors as indicated on patent applications. Hence, it is reasonable to expect that a patent based on an invention from an IBM laboratory in Japan would be coded as a "Japanese" patent. The patent might be assigned to IBM, Inc., or it might be assigned to an affiliate or subsidiary organized in Japan. Either way, in principle, it would be treated as if it were an IBM patent, so long as the *Who Owns Whom* directory includes the ownership link. Certainly, it is possible for some subsidiaries and affiliates to be omitted in this classification, which would mean that the foreign patent counts of their parent firms are systematically biased downward. Further, to the extent that the creation of such foreign affiliates or the assignment of patents to them has changed over time, the *change* in foreign patents for these firms might be systematically biased. There is no obvious reason, however, that such an undercount of foreign patents would be correlated with the other variables of interest.

For the purpose of estimation the data are combined to form two observations for each firm, one corresponding to the 1983–1986 period, and a second corresponding to the 1988–1991 period. Foreign and domestic patents are summed over the four years that constitute each period. The specification of equation (12) that is then estimated is one in which the dependent variable is the difference between the number of foreign patents taken during the 1988–1991 period and the number taken during the 1983–1986 period. Similarly, the change-in-domestic-patents variable that appears on the right side of equation (12) equals the difference between the number of domestic patents taken during the 1988–1991 period and the number taken during the 1983–1986 period.

Table 8.2 presents country-level information on foreign patents by firms in the sample, along with other indicators of activity by the foreign affiliates of U.S. multinationals. Foreign patenting is concentrated in a relatively small number of technologically advanced countries, which is not surprising; nor is it surprising that R&D spending by the foreign affiliates of U.S. multinationals is concentrated in roughly the same countries. Indeed, the five foreign countries (the United Kingdom, Japan, Germany, Canada, and France) with the most patents attributed to resident inventors over the period 1988–1991 lead all others in R&D spending by U.S. multinationals in 1989. To be sure, there is important variation among countries, and most importantly, the vast majority of U.S. patents taken out by sample firms have inventors that are residents of the United States. The

22. Jaffe, Trajtenberg, and Henderson (1993) investigated the extent of geographic dispersion among the inventors on a given patent. They found that all inventors on a given patent listed the same country of residence on 98 percent of all patents (including those with a single inventor).

**Table 8.2          Foreign Patent and R&D Activity of U.S. Firms**

| | Patents 1983–1986 | Patents 1988–1991 | Net PPE 1989 | Sales 1989 | R&D Spending 1989 |
|---|---|---|---|---|---|
| Australia | 14 | 17 | 12,113 | 37,745 | 191 |
| Austria | 2 | 1 | 919 | 5,550 | 16 |
| Bahamas | 0 | 1 | 616 | 1,529 | * |
| Belgium | 109 | 106 | 4,811 | 30,085 | 317 |
| Brazil | 4 | 6 | 9,223 | 30,588 | 90 |
| Canada | 152 | 305 | 63,636 | 173,251 | 914 |
| Chile | 1 | 1 | 718 | 1,981 | 1 |
| Colombia | 0 | 1 | 1,959 | 3,895 | 2 |
| Denmark | 3 | 10 | 923 | 4,119 | d |
| Dominican Republic | 0 | 0 | 281 | 578 | * |
| Ecuador | 1 | 0 | 196 | 578 | * |
| Egypt | 1 | 0 | 1,313 | 1,871 | * |
| France | 148 | 214 | 11,093 | 70,761 | 545 |
| Germany | 360 | 418 | 21,066 | 106,366 | 1,496 |
| Greece | 3 | 1 | 174 | 1,932 | 1 |
| Guatemala | 1 | 0 | 133 | 672 | * |
| Hong Kong | 4 | 7 | 3,174 | 16,408 | 9 |
| India | 1 | 10 | 76 | 323 | 2 |
| Indonesia | 1 | 0 | 4,644 | 6,120 | 2 |
| Ireland | 7 | 37 | 1,874 | 11,415 | 134 |
| Israel | 11 | 53 | 326 | 1,042 | 29 |
| Italy | 35 | 50 | 6,386 | 45,265 | 294 |
| Japan | 174 | 483 | 7,830 | 58,420 | 488 |
| Luxembourg | 26 | 21 | 633 | 1,443 | d |
| Malaysia | 3 | 10 | 2,212 | 5,419 | 3 |
| Mexico | 1 | 1 | 3,929 | 16,437 | 37 |
| Netherlands | 52 | 84 | 8,182 | 45,408 | 360 |
| New Zealand | 1 | 1 | 775 | 3,153 | 4 |
| Nigeria | 0 | 0 | 706 | 2,250 | * |
| Norway | 4 | 4 | 5,865 | 7,616 | 27 |
| Philippines | 2 | 2 | 531 | 2,905 | 5 |
| Singapore | 1 | 26 | 2,153 | 15,102 | 25 |
| South Africa | 2 | 4 | 449 | 2,653 | 9 |
| South Korea | 6 | 4 | 641 | 2,463 | 5 |
| Spain | 6 | 8 | 4,514 | 23,712 | 115 |
| Sweden | 13 | 12 | 732 | 7,703 | 33 |
| Switzerland | 93 | 88 | 1,977 | 36,231 | 67 |
| Taiwan | 0 | 4 | 1,047 | 6,773 | 23 |
| United Kingdom | 540 | 749 | 42,418 | 167,186 | 1,673 |
| Venezuela | 0 | 3 | 461 | 2,677 | 9 |
| United States | 28,516 | 39,143 | | | |

*Note:* Columns (1) and (2) report total numbers of U.S. patents granted to the 378 U.S. firms in the sample and assigned to inventors located in designated countries. Column (3) reports aggregate values (in $ millions) of the local property, plant, and equipment of majority-owned nonbank affiliates of nonbank U.S. parent firms in 1989. Column (4) reports aggregate sales (in $ millions) of majority-owned nonbank affiliates of nonbank U.S. parent firms in 1989. Column (5) reports aggregate R&D expenditures (in $ millions) on behalf of majority-owned nonbank affiliates of nonbank U.S. parent firms in 1989. d = data suppressed to protect the identity of individual survey respondents. * = R&D spending of less than $500,000. Data reported in columns (3)–(5) are drawn from U.S. Department of Commerce (1992).

**Table 8.3**                **R&D Activity and Patenting Behavior**

| | ln(total patents, 1982–1985) | | ln(1 + total patents, 1982–1985) | |
|---|---|---|---|---|
| Constant | 0.8714 | −0.9037 | −1.0570 | −1.8438 |
| | (0.1478) | (0.3452) | (0.1797) | (0.3429) |
| ln(R&D, 1986) | 0.8376 | 0.4726 | 0.7317 | 0.5569 |
| | (0.0371) | (0.0735) | (0.0369) | (0.0740) |
| Patents dummy | | | 3.1103 | 3.0377 |
| | | | (0.2063) | (0.2178) |
| ln(Assets, 1986) | | 0.4470 | | 0.2151 |
| | | (0.0787) | | (0.0857) |
| $R^2$ | .690 | .728 | .782 | .788 |
| $N$ | 231 | 231 | 292 | 292 |

*Note:* The table reports estimated coefficients from ordinary least squares (OLS) regressions. The dependent variable in the regressions reported in columns (1) and (2) is the log of the number of new patents (domestic plus foreign) taken out between 1982 and 1985. Observations are included in the samples analyzed in these regressions only if they have nonzero and nonmissing patent and R&D data. The dependent variable in the regressions reported in columns (3) and (4) is the log of 1 plus the number of new patents (domestic plus foreign) taken out between 1982 and 1985. Observations are included in the samples analyzed in these regressions only if they have nonzero and nonmissing R&D data. "ln(R&D, 1986)" is the log of total R&D expenditures in 1986. "Patents dummy" is a dummy variable that equals 1 if a firm took out nonzero patents between 1982 and 1985, and equals 0 otherwise. "ln(Assets, 1986)" is the log of total firm assets in 1986. Heteroskedasticity-consistent standard errors are in parentheses.

foreign data presented in table 8.2, however, serve to confirm the reasonableness of the patent attribution method on which is based the empirical work that follows.

## 8.4  Results

As a prelude to estimating the model implied by equation (12), the regressions reported in table 8.3 look simply at the firm-level relationship between R&D and patents as it is evident in the data. Columns (1) and (2) of table 8.3 present estimates in which the dependent variable is the log of total (worldwide) firm patents over the 1982–1985 period, and the independent variables include the log of R&D spending in 1986 and log of total firm assets in 1986. The sample analyzed in these regressions is limited to firms with nonzero patents over 1982–1985, and those with positive R&D spending and total assets in 1986.

Consistent with other work,[23] the results indicate a strong correlation between patenting and R&D activity, one that is not simply a function of firm size (as measured by assets). The regression of log of patents on log R&D (reported in column (1)) shows slightly less than constant returns of patents to R&D, although this result is somewhat sensitive to how the

23. See, e.g., Bound, Cummins, Griliches, Hall, and Jaffe (1984).

observations with no patents are treated. When log of total assets is added to the regression, as it is in the regression reported in column (2), log assets absorbs part of the explanatory power of log R&D, but the results continue to imply a patent production function with approximately constant returns to scale. Columns (3) and (4) of table 8.3 report regressions using a larger sample of firms that includes those with no patents during the 1982–1985 period. The dependent variable in these regressions is now the log of 1 plus patents, and the right-hand side variables now include a dummy variable that takes the value 1 if a firm has nonzero patents over this time period. The results reported in columns (3) and (4) are qualitatively similar to those reported in columns (1) and (2), in that a strong positive relationship between patents and R&D spending exhibits decreasing returns.

The consistency of the firm-level patent data with country and firm characteristics (as evidenced in tables 8.2 and 8.3) offers the prospect of informative estimation of variants of equation (12) using these data. Table 8.4 presents means and standard deviations of the regression variables, and the initial regression results are presented in table 8.5. The specification estimated in these regressions is

$$(13) \qquad P^*_{it} - P^*_{it-1} = \beta_1(P_{it} - P_{it-1}) + \beta_2\alpha_{it} + \beta_3\lambda_{it} + \beta_4 X_{it} + \varepsilon_{it},$$

$$\lambda_{it} \equiv \left[\frac{(1 - \alpha_{it}\tau_t)}{(1 - \beta_{it}\tau_t)}\right] - \left[\frac{(1 - \alpha_{it-1}\tau_{t-1})}{(1 - \beta_{it-1}\tau_{t-1})}\right].$$

Comparing equations (13) and (12), it follows that the regression coefficients can be interpreted as $\beta_1 = (c^*/c)$, $\beta_2$ equals the product of $(c^*/c)$ and a linearization of the $f(\cdot)$ function, and $\beta_3$ captures a different linearization of the $f^*(\cdot)$ function. The reason that the first difference of the $f(\cdot)$ function may be represented in equation (13) simply by $\alpha_{it}$ is that all firms were entitled to deduct their full R&D expenses in the period before 1986, and all faced the same statutory taxes after 1986, so that this term differs between firms only in $\alpha_{it}$. The variable $X_{it}$ represents firm-specific characteristics (including a constant term).

Column (1) of table 8.5 reports estimates of equation (13) without including firm-specific characteristics (other than constants). The estimated coefficients are consistent with the evidence reported in other tables and with a generally complementary relationship between domestic and foreign innovative activity. The estimated value of $\beta_1$ is approximately 0.06, which means that shocks to domestic patenting translate rather little into changes in foreign patents—reflecting the much larger share of U.S. inventors than foreign inventors among the patents taken out by U.S. firms. The estimated value of $\beta_2$ is positive but not significant, although this is not of great consequence because $\alpha_{it}$ is included in equation (13) merely in order to control for changes in domestic patenting due to tax changes rather than firm-specific shocks.

**Table 8.4**     **Means and Standard Deviations of Regression Variables**

| Variable | Mean | Standard Deviation | N |
|---|---|---|---|
| *R&D Sample (table 8.3)* | | | |
| ln(total patents, 1982–85) | 3.5225 | 1.9805 | 231 |
| ln(1 + total patents, 1982–85) | 3.5571 | 2.4662 | 292 |
| ln(R&D, 1986) | 2.8121 | 2.0368 | 292 |
| Patents dummy | 0.8219 | 0.3832 | 292 |
| ln(Assets, 1986) | 6.5559 | 1.8240 | 231 |
| *Foreign Patents Sample (tables 8.5 and 8.6)* | | | |
| Change in foreign patents | 3.0317 | 14.8684 | 378 |
| Change in domestic patents | 35.2116 | 178.7609 | 378 |
| R&D expense deductibility, 1991 | 0.8806 | 0.1315 | 378 |
| Change in R&D tax incentives (foreign) | −0.1126 | 0.0713 | 378 |
| Percent foreign sales, 1991 | 0.3242 | 0.1946 | 378 |
| First-period foreign patents | 5.3810 | 21.1604 | 378 |
| Foreign patents ∗ R&D expense deductibility | 4.6951 | 18.4840 | 378 |
| Foreign patents ∗ R&D incentives (foreign) | −0.6773 | 2.8683 | 378 |

*Note:* The table presents means and standard deviations of variables used in the regressions.

**Table 8.5**     **Foreign Patents and Domestic Tax Incentives**

| | Dependent Variable: Change in Number of Foreign Patents | |
|---|---|---|
| Constant | −14.4802 | −11.9398 |
| | (7.4138) | (7.3321) |
| Change in domestic patents | 0.0590 | 0.0587 |
| | (0.0144) | (0.0143) |
| R&D expense deductibility, 1991 | 13.5946 | 9.5607 |
| | (7.1326) | (7.1384) |
| Change in R&D tax incentives (foreign) | −30.7697 | −26.4124 |
| | (12.8296) | (12.3228) |
| Percent foreign sales, 1991 | | 4.6708 |
| | | (2.4622) |
| $R^2$ | .513 | .516 |
| N | 378 | 378 |

*Note:* The table reports estimated coefficients from OLS regressions. The dependent variable is the difference between the number of new foreign patents taken out during 1988–1991 (inclusive) and the number taken out during 1983–1986 (inclusive). "Change in domestic patents" is the difference between the number of new domestic patents taken out during 1988–1991 (inclusive) and the number taken out during 1983–1986 (inclusive). "R&D expense deductibility, 1991" equals the fraction of domestic R&D expenses that firms can deduct against their domestic tax liabilities in 1991. "Change in R&D tax incentives (foreign)" equals the change in the required cost of capital for a $1 investment in domestic R&D intended to enhance foreign profitability. "Percent foreign sales, 1991" equals the fraction of a firm's sales that are foreign in 1991. Heteroskedasticity-consistent standard errors are in parentheses.

The negative and significant estimated value of $\beta_3$ implies that greater deductibility of R&D expenses in 1991 is associated with increased foreign patenting. Specifically, lower tax costs of performing R&D in the United States for use abroad are associated with greater foreign patents in the second (1988–1991) period relative to the first (1983–1986). In order to interpret the magnitude of the estimated value of $\beta_3$, it is important to bear in mind the construction of the R&D tax incentive variable, and specifically, the use of average foreign tax rates in place of $\beta_{it}$. Because a 10 percent difference in average foreign tax rates is generally sufficient to move firms between excess and deficit foreign tax credit status, it follows that the estimated value of $\beta_3$ (without this correction) overstates by a factor of ten the impact of changes in the tax treatment of royalties. The estimated coefficient of $-30.8$ in column (1) therefore implies that changing the domestic taxation of foreign source royalties from taxable to not taxable, would, for a firm with the mean value of $\alpha_{it} = 0.88$, be responsible for 1.1 additional foreign patents over the 1988–1991 period. Given the sample mean value of 5.4 foreign patents over the 1983–1986 period, this estimate implies that the cross elasticity of foreign patents with respect to the after-tax cost of domestic R&D directed at foreign markets is between 0.2 and 0.4. This estimate is of the same order of magnitude, though of a different sign, as estimates of international R&D and royalty substitutability reported by Hines (1995). These behavioral elasticities are considerably smaller than an own-price R&D demand elasticity of unity or greater, as reported by Hall (1993) and Hines (1993).

Column (2) of table 8.5 presents estimated coefficients from a regression that adds as an independent variable the 1991 ratio of foreign to total sales. The purpose of this somewhat ad hoc addition is to control for a form of unobserved heterogeneity, in which firms that differ in their degrees of multinationality also differ in other unobserved dimensions that affect changes in foreign patenting. Firms with greater foreign sales in 1991 show faster growth of foreign patenting, although in other ways the results presented in column (2) differ little from those presented in column (1). The estimated tax effects in the column (2) regression are somewhat smaller than those in the first specification of the equation, but remain significant and of the same sign.

Table 8.6 reports results from a different specification of equation (12):

$$(14)\quad P_{it}^* - P_{it-1}^* = \beta_1(P_{it} - P_{it-1}) + \beta_2 P_{it-1}^* + \beta_2 P_{it-1}^* \alpha_{it} + \beta_3 P_{it-1}^* \lambda_{it}$$
$$+ \beta_4 X_{it} + u_{it},$$

$$\lambda_{it} \equiv \left[ \frac{(1 - \alpha_{it}\tau_t)}{(1 - \beta_{it}\tau_t)} \right] - \left[ \frac{(1 - \alpha_{it-1}\tau_{t-1})}{(1 - \beta_{it-1}\tau_{t-1})} \right].$$

The specification in equation (14) is a close variant of equation (13), the difference being that the independent variables are now interacted with

**Table 8.6**          **Foreign Patents and Domestic Tax Incentives**

| | Dependent Variable: Change in Number of Foreign Patents | | | |
|---|---|---|---|---|
| Constant | 0.4650 | | −0.3125 | |
| | (0.3300) | | (0.0094) | |
| Change in domestic patents | 0.0441 | 0.0443 | 0.0441 | 0.0441 |
| | (0.0094) | (0.0093) | (0.0094) | (0.0094) |
| First-period foreign patents | −7.0090 | −6.9122 | −6.9873 | −7.0120 |
| | (2.9126) | (2.8834) | (2.9001) | (2.9079) |
| Foreign patents * R&D expense | 6.1417 | 6.0594 | 6.1158 | 6.1389 |
| deductibility | (2.2333) | (2.5081) | (2.5218) | (2.5281) |
| Foreign patents * R&D incentives | −14.6054 | −14.4423 | −14.5892 | −14.6249 |
| (foreign) | (5.8364) | (5.7862) | (5.8173) | (5.8309) |
| Percent foreign sales, 1991 | | | 2.4524 | 1.7459 |
| | | | (1.9554) | (1.1536) |
| $R^2$ | .640 | .654 | .641 | .656 |
| $N$ | 378 | 378 | 378 | 378 |

*Note:* The table reports estimated coefficients from OLS regressions. The dependent variable is the difference between the number of new foreign patents taken out during 1988–1991 (inclusive) and the number taken out during 1983–1986 (inclusive). "Change in domestic patents" is the difference between the number of new domestic patents taken out during 1988–1991 (inclusive) and the number taken out during 1983–1986 (inclusive). "First-period foreign patents" is the number of foreign patents taken out between 1983 and 1986. "Foreign patents * R&D expense deductibility" equals the product of foreign patents taken out between 1983 and 1986 *and* the fraction of domestic R&D expenses that firms can deduct against their domestic tax liabilities in 1991. "Foreign patents * R&D incentives (foreign)" equals the product of foreign patents taken out between 1983 and 1986 *and* the change in the required cost of capital for a $1 investment in domestic R&D intended to enhance foreign profitability. "Percent foreign sales, 1991" equals the fraction of a firm's sales that are foreign in 1991. Heteroskedasticity-consistent standard errors are in parentheses.

numbers of foreign patents over 1983–1986. The specification in equation (14) is intended to provide a natural scaling for the price-type variables that appear on the right side of equation (12).

The results reported in table 8.6 are quite consistent with those reported in table 8.5. Firms with rapidly growing domestic patenting exhibit faster than average growth of foreign patenting. Of particular interest is the estimated −14.6 value of $\beta_3$ in the regression reported in column (1). Again taking a 10 percent change in the average foreign tax rate to be sufficient to change foreign tax credit status, it follows that the −14.6 coefficient implies roughly a 0.5 cross-price elasticity of foreign R&D with respect to the cost of domestic R&D directed at foreign markets. As is evident from the results reported in columns (2) through (4) of table 8.6, minor specification changes affect this estimated behavioral elasticity very little.

## 8.5   Conclusion

This study considers the effect of changes in the after-tax cost of R&D on subsequent patenting by U.S. firms in the United States and abroad.

The purpose is to estimate the impact of tax policy on the location of successful inventive activity. Tax policy affects patent location by influencing the location of R&D and therefore the likelihood of producing patentable inventions. Recent U.S. tax changes affect some U.S. firms more strongly than others, making it possible to estimate the effect of tax policies on innovation by comparing reactions to the changes.

The results indicate that firms for which after-tax costs of performing R&D in the United States for use abroad rose most rapidly after 1986 exhibited the slowest growth of foreign patenting in subsequent years. Estimated cross-price elasticities of foreign patenting with respect to the cost of domestic R&D directed at foreign markets vary between 0.2 and 0.5. This suggests not only that tax incentives influence subsequent patenting patterns, but that foreign and domestic innovative activities are complements at the firm level. Although this is an intuitively appealing finding, it is inconsistent with available evidence of the international substitutability of R&D activity as measured at the aggregate level. This raises the interesting possibility that domestic and foreign innovation, although complements for individual firms, become substitutes between economies due to induced effects on the composition of industry or for other reasons.

# References

Altshuler, Rosanne, and T. Scott Newlon. 1993. The effects of U.S. tax policy on the income repatriation patterns of U.S. multinational corporations. In *Studies in international taxation,* ed. Alberto Giovannini, R. Glenn Hubbard, and Joel Slemrod, 77–115. Chicago: University of Chicago Press.

Altshuler, Rosanne, T. Scott Newlon, and William C. Randolph. 1995. Do repatriation taxes matter? Evidence from the tax returns of U.S. multinationals. In *The effects of taxation on multinational corporations,* ed. Martin Feldstein, James R. Hines Jr., and R. Glenn Hubbard, 253–72. Chicago: University of Chicago Press.

Blomström, Magnus. 1991. Host country benefits of foreign investment. In *Foreign investment, technology and economic growth,* ed. Donald McFetridge, 93–108. Calgary: University of Calgary Press.

Blomström, Magnus, and Ari Kokko. 1995. Policies to encourage inflows of technology through foreign multinationals. *World Development* 23 (3): 1–10.

Bound, John, Clint Cummins, Zvi Griliches, Bronwyn Hall, and Adam Jaffe. 1984. Who does R&D and who patents? In *R&D, patents and productivity,* ed. Zvi Griliches, 21–54. Chicago: University of Chicago Press.

Davidson, W. H., and Donald G. McFetridge. 1984. International technology transactions and the theory of the firm. *Journal of Industrial Economics* 32 (3): 253–64.

Dun & Bradstreet Ltd. 1989. *Who owns whom directory of corporate affiliations,* various vols. High Wycombe, U.K.: Dun and Bradstreet International.

Ethier, Wilfred J., and James R. Markusen. 1996. Multinational firms, technology diffusion and trade. *Journal of International Economics* 41 (1–2): 1–28.

Griliches, Zvi. 1992. The search for R&D spillovers. *Scandinavian Journal of Economics* 94 (Suppl.): 29–47.

Hall, Bronwyn H. 1993. R&D tax policy during the 1980s: Success or failure? In *Tax policy and the economy,* vol. 7, ed. James M. Poterba, 1–35. Cambridge: MIT Press.

Hall, Bronwyn H., Adam B. Jaffe, and Manuel Trajtenberg. 2000. Market value and patent citations: A first look. NBER Working Paper no. 7741. Cambridge, Mass.: National Bureau of Economic Research, June.

Hartman, David G. 1985. Tax policy and foreign direct investment. *Journal of Public Economics* 26 (1): 107–21.

Hines, James R., Jr. 1991. The flight paths of migratory corporations. *Journal of Accounting, Auditing, and Finance* 6 (4): 447–79.

Hines, James R., Jr. 1993. On the sensitivity of R&D to delicate tax changes: The behavior of U.S. multinationals in the 1980s. In *Studies in international taxation,* ed. Alberto Giovannini, R. Glenn Hubbard, and Joel Slemrod, 149–87. Chicago: University of Chicago Press.

Hines, James R., Jr. 1994. No place like home: Tax incentives and the location of R&D by American multinationals. In *Tax policy and the economy,* vol. 8, ed. James M. Poterba, 65–104. Cambridge: MIT Press.

Hines, James R., Jr. 1995. Taxes, technology transfer, and the R&D activities of multinational firms. In *The effects of taxation on multinational corporations,* ed. Martin Feldstein, James R. Hines Jr., and R. Glenn Hubbard, 225–48. Chicago: University of Chicago Press.

Hines, James R., Jr. 1997. International taxation and corporate R&D: Evidence and implications. In *Borderline case: International tax policy, corporate research and development and investment,* ed. James M. Poterba, 39–52. Washington, D.C.: National Academy Press.

Hines, James R., Jr., and R. Glenn Hubbard. 1990. Coming home to America: Dividend repatriations by U.S. multinationals. In *Taxation in the global economy,* ed. Assaf Razin and Joel Slemrod, 161–200. Chicago: University of Chicago Press.

Hines, James R., Jr., and Eric M. Rice. 1994. Fiscal paradise: Foreign tax havens and American business. *Quarterly Journal of Economics* 109 (1): 149–82.

Jaffe, Adam B., Manuel Trajtenberg, and Rebecca Henderson. 1993. Geographic localization of knowledge spillovers as evidenced by patent citations. *Quarterly Journal of Economics* 108 (3): 577–98.

Jaffe, Adam B., and Manuel Trajtenberg. 1999. International knowledge flows: Evidence from patent citations. *Economics of Innovation and New Technology* 8 (1): 105–36.

Lipsey, Robert E., Magnus Blomström, and Irving B. Kravis. 1990. R&D by multinational firms and host country exports. In *Science and technology: Lessons for development policy,* ed. Robert E. Evenson and Gustav Ranis, 271–300. Boulder, CO: Westview Press.

Mansfield, Edwin, and Anthony Romeo. 1980. Technology transfer to overseas subsidiaries by U.S.-based firms. *Quarterly Journal of Economics* 95 (4): 737–50.

Mansfield, Edwin, David Teece, and Anthony Romeo. 1979. Overseas research and development by U.S.-based firms. *Economica* 46 (182): 187–96.

Scholes, Myron S., and Mark A. Wolfson. 1992. *Taxes and business strategy: A planning approach.* Englewood Cliffs, N.J.: Prentice-Hall.

Standard and Poors Compustat Service. Available at http://garnet.acns.fsu.edu/~ppeters/fin6842/exer/compu.html.

Teece, David J. 1976. *The multinational corporation and the resource cost of international technology transfer.* Cambridge, Mass.: Ballinger.

Turro, John. 1993. U.S. enacts controversial budget legislation. *Tax Notes International* 16 (7): 435–38.

U.S. Congress. Joint Committee on Taxation. 1993. *Summary of the President's revenue proposals.* 103d Cong., 1st sess. Washington, D.C.: GPO.

U.S. Department of Commerce. Bureau of Economic Analysis. 1985. *U.S. direct investment abroad: 1982 benchmark survey data.* Washington, D.C.: GPO.

U.S. Department of Commerce. Bureau of Economic Analysis. 1992. *U.S. direct investment abroad: 1989 benchmark survey, final results.* Washington, D.C.: GPO.

U.S. Department of Commerce. Bureau of Economic Analysis. 1996. *U.S. direct investment abroad: 1994 benchmark survey, final results.* Washington, D.C.: GPO.

U.S. Department of the Treasury. 1983. *The impact of the section 861–8 regulation on U.S. research and development.* Washington, D.C.: GPO.

U.S. Department of the Treasury. 1995. *The relationship between U.S. research and development and foreign income.* Washington, D.C.: U.S. Department of the Treasury.

Wang, Jian-Ye, and Magnus Blomström. 1992. Foreign investment and technology transfer: A simple model. *European Economic Review* 36:137–55.

Zejan, Mario C. 1990. R&D activities in affiliates of Swedish multinational enterprises. *Scandinavian Journal of Economics* 92:487–500.

## Comment    Austan Goolsbee

In this paper, Hines and Jaffe take up the important issue of whether domestic and foreign R&D are substitutes or complements. To do so, they use an interesting but indirect test based on changes to the tax price of doing R&D in the two locations. They show that R&D tax policy in the 1980s changed the relative incentive to engage in R&D domestically but in a way that varied across companies depending on each one's foreign tax status. Using an extensive data source on foreign patents, they use this cross-sectional variation to show that firms whose *domestic* tax prices rose the most had the slowest growth rates of *foreign* patenting, and thus that the two types of R&D must be complements.

The topic itself is quite important in ongoing discussions about tax and R&D policy. R&D is subsidized or encouraged in most developed countries for the presumed spillovers. Often the country's policy makers perceive that their R&D efforts are directly competing with the policies of the other nations, but if there are strong complementarities, this will not be the case.

First, let me discuss the precise experiment they analyze. The paper begins with a firm investing in a foreign location and trying to decide whether to do the R&D in the United States and then sell the product in

Austan Goolsbee is associate professor of economics at the University of Chicago Graduate School of Business and a faculty research fellow of the American Bar Foundation and the National Bureau of Economic Research.

the foreign country (and pay royalties back to the United States), or to do the R&D and sell the product in the foreign country. Obviously the relative tax treatment of R&D in the two countries will matter for the decision and we know that the tax treatment varied substantially (perhaps too much!) throughout the 1980s.

Normally, in a case like this, the researcher has only a time series on tax policy and it is difficult to identify the impact of taxes from other time series variables. Hines and Jaffe make the important observation that the changes to tax policy also generate cross-sectional variation in the relative R&D price.

Oversimplifying somewhat, before the Tax Reform Act of 1986 (TRA 1986), companies could deduct all of their U.S. R&D expenses from their U.S. income. After 1986, they could deduct only part of it from U.S. income because the rest was viewed to be intended for foreign markets. Other countries, however, do not give these companies any credit for this U.S. R&D, so the impact of this change varies by foreign tax status. For firms with deficit credits (also known as excess limits), whose foreign tax rates are lower than the U.S. rate, this is not a problem. Firms with excess credits, however, whose foreign tax rates are higher than the U.S. rate, lose the deductions because they have already "maxed out," if you will. Hines and Jaffe argue, therefore, that changes to the allocation rules pre- and post-TRA 1986 should impact the R&D of excess credit companies differently than they would deficit credit companies. Assuming that unobservable factors affect both of these types of companies equally, it is possible to identify the impact of taxes based on the change in the cross-sectional R&D price.

Because no data on the domestic and foreign R&D by firm are readily available to examine this issue, Hines and Jaffe turn to the extremely detailed NBER/Case Western Reserve University (CWRU) database on foreign patents of U.S. companies described in Jaffe and Trajtenberg (1999). This data is an exciting resource for economists and it is good to see it filtering into public economics and tax work. Essentially they can get a measure of the foreign tax rate from Standard and Poors Compustat Service and, classifying patents as a proxy for foreign R&D, look at the natural experiment just described.

The results show that there must be very substantial complementarity between domestic and foreign R&D. As this is an indirect test based on a natural experiment methodology, it is important to consider the plausibility of the magnitudes and the validity of the experiment before being fully convinced by this type of evidence.

The first quibble I have with the paper is that I do not think that the coefficients are estimated as precisely as the tables portray. There are two time periods in the study (a before and after), and 378 firms; but the 378 firms are unlikely to be completely independent of one another. In the extreme, one might argue that the identification comes strictly from comparing two types of firms—deficit and excess credit. Accounting for the dependence of the residuals across firms within tax status classes would make the standard errors larger, possibly a great deal larger.

My second reservation about the results relates to their magnitude. The paper notes that the results in table 8.4 suggest that for the average firm, moving from taxable to nontaxable would result in eleven additional foreign patents from 1988 to 1991. Note, however, that the mean number of foreign patents is only 5.4—so this is more than a 100 percent increase. The means in table 8.2 do not make it easy to calculate an elasticity, but my back-of-the-envelope computation suggests an elasticity of around −2. Remember, this is not a standard own-price elasticity. It is more like a *cross*-price elasticity, and as such is very large, indeed. Hines (1993) found that the own-price elasticity of domestic R&D in this same context was between −1.2 and −1.8. This very strong complementarity result is even more puzzling when we consider the findings of Hines (1995), using aggregate data, that foreign and domestic R&D are *substitutes*.

Further, the magnitude is probably biased toward zero by the role of measurement error and policy uncertainty. As Hines and Jaffe painstakingly recount the myriad changes to the international R&D incentives over the time period, one cannot help but notice how frequently the major changes take place. In the empirical work, they divide the sample into two parts: 1983–1986 and 1988–1991. This type of grouping is probably the right thing to do given the numerous changes, but it should introduce significant measurement error. It is hard to imagine any firm taking existing, statutory tax policy as being permanent, and this expectations problems is likely to bias the results downward.

Regardless, given the natural experiment methodology, it is not unusual to ask whether this is a valid experiment and whether there is a valid control group. The basis of the paper is a comparison of the patent responses of excess and deficit credit firms in the two periods. One may not be a valid control group for the other, however, even when eliminating aggregate factors. It would take some more convincing to establish the validity.

By definition, the two groups must be investing in different countries, for example. It would be helpful to know whether low-tax countries (which are, on average, the investment locations of deficit credit firms) are concentrated in certain geographic regions, and so on. Over the 1980s, there were some major economic shifts that were not neutral across regions, that might influence patenting probabilities, and that are probably correlated with the tax changes. Things like the tremendous fall of oil prices or the dramatic shifts in exchange rates around the same time as TRA 1986 are likely to have impacted companies differently if they had invested in Asia versus Europe versus the Middle East, for example; and, as omitted variables correlated with the tax change, could generate the tax results. In the years after TRA 1986, there were also some substantial tax changes in other countries that may have similarly influenced incentives. Each of these issues deserves more discussion to assure us that the estimated impact is not spurious.

To summarize, in this paper, Hines and Jaffe present a creative approach to establishing the complementarity of foreign and domestic R&D and the results are striking but not conclusive. It is, perhaps, unrealistic to expect that we would find the results completely definitive because they are based on indirect evidence and one can always quibble with the data or the experiment in such studies. I hope that their effort, however, will encourage others to use tax policy as the source of experiments that can illuminate important areas of research on R&D.

## References

Hines, James R., Jr. 1993. On the sensitivity of R&D to delicate tax changes: The behavior of U.S. multinationals in the 1980s. In *Studies in international taxation,* ed. Alberto Giovannini, R. Glenn Hubbard, and Joel Slemrod, 149–87. Chicago: University of Chicago Press.

Hines, James R., Jr. 1995. Taxes, technology transfer, and the R&D activities of multinational firms. In *The effects of taxation on multinational corporations,* ed. Martin Feldstein, James R. Hines Jr., and R. Glenn Hubbard, 225–48. Chicago: University of Chicago Press.

Jaffe, Adam B., and Manuel Trajtenberg. 1999. International knowledge flows: Evidence from patent citations. *Economics of Innovation and New Technology* 8 (1): 105–36.

Standard and Poors Compustat Service. Available at http://garnet.acns.fsu.edu/~ppeters/fin6842/exer/compu.html.

# Taxation and the Sources
# of Growth
# Estimates from U.S.
# Multinational Corporations

Jason G. Cummins

## 9.1 Introduction

Numerous careful studies of productivity have been made at the firm level (for surveys, see Mairesse and Sassenou 1991; Griliches and Mairesse 1995). None of these studies, however, focus on U.S. multinational corporations (MNCs) despite their important role in the global economy.[1] In this study, I fill that gap by estimating the parameters of the MNC's production technology and using them to study the sources of firm growth. This exercise is only a first step, albeit a necessary one, toward better understanding the effects of tax policy in an increasingly integrated global economy. It certainly is not sufficient because it ignores the effect of tax policy on the wider economy in general and on solely domestic firms in particular.

The growth-accounting exercise is guided by a theoretical model that highlights how capital income tax policy can affect the dynamics of productivity. In the canonical Solow (1957) growth model, tax policy can affect the growth rate of output by changing the growth rates of factor inputs such as capital and labor. However, in this model tax changes cannot affect total factor productivity (TFP) directly because improvements in productivity are disembodied (i.e., technical change arrives as manna

Jason G. Cummins is assistant professor of economics at New York University and a research associate of the Institute for Fiscal Studies.

The author thanks James R. Hines Jr., Sam Kortum, Ned Nadiri, conference participants, and participants at the NBER Summer Institute for helpful comments and suggestions. He gratefully acknowledges financial support from the C. V. Starr Center for Applied Economics.

1. Many studies compare country-, industry-, and firm-level productivity among countries (see, e.g., Hulten 1990). However, these studies ignore MNCs, which operate in many different countries, by assuming that firms are based in only a single country.

from heaven). However, when technical change is embodied in capital (see, e.g., Solow 1960; Domar 1963; Jorgenson 1966), tax policy can affect TFP through investment.[2] To gauge whether this role for tax policy is economically important, I construct a vintage capital model, based on Hulten (1992), with both embodied and disembodied technical change and use it to decompose the sources of growth of U.S. MNCs.

The standard econometric approach for obtaining the technological parameters that can be used to study growth is to estimate the system of factor share equations derived from the cost function dual to the production function.[3] These estimates can be used to calculate the measures of interest, such as factor shares, returns to scale, and TFP. However, this approach is unsuitable for firm-level data because the input prices paid by firms are usually unobserved.[4]

An alternative that exploits the rich firm-level variation in input quantities is to estimate the production function itself (recently, Mundlak 1996 has advocated a return to estimating the primal technology). There are two problems with this approach. First, more variable inputs, such as materials and labor, are more highly correlated with the current realization of any shock that is observable to the firm (e.g., a productivity shock); and second, input demands are endogenous because they are determined in part by the firm's expectations of the realizations of shocks when those inputs will be used. As a consequence, inputs in place will be correlated with the current realization of the shock, and this will generate a simultaneous equations bias. Hence, standard econometric techniques provide biased estimates of the input demand and production parameters. In order to obtain unbiased parameter estimates, I use a semiparametric procedure developed by Olley and Pakes (1996).[5]

2. It is important to recognize that I am using TFP, not average labor productivity, as the measure of technical progress. Investment affects average labor productivity regardless of whether technical change is embodied or disembodied, whereas it affects TFP only when technical change is embodied.

3. The traditional approach to productivity analysis is to use the index number methodology to calculate productivity indexes. The approach is simple because direct estimation of the underlying technology is unnecessary. However, for the index number approach to provide meaningful estimates of technical change, some strong assumptions must be maintained. It is necessary to assume constant returns-to-scale technology, competitive input and output markets, and instantaneous adjustment of all inputs to their desired demand levels. If any of these assumptions is violated, the productivity measure based on the index number approach will yield biased estimates of technical change. The econometric approach taken in this paper allows one to assess the validity of at least some of these assumptions by estimating the characteristics of the underlying technology. (For a survey of the econometric approach to productivity analysis see Nadiri and Prucha 1997.)

4. Griliches (1979) argues that even if such data existed they would not contain sufficient variation for estimation.

5. This approach is not without drawbacks, either. For example, under imperfect competition, when real output is constructed with common deflators across firms, the parameters of the production technology are biased downward in most circumstances (Klette and Griliches 1996).

Using this alternative approach, I quantitatively examine the sources of output and productivity growth by decomposing the contributions of factor inputs (i.e., scale effects) and TFP. The results are quite surprising. Factor input growth, not TFP, is responsible for output growth in the MNCs in the sample. TFP actually declines over the sample period (1981–95), although this masks a steeper drop in the 1980s followed by a sharp recovery in the early 1990s. Among the inputs, growth in parent and affiliate capital is the most important. The importance of foreign direct investment (FDI) is especially striking. It contributes more to output growth than the sum of the contributions of parent employment, affiliate employment, and materials.

The estimates can be used to study the determinants of productivity growth and, in particular, to distinguish between different sources of growth. For example, the recent mini-boom in productivity comes from a reallocation of output to more productive firms, not a general increase in productivity. The results also indicate that there is substantial heterogeneity in MNC productivity. In the time and cross-sectional dimensions, MNCs' productivities differ widely depending on the countries in which their affiliates are located.

Finally, I quantify how tax policy affects MNC productivity by linking changes in the after-tax price of capital with embodied technical change. *Embodiment* means that new capital is more productive than old capital. The estimates imply that the parent's best practice technology is 66 percent higher than the average level of technology but that the affiliates' best is indistinguishably different from average. This means that there is an economically significant disadvantage for a parent's operating the average capital good relative to the frontier one. This suggests that productivity can be increased by decreasing the average age of capital. Hence, changes in the after-tax price of capital can result in investment that translates directly into productivity growth.

## 9.2 Theoretical Model

As technical change occurs, new assets acquired often embody efficiency improvements. Take computers as perhaps the most obvious example. Controlling for depreciation and inflation, a computer purchased in 2000 is much different from one purchased in 1990. The reason is that the newer one incorporates the technological improvements that make it more efficient per dollar of investment. Technical change that is not incorporated into specific assets is *disembodied.* An example of this type of technical change is Frederick Winslow Taylor's time and motion studies, which improved how factors of production interact, rather than the inputs themselves.

In mathematical terms, when technical change is disembodied, the capital stock, $K_t$, is equal to the weighted sum of undepreciated capital from each vintage:[6]

(1)                    $K_t = I_t + (I - \delta)I_{t-1} + \cdots + (1 - \delta)^t I_0,$

where $I_t$ is investment in year $t$ and $\delta$ is the constant rate of geometric depreciation. In this case, technical progress generates greater output regardless of whether the firm invests. When technical change is embodied in capital, the capital stock is computed by defining investment in terms of efficiency units, $H_t$:

(2)                          $H_t = \Phi_t I_t,$

where $\phi_t$ is the level of frontier technology in year $t$. The growth rate of $\phi$ is the growth rate of embodied technical change. In contrast to when technical change is disembodied, in this case, technical progress generates greater output only when the firm invests.

The capital stock measured in efficiency units is equal to

(3)        $J_t = H_t + (1 - \delta)H_{t-1} + \cdots + (1 - \delta)^t H_0$

$= \Phi_t I_t + (1 - \delta)\Phi_{t-1} I_{t-1} + \cdots + (1 - \delta)^t \Phi_0 I_0.$

The difference between $K_t$ and $I_t$ is given by the average embodied technical efficiency, $\Psi_t$, defined as the weighted average of the frontier efficiency levels of each past vintage of investment:

(4)  $\Psi_t = \dfrac{I_t}{K_t}\Phi_t + \dfrac{(1 - \delta)I_{t-1}}{K_t}\Phi_{t-1} + \dfrac{(1 - \delta)^2 I_{t-2}}{K_t}\Phi_{t-2} + \cdots = \dfrac{J_t}{K_t}.$

The after-tax price of investment measured in units of $I_t$ is $P_t^I$ and, similarly, $P_t^K$ is the price of using one unit of $K_t$ for one period.[7] Letting $P_t^H$ and $P_t^I$ denote the corresponding prices of investment and capital in efficiency units, I can use the accounting identities, $P_t^I I_t = P_t^H H_t$ and $P_t^K K_t = P_t^J J_t$, to express $\phi_t$ and $\Psi_t$ in terms of prices:

(5)                  $\Phi_t = \dfrac{P_t^I}{P_t^H}; \qquad \Psi_t = \dfrac{P_t^K}{P_t^J}.$

To this point it has been assumed that there is only a single capital good, but MNCs use different capital goods in each location where they operate.[8]

---

6. The firm index $i$ is suppressed to economize on notation except where essential.

7. To economize on notation, tax terms are suppressed. In the empirical work I incorporate data on the after-tax prices of investment.

8. It is likely that capital is heterogeneous within each location, as well as across locations, but this has to be ignored because the data on MNCs do not detail different types of investment goods. Cummins and Dey (1997) use firm-level panel data to estimate a model with heterogeneous capital goods, although they cannot distinguish the location of capital.

Specifically, the MNC uses a vector of quasi-fixed factors of production consisting of the parent and affiliates' beginning-of-period quality-adjusted capital, $J_t = (J_{jt})_{j=1}^n$, where $j$ indexes the $n$ locations of capital. The variable factors of production are labor, $L_t = (L_{jt})_{j=1}^n$ and materials, $M_t$. The firm produces gross output, $Y$, using a quasi-concave production function

(6)
$$Y_t = F(J_t, L_t, M_t, t \mid \alpha),$$

where $t$ is introduced as an argument to account for disembodied technical change; and $\alpha$ is a parameter vector describing the technical coefficients of production. According to this formulation, inputs that are spatially separate are included in a single production technology. This technology, however, is empirically cumbersome because MNCs vary in the number of countries in which they operate. Additional structure is imposed by assuming that affiliates' factor inputs are weakly separable from other inputs. In this case, the parent firm's inputs can be separated from the aggregates of the affiliates' inputs:

(7)
$$Y_t = F(J_{dt}, J_{ft}, L_{dt}, L_{ft}, M_t, t \mid \alpha),$$

where $d$ and $f$ index the domestic parent and aggregate foreign affiliate, respectively.

The logarithmic time derivative of equation (7) relates the growth rate of output and the share-weighted growth rates of quality-adjusted capital, labor, and materials:

(8)
$$\hat{Y}_t = \alpha_{L_d}\hat{L}_{dt} + \alpha_{L_f}\hat{L}_{ft} + \alpha_{J_d}\hat{J}_{dt} + \alpha_{J_f}\hat{J}_{ft} + \alpha_M\hat{M}_t + \lambda_t,$$

where hats over output and inputs denote their growth rates; $\lambda_t$ is the rate of disembodied technical change in year $t$; and, assuming perfect competition and constant returns to scale, the $\alpha$'s denote the factor shares, $S$. For example, the capital shares are

(9)
$$\alpha_{J_d} = \alpha_{K_d} = S_{K_d} = \frac{P_{dt}^J J_{dt}}{V_t} = \frac{P_{dt}^K K_{dt}}{V_t};$$

$$\alpha_{J_f} = \alpha_{Kf} = S_{K_f} = \frac{P_{ft}^J J_{ft}}{V_t} = \frac{P_{ft}^K K_{ft}}{V_t},$$

where $V_t$ is the value of input and output.

Equation (8) is the theoretical basis for decomposing the sources of output growth, but it suffers from a practical drawback. In most data sets quality adjustment is unobserved. Hence, to study the sources of growth, the share-weighted growth rate of quality-adjusted capital must be separated into quality unadjusted units, which are observable, and the growth rates of the two types of embodied technical change, which are unobservable:

$$(10) \qquad \hat{Y}_t = \alpha_{L_d} \hat{L}_{dt} + \alpha_{L_f} \hat{L}_{ft} + \alpha_{K_d} \hat{K}_{dt} + \alpha_{K_f} \hat{K}_{ft}$$

$$+ \alpha_M \hat{M}_t + \alpha_{K_d} \Psi_{dt} + \alpha_{K_f} \Psi_{ft} + \lambda_t,$$

where $\psi_{jt}$ is the growth rate of $\Psi_{jt}$. The terms $\alpha_{K_d} \psi_{dt}$ and $\alpha_{K_f} \psi_{ft}$ summarize quality change resulting from technology embodied in domestic and foreign capital input, respectively. Notice that when there is no disembodied technical change, $\lambda_t = 0$, technical change is entirely embodied.

Finally, the growth rate of output can be equated with the share-weighted sum of the growth rates of inputs and the growth rate of total factor productivity, $\widehat{\text{TFP}}_t$:

$$(11) \quad \hat{Y}_t = \alpha_{L_d} \hat{L}_{dt} + \alpha_{L_f} \hat{L}_{ft} + \alpha_{K_d} \hat{K}_{dt} + \alpha_{K_f} \hat{K}_{ft} + \alpha_M \hat{M}_t + \widehat{\text{TFP}}_t.$$

In the empirical productivity literature, $\widehat{\text{TFP}}_t$ is typically interpreted as an estimate of the growth rate of disembodied technical change. However, in this model total factor productivity growth is composed of both embodied and disembodied improvements in productivity:

$$(12) \qquad \widehat{\text{TFP}}_t = \alpha_{K_d} \Psi_{dt} + \alpha_{K_f} \Psi_{ft} + \lambda_t.$$

Although the growth rate of the average level of productivity, $\psi_{jt}$, is unobservable, it does depend on observable variables. Specifically, it is a function of current investment and the average level of productivity in the preceding year. For example, if a firm's capital stock is relatively new, current investment will have a modest impact on the growth rate of its average productivity. In contrast, investment by a firm with a relatively old capital stock will have a substantial impact on the growth rate of its average productivity. The elasticity of embodiment, $\varepsilon_{jt}$, which defines the percent difference between the current best practice technology and the average level of technology, formalizes the connection (see Hulten 1992):

$$(13) \qquad \Psi_{jt} = \frac{\Phi_{jt} - \Psi_{j,t-1}}{\Psi_{j,t-1}} \frac{I_{jt}}{K_{j,t-1}} = \varepsilon_{jt} \frac{I_{jt}}{K_{j,t-1}}.$$

Equations (12) and (13) define the growth in embodied technical change, $\widehat{EP}_t$:

$$(14) \qquad \widehat{EP}_t = \alpha_{K_d} \Psi_{dt} + \alpha_{K_f} \Psi_{ft}$$

$$= \alpha_{K_d} \varepsilon_{dt} \frac{I_{dt}}{K_{d,t-1}} + \alpha_{K_f} \varepsilon_{ft} \frac{I_{ft}}{K_{f,t-1}}.$$

According to this relationship, the growth in embodied technical change is a function of current investment, the factor shares, and the elasticities of embodiment. Given the investment-capital ratios, the production function parameters, and $EP_t$, this equation can be used to infer the value of the elasticity of embodiment.

The effect of investment on productivity is made explicit by rewriting equation (10) using equation (14):

$$(15) \quad \hat{Y}_t = \alpha_{L_d}\hat{L}_{dt} + \alpha_{L_f}\hat{L}_{ft} + \alpha_{K_d}(1 + \varepsilon_{dt})\hat{K}_{dt} + \alpha_{K_f}(1 + \varepsilon_{ft})\hat{K}_{ft}$$

$$+ \alpha_M \hat{M}_t + \alpha_{K_d}\varepsilon_{dt}\delta + \alpha_{K_f}\varepsilon_{ft}\delta + \lambda_t.$$

When capital is measured in unadjusted units the correct output elasticity for growth accounting must be marked up by the elasticity of embodiment. Estimates of the parameters of the production technology ignore this additional output growth from capital because $\alpha_j\psi_j$ is in the residual. I will use an indirect technique, described next, to infer $\varepsilon_j$ and thereby arrive at the true output elasticity of capital.

The link between tax policy and embodied technical change is completed by specifying the relationship between the after-tax price of capital and investment. In the empirical investment literature this is done using marginal $q$, defined as the ratio of the marginal after-tax cost of investment, including adjustment costs, to its market price:

$$(16) \quad q_{jt} = \frac{C_{I_{jt}} + P^I_{jt}}{P^I_{jt}},$$

where $C_{I_{jt}}$ is the marginal adjustment cost for investment in location $j$.

Consistent with studies in the investment literature, I assume that marginal adjustment costs are linear, $C_{I_{jt}} = \beta_j(I_{jt}/K_{j,t-1}) + v_t$, where $\beta_j$ are the parameters describing the technical coefficients of adjusting the capital stock and $v_t$ is a structural disturbance to the adjustment cost technology ($E_t[v_t] = 0$, $E_t[v_t^2] = \sigma_v^2$). Provided the firm's net revenue and adjustment cost functions are linear homogeneous, and the firm operates in perfectly competitive markets, Hayashi and Inoue (1991) and Chirinko (1993a) prove that Tobin's average $Q$—defined as the ratio of the market value of the firm to the replacement cost of its capital stock—can be substituted for the marginal $q$'s in equation (16). Then the following investment equation can be estimated as

$$(17) \quad Q_t = \sum_{j=1}^{n} \frac{K_{jt}}{K_t} q_{jt} = \beta_0 + \beta_d \frac{I_d}{K_{d,t-1}} + \beta_f \frac{I_f}{K_{f,t-1}} + v_t,$$

where $\beta_0$ is introduced as an intercept. Although the focus of this paper is not on investment behavior, I estimate the adjustment cost parameters in equation (17) for the firms in the sample because they govern how responsive investment is to changes in average $Q$. If the adjustment costs are large (large $\beta$'s), changes in $Q$—resulting from, for example, changes in capital income tax policy—will translate into small increases in productivity, regardless of the magnitude of the elasticity of embodiment.

It is important to notice that the size of the adjustment costs are unrestricted in this specification. One might suspect that foreign affiliates' adjustment costs would be lower because their operations are likely to be younger than the parents'; but a sensible case can be made for why adjustment costs may be higher. For example, if adjustment costs for installing capital depend primarily on the flexibility of the labor force, one might expect that it would be more disruptive to the production process to install a machine in a factory in Paris, France, than to install the identical one in Paris, Texas. In some cases, the distinction between domestic and foreign is quite artificial, but this does not pose a conceptual challenge to the approach. Consider the auto industry, in which many assembly plants are similar in the United States and Canada. If U.S. MNCs are, on average, like those in the auto industry, one would expect parent and affiliate adjustment costs to be similar. To the extent that the parent or subsidiary changes its adjustment cost technology, say, by building a new factory in Ontario or Ohio, this will be reflected in the estimates.

In summary, it is tricky to find the true contribution of capital to output growth when the quality of capital goods is unobserved, as it is in most data sets. In order to find the actual contribution, an indirect approach must be used. The key to this indirect approach is inferring the firm's elasticity of embodiment, which defines the bang-for-the-buck from investing in the best available technology. The idea captured by this elasticity is that the contribution to growth of a new computer is higher for a firm using vintage 1950s adding machines than for a firm using one-year-old computers. Then the true contribution of capital to output growth can be found by marking up its observed contribution by this elasticity. Finally, the effects of policy changes can be analyzed by linking investment in new, more efficient capital goods to the $Q$ model, which summarizes the net return to investment by incorporating variable such as taxes and interest rates.

## 9.3 Empirical Methodology

To sort out the contributions of different factors to output growth, I estimate the production technology introduced in the previous section. Then I can separate the contributions of embodied and disembodied technological change, and use this separation as the basis for inferring the elasticity of embodiment.

An MNC's production technology is likely to be a complicated function, which argues for using a flexible functional form to approximate it. However, estimates of output elasticities are usually qualitatively unaffected if a first-order approximation to the technology is used (Griliches and Mairesse 1995). Hence the Cobb-Douglas is generally used for growth accounting:

$$(18) \qquad y_t = \alpha_{L_{dt}} l_{dt} + \alpha_{L_{ft}} l_{ft} + \alpha_{K_d} k_{dt} + \alpha_{K_f} k_{ft}$$

$$+ \alpha_M m_t + \sum_{t=1}^{T} \alpha_t D_t + u_t,$$

where lowercase letters represent the logarithms of variables; $D_t$ are year dummy variables, where $T$ is the total number of years in the panel. Total factor productivity is the sum of the dummy variables and the residual, $u_t$ (i.e., the residual growth rate of output not attributable to the factor inputs).

The problem in consistently estimating the parameters in equation (18) is that inputs in place are correlated with $u_t$. This occurs because current input choices are a function of current and expected future realizations of technology shocks that are unobserved by the econometrician. Any econometric procedure that fails to account for the endogeneity will yield biased estimates of the input coefficients. The bias can be severe for the more variable inputs because they are more highly correlated with current realizations of technical change. However, the bias will also occur for quasi-fixed inputs because demand for them depends on expected future technology so that those in place are also correlated with $u_t$. In the results, the estimates using ordinary least squares (OLS) are compared to those from the semiparametric procedure introduced by Olley and Pakes (1996) that corrects for the bias (see Cummins 1999 for details on the estimation procedure).

Using the unbiased estimates, total factor productivity for each firm, $\text{TFP}_{it}$, where the firm index $i$ is introduced, is calculated as

$$(19) \qquad \text{TFP}_{it} = Y_{it} / \exp(\alpha_{L_{dt}} l_{idt} + \alpha_{L_{ft}} l_{ift} + \alpha_{K_d} k_{idt}$$

$$+ \alpha_{K_f} k_{ift} + \alpha_M m_{it}) = \frac{Y_{it}}{Z_{it}}.$$

Aggregate $\text{TFP}_t$ is the output-weighted average of firm-level $\text{TFP}_{it}$:

$$(20) \qquad \text{TFP}_t = \sum_{i=1}^{N} \text{TFP}_{it} s_{it} \quad \text{where } s_{it} = \frac{Y_{it}}{\sum_{i=1}^{N} Y_{it}},$$

and $N$ is the number of MNCs. Aggregate $\text{TFP}_t$ can be decomposed as the sum of unweighted aggregate productivity, $\overline{\text{TFP}}_t$, and the sample covariance between $\text{TFP}_t$ and output:

(21)    $$TFP_t = \overline{TFP_t} + \sum_{i=1}^{N}(s_{it} - \bar{s}_t)(\overline{TFP_{it}} - \overline{TFP_t}).$$

The larger the covariance, the higher the share of output that goes to more productive firms. This decomposition can be used to answer whether productivity changes result from changes in average productivity or from a reallocation of inputs to more productive firms.

Embodied technical change can be distinguished from disembodied technical change using the coefficient estimates on the year dummy variables:

(22)    $$EP_{it} = TFP_{it} - \exp\left(\sum_{t=1}^{T}\alpha_t D_t\right).$$

This value can be used to calculate $\widehat{EP_{it}}$. Then, when a disturbance is appended to equation (14), the regression of $\widehat{EP_{it}}$ on $\alpha_j I_{jt}/K_{jt}$ provides estimates of $\varepsilon_{jt}$. This is a purely statistical relationship because investment is likely to be endogenous, so it is used only to gain a sense of the magnitude of the mean elasticity of embodiment across firms and over the sample period.

### 9.4    Data

The production function is estimated using a firm-level panel data set constructed from several sources. A detailed description of how the variables are constructed is contained in appendix A. In this section, important data issues for estimation are outlined and some features of the sample are presented.

The data on the U.S. parent firms are from Standard and Poors Compustat Service industrial and full-coverage files. The data on affiliates are from the Compustat geographic segment file (for a detailed description see Cummins and Hubbard 1995). The geographic segment file reports only a limited set of information on the foreign operations of MNCs: capital expenditures, tangible fixed assets, operating income, depreciation, and sales. The data are recorded for seven years at a time. I combine 3 seven-year panels to obtain a data set extending from 1980 to 1995.[9] The tax parameters are updated and expanded from Cummins, Hassett, and Hubbard (1995). There are about 200 parent and affiliates with complete data for at least one year.

As discussed in the presentation of the theoretical model, MNCs vary in the number of different locations in which they operate. When this is the case, it makes the specification of the production technology problematic.

---

9. Due to differences in accounting reporting requirements prior to 1980, the panel begins in 1980.

Consider how to estimate the parameters of the Cobb-Douglas production function when, for example, some MNCs operate in ten foreign countries while the rest operate in a single foreign country. The parameters for the nine countries in which some firms in the sample have no operations are unidentified. Indeed, it would be necessary to formulate a model to explain why firms locate in different numbers of countries. To enable comparison among MNCs, I assume that all the MNCs' foreign affiliates can be aggregated into a single foreign affiliate. This is a strong assumption that is likely invalid (see, e.g., Cummins 1999), but the bias is unlikely materially to affect estimated output elasticities (Griliches 1979), which are the focus for growth accounting. The individual countries for which Compustat reports affiliate data are Australia, Canada, France, Germany, Japan, and the United Kingdom.[10] When an MNC reports operations for more than one country I aggregate them and denote the affiliate's country as "multiple." These six countries receive the majority of American MNCs' FDI.

In the geographic segment file, affiliates' data are reported in nominal U.S. dollars. There are a number of different methods to translate variables measured in different currencies into real figures that are comparable across time and across countries. I use a method suggested by Leamer (1988) that translates foreign currencies into U.S. dollars in each year using the current exchange rate and then divides by the U.S. price deflator to form the real series. Because the parent's and affiliate's data are already reported in U.S. dollars in the geographic segment file, I assume that firms accurately translate host-country currencies into U.S. dollars in each year using the current exchange rate—as they are required to do under FASB regulations. Then the real series are obtained by dividing the variables by the U.S. price deflator. Leamer (1988) concludes that this method performs well relative to others in constructing comparable investment and capital stock series. To the extent that there is mismeasurement due to exchange rate fluctuations, it is unlikely that the qualitative empirical results would be affected because there are year effects in the regressions. However, the year effects would no longer be pure measures of disembodied technical change.

Summary statistics for the data used in estimation are given in table 9.1. The number of MNCs in the sample increases from twenty-eight firms in 1981 to ninety-one firms in 1995. The total number of observations is 1,012. The sample variables are MNCs' gross output ($Y$), parent and affiliate capital ($K_d$ and $K_f$) and labor ($L_d$ and $L_f$), and materials ($M$). Included in the table are the means, medians, and standard deviations of the variables. The sample statistics indicate wide variation in the size of firms and the composition of their capital stocks. Despite entry into the sample, the sample statistics are broadly similar over time. The exceptions to this

---

10. Mexico and Brazil are also reported but are excluded.

**Table 9.1**  **Means, Medians, and Standard Deviations of Selected Sample Variables**

| Year | N | Gross Output | Parent Employees | Affiliate Employees | Parent Capital | Affiliate Capital | Materials |
|------|---|------|------|------|------|------|------|
| 1981 | 28 | 441.1 | 2,334.4 | 530.1 | 304.2 | 39.0 | 330.8 |
|      |    | (82.3) | (661.0) | (206.0) | (43.8) | (10.8) | (30.7) |
|      |    | [1,475.6] | [7,013.2] | [1,430.1] | [758.1] | [97.0] | [1,316.9] |
| 1982 | 28 | 338.1 | 2,153.3 | 465.2 | 307.6 | 29.1 | 234.8 |
|      |    | (67.8) | (575.5) | (162.5) | (45.2) | (10.9) | (27.6) |
|      |    | [1,027.4] | [6,257.6] | [1,276.1] | [748.9] | [58.4] | [876.4] |
| 1983 | 34 | 298.9 | 2,179.1 | 474.5 | 287.1 | 27.5 | 203.2 |
|      |    | (45.1) | (306.0) | (162.5) | (31.1) | (7.8) | (19.7) |
|      |    | [1,023.0] | [7,566.6] | [1,544.1] | [783.3] | [63.5] | [840.4] |
| 1984 | 45 | 373.9 | 2,538.9 | 546.0 | 461.7 | 63.9 | 237.9 |
|      |    | (63.8) | (458.0) | (190.0) | (41.3) | (9.4) | (30.9) |
|      |    | [997.1] | [7,072.4] | [1,308.9] | [1,207.6] | [135.2] | [813.9] |
| 1985 | 46 | 458.6 | 3,974.5 | 889.6 | 637.4 | 69.0 | 278.3 |
|      |    | (81.9) | (762.0) | (290.5) | (52.6) | (10.8) | (37.1) |
|      |    | [1,105.9] | [10,233.0] | [1,929.0] | [2,338.9] | [156.6] | [869.6] |
| 1986 | 55 | 528.0 | 4,462.2 | 1,116.2 | 385.6 | 58.4 | 350.0 |
|      |    | (88.7) | (800.0) | (255.0) | (69.4) | (10.7) | (46.6) |
|      |    | [1,248.3] | [11,082.0] | [2,672.3] | [791.4] | [122.7] | [957.9] |
| 1987 | 68 | 492.5 | 3,369.6 | 818.8 | 394.2 | 77.9 | 337.5 |
|      |    | (73.8) | (624.5) | (208.5) | (38.9) | (11.2) | (41.0) |
|      |    | [1,280.5] | [9,429.0] | [2,022.3] | [840.5] | [199.7] | [1,015.7] |
| 1988 | 79 | 641.4 | 4,565.7 | 1,090.7 | 415.3 | 88.1 | 448.4 |
|      |    | (67.9) | (440.0) | (205.0) | (39.7) | (9.9) | (37.4) |
|      |    | [1,890.8] | [13,583.0] | [3,100.1] | [989.2] | [227.5] | [1,528.6] |
| 1989 | 77 | 662.9 | 4,734.5 | 1,210.3 | 374.1 | 97.5 | 460.6 |
|      |    | (77.3) | (434.0) | (200.0) | (45.9) | (10.5) | (46.3) |
|      |    | [1,967.1] | [13,840.0] | [3,439.8] | [740.9] | [247.3] | [1,575.1] |
| 1990 | 88 | 630.9 | 4,122.1 | 1,116.3 | 638.1 | 160.1 | 425.8 |
|      |    | (64.1) | (463.0) | (213.0) | (46.0) | (13.1) | (36.0) |
|      |    | [1,862.1] | [13,596.0] | [3,331.9] | [2,499.2] | [571.9] | [1,451.5] |
| 1991 | 90 | 654.6 | 3,611.2 | 1,334.5 | 815.8 | 171.8 | 453.2 |
|      |    | (73.9) | (460.5) | (199.0) | (46.2) | (12.0) | (39.4) |
|      |    | [1,830.1] | [11,295.0] | [4,608.1] | [2,743.0] | [570.7] | [1,446.2] |
| 1992 | 90 | 630.4 | 4,161.7 | 664.8 | 883.3 | 158.9 | 439.3 |
|      |    | (92.4) | (479.5) | (176.0) | (64.9) | (13.0) | (49.3) |
|      |    | [1,721.0] | [14,211.0] | [1,187.8] | [2,971.5] | [507.0] | [1,381.8] |
| 1993 | 90 | 736.5 | 3,857.9 | 1,039.5 | 956.9 | 169.7 | 535.8 |
|      |    | (119.9) | (684.0) | (223.0) | (91.2) | (16.3) | (66.0) |
|      |    | [1,959.0] | [12,527.0] | [2,922.5] | [3,311.0] | [537.6] | [1,634.9] |
| 1994 | 103 | 602.4 | 3,047.2 | 821.9 | 883.5 | 137.0 | 443.6 |
|      |    | (95.4) | (492.0) | (167.0) | (83.0) | (12.0) | (45.7) |
|      |    | [1,819.5] | [11,438.0] | [2,679.3] | [3,273.2] | [492.8] | [1,537.8] |
| 1995 | 91 | 696.2 | 3,340.9 | 918.4 | 938.6 | 154.4 | 520.5 |
|      |    | (92.22) | (492.0) | (173.0) | (96.6) | (16.4) | (50.3) |
|      |    | [1,976.5] | [12,234.0] | [2,867.7] | [3,266.5] | [526.9] | [1,669.7] |
| Total | 1,012 | 589.9 | 3,679.9 | 934.7 | 650.4 | 117.7 | 413.5 |
|       |    | (78.8) | (532.0) | (200.0) | (58.3) | (11.9) | (40.2) |
|       |    | [1,692.2] | [11,745.0] | [2,813.8] | [2,363.7] | [413.2] | [1,378.5] |

*Note:* The data set is an unbalanced panel of U.S. MNCs. The total number of MNCs in the sample in each year is reported in column (2). For each MNC there are data on capital and labor for the parent and its affiliates (which are aggregated across countries into a single affiliate). Data on gross output and materials are for the MNC as a whole. Variables are in $ millions (1987), except "Employees" which are in units. Medians of the variables are in parentheses below the means. Standard deviation of the variables are in square brackets below the means.

are the large jumps in both parent and affiliate mean capital stocks in 1990 and 1991. These increases were not accompanied by increases in other factor inputs. The number of firms declines in 1995 because the U.S. Securities and Exchange Commission (SEC), in Financial Reporting Release no. 44, eliminated the requirement that firms report detailed data about their property, plant, and equipment (see http://www.sec.gov/rules/final/dissuer.txt).

## 9.5  Empirical Results

I present the empirical results in three parts. The first subsection contains the estimates of the production function, which form the basis of the decomposition of the sources of growth in the second. In the last subsection I highlight the role of tax policy in the growth of MNCs by showing how it can affect productivity directly through investment by changing the after-tax price of capital.

### 9.5.1  Production Function Estimation

Table 9.2 presents the estimates of the parameters of the MNC's Cobb-Douglas production function. Standard errors on the estimates are in parentheses. (All of the parameter estimates are statistically significant from zero at better than the 1 percent level.) In each of the specifications, year effects are estimated but not reported. For comparison to the literature both value-added and gross output production functions are estimated. In the first two columns the dependent variable is value added, and in the last two gross output is used.[11] The former is the more common specification because government statistical agencies report a variety of measures of real value added (e.g., GDP), but not price and quantity data on gross output and intermediate inputs. Some form of separability is required to derive the value-added specification—perfect substitutability or complementarity of materials with other factors of production suffices—so the gross output specification is preferable for its generality. In theory, the parameter estimates in the gross output specification equal those from the value-added specification multiplied by $(1 - \alpha_M)$. A comparison between the results shows that this condition is not satisfied suggesting that the value-added specification is misspecified. This misspecification could result in mistaken inference about the sources of growth (see Bruno 1984; comments by Baily 1986; Grubb 1986). I concentrate, then, on the results in columns (3) and (4).

Comparing the estimates from OLS in column (3) to the ones from the

---

11. There were sixteen values of value added, defined as gross output less materials, that were negative and had to be deleted. Thus the number of observations in columns (1) and (2) is sixteen less than in (3) and (4).

Table 9.2    Cobb-Douglas Production Function Parameter Estimates

| Parameter | Value Added | | Gross Output | |
|---|---|---|---|---|
| | OLS (1) | Semiparametric (2) | OLS (3) | Semiparametric (4) |
| $L_d$ | 0.602 | 0.611 | 0.288 | 0.281 |
| | (0.031) | (0.033) | (0.018) | (0.019) |
| $L_f$ | 0.112 | 0.102 | 0.065 | 0.074 |
| | (0.028) | (0.029) | (0.016) | (0.017) |
| $K_d$ | 0.259 | 0.207 | 0.171 | 0.131 |
| | (0.018) | (0.023) | (0.011) | (0.012) |
| $K_f$ | 0.055 | 0.041 | 0.058 | 0.085 |
| | (0.013) | (0.024) | (0.008) | (0.013) |
| $M$ | — | — | 0.427 | 0.423 |
| | | | (0.010) | (0.011) |
| $N$ | 996 | 996 | 1,012 | 1,012 |

*Note:* The dependent variable in columns (1) and (2) is value added. The dependent variable in columns (3) and (4) is gross output. Standard errors on parameter estimates are in parentheses. The semiparametric estimator is described in the text and in detail in Cummins (1999).

semiparametric estimator in column (4) shows that the OLS estimates of the share of domestic capital are biased upward and the estimates of the affiliate inputs are biased downward. In terms of accounting for growth, the OLS estimates would imply a larger contribution from parents' capital and smaller contributions from affiliates' factors. The implied returns to scale in column (3) are 1.01, and 0.99 in column (4). The estimated parameters then are approximately equal to their factor shares when perfect competition is assumed. The estimates of the parents' employment share and materials are virtually identical using either estimator. This is somewhat surprising, because variable factors are more likely to be correlated with current realizations of shocks. However, the year effects may capture these shocks, in which case the estimates of the variable factors would be unaffected by using the semiparametric technique. In column (4), the total share of parents' inputs is about 0.41 and the total share of affiliates' inputs is about 0.16. Notably, the ratio of the parents' output elasticity of capital to its output elasticity of labor is about 0.45, whereas the affiliates' ratio is about 1.1. If the ratio of the rental price of capital and the wage are the same in the United States and abroad, the ratios of the output elasticities are proportional to the capital-labor ratio, implying that the affiliates are much more capital intensive.

### 9.5.2    Sources of MNC Growth

Table 9.3 contains the aggregate indexes of factor inputs. Each index is calculated as the annual average of the firm-level factor inputs using gross

Table 9.3                    Sources of Growth: Aggregate Factor Input Indexes

| Year | Parent Labor | Affiliate Labor | Parent Capital | Affiliate Capital | Materials |
|------|--------------|-----------------|----------------|-------------------|-----------|
| 1981 | 1.00 | 1.00 | 1.00 | 1.00 | 1.00 |
| 1982 | 0.82 | 0.82 | 0.90 | 0.94 | 0.61 |
| 1983 | 1.09 | 1.09 | 0.99 | 1.17 | 0.65 |
| 1984 | 0.83 | 0.77 | 1.20 | 1.62 | 0.51 |
| 1985 | 0.99 | 0.95 | 2.04 | 2.09 | 0.50 |
| 1986 | 1.13 | 1.36 | 1.35 | 1.82 | 0.56 |
| 1987 | 1.04 | 1.13 | 1.42 | 2.30 | 0.64 |
| 1988 | 1.72 | 1.93 | 2.00 | 3.64 | 1.07 |
| 1989 | 1.77 | 2.16 | 1.89 | 4.11 | 1.11 |
| 1990 | 1.71 | 2.08 | 3.33 | 6.85 | 1.01 |
| 1991 | 1.36 | 2.69 | 3.87 | 7.37 | 0.97 |
| 1992 | 1.66 | 0.63 | 4.02 | 6.44 | 0.91 |
| 1993 | 1.28 | 1.59 | 4.07 | 5.93 | 1.05 |
| 1994 | 1.27 | 1.57 | 4.38 | 5.83 | 1.10 |
| 1995 | 1.27 | 1.57 | 4.54 | 6.43 | 1.13 |
| Average Annual Share-Weighted Growth Rates (%) | | | | | |
| 1981–95 | 0.48 | 0.24 | 1.49 | 1.21 | 0.37 |
| 1981–85 | −0.06 | −0.09 | 2.56 | 1.72 | −6.76 |
| 1986–90 | 3.11 | 0.84 | 3.32 | 3.34 | 6.73 |
| 1991–95 | −0.50 | −0.93 | 0.53 | −0.29 | 1.67 |

Note: Each aggregate index is calculated as the annual average of the firm-level factor inputs using gross output shares as weights. Average annual share-weighted growth rates use the estimates in column (4) of table 9.2 as shares.

output shares as weights (i.e., the same way aggregate TFP is defined in equation [20]). The first year of the sample, 1981, is used as the base of the index. Relative to capital inputs there is little growth in labor or material inputs. The growth in affiliate capital is largest, increasing at more than 14 percent annually over the entire period. This increase, however, is insufficient to understand FDI's contribution to growth, because it is unweighted by its share in output.

To calculate average annual share-weighted growth rates, the parameter estimates in column (4) of table 9.2 are used as shares. In the bottom panel of the table the average annual growth rates are presented for the whole period and 3 five-year subperiods. Over the entire period the share-weighted growth rates of capital are the largest contributors to growth. Although the parents' capital growth rate contributes the most to growth, the affiliates' capital contributes more than the sum of all the other factors. As emphasized by Hulten (1978), growth in intermediate inputs (i.e., materials) is partly due to technical change. Thus even the contribution of materials to growth may reflect improvements in the quality of capital. Based on these results, MNCs' capital is the most important source of growth, with FDI nearly as important as domestic capital growth. This pattern is broadly consistent in the three subperiods, although the contributions of capital are smaller recently.

In table 9.4, TFP and its components are presented. The aggregate productivity indexes are calculated as the annual average of the firm-level productivity estimates from the semiparametric specification in column (4) of table 9.2. The weighted index in column (1) uses firm-level gross output shares as weights (see equation [20]). The percent of embodied and disembodied technical change in columns (2) and (3) are their shares in TFP, calculated as the ratio of embodied or disembodied technical change (from equation [22]) to TFP. The unweighted index of TFP is in column (4). The percent of embodied and disembodied technical change in unweighted TFP are in columns (5) and (6). Finally, the difference between the weighted and unweighted indexes is $\text{Cov}(\text{TFP}_{it}, Y_{it})$, the sample covariance between TFP and gross output.

Both weighted and unweighted TFP have declined over the sample period. Thus $\text{TFP}_t$ has actually retarded growth. This is a somewhat usual result, as TFP is often the single most important contributor to growth. For example, in the original growth-accounting study, Solow (1957) found that technical change accounted for the greatest share of growth; Hulten (1992) found that TFP was the largest contributor over the period 1949–83. Nevertheless, a number of studies have used microdata and have found that productivity has declined, even in industries in which this result might seem contrary to conventional wisdom. For example, Olley and Pakes (1996) find that weighted TFP in the telecommunications industry declined by 3 percent from 1974 to 1987; unweighted productivity declined by 34 percent over the same period. (For a survey of other studies with similar results, see Nadiri and Prucha 1997.) Disembodied change accounts for more than 70 percent of TFP. This finding is similar to that in Hulten (1992) in which disembodied productivity accounted for about 80 percent of TFP. Embodied change accounts for a declining share of TFP in the 1980s but sharply rises in the 1990s. The unweighted TFP index is also declining. In the unweighted index, however, the share of disembodied technical change is increasing consistently through the sample period.

The final column is the difference between the two indexes, or the sample covariance between output and productivity. When this covariance is positive the share of output that goes to more productive firms is higher, and thus aggregate productivity is higher. Until 1992 the covariance is relatively small. After 1992 the data indicate that there was a substantial reallocation of output toward more productive firms. This could result from reallocating factor inputs toward more productive firms or from using the existing factor inputs more efficiently in more productive firms. Unfortunately, the econometric approach is not rich enough to disentangle the contributions of these two alternatives.

**Table 9.4    Sources of Growth: Aggregate Total Factor Productivity Indexes**

| Year | Weighted TFP Index | Percent Disembodied | Percent Embodied | Unweighted TFP Index | Percent Disembodied | Percent Embodied | Cov(TFP$_{it}$, Y$_{it}$) |
|------|------|------|------|------|------|------|------|
| 1981 | 1.00 | 78.3 | 21.7 | 0.89 | 87.8 | 12.2 | 0.11 |
| 1982 | 0.91 | 79.7 | 20.3 | 0.86 | 84.3 | 15.7 | 0.05 |
| 1983 | 0.86 | 84.2 | 15.8 | 0.81 | 88.9 | 11.1 | 0.04 |
| 1984 | 0.86 | 85.0 | 15.0 | 0.84 | 87.6 | 12.4 | 0.03 |
| 1985 | 0.85 | 86.4 | 13.6 | 0.83 | 88.1 | 11.9 | 0.02 |
| 1986 | 0.78 | 82.0 | 18.0 | 0.78 | 82.4 | 17.6 | 0.00 |
| 1987 | 0.81 | 87.8 | 12.2 | 0.77 | 93.0 | 7.0 | 0.05 |
| 1988 | 0.82 | 89.2 | 10.8 | 0.80 | 91.2 | 8.8 | 0.02 |
| 1989 | 0.79 | 89.7 | 10.3 | 0.76 | 93.1 | 6.9 | 0.03 |
| 1990 | 0.78 | 89.2 | 10.8 | 0.76 | 91.4 | 8.6 | 0.02 |
| 1991 | 0.76 | 88.1 | 11.9 | 0.75 | 89.4 | 10.6 | 0.01 |
| 1992 | 0.77 | 92.4 | 7.6 | 0.80 | 88.9 | 11.1 | −0.03 |
| 1993 | 0.87 | 81.3 | 18.7 | 0.78 | 90.2 | 9.8 | 0.09 |
| 1994 | 0.89 | 74.4 | 25.6 | 0.72 | 91.6 | 8.4 | 0.17 |
| 1995 | 0.91 | 72.8 | 27.2 | 0.72 | 92.6 | 7.4 | 0.20 |

*Note:* The aggregate productivity index is calculated as the annual average of the firm-level productivity estimates from the semiparametric specification in column (4) of table 9.2. "Weighted TFP Index" uses firm-level gross output shares as weights. "Percent Disembodied" technical change is the share of productivity attributable to year dummy variables in TFP. "Percent Embodied" technical change is the share of productivity not attributable to year effects in TFP. The difference between the weighted and unweighted indexes is Cov(TFP$_{it}$, Y$_{it}$), the sample covariance between TFP and gross output.

Figures 9.1 and 9.2 illustrate this boom. The first plots the two indexes from table 9.4 and the second plots the growth rates of the indexes. The boom in productivity is quite pronounced. In addition, the other striking feature is the drop in productivity in 1986. A complete analysis of these changes is beyond the scope of this paper and, indeed, would require a rather complicated dynamic general equilibrium model. However, it is possible to speculate on the sources of these two productivity changes. First, the boom in productivity coincides with the North American Free Trade Agreement (NAFTA), suggesting that productivity may be associated with freer trade. I investigate this possibility in figures 9.3 and 9.4. Figure 9.3 depicts the productivity indexes for firms with Canadian affiliates. The boom is even more dramatic for these MNCs than for MNCs overall. In addition, comparison of the weighted index to the unweighted index shows that the boom was caused by a dramatic reallocation of output from less productive to more productive firms. Figure 9.4 depicts the productivity indexes for firms with affiliates in countries besides Canada. Productivity in these MNCs has been declining steadily since the late 1980s. There is also little difference between the weighted and unweighted indexes, indicating that the productivity drop results from a decline in average productivity. The second feature of these figures, the drop in productivity in 1986, is intriguing because it may be correlated with the increase in the after-tax cost of equipment capital from the Tax Reform Act of 1986. (I investigate this possibility more formally and generally in table 9.6 using regression analysis.)

Table 9.5 compares aggregate TFP by the location of the MNCs' affiliates. Most of the MNCs in the sample report data for only a single foreign affiliate, but about a quarter of the MNCs report affiliate data in multiple countries. These firms are in the row labeled "Multiple" in the table. The format of the table is the same as in table 9.4, except instead of comparing productivity over time relative to a base year, the table compares productivity among MNCs, relative to the productivity of the MNCs with Canadian affiliates. The weighted TFP index in column (1) is calculated as the affiliate country average of the firm-level productivity estimates from the semiparametric specification in column (4) of table 9.2. Only the MNCs with Japanese affiliates have higher weighted TFP than those in Canada. Perhaps surprisingly, Australia and the United Kingdom have the lowest productivity. There is substantial heterogeneity in the percent of disembodied versus embodied technical change. In Australia there is almost no embodied technical change, although it accounts for about 21 percent of productivity in Japan. The unweighted TFP index is in column (4). Relative to Canadian affiliates, no other countries' affiliates have greater unweighted productivity. Finally, in column (7), the covariance between TFP and output is usually positive. Thus average productivity is greater for the MNCs with affiliates in these countries because of a reallocation of output

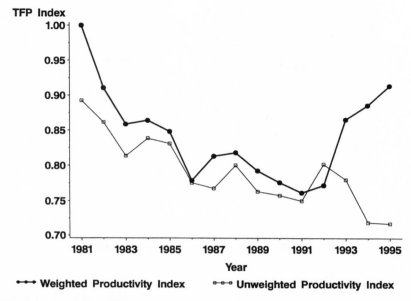

Fig. 9.1    Aggregate TFP indexes

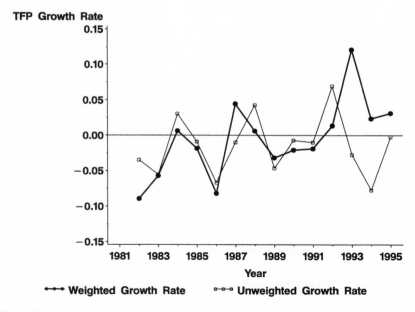

Fig. 9.2    Growth rates of weighted and unweighted TFP

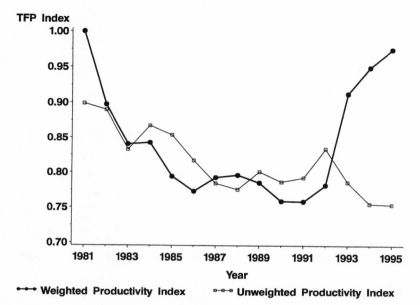

Fig. 9.3    Aggregate TFP indexes: Canadian affiliates

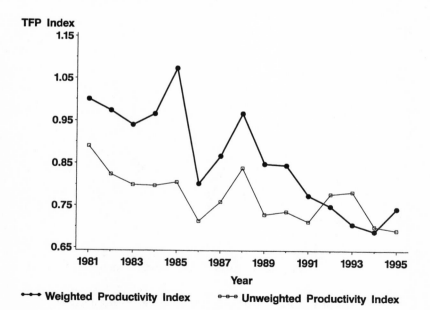

Fig. 9.4    Aggregate TFP indexes: non-Canadian affiliates

**Table 9.5**    **Aggregate Total Factor Productivity: Cross-Sectional Comparison**

| Affiliate Country | Weighted TFP Index | Percent Disembodied | Percent Embodied | Unweighted TFP Index | Percent Disembodied | Percent Embodied | Cov(TFP$_{it}$, $Y_{it}$) |
|---|---|---|---|---|---|---|---|
| Australia | 0.83 | 99.8 | 0.2 | 0.84 | 99.2 | 0.8 | −0.01 |
| Canada | 1.00 | 82.8 | 17.2 | 0.96 | 86.9 | 13.1 | 0.04 |
| France | 0.94 | 86.3 | 13.7 | 0.79 | 101.4 | −1.4 | 0.14 |
| Germany | 0.86 | 95.0 | 5.0 | 0.85 | 97.2 | 2.8 | 0.01 |
| Japan | 1.03 | 79.2 | 20.8 | 0.88 | 91.6 | 8.4 | 0.15 |
| United Kingdom | 0.84 | 96.9 | 3.1 | 0.88 | 94.3 | 5.7 | −0.04 |
| Multiple | 0.99 | 83.5 | 16.5 | 0.92 | 91.0 | 9.0 | 0.07 |

*Note:* The aggregate productivity index is calculated as the affiliate country average of the firm-level productivity estimates from the semiparametric specification in column (4) of table 9.2. Canada is the base of the index. "Weighted TFP Index" uses firm-level gross output shares as weights. "Percent Disembodied" technical change is the share of productivity attributable to year dummy variables in TFP. "Percent Embodied" technical change is the share of productivity not attributable to year effects in TFP. The difference between the weighted and unweighted indexes is Cov(TFP$_{it}$, $Y_{it}$), the sample covariance between TFP and gross output.

from less productive to more productive MNCs. The exceptions are Australia and the United Kingdom, where the covariance is negative but close to zero. In these countries, changes in average productivity, not a reallocation of output from less productive to more productive firms, drives productivity growth.

### 9.5.3    Linking Taxation, Investment, and Productivity

The estimates in table 9.6 provide the basis for exploring the connection between changes in the after-tax price of capital and productivity. According to the model, technical change is embodied in new capital, so tax policy can affect productivity directly through investment by changing the after-tax price of capital. The connection is made using equation (14), which translates investment into productivity, and equation (17), which translates changes in the value of a marginal unit of capital into investment. Both adjustment costs and the elasticity of embodiment are important in linking changes in policy with changes in productivity. When either the elasticity of embodiment is small or adjustment costs are large, changes in tax policy can have only a minor impact on productivity. For example, consider a firm with a relatively old capital stock and, hence, a large elasticity of embodiment. If the firm faces high adjustment costs, changes in the cost of capital will have a small effect on investment and productivity. However, if adjustment costs are modest, the same changes will have a large effect on investment and productivity. In contrast, there is little room for even large investment responses to have an effect on productivity in a firm with a relatively new capital stock because the elasticity of embodiment is small.

The first two columns present OLS estimates of the adjustment cost parameters from the investment equation (17). This approach uses average $Q$ as the dependent variable when estimating the adjustment costs parameters. This approach is novel; only Barnett and Sakellaris (1996) have estimated a similar investment equation. There are a number of advantages to this specification. First, measurement error in average $Q$ is more severe than is measurement error in the investment-capital ratios. Because measurement error in the dependent variable does not affect the parameter estimates, the resulting estimates are likely to be less biased compared to those when $Q$ is used as the regressor. Second, the extension of the usual single capital good investment equation to the case of multiple capital goods indexed by location is natural in this specification; the investment-capital ratios of additional locations are included only as additional regressors.[12]

---

12. Cummins and Dey (1997) show that a more general model with heterogeneous capital goods is preferable to this approach. However, their econometric approach is considerably more complex. Because the focus of this paper is not on investment behavior per se, I adopt this more transparent specification. For the same reason, I ignore a number of important econometric issues involved in estimating even this simpler investment equation.

**Table 9.6**    **Investment and Embodied Technical Change: Estimates of Adjustment Cost Parameters and the Elasticities of Embodiment**

| Parameter | Investment Equation | | Embodiment Equation |
|---|---|---|---|
| | (1) | (2) | (3) |
| $\beta_{K_d}$ | 4.40 | 3.39 | — |
| | (0.511) | (0.811) | |
| $\beta_{K_f}$ | 1.67 | 1.70 | — |
| | (0.440) | (0.642) | |
| $\varepsilon_{K_d}$ | — | — | 0.664 |
| | | | (0.381) |
| $\varepsilon_{K_f}$ | — | — | −0.150 |
| | | | (0.182) |
| $N$ | 742 | 291 | 358 |

*Note:* The investment relationship estimated is defined by equation (17). The embodiment relationship estimated is defined by equation 14. The dependent variable in column (1) is tax-adjusted $Q_{it}$. The dependent variable in column (2) is real $Q_{it}$. The dependent variable in column (3) is the growth of embodied technical change $EP_{it}$, defined as the growth in the part of TFP not attributable to year effects. Standard errors on parameter estimates are in parentheses.

It is important to highlight the role of the sources of variation in the data. Variation in the after-tax price of capital is *not* essential for estimating equation (17), unlike in the usual specification in which tax-adjusted $Q$ is the regressor. For example, if $Q$ is subject to additive measurement error as a result of removing the tax adjustment, then the estimates of equation (17) are still consistent. Taxes are nonetheless included in the model so that the elasticity of investment with respect to its after-tax price can be calculated and used for policy experiments.

In the first column the dependent variable is tax-adjusted average $Q$ (for details on the construction of this variable, see Cummins, Hassett, and Hubbard 1994). The parameter estimates are statistically significant and imply marginal adjustment costs of investment that are small compared to those in many studies (see, e.g., Chirinko 1993b). The estimates for the parents' adjustment costs are similar to those obtained by Cummins et al. (1994) for U.S. firms in the "natural experiment" years using the usual empirical approach to estimate the $Q$ model. The estimates for the affiliates are similar to those for affiliates in Altshuler and Cummins (1999) and Cummins and Hubbard (1995). The number of observations drops because some of the data necessary to calculate tax-adjusted $Q$ are missing. In column (2) the dependent variable is real $Q$ constructed by Cummins, Hassett, and Oliner (1999) from securities analysts' earnings expectations. This measure has theoretical and empirical appeal because it relies on professionals to forecast the value of the firm, rather than on market data, which tend to be quite noisy measures of fundamentals. The parameter estimates are both statistically significant and imply lower adjustment costs for parent investment and about the same costs for affiliate investment. There are only 291 observations because real $Q$ is frequently missing. These estimates suggest that adjustment costs are relatively modest, which at least opens the possibility for tax policy to affect productivity.

In column (3), I use equation (14) to explore the connection between investment and the growth in embodied productivity. OLS is used to estimate the relationship by appending a stochastic disturbance to the equation. The disturbance is assumed to be uncorrelated with the regressors.[13] As a result, the coefficient estimates must be treated with caution. The dependent variable is the growth rate of embodied productivity, defined in equation (22), and the regressors are the investment-capital ratios multiplied by their estimated capital shares, $\alpha_{K_d} = 0.131$ and $\alpha_{K_f} = 0.085$.[14] The number of observations is only 352 for two reasons: Once-lagged embodied technical change is needed to construct the growth rate; and observations were deleted if the estimated embodied productivity was negative—which is empirically possible given the decomposition of TFP into embodied and disembodied components, but theoretically impossible. The estimate of the elasticity of embodiment is 0.664 and statistically significant at the 10 percent level. The estimate of the affiliate's average elasticity of embodiment is $-0.150$, which is nonsensical, but it is statistically insignificant from zero.[15] Although there are a number of important caveats in interpreting these results, they imply that the best practice technology is 66 percent higher than the average level in parents, but indistinguishably different from the average in affiliates. While there is no data on the average age of the parents' and affiliates' capital stock, it is likely that the parents' stock is older. Hence, despite the numerous assumptions underlying this approach, the results are at least sensible.

The sizes of these elasticities affect the contribution of capital to growth. Recall from equation (15) that the true contribution of quality unadjusted capital is marked up by the elasticity of embodiment. This implies that the true output elasticity for parent capital is 0.22 instead of 0.13, whereas

13. It would be preferable to relax the assumption that the disturbance is orthogonal to the regressors and use an instrumental variable estimator such as generalized method of moments (GMM). However, such an approach is infeasible because the lagged (period $t-2$ and $t-3$) dependent variables that are suitable instruments are missing too frequently.

14. All the variables in the regression are generated regressors. The dependent variable is the growth rate of a residual from the estimation of the production function. Measurement error in the dependent variable, however, does not affect the coefficient estimates. The regressors are "generated" because the capital shares are estimated. For my purposes, however, this is unimportant, because Pagan (1984) shows that the OLS estimator provides asymptotic $t$-statistics that are valid for the hypothesis test that the coefficient estimate on the generated regressor is zero.

15. The OLS estimates of these elasticities using the growth rate of the aggregate index of embodied technical change and the growth rate of the indexes of parent and affiliate capital multiplied by their estimated capital shares are 2.69 and $-1.76$, respectively. Neither estimate is statistically significant because there are only 14 observations.

the output elasticity of affiliate capital is unaffected. Using this value to recalculate the annual share-weighted growth rate of parent capital in the bottom panel of table 9.3 increases its contribution to growth from 1.49 to 2.48 percent. In studies that ignore quality adjustment, this additional contribution to growth is spuriously attributed to TFP, not to capital. These results highlight that investment affects output growth through two channels, increasing both quality unadjusted capital and embodied productivity. As is clear from comparing the parents' and affiliates' elasticity of embodiment, this effect diminishes as the average age of the capital falls. Hence, increases in embodied productivity have only a transitory effect, raising the level of output but not permanently changing its growth rate.

## 9.6   Conclusion

The growth accounting for U.S. MNCs indicates that broad similarity in some dimensions but significant differences in others. Across firms, parent investment and FDI—in spite of capitals' relatively modest share in output—are the most important sources of MNC growth. Indeed, FDI is nearly as important as domestic investment and contributes more to growth than the sum of the contributions of parent and affiliate employment, and materials.

Productivity declined throughout the 1980s and recovered in the 1990s. This general trend masks two very different experiences. MNCs with Canadian affiliates have had a productivity boom since 1992, whereas MNCs with affiliates elsewhere have continued their slides. There are wide cross-sectional differences among MNCs depending on where their affiliates operate. The MNCs with affiliates in the United Kingdom are nearly the least productive.

A number of previous studies have highlighted the important role played by capital in growth accounting when technical progress is embodied. Most of these studies concluded that embodiment was empirically unimportant. For example, Hulten (1992) echoed Denison (1964) by finding that changes in the age structure of capital have had little effect on output growth. Other studies have found the opposite. For example, Bahk and Gort (1993) show that quality improvements are associated with statistically and economically significant growth effects. Specifically, they find that a one-year change in the average age of the capital stock is associated with a 2.5–3.5 percent change in output. In this study, improvements in the quality of capital are important as well. The already large contribution of parent capital to growth are marked up significantly because of embodied technical change. Because the parents' elasticity of embodiment is large and adjustment costs of investment are small, changes in the after-tax price of capital result in robust investment, which translates directly into productivity gains. This connection suggests the possibility that tax incentives for capital increase productivity and growth.

## Appendix
### Dataset Construction

The variables used for econometric estimation are constructed as follows. Gross output is the sum of three items: the sum of net sales in the geographic segments; the parent's domestic net sales; and, when reported, the change in finished goods inventory. The replacement value of the parent's and affiliates' capital stock (hereafter capital stock) is constructed from the net stock of tangible fixed assets using the perpetual inventory method with the initial observation set equal to the book value of the firm's first reported observation.[16] The depreciation rate of parent and affiliate capital is assumed identical and calculated using depreciation rates in Hulten and Wykoff (1981). Net investment is the change in each capital stock. Gross investment is the sum of net investment and depreciation.

Total labor input is defined as total employees.[17] I use an auxiliary data set to construct the parent's and affiliates' labor input from total employees. The U.S. Bureau of Economic Analysis (BEA) reports parent employment by industry and foreign affiliate employment by country and industry in an annual survey (for a detailed description of the data, see U.S. Department of Commerce 1995). Using these data, I construct the percentage of total employment accounted for by the parent and its affiliates by industry. I then match these industry weights to the firm-level data and construct parent and affiliate employees as the respective weight multiplied by total employees. The BEA's industry classification fails to correspond exactly to the firm-level Standard Industry Classification (SIC) codes. Typically, the BEA industry classification corresponds to a two- or three-digit SIC code, but in some cases it corresponds to a one- or four-digit code. Parent and affiliate employment are constructed using the most disaggregated BEA weight available. In most cases this is a good approximation of parent and affiliate employment because the survey from which the weights are constructed includes the MNCs in our firm-level data.[18]

16. Major capital stock changes are deleted to eliminate clear discontinuities in the identity of the firm or measurement error. Second, the geographic segment file provides a footnote if the data reflect the results of a merger or acquisition. Firms recording this footnote are deleted.

17. Labor and related expense is not reported frequently enough to be empirically useful.

18. I checked the accuracy of this method by comparing the employee numbers to those from the companies' annual reports. I picked a random sample of twenty MNCs from the sample and found that in most cases our method gave numbers within 10 percent of those reported in their 1993 annual report.

Material input is calculated by separating labor expense from total expense, defined as the sum of cost of goods sold, and, when reported, selling, general, and administrative expense. Total labor expense is calculated as the average sectoral labor cost per employee multiplied by total employees and deflated by the price index for total compensation. The average sectoral labor cost is computed using the Bureau of Labor Statistics' (BLS) annual survey of employer cost for employee compensation, which contains sector-level wage data (the sum of salary and benefits). The BLS began this survey in 1986, so the values for earlier years are obtained by extrapolating backward using the sector-level employment cost index. I assume a 2,040-hour work year to calculate the annual salary. Then materials are calculated as total expense less labor expense. Value added is gross output less materials.

The construction of average $Q$ and real $Q$ are complicated and are both described in detail in Cummins et al. (1999).

Home-and host-country tax variables (federal and subfederal corporate income tax rates, investment tax credits, depreciation allowances, and withholding tax rates on repatriated dividends) are updated and expanded from Cummins et al. (1995).[19] The price of capital and output goods are, respectively, the property, plant, and equipment deflator (PPE) and the GDP deflator of the United States. All capital and investment variables are deflated by the U.S. PPE deflator and output is deflated by the U.S. GDP deflator.

# References

Altshuler, Rosanne, and Jason G. Cummins. 1999. Tax policy and the dynamic demand for domestic and foreign capital by multinational corporations. New York University. Mimeograph.

Bahk, Byong-Hyong, and Michael Gort. 1993. Decomposing learning by doing in new plants. *Journal of Political Economy* 101 (4): 561–83.

Baily, Martin Neil. 1986. Productivity growth and materials use in U.S. manufacturing. *Quarterly Journal of Economics* 101 (1): 185–95.

Barnett, Steven A., and Plutarchos Sakellaris. 1999. A new look at firm market value, investment, and adjustment costs. *Review of Economics and Statistics* 81 (2): 250–60.

Bruno, Michael. 1984. Raw materials, profits, and the productivity slowdown. *Quarterly Journal of Economics* 99 (1): 1–29.

Chirinko, Robert S. (1993a). Investment, Tobin's $Q$, and multiple capital inputs. *Journal of Economic Dynamics and Control* 17 (5/6): 907–28.

Chirinko, Robert S. 1993b. Business fixed investment spending: A critical survey of modeling strategies, empirical results, and policy implications. *Journal of Economic Literature* 31 (4): 1875–1911.

---

19. Ken McKenzie kindly supplied some of the Canadian tax parameters.

Cummins, Jason G. 1999. The giant sucking sound: Structural estimates of factor substitution from firm-level panel data on multinational corporations. Mimeograph.

Cummins, Jason G., and Matthew Dey. 1997. Taxation, investment, and firm growth with heterogeneous capital. Mimeograph.

Cummins, Jason G., Kevin A. Hassett, and R. Glenn Hubbard. 1994. A reconsideration of investment behavior using tax reforms as natural experiments. *Brookings Papers on Economic Activity,* issue no. 2: 1–74.

Cummins, Jason G., Kevin A. Hassett, and R. Glenn Hubbard. 1995. Tax reforms and investment: A cross-country comparison. *Journal of Public Economics* 62:237–73.

Cummins, Jason G., Kevin A. Hassett, and Steven D. Oliner. 1999. Investment behavior, observable expectations, and internal funds. Mimeograph.

Cummins, Jason G., and R. Glenn Hubbard. 1995. The tax sensitivity of foreign direct investment: Evidence from firm-level panel data. In *The effects of taxation on multinational corporations,* ed. M. Feldstein, J. R. Hines, and R. G. Hubbard, 123–47. Chicago: University of Chicago Press.

Denison, Edward F. 1964. The unimportance of the embodiment question. *American Economic Review* 54 (1): 90–94.

Domar, Evesy D. 1963. Total factor productivity and the quality of capital. *Journal of Political Economy* 71 (3): 586–88.

Griliches, Zvi. 1979. Issues in assessing the contribution of research and development to productivity growth. *Bell Journal of Economics* 10 (1): 92–116.

Griliches, Zvi, and Jacques Mairesse. 1995. Production functions: The search for identification. NBER Working Paper no. 5067. Cambridge, Mass.: National Bureau of Economic Research, March.

Grubb, David. 1986. Raw materials, profits, and the productivity slowdown: Some doubts. *Quarterly Journal of Economics* 101 (1): 175–84.

Hayashi, Fumio, and Tohru Inoue. 1991. The relation between firm growth and $Q$ with multiple capital goods: Theory and evidence from panel data on Japanese firms. *Econometrica* 59 (3): 731–53.

Hulten, Charles R. 1978. Growth accounting with intermediate inputs. *Review of Economic Studies* 45 (3): 511–18.

Hulten, Charles R. 1990. Introduction. In *Productivity growth in Japan and the United States,* ed. C. R. Hulten, 1–27. Chicago: University of Chicago Press.

Hulten, Charles R. 1992. Growth accounting when technical change is embodied in capital. *American Economic Review* 82 (4): 964–80.

Hulten, Charles R., and Frank Wykoff. 1981. Measurement of economic depreciation. In *Depreciation, inflation, and the taxation of income from capital,* ed. C. R. Hulten, 81–125. Washington, D.C.: Urban Institute.

Jorgenson, Dale W. 1966. The embodiment hypothesis. *Journal of Political Economy* 74 (1): 1–17.

Klette, Tor J., and Zvi Griliches. 1996. The inconsistency of common scale estimators when output prices are unobserved and endogenous. *Journal of Applied Econometrics* 11 (4): 343–61.

Leamer, Edward. 1988. The sensitivity of international comparisons of capital stock measures to different "real" exchange rates. *American Economic Review* 78 (2): 479–83.

Mairesse, Jacques, and Mohamed Sassenou. 1991. R&D and productivity: A survey of econometric studies at the firm level. NBER Working Paper no. 3666. Cambridge, Mass.: National Bureau of Economic Research, March.

Mundlak, Yair. 1996. Production function estimation: Reviving the primal. *Econometrica* 64 (2): 431–38.

Nadiri, M. Ishaq, and Ingmar R. Prucha. 1997. Dynamic factor demand models and productivity analysis. New York University, Department of Economics. Mimeograph.

Olley, G. Steven, and Ariel Pakes. 1996. The dynamics of productivity in the telecommunications equipment industry. *Econometrica* 64 (6): 1263–97.

Pagan, Adrian. 1984. Econometric issues in the analysis of regression with generated regressors. *International Economic Review* 25 (1): 221–47.

Solow, Robert M. 1957. Technical change and the aggregate production function. *Review of Economics and Statistics* 39 (3): 312–20.

Solow, Robert M. 1960. Investment and technical progress. In *Mathematical methods in the social sciences,* ed. K. Arrow, S. Karlin, and P. Suppes, 89–104. Stanford: Stanford University Press.

U.S. Department of Commerce. 1995. *Survey of current business.* Vol. 75 (3). Washington, D.C.: GPO.

# Comment   Samuel S. Kortum

What is the contribution of different factors of production and technological change to the growth of MNCs since the 1980s? Would changes in the taxation of these corporations substantially alter their growth? Cummins approaches the first question with new data on U.S.-based multinationals that allow him to identify the impact of parent and affiliate capital and labor. For the second question he adopts a model in which technological change is embodied in investment goods, so that a jump in investment raises productivity as well as the capital stock. He concludes that capital—with a surprisingly large contribution of affiliate capital—played the major role in the growth of MNCs. Technological change contributed little. On the second question, Cummins suggests that the productivity gains from an investment-promoting tax policy could be substantial.

I argue that these conclusions should be tempered. With respect to the first question, I raise some questions concerning the specification of the MNC's production function. For the second, I show that the productivity impact of higher investment is fleeting. Nevertheless, I applaud Cummins on his research agenda concerning MNCs and on his empirical strategy in particular. Given their growing importance in the world economy, it is crucial that economists get a better handle on the workings of the MNC. By linking data on parents and their affiliates, Cummins can do just that. Many others will likely follow his lead.

I begin by discussing the MNC's production function. In the paper, the output of the entire MNC is aggregated, whereas the capital and labor of both affiliate and parent enter as four distinct inputs into a Cobb-Douglas

Samuel S. Kortum is assistant professor of economics at Boston University and a faculty research fellow of the National Bureau of Economic Research.

production function. A more natural assumption is that the Cobb-Douglas production function applies separately to the output of the parent and the output of its affiliates. If so, and if affiliates are growing faster than their parents, then the paper's estimates of disembodied technological change are biased down in the earlier years of the sample and biased up in the later years. This argument could explain the finding that disembodied technological change is negative in the first half of the sample, then recovers in the latter half.

I then probe the model of capital embodied technological change that the paper adopts. Although introducing embodied technology augments capital's contribution to growth in an accounting sense, it turns out to make little difference to the output effect of a policy-induced increase in investment. The impact on productivity of a jump in investment, driven by changes in the age distribution of capital, is short lived and eventually reverses itself. I make this point analytically and with a simulation based on parameter values from the paper.

### The Multinational's Production Function

Because production by a domestic parent $Y_d$ and its foreign affiliate $Y_f$ take place in separate locations, it makes sense to explain each in terms of its own production function. Ignoring materials inputs, we have $Y_d = F_d(K_d, L_d, A_d)$ and $Y_f = F_f(K_f, L_f, A_f)$. Of course there may be links between production of the parent and its affiliate. The most plausible link, and a possible reason for the MNC to exist in the first place, is that the affiliate inherits its technology $A_f$ in part from the knowledge $A_d$ of its parent. An exploration of this link, however, is for another paper.

The present paper is concerned with decomposing the growth of the output of the entire multinational $Y = Y_d + Y_f$. It begins with a production function for $Y$, which in the empirical work is a Cobb-Douglas function of $K_d$, $K_f$, $L_d$, and $L_f$. In growth rates (denoted by hats)

$$(1) \qquad \hat{Y} = \hat{A} + \alpha_{K_d}\hat{K}_d + \alpha_{K_f}\hat{K}_f + \alpha_{L_d}\hat{L}_d + \alpha_{L_f}\hat{L}_f,$$

a simplified version of equation (10) in Cummins's paper.

Suppose we adopt the Cobb-Douglas functional form (with parameters $\beta$) but maintain the principle that a separate production function governs the output of the parent and the affiliate. The resulting equation for output growth is

$$(2) \qquad \hat{Y} = s_d\hat{A}_d + (1 - s_d)\hat{A}_f + s_d\beta_{K_d}\hat{K}_d + (1 - s_d)\beta_{K_f}\hat{K}_f$$
$$+ s_d\beta_{L_d}\hat{L}_d + (1 - s_d)\beta_{L_f}\hat{L}_f,$$

where $s_d = Y_d/Y$ is the parent's share of the multinational. In equation (2), the output elasticity of affiliate capital is automatically larger in an MNC where affiliates play a larger role. This implication is intuitive and its absence from equation (1) raises questions about that specification. Doubling the capital stock of an affiliate, if it is tiny relative to the parent, is unlikely to produce a large percentage increase in the MNC's total output. A similar argument applies over time.

With globalization of production, affiliates will become a larger share of multinational output and $s_d$ will fall over time. If equation (2) is correct, then the estimates of equation (1) will be time averages of the corresponding coefficients in equation (2). The true output elasticities of $K_f$ and $L_f$ will be less than the estimated elasticities in the early years and greater toward the end of the sample (the opposite will be the case with the output elasticities of $K_d$ and $L_d$). However, with affiliates growing faster than parents, presumably $\hat{K}_f > \hat{K}_d$ and $\hat{L}_f > \hat{L}_d$ (table 9.3 of the paper verifies these inequalities). It follows that the rate of disembodied technological change inferred from the estimates will be less than the true rate $s_d \hat{A}_d + (1 - s_d)\hat{A}_f$ early in the sample and greater than the true rate toward the end.

### Technology Embodied in Capital

With personal computers everywhere, we are accustomed to technological change arriving in new equipment. The model of capital embodied technology captures that feature of reality in a simple way. Physical investment $I$ is the rate at which new machines are brought into production. Adding up machines (allowing for a geometric depreciation rate $\delta$), the capital stock $K$ satisfies $\dot{K} = I - \delta K$. If the capability of new machinery is improving at rate $a > 0$, then investment in efficiency units is $H_t = e^{at}I_t$. The effective capital stock $J$ (which is what should enter the production function) satisfies $\dot{J} = H - \delta J$. Assuming a Cobb-Douglas production function with a capital elasticity $\alpha_K$, the contribution of capital to output growth is $\alpha_K \hat{J}$.

The elasticity of embodiment $\varepsilon = [(H/J) - (I/K)]/(I/K)$ summarizes what we need to know about the age of machinery. Multiplying the elasticity by 100, it represents the percentage change in the effective capital stock brought about by replacing all existing machines with new ones (holding fixed $K$). The contribution of capital to output growth can be expressed, like the paper's equation (15), as $\alpha_K \hat{J} = \alpha_K(1 + \varepsilon)\hat{K} + \alpha_K \varepsilon \delta$. Because not all machinery is brand new, $\varepsilon > 0$. Hence, according to the accounting equation, capital contributes more to growth because it embodies new technology (i.e., the output elasticity of $K$ exceeds $\alpha_K$), but this interpretation may be misleading.

When we look at what tax policy might achieve, the role of capital embodied technology turns out to be modest and transitory. The contribution of capital to output growth consists of three parts: (1) the physical capital effect $\alpha_K \hat{K}$, (2) the technological change effect $\alpha_K a$, and (3) the capital age effect $\alpha_K \hat{X}$, where $X = (J/K)(I/H) = 1/(1 + \varepsilon)$. The physical capital effect

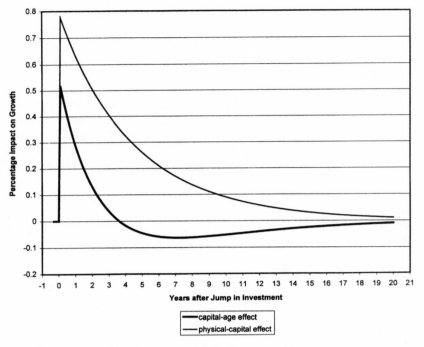

**Fig. 9C.1   Effects on growth of a permanent 10 percent jump in investment**

is the same as in the standard model and the technological change effect is exogenous. Any new action must come through the capital age effect. Surprisingly, however, tax policies that permanently raise the level of investment have no long-run effect on the age distribution of capital. Not only is there no permanent growth effect through the age channel, there is not even a permanent level effect. The only long-run impact of tax policy is through the traditional channel of a permanently higher physical capital stock.

To see this, assume that investment grows at a constant rate $g$ (a policy change can be thought of as a discontinuous jump in the path of investment). Eventually $K$ will also grow at approximately rate $g$. In a steady-state situation with stocks and flows growing at the same rate, $I/K = g + \delta$ and $H/J = g + \delta + a$. It follows that $\varepsilon = a/(g + \delta)$. The *level* of investment, which could perhaps be raised permanently by policy, does not matter in the long run for the age distribution of capital. In the short run, however, a jump in the level of investment begins to reduce the average age of capital. We now turn to the dynamics whereby the age of capital first falls and then rises again to its original level.

We simulate the path of the capital age effect $\alpha_K \hat{X} = \alpha_K [(H/J) - (I/K) -$

*a*] following a 10 percent jump in the level of investment. For the simulation, (1) we initialized $H/J$ and $I/K$ at their steady-state values (prior to the jump in investment); (2) we set the depreciation rate at $\delta = 0.1$; (3) we set investment growth at $g = 0.11$ (the growth of parent capital from table 9.3); (4) we set embodied technological change at $a = 0.14$, so that the steady-state elasticity of embodiment is 2/3 (as in table 9.6); and (5) we set $\alpha_K = 0.37$ based on the estimates in the last column of table 9.2 (dividing the sum of the capital elasticities by $1 - \alpha_M$). Note that our parameter choices, although perhaps extreme, are designed to give the capital age effect its best shot.

Figure 9C.1 shows what happens. Initially, the capital age effect (the fat line) contributes half a percentage point to growth, exactly what is predicted by equation (14) in the paper ($10\alpha_K \varepsilon I/K = 10\alpha_K a = 0.5$). However, the capital age effect has turned negative by four years out and stays negative thereafter while slowly diminishing toward zero. For comparison, we also plot (as a thin line) the traditional physical capital effect (less its steady-state value of $\alpha_K g$). Although the capital age effect is more than half as large as the physical capital effect in the first year, it falls much more rapidly.

The bottom line is that one should not expect a big or long lasting contribution from the capital age effect. Consequently, because the capital age effect is the mechanism by which tax policy could raise productivity, one should not hope for big productivity effects. The growth impact of rising physical capital dwarfs the impact of shifts in the age distribution of capital.

# Contributors

Rosanne Altshuler
Department of Economics
75 Hamilton Street
Rutgers University
New Brunswick, NJ 08901

Kimberly A. Clausing
Department of Economics
Reed College
3203 SE Woodstock Blvd.
Portland, OR 97202

Julie H. Collins
Kenan-Flagler Business School
University of North Carolina
CB 490, McColl Building
Chapel Hill, NC 27599

Jason G. Cummins
Department of Economics
New York University
269 Mercer Street, 7th Floor
New York, NY 10003

Timothy J. Goodspeed
Department of Economics
Hunter College
695 Park Avenue
New York, NY 10021

Austan Goolsbee
Graduate School of Business
University of Chicago
1101 E. 58th Street
Chicago, IL 60637

Harry Grubert
Office of International Tax Analysis
U.S. Department of the Treasury
Room 4209, Main Treasury
15th and Pennsylvania NW
Washington, DC 20220

John R. M. Hand
Kenan-Flagler Business School
University of North Carolina,
    Chapel Hill
Campus Box 3490, McColl Building
Chapel Hill, NC 27599

Kevin Hassett
American Enterprise Institute
1150 17th Street NW
Washington, DC 20036

James R. Hines Jr.
Business School
701 Tappan Street
University of Michigan
Ann Arbor, MI 48109

Adam B. Jaffe
MS 021
Brandeis University
Waltham, MA 02454

Deen Kemsley
School of Business
607 Uris Hall
Columbia University
3022 Broadway
New York, NY 10027

Samuel S. Kortum
Department of Economics
Boston University
270 Bay State Road
Boston, MA 02215

Jack M. Mintz
Rotman School of Business
University of Toronto
150 St. George Street
Toronto, Ontario M5S 3E6 Canada

T. Scott Newlon
Horst Frisch Incorporated
Watergate Office Building
2600 Virginia Avenue NW, Suite 300
Washington, DC 20037

William C. Randolph
Director, International Taxation
Office of Tax Analysis
U.S. Department of the Treasury
1500 Pennsylvania Ave., Rm 3045
Washington, DC 20220

Douglas A. Shackelford
Kenan-Flagler Business School
University of North Carolina,
    Chapel Hill
Campus Box 3490, McColl Building
Chapel Hill, NC 27599

Joel B. Slemrod
Director, Office of Tax Policy Research
University of Michigan Business
    School
701 Tappan Street, Room A2120D
Ann Arbor, MI 48109

Deborah L. Swenson
Department of Economics
University of California
Davis, CA 95616

Shang-Jin Wei
The Kennedy School of Government
Harvard University
79 JFK Street
Cambridge, MA 02138

Bernard Yeung
New York University
Stern School of Business
44 W 4th Street Rm 7/65
New York, NY 10012

# Author Index

# Subject Index

271